W9-BOY-164

Better Homes and Gardens®

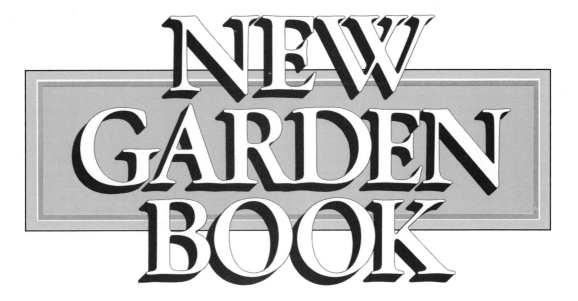

NEW GARDEN BOOK

© Copyright 1990 by Meredith Corporation, Des Moines, Iowa.
First Edition, 1951: *Garden Book*.
Second Edition, 1968: *New Garden Book*.
Third Edition, 1979: *Complete Guide to Gardening*.
All Rights Reserved. Printed in the United States of America.
Fourth Edition. Printing Number and Year: 5   96 95 94 93
Library of Congress Catalog Card Number: 89-63159
ISBN: 0-696-00042-3
ISBN: 0-696-02557-4 (trade paperback)

BETTER HOMES AND GARDENS® BOOKS

Editor
Gerald M. Knox

Art Director
Ernest Shelton

Managing Editor
David A. Kirchner

Project Editors
James D. Blume, Marsha Jahns

Project Managers
Liz Anderson, Jennifer Speer Ramundt, Angela K. Renkoski

Associate Art Directors
Neoma Thomas, Linda Ford Vermie, Randall Yontz

Assistant Art Directors
Lynda Haupert, Harijs Priekulis, Tom Wegner

Graphic Designers
Mary Schlueter Bendgen, Mike Burns, Brenda Drake Lesch

Art Production
Director, John Berg; Associate, Joe Heuer;
Office Manager, Michaela Lester

President, Book Group
Jeramy Lanigan

Vice President, Retail Marketing
Jamie L. Martin

Vice President, Administrative Services
Rick Rundall

Better Homes and Gardens® magazine
President, Magazine Group: James A. Autry
Editorial Director: Doris Eby
Garden and Outdoor Living Editor: Douglas A. Jimerson

Meredith Corporation Officers
Chairman of the Executive Committee: E. T. Meredith III
Chairman of the Board: Robert A. Burnett
President: Jack D. Rehm

NEW GARDEN BOOK

Project Editor
James D. Blume

Contributing Project Editor
David A. Walsh

Graphic Designer
Harijs Priekulis

Contributing Photographers
Crandall & Crandall, deGennaro Studios,
Peter Krumhardt

Contributing Illustrators
Timothy A. Clark, Michael Eagleton, Mike Henry,
Jim Stevenson

Consultant
Jane Austin McKeon

Electronic Text Processor
Paula Forest

CONTRIBUTING WRITERS

Monica Brandies
Once an Iowa gardener and a commercial greenhouse operator, Floridan Monica Brandies covers gardening for several newspapers and national magazines.

Lorraine Burgess
Lorraine Burgess of Colorado Springs contributed to the *Complete Guide to Gardening* and *Annuals You Can Grow,* both from Better Homes and Gardens® Books.

Thomas E. Eltzroth
Thomas E. Eltzroth, a horticulture professor at California Polytechnic State University, has cowritten gardening books and is a professional horticultural photographer.

Cathy Howard
An Oregon writer, Cathy Howard also is a field editor for *Better Homes and Gardens®* magazine.

Ann Reilly
A New York native, Ann Reilly contributed to Better Homes and Gardens® *Annuals You Can Grow, Roses You Can Grow,* and *Step-by-Step Successful Gardening.*

John Whitman
Minnesotan John Whitman, once a grower for one of the country's largest nurseries, wrote *Starting from Scratch: A Guide to Indoor Gardening.*

Thomas Wirth
A Massachusetts landscape architect, Thomas Wirth has written for the television shows "Victory Garden" and "This Old House," and is the author of *The Victory Garden Landscape Guide.*

INTRODUCTION

Almost as much as they enjoy growing the perfect flower, sweetest fruit, or greenest lawn, gardeners like sharing gardening tips. That's why we at Better Homes and Gardens® Books have been thrilled that millions of gardeners have sought the advice of the *New Garden Book*—first published in 1951—and put it into successful practice. Now we're happy to bring you this up-to-date edition. Like a good gardener, today's *New Garden Book* makes best use of both the latest gardening information and the tested techniques from yesteryear. With the *New Garden Book* as your consultant and companion, you can rest assured that yours will be the better garden you've always dreamed of.

CONTENTS

GARDENING BASICS

E veryone's vision of paradise includes a garden, lush with green plants, awash in the fragrance and colors of flowers, and filled with sweet-tasting produce, freshly picked and prepared. It is the delight in doing our part to help fulfill this dream that makes us the gardeners we are.

CONSIDER YOUR CLIMATE

Key to successful gardening is knowing what plants are best suited for your area and when to plant them. This is true for every type of gardening. Climate maps, such as the one at right, give a good idea of the extremes in temperature by zones. By choosing plants best adapted to the different zones, and by planting them at the right time, you will have many more successes. The zone-number listings found in this book tell you the coldest temperature a plant typically can endure.

MICROCLIMATES COUNT

Skilled gardeners use climate maps only as general guides, however, for selecting the right plants. These experienced gardeners realize that within 1 square mile of their homes may be dozens of microclimates, each different from the others. Even in a single yard you may find a half dozen or more different situations that will affect the choice of plants and their planting times. Here are a few factors to keep in mind.

Plants react to exposure. Southern and western exposures are sunnier and warmer than northern or eastern ones. Light conditions differ greatly even in a small yard. Match your plants' needs to the correct exposure.

Wind can damage many plants, by either drying the soil or knocking over fragile growth. Protect plants from both summer and winter winds to increase their odds of survival and to save yourself the time and energy of staking plants and watering more frequently.

Consider elevation, too, when selecting plants. Cold air sweeps down hills and rests in low areas. These frost pockets are fine for some plantings, deadly for others. Plant vegetation that prefers a warmer environment on the tops or sides of hills, never at the bottom.

Use fences, the sides of buildings, shrubs, and trees to your advantage. Watch the play of shadows, the sweep of winds, and the flow of snowdrifts in winter. These varying situations are ideal for some plants, harmful to others. In short, always figure out how to make the most of everything your yard offers you.

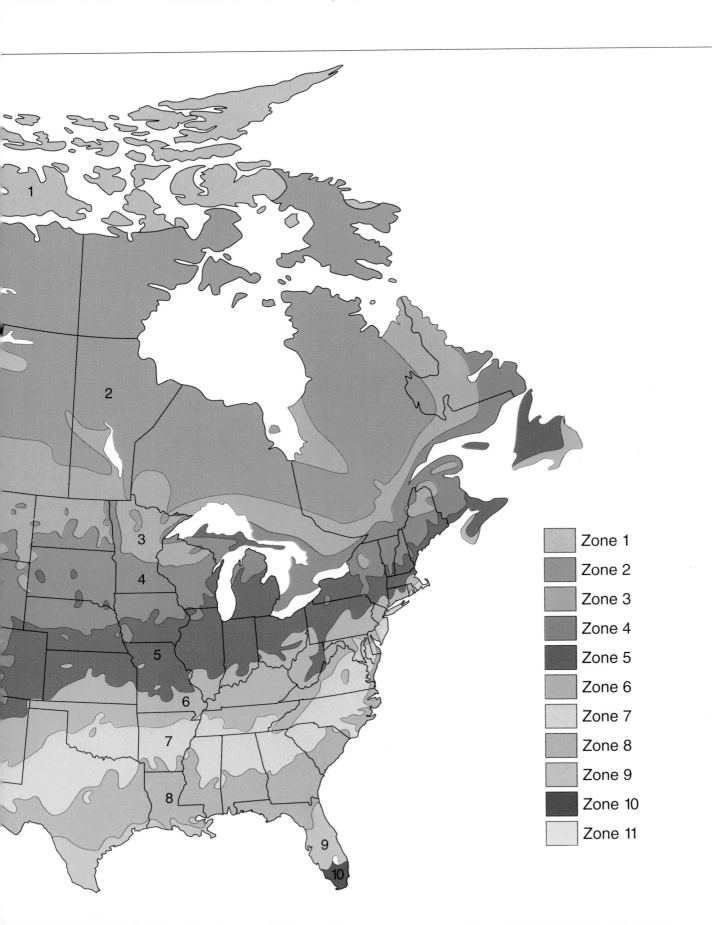

Zone 1
Zone 2
Zone 3
Zone 4
Zone 5
Zone 6
Zone 7
Zone 8
Zone 9
Zone 10
Zone 11

KNOW YOUR SOIL

Good soil is essential to successful gardening. But if your garden soil isn't ideal—or even fair—don't despair. You can improve it.

Good garden soil—called loam—has certain characteristics, all of which help plants grow vigorously. Loam has a nice feel to it. When you squeeze it lightly in your hand, it holds shape. But if you squeeze harder, it crumbles. Good loamy soil is so easy to work you can dig a hole in it with your bare hand.

Good soil contains food for microorganisms, plus all essential nutrients for plants. Because of its high content of decayed organic matter, loam retains those nutrients, as well as moisture.

Since most soils are not good soils in the beginning, gardeners improve them by following the basic steps outlined here.

DETERMINE YOUR SOIL TYPE

The soil in most home gardens falls into certain general categories. If you have rocky soil, it is almost impossible to dig or cultivate. If you have clayey soil, it is compacted and difficult to work when dry. During rains, it turns slick and greasy. Sandy soil is just the opposite—so loose it won't even form a ball when squeezed in your hand. You can feel its graininess when you rub it between your fingers. Silty soil falls in between sandy and clayey soils. Its particles create a slippery surface when wet, but don't compact like clay when dry. Mucky soils look and feel like peat.

■ Improving your soil

The goal of home gardeners is to turn whatever kind of soil they have into loam. If your soil falls short of the ideal, try these tips.

For rocky soils, bring in loam and make raised beds; these work beautifully for both vegetables and flowers. Buying soil is expensive, but converting rocky soil to loam is next to impossible.

For clayey, sandy, and silty soils, add lots of organic matter as outlined on the opposite page. Organic matter will make clayey soil loose and airy. It gives body to sandy and silty soils, helping them retain nutrients and water, which normally would wash away or evaporate.

Mucky soils—found in wet, low-lying areas—are good for a few specific crops, but not for many. Your best bet is to find a new garden location better suited to a wider variety of vegetables and flowers.

WORK YOUR SOIL

To get good garden soil, you must work it. Some gardeners dig up areas by hand with a garden fork or spade. Others prefer renting or buying a power tiller for this job. The initial preparation of a garden area is the hardest of all. In subsequent years, working the soil gets easier and easier.

Work the soil to a depth of at least a foot. Some experts consider 2 feet to be the minimum, but most crops will thrive in soil loosened to the lesser depth.

Work only when the soil is slightly moist, especially if it has a clay base. Clayey soil,

Soil high in clay, left, forms a tight, sticky mass if squeezed when wet. Sandy soil, center, feels grainy and crumbles when wet. To improve either type of soil, add lots of organic matter.

Loam, right—the ideal soil—molds into a loose mound when squeezed lightly. Squeezed harder, however, it crumbles. Loam consists of sand, clay, silt, and organic matter in just the right combination.

worked when soggy, will form clods that dry brick hard. If the soil is dusty, on the other hand, it also is hard to work.

Whenever possible, work your garden in the fall. If you cut into sod, remove all the grass to prevent it from resprouting later. Remove all rocks and debris, which only interfere with gardening. Use an iron rake to separate them from the soil. Break up all clods, but let the soil surface stay rough. The more soil exposed during the winter, the better; exposed soil breaks down into a better texture.

TEST YOUR SOIL

Getting your soil to feel right is just one step in the right direction. You also must know whether your soil is alkaline, neutral, or acidic.

To determine this, you'll need to have a soil test done. Most public universities will test your soil for a minimal charge. Or, you can buy tester kits through mail-order gardening catalogs.

When tested, your soil will be rated on a pH scale, which runs from 1 (highly acidic) to 14 (highly alkaline). Most soils fall into the range of 5 to 8. Although plants tolerate a wide range of pH values, most prefer a pH between 6.2 and 7.2 (nearly neutral).

Besides the rating, the soil test also will tell you exactly what you need to do to make your soil fall into the preferred range. And you'll learn if your soil lacks any nutrients.

Although some gardeners grow good crops without soil tests, most gardeners use these tests to help them improve their crops.

ADD ORGANIC MATTER

Good garden soil is like a living creature. Although it's made up of many inorganic compounds, it's also populated with billions of microorganisms. Most of these, including many forms of fungi and bacteria, are helpful; some are not. You'll find worms and numerous insects, too—again, mostly beneficial. Thinking of soil as alive is critical to good gardening. Things alive require special care and sensitivity.

The key to keeping a garden soil alive is to provide it with a constant source of nourishment in the form of organic matter. Anything once alive can serve as food for the soil's microorganisms, as well as for worms. In the home garden, this organic matter typically comes in the form of compost (see page 16), rotted manure, straw, grass clippings, shredded leaves, and peat. The soil's living organisms break these materials down into humus, a rich, dark brown substance that does wonders for garden soil.

Humus keeps the garden moist during hot weather. It keeps soil loose so plant roots can grow in it freely. It gives off slow, mild doses of nutrients—like a time-release capsule—and helps soil retain chemical fertilizers. It stops runoff and erosion. It attracts worms, which feed on it and leave behind castings rich in nitrogen. And it helps plants resist disease and insects through increased vigor. For the gardener, humus is the equivalent of "black gold."

Working your garden soil will go a long way to improving it. For small gardens, you can use a garden fork or spade. For a large area, however, a power tiller is convenient, perhaps even necessary.

11

CHOOSING AND USING FERTILIZERS

All plants need fertilizers to grow well. Whether you fertilize your garden according to the specific recommendations of a soil test (see page 11) or on a more casual basis is up to you.

Fertilizers fall into two general categories: organic and inorganic. Organic fertilizers are those formed naturally, including such things as compost, mulch, and manure. Inorganic fertilizers are man-made or mined, often referred to as chemical fertilizers.

Organic fertilizers break down slowly and give small amounts of essential nutrients to plants. Inorganic fertilizers act quickly, giving large amounts of these same essential nutrients to plants. The amount of nutrients provided varies with the composition of each fertilizer.

Both organic and inorganic fertilizers contain three essential—or primary—nutrients vital to good plant growth: nitrogen, phosphorus, and potassium (or potash).

MAKING YOUR OWN FERTILIZER

Some gardeners use only organic fertilizers in their gardens. They make compost from kitchen scraps, garden debris, and grass clippings (see page 16). Compost has a low concentration of essential nutrients, but does supply these steadily over a long time. The compost, once mixed into the soil, also attracts worms, which add nitrogen to the soil through their excretions, called castings. And when worms die, their decomposing bodies supply even more nitrogen.

Organic gardeners also tend to grow nitrogen-fixing crops in their gardens, either for food or as cover crops. Any member of the pea or bean family discharges nitrogen into the soil through nodules in its roots. And by tilling these plants into the soil, you can improve its fertility.

BUYING FERTILIZER

Common organic fertilizers are for sale in most garden centers. The most popular are blood meal, bonemeal, various types of dried cow manure, sludge, and kelp. These fertilizers contain

Nitrogen gives plants their rich green color. It promotes rapid growth of stems and leaves. Plants and soil microorganisms need lots of nitrogen, so replenish it regularly.

Phosphorus is essential for flowering, fruiting, and rapid root growth. Mix plenty of phosphorus into the soil at planting time to get it close to the plant's roots.

Potassium is vital to many phases of plant growth, especially root formation and seed production. As with phosphorus, mix it into the soil at planting time.

varying percentages of essential nutrients, which are listed on the fertilizer labels. These products are often quite expensive compared with the amounts of nutrients in them.

Man-made fertilizers are less expensive than most organic fertilizers. The percentages of nutrients are printed on the container. The numbers indicate the percentage of nitrogen (N), phosphorus (P), and potassium (K) in the package. For example, a 10–10–10 fertilizer contains, by weight, 10 percent of each nutrient; the remainder is inert matter.

Since some plants grow better with different formulations, you'll have to match the nutrient content to the needs of each plant. The choice of fertilizer also varies with the time of year you apply it. (For particulars, see the chart at right or refer to the discussions of specific plants throughout the book.)

APPLYING FERTILIZERS

Organic fertilizers are safe to use at any stage of growth. Mix them into the soil, sprinkle them alongside plants, or spray leaves with diluted material (such as kelp) for foliar feedings. Except for fresh manure, these fertilizers will not burn stems or foliage. Use organic fertilizers wisely by concentrating them where they will do the most good: in the planting hole, at the base of each plant, or directly in a furrow.

Add organic fertilizers to water to form manure tea. Pour this over young plants as a transplant solution or use it on mature plants to stimulate growth.

Inorganic fertilizers are much stronger than organic ones. To guard against fertilizer burn, avoid getting inorganic fertilizers in undiluted granular form on seeds, roots, stems, or leaves of plants. Never use inorganic fertilizer around germinating seedlings for the same reason. The seedlings often will wilt and die if sprinkled with fertilizer granules.

Mix granular inorganic fertilizers into the soil in spring. Or put them right into the furrow or planting hole, covering them with just enough soil to keep them from touching seeds or the roots of transplants.

One teaspoon of inorganic fertilizer mixed into a gallon of water makes a good transplant solution. Each time you plant seedlings, pour 2 cups of the solution around the young plants to help them overcome transplant shock. Diluted inorganic fertilizer will not burn plants if the solution is weak.

Use inorganic fertilizer throughout the season to stimulate growth. Sprinkle it around a plant's base or along a row edge, following the recommendations in the chart, above right.

WHEN TO FEED

Plant Group	Feeding Schedule	Comments
Annuals	Spring and summer	Mix fertilizer into soil before planting. Refeed when you pinch off growing tips or cut back scraggly plants.
Berries	Before spring growth	Side-dress in summer but not late in the season. Late feeding can cause weak growth vulnerable to winter damage.
Bulbs, tubers	Spring and fall	Mix fertilizer into soil under bulbs and tubers at fall planting. Sprinkle soil surface with fertilizer each spring as growth emerges.
Evergreens	Early spring	Use acidic fertilizers for azaleas and camellias. Get fertilizers as deep into the soil as possible.
Houseplants	All year	Increase feeding in spring and summer. Cut back in fall and winter.
Lawns	Early spring to fall	Apply fertilizer to lawn before any growth in spring; will help crowd out weeds. Use low-nitrogen fertilizers late in the season.
Perennials	When growth starts	Repeat again when buds form. Follow more specific recommendations for individual plants (see pages 150–173).
Trees	Spring	Use any method that will get fertilizers deep into the soil.
Vegetables	Throughout season	Mix fertilizer into soil in spring. Side-dress as indicated for individual plants (see pages 296-317).
Woody plants	Early spring	Side-dress young plants again in summer, older plants after any pruning.

■ Limestone

A soil test may show the need for calcium, magnesium, or other nutrients, which varying forms of limestone can supply. The test will tell which form to buy since each affects soil pH differently. Follow directions exactly and never apply lime without testing the soil. Since every soil is different, there is no general rule for using lime.

WATERING

Water is essential to all plants and grasses, but in varying degrees. Too much water can be just as deadly to some plants as too little is to others. Know the water needs of your plants and lawn.

Knowing how and when to water will help you get the very most from your plants. Smart watering also will save you money.

All plants need water—in varying amounts—to survive. Some plants like it dry; others tolerate drought but prefer moisture. Some like it moist; still others like it wet or soggy.

Identifying the water needs of each plant is a critical step in good gardening. You can do this only on a plant-by-plant basis. You'll find much of the necessary information in this book. As added help, read the labels of individual plants you purchase.

Although 1 inch of rain (or water) a week often is enough, there is no hard-and-fast rule about watering. Many garden plants have different watering needs. Temper the inch-a-week general guideline with the following advice.

KNOW YOUR WATER

Whenever possible, use hard water from a well instead of softened water. Softened water costs more, and vegetables, flowers, shrubs, trees, and lawns get no benefits from the salts contained in it.

If your area has extremely hard water with a high pH, heavy watering can change the pH of the soil. This change usually makes little difference except with acid-loving plants such as blueberries, azaleas, and rhododendrons. When growing plants that require specific pH levels, test your soil more frequently and alter the pH as needed.

WATER THE RIGHT WAY

Plants respond to deep watering, not to shallow sprinklings; so whenever you water, drench the soil to a depth of 6 inches or more. To see whether water is getting that deep, dig your hand or poke a tool such as a garden trowel into the soil. A heavy, deep watering from time to time is better for most plants than frequent,

shallow waterings. Since deep watering requires time, use flood irrigation, drip irrigation, or sprinklers to do the job right.

If you use sprinklers, sprinkle during the early morning. Avoid windy or super-hot days to reduce evaporation loss.

Flood irrigation—simply letting water spill over the ground from a hose—works on certain crops such as corn or strawberries. It's also one of the simplest ways to water pine trees and shrubs during dry spells. Less water is lost to evaporation using this method than with traditional sprinklers.

For drip irrigation, the system can be as simple as a hose with holes in it or as complex as a commercial setup that covers acres. Use drip-irrigation systems to efficiently water just the roots of plants in dry areas. To save even more water, place the hoses or feeders under plastic.

For extremely efficient watering, punch holes in a jug or can. Place it next to a specific plant (above or below the ground), and fill it with water. This works well for melons and flowering shrubs.

■ Water whenever plants need it

Stress caused by lack of water will affect the taste of vegetables. Under stress, most flowers grow poorly, as do trees, shrubs, and lawns.

Wilting in the early morning or late evening indicates stress. Get water to plants immediately. If a plant wilts only in the heat of midday, though, stress may or may not be present. Check the plant again in the evening to see whether it has bounced back.

CONSERVING WATER

Water is one of the most precious resources today. In areas prone to drought, it can be so scarce that conservation becomes one of the main concerns of every gardener. One of the simplest and most effective ways to preserve water is to change your soil so it retains every drop for as long as possible.

Do this by adding organic matter to the soil every year. How you add organic matter makes little difference. You can grow cover crops (known as green manure), use organic mulches (such as grass clippings, shredded leaves, or straw), or add compost (see page 16), peat, and rotted manure. All of these break down into humus, which absorbs and holds water in the soil for days.

Also, to help conserve moisture and discourage weeds, apply mulches around plants (see page 17). Weeds compete with cultivated plants for water and valuable nutrients.

CHOOSE SUITABLE PLANTS

One last smart-watering technique is to match your yard's plants to your climate. All plants vary in their water needs. In dry areas, to get stunning gardens without the expense of constant watering, grow plants that can tolerate drought. In wet areas, grow plants suited for high-moisture situations. This simple strategy, so often ignored, is one of the best ways to get beautiful gardens and yards inexpensively.

Horticulturists are constantly breeding plants that tolerate varied climatic conditions. Read catalogs carefully to choose the newest and best varieties for your area.

Trickle or drip-irrigation systems lead water right to the plants' roots. This efficient use of water saves time and money. Systems can be as simple a soaker hose or as complex as this one used to water a large vegetable garden.

COMPOSTING

Everything that dies breaks down into a brown, fluffy material called compost or humus, which is essential to soil vitality and vigorous plant growth. In nature, humus forms at the rate of an inch or so a century. Gardeners use several techniques to help nature make humus faster. These techniques can be simple or involved, depending upon how quickly you want to develop humus. The faster you want it, the more you must help things along.

THE SLOW AND EASY WAY

If you're in no hurry, make compost the simple way. Stack all dead material in a pile at one corner of your garden. Or put it in the center of a ring-shaped wire enclosure. Put all weeds, grass clippings, leaves, and kitchen scraps—including bones with meat on them—into the pile. Over a period of time, these will break down into compost. (Though the bones won't decompose, the meat on them will, providing a rich supply of nitrogen. The temperature of the compost pile will keep any rodents at bay. Remove the bones when completely bare.) This method takes one to two years to form humus.

QUICK COMPOSTING

If you want to speed up the process, follow these simple steps.

Scratch up the soil in a 4x4-foot area to expose soil microorganisms. If you prefer to contain compost and make it more attractive to the eye, enclose the area. Use wire, concrete blocks, or pieces of wood. Leave air spaces on the sides. The gaps help oxygen-loving microorganisms survive and multiply.

Throw organic matter into the enclosure whenever available. Use kitchen scraps, weeds, grass clippings, leaves, small branches, and any other debris that will decompose.

Shred all material into the smallest pieces possible. Fine shredding exposes more surface to the feeding microorganisms.

Occasionally, sprinkle some soil into the pile to bring in millions of fresh microorganisms.

Keep the organic matter moist, but not soggy. If the pile dries out, it won't break down properly. Water the pile in dry weather.

Sprinkle a handful of fertilizer into the pile from time to time. The nitrogen encourages the composting process.

Turn the pile whenever you want, as long as you don't turn it more often than once a week. Turning the pile mixes up the debris, moistens everything, and supplies new oxygen to the microorganisms.

The compost heats up tremendously when it starts to break down. Stick your hand into the pile to feel the warmth. The hotter it is, the better. This heat can be so intense that it kills bacteria and weed seeds.

Your compost pile will shrink to a fraction of its initial size, which is normal. As materials break down, they take up less and less space.

This accelerated composting process requires some energy, but doesn't have to be any more involved than outlined here. And you can have compost in as little as three to eight weeks, depending upon the organic material composted.

Dual compost bins are tidy and efficient. While you fill one, the second is already working. As you remove compost from the first bin, place any "undigested" debris in the other bin for further composting.

MULCHES

There are two types of mulches (anything that covers the surface of the ground is called a mulch)—organic and inorganic. The most popular organic mulches (things once alive) are ones readily available and almost all are inexpensive: compost, grass clippings, pine needles, sawdust, and shredded leaves or bark. Popular inorganic mulches are plastic—both clear and black—and rocks.

Organic mulches break down in the soil and need regular replacing. Inorganic mulches—such as stone and man-made materials—do not break down, and are more permanent.

Mulches do a number of good things for the yard and garden. Organic mulches keep the soil moist and cool. They also break down, providing food for soil microorganisms and worms. This nourishment keeps the soil alive and adds valuable nutrients to it. Organic mulches also stop many weeds from growing, although they cannot stop all weeds. Fortunately, the few that do pop through the mulch are easy to pull because the earth under the mulch is moist. Mulches also prevent erosion on steep slopes and help protect the soil from compacting, which can hinder root growth.

Inorganic mulches raise the temperature of the soil and benefit warmth-loving plants the most. Clear plastic raises temperatures faster than black plastic, but it allows some weeds to sprout under it. Black plastic kills all weeds. Whenever using plastics, always water the ground before laying them down.

Rocks of varying size make good mulches, and come in many colors and shades, which can add to a garden's good looks. Some gardeners put plastic underneath the rocks to stop weeds from sprouting.

One of the best uses of small rocks is in rock gardens, often planted with low-growing flowers and sprawling foliage plants. If chosen correctly, the rocks will retain moisture in the soil yet allow rainwater to penetrate easily.

MULCHES

Kind	Minimum Depth	Comments
Bark (shredded)	2 inches	Attractive and long lasting, but expensive.
Corncobs (ground)	3 inches	Good where available. Slightly acidic.
Cottonseed hulls	3 inches	Nice appearance, but tend to scatter. Keep moist.
Grass clippings	2 inches	Readily available at no cost. Effective and a favorite of earthworms. Replenish often. Compost grass sprayed with weed killer before using as mulch.
Leaves (shredded)	2 inches	Shred all leaves before using as mulch. Break down rapidly and attract earthworms.
Peanut hulls	3 inches	Good where available. Will blow around.
Pine needles	3 inches	Easy to use, slightly acidic, and prone to burning. Hold up well and drain freely. Pine boughs make superb winter mulch.
Plastic (black, clear)	6 mils	Water ground before laying plastic. Cut holes for plants. Excellent for plants that like warm soil.
Sawdust	2 inches	Readily available and inexpensive in many areas. Tends to be acidic (good for azaleas, blueberries, and rhododendrons). Compost first, or add lots of nitrogen to soil during use.
Seaweed	3 inches	Easy to use and inexpensive along coasts. Salt washes off in rain. Can smell.
Straw	4 inches	Superb summer or winter mulch. Becoming expensive. Attracts worms.
Stone (or rock)	2 inches	Nice texture and shape. Good in rock gardens. Difficult to deal with in borders or raised beds; loose rocks can become a problem along pathways.
Tobacco stems	3 inches	Long lasting and good color, but can carry tobacco mosaic virus.

TOOLS

If there is any rule for tools, it is that they should match the job. Good tools solve problems; poor tools don't.

The choice of tools is personal, usually reflecting the gardening style and temperament of each gardener. You may be satisfied with a few basic tools that not only do the job, but do it well. Or you may prefer elaborate tools, such as power shredders, power tillers, and trimmers. For small gardens and yards, power tools often are a matter of choice. For large areas, though, power tools usually are essential, despite their cost and need for regular maintenance.

BASIC TOOLS AND SUPPLIES

The following list includes the tools or supplies often used in the average garden. The only power tool listed is a power tiller, the single most popular item for large gardens.

■ Cultivator	■ Insecticide	■ Rake (iron)
■ Fertilizer	■ Knife (pocket)	■ Spade
■ Fungicide	■ Labels	■ Sprinkler
■ Garden fork	■ Nozzle	■ String
■ Gloves	■ Pail	■ Trowel
■ Hoe	■ Power tiller	■ Watering can
■ Hose	■ Pruners	■ Wheelbarrow

A TOOL PRIMER

Mail-order catalogs describe hundreds of tools. Leaf through these to learn what's available. If you're unsure about a tool's value, borrow or rent it first to see just how well it works for you.

■ Begin with the basics

Most gardeners start with a few simple tools. With no more than a trowel, spade, iron rake, hose, and hoe, a good gardener can create a bountiful paradise. You can add other tools as needed.

■ Keeping costs in line

Tools can be expensive. As with most products, shop around. High price doesn't always indicate good quality.

You'll often find good-quality tools at garage sales. Even after years of use, good used tools are better than inferior new ones.

Make your own tools to help keep costs down. Many gardeners prefer homemade items to more expensive, but similar, products available in stores or catalogs. The pointed end of a broken hoe handle serves well as a dibble. An old hose with holes poked in it can become a trickle irrigation system. And rotary lawn mowers can do some of the work of shredders. Run the mower through a pile of leaves several times—presto, instant mulch.

■ Taking care of tools

Tools rust quickly when left outside, so bring them in each day. Especially convenient is a tool shed near the garden. This saves steps, and protects tools from the elements. Or, install pegboard with fasteners on garage walls and store your tools there. This works well, is inexpensive, and uses space normally wasted.

Clean tools after each use. Scrape all soil from the metal. Spraying off soil with a hose works quickly and well, as long as you dry the metal immediately afterward and coat it with oil.

■ Use tools safely

Tools can cause serious injury. Place them where they can't hurt anyone. The prongs of an iron rake accidentally left lying in a garden, for example, can easily puncture bare feet.

Keep tools sharp. Sharp tools work efficiently, save labor, and cause fewer injuries. Study tools or manuals to know which edges to sharpen (the inside edge of a hoe, for example).

Tighten screws and bolts regularly. Heavy use can loosen them, making some tools next to useless and potentially dangerous.

Wipe wooden handles with linseed oil. This keeps the wood moist, resulting in fewer blisters for the gardener.

Store all poisons in a locked cabinet out of the reach of children and away from pets.

A tool shed close to the garden saves energy and time. Sheds can be just big enough to hold tools, or large enough for tools plus yard supplies. A shed can be attractive, too, as shown here.

LANDSCAPING

Careful landscaping can dramatically change the way you look at—and enjoy—your yard. You can screen out unsightly views or create dazzling new ones. You can extend your home's living area with a deck or patio, or you can capture a nook in the yard with plants. To start, thoroughly study your family's needs and wishes. Then plan in detail the landscape that meets them.

POINTS OF VIEW

No landscape architect knows as well as you just what your family wants and needs. Here are some points to consider when improving your yard.

■ The view from the street

The front entranceway often is planted by the builder for instant effect. These original plants may die, grow out of bounds, or prove to be poor choices. Replace them as needed with carefully selected shrubs, ground covers, and flowers for neat but interesting appearance. Add trees to frame and shade the house. And, if needed, replace walkways and driveways to make them safer and integral parts of the overall landscape look.

■ The view from indoors out

Most people look out at their yard much more often than they actually go there. The views from the most-used windows can lift your spirits if they include your children at play, buds swelling on a crab apple tree when winter wanes, or a lineup of bathers at the birdbath on a summer afternoon. Other sights—such as your neighbor's trash—can irritate or depress you. Hide them with shrubs or vines.

■ The practical view

Cluster all service areas—clotheslines, dog runs, compost piles, and such—where they are most convenient, usually close to the kitchen door. Then use fences, shrubs, or vines to play down their presence. Wise plantings also can stop the wind from yanking the storm door out of your grasp, keep your house warmer in winter and cooler in summer, and cut your energy and water bills.

■ The beautiful view

Rooms that open onto gardens, patios, decks, and pools expand and enhance your living space. With sheltering fences and plantings for privacy, you can entertain in elegance or relax in sweet-scented, shady seclusion. After all, the soul usually thrives best in a place that's safe and unseen, yet offers a view beyond.

(Above) Good landscaping—including new plantings and a side courtyard—turns a so-so yard into an eye-catcher.

(Left) Once a youngster's play area, this small yard is now a restful, private adult retreat.

(Opposite) Well-conceived plans turn a narrow backyard into a large outdoor living, dining, and play area.

CHOOSING PLANTS

(Above) This elegant entrance gains even greater beauty from plantings specially selected to remain in scale. Small trees and shrubs keep the setting intimate and inviting. Low plantings accent, but don't hide, the windows.

(Opposite) Plantings can enhance even the most dramatic deck. Here, they offer privacy without obstructing the unmatchable view, plus add color and greenery without creating undue maintenance chores.

The right plants can mean the difference between a good landscaping job and a great one. They can give you shade, beauty, color, fruit, and fascination—or problems. Take time to know what each plant, tree, or shrub will do before adding it to your yard.

PLANT CONSIDERATIONS

Trees take a long time to mature. So, if you are blessed with good trees, do all you can to design your landscaping around them. And be sure to protect them from unnecessary grade changes, soil compaction, mechanical injury, and pests and diseases.

When choosing a new plant, consider hardiness first. Will the plant thrive in your climate? Pampering a few exotic favorites may be fun, but for ease of maintenance, the bulk of any planting should be naturally adapted to the area. Find your hardiness zone (see pages 8–9) and make sure the plants you like will feel at home in your area, remembering that every yard can have its own microclimates that don't fit quite squarely under your area's zone classification.

Proper size means easy maintenance. Planting tall shrubs in front of windows or spreading shrubs too close to walks leads to constant pruning. And be sure to look up and check for utility wires when planting trees; otherwise, someone someday could prune your tree beyond recognition. To fill in beneath wires, plant short trees, such as magnolia or hawthorn.

Consider a plant's season of interest, planning bloom and fruit-bearing times for maximum enjoyment and convenience. For example, dogwoods are beautiful in spring bloom, have brilliant autumn color, and display an interesting shape in winter. Evergreens will frame your home all year.

Each plant has pros and cons you must weigh. Viburnums, for example, are lovely in bloom, but can bear fruit that's squishy on a walkway. Lovely spring bulbs become scraggly while their foliage dies down. Acorns dropped on a patio need sweeping; dropped on a woodland setting, however, they become a mulch for wildflowers.

THE XERISCAPE CONCEPT

Spreading across the country from the Sunbelt is a sound conservation concept called xeriscaping. Through careful design and plant selection—plus soil improvement, mulching, proper irrigation, and maintenance—xeriscaping helps ensure successful growth yet cuts watering requirements drastically.

In a xeriscape, a plant's water needs determine where it goes. Near the house are the showy, thirsty plants that create an oasis of green foliage and colorful blossoms. Farthest from the house are the natural or xeric zones. Plants in these spaces can live on water from the area's rainfall alone. In between the two extremes are drought-tolerant plants that need infrequent watering.

Xeriscapers consider turf size and shape, too, because grass takes more water and care than any other part of the landscape. Plantings, ground covers, meadows, mulches, decks, and walkways reduce lawns to a size that's both enjoyable and workable.

WHERE TO PLANT TREES AND SHRUBS

Woody plants give substance and three-dimensional shape to your yard. They soften and blend in the lines of the house so it looks as if it belongs. Careful placement of trees and shrubs can not only increase the beauty of your house, but also add to its value.

TREES

Large and durable, trees take little maintenance; yet, in return, they give us shade, texture, fragrance, flowers, autumn color, and interesting berries, bark, and winter shape.

Because trees are so permanent, deciding where to plant them can seem frightening. To make wise decisions, study all you can about the various kinds of trees. Look at other examples in your neighborhood and ask your county extension office or nursery for advice. Visit an arboretum if you can.

Keep in mind your special growing conditions, such as an area's tendency for drought, flooding, salt air, city pollution, and high winds. Select trees you know can withstand—or even thrive on—local conditions.

Always envision the tree at its mature size. Be sure the full-grown tree will have room, and that whatever surrounds it will set it off. A background of evergreens, for example, will accent a magnolia's white blooms.

Use your best instincts and common sense when selecting trees and sites, making sure you don't plant trees where they would block your view from the house windows or from the car as you enter the street.

Once you've made your decisions, plant your trees as early as possible in your landscaping schedule; they take longest to grow, yet add the most to your yard.

■ Tree sites

Plant evergreens on the north and west sides of your house, or between the house and the coldest winds, to cut your heating costs and increase your comfort in winter.

Deciduous trees are the best choice for the south and east. They provide shade through the heat of the day in the summer. In winter, their bare branches let the sun shine in to warm and brighten your rooms.

Deciduous trees offer a great variety of sizes and shapes. Columnar trees—such as gray birch, white and Lombardy poplar, arborvitae, and special varieties like the 'Sentry' maple and 'Sentry' ginkgo—take up very little room on the ground, yet grow tall and stately. They make excellent hedges along property lines to screen views or block the wind.

Vase-shaped and spreading trees—like the red and white oaks, sugar maple, and sycamore—produce lots of shade. Prune their lower branches as the trees mature to help increase air circulation.

Weeping trees like the willow, beech, and weeping cherry need room to spread because they will grow as wide as they do tall.

Even a small side yard has room for trees if you pick the right ones, such as katsura, dogwood, magnolia, redbud, snowdrop, or smoke.

Pyramid shapes are natural to the pin oak, small-leaved linden, sweet gum, and larch. They look formal and work well on lawns or along the street.

Small flowering trees—such as dogwood, crab apple, flowering cherry, hawthorn, and magnolia—make excellent accent trees. They are ideal beneath electric lines where they can fill the skyline and view, yet not interfere with the wires.

■ How many trees?

The number of trees to plant is a personal choice. Mother Nature crowds them close together in forests with delightful effects. If you are willing to crowd and control, you can do likewise. You can always remove a tree if you have too many. But if some die and you have too few, it takes years to grow more.

To fill empty spaces the first few years, plant fast-growing, temporary trees such as poplar, silver maple, alder, and black locust. Be sure these trees don't crowd or compete for water and nutrients with the choice plants, and cut them down as the permanent trees grow.

SHRUBS

Unlike trees, shrubs can grow to maturity in just a few years. Like trees, though, shrubs offer a wide selection of sizes, blooms, foliage color and texture, and fruit production. Use them lavishly, but prudently. Avoid too many shrubs or shrubs that spread too much. Going overboard with shrubs will smother the lines of your house or take up too much yard.

Usually, a grouping of at least three shrubs of the same kind and color will give a much more striking, pleasing, and unifying result than if you use too great a variety. If you do choose a mixed-shrub border, avoid the tall-short look. Blend textures, colors, and bloom times.

Whether tree or shrub, all woody plants soon claim their own space; young ones, though, grow better if surrounded by mulch. If you choose not to mulch, set cultivated plants around tree or shrub trunks; the cultivated plants will remind you to feed and water your young woody plants. Lawns or wild plants are the worst early companions. They lead to neglect or damage from lawn mowers.

PLANTING DISTANCES

Dwarf fruit and small flowering trees are ideal for small lots. Plant them at least 8 feet from buildings and 10 feet from other small trees so their branches will touch but not entwine.

Put most foundation plantings 3 feet from the house; spreading junipers 4 feet. Be careful not to put the plants directly under the drip line. If the roof extends beyond the planting, you'll have to water accordingly.

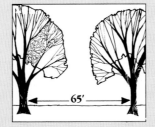

Large trees with wide-spreading branches need 65 feet between trunks for their ideal growth. Given the room, most trees will spread their branches and roots as wide as their height.

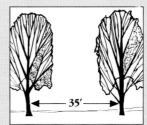

Nonspreading trees still need up to 35 feet between trunks to develop and show their natural forms. For uniform growth in a formal row, buy grafted stock.

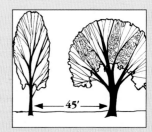

Nonspreading trees planted with spreading varieties will compete for nutrients and light. For full development, space them 45 feet apart. Willow and poplar trees have invasive roots, so plant them 65 feet or more from water pipes.

ANALYZING YOUR LOT AND YOUR NEEDS

While all the decisions about plants simmer in your subconscious, you need to ask—and answer—some questions about your lot and your needs. Only by doing so can you come up with a concept and a plan to achieve your landscaping goals.

EXAMINING YOUR NEEDS

What do you have? Learn the identity and value of the trees and shrubs already growing in your yard. When do they bloom? What are their fall colors? Which ones do you want to save or accent? You may want to remove the less desirable or move the misplaced.

What do you want and need? Some families need a swing set and a vegetable garden; others, a patio and a pool. Write down all considerations and incorporate the most important.

What will your wants and needs cost in time, energy, and money? A good plan can save all three—and be done in stages to stagger costs.

Is there a landscape style you favor, and will it fit in with your house and lot? What plants or structural features will best develop that style?

What are the different microclimates in your yard? Think of ways to take advantage of them. For example, put tender plants on the south side of the house where they will get the most protection. Plant fruit trees where the late-winter sun will not lure peaches into bloom before the last frost. Construct the pool where the sun is brightest, and build the path from the car to the kitchen in a wind-protected location.

Where do shadows fall? How do they change through the seasons? Fruit and vegetables need all the sun they can get. You can choose specific flowers, ground covers, and shrubs to thrive in sun or shade.

Are there underground cables or water lines you must not break? Utility companies usually will show you where the lines are. Some may be marked on building plans.

Will any of your changes affect your neighbors? If so, talk to them early in the planning stage to avoid misunderstandings.

Do you have drainage problems or grades that will need changing? For big or complicated jobs, call in experts. They will save you money in the long run.

A "before" nightmare! Here, shrubs are overgrown and out of shape. The trash can is more necessary than lovely. Overall, the yard lacks charm. To find out what the homeowners did to add charm, see pages 29–35.

A CASE STUDY: ANALYSIS

It takes courage to say, "The shrubs and grass must go." But courage is what's needed.

This yard had fine trees, but the shrubbery was scraggly and dull, and the lawn patchy. Overall, the landscaping looked boring.

The homeowners wanted to accent the trees, brighten and dramatize the entry, and tie the house to the site with plants that offered more year-round interest. Additionally, the backyard needed an easy access from the front, more plantings, and a focal point.

By analyzing their landscape problems and needs first, the homeowners were able to transform a so-so yard into sensational surroundings.

Blah entry
This yard has neither color nor charm. It expresses no welcome and emphasizes the plainness of the house.

Vexing slopes
The land falls away to the right of the house and rises to the left. Such slopes add interest if landscaped well, are obstacles otherwise.

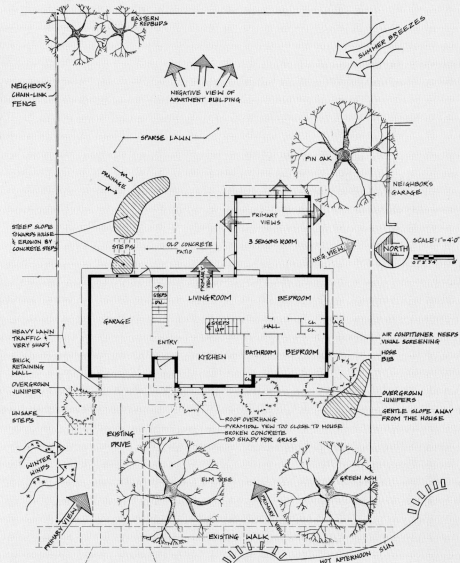

Eroded soil
At the back of the house, the stairs are a case of a missed opportunity for special plantings.

Patchy turf
Bare spots in the lawn from too much shade detract from the appearance of the front and back yards.

29

GETTING A PLAN ON PAPER

You can do landscaping plans in your head, but the work and the results will be haphazard at best. Mistakes that would easily show up on a scaled plan may not become glaring in reality until years of work—and growth—have gone wasted.

CURRENT SITE

Check for any plans of your lot that may already be available from the builder or architect, or from the local Federal Housing Administration or Veterans Administration office. Or see whether a loan plat is on file with your deed or with your mortgage company. Get copies of any plans; they will save you time.

Also ask the builder, architect, or FHA official whether any topographical data is on file. This may show grade changes and drainage.

You may need a surveyor if plans are missing or incomplete, if your lot is irregularly shaped, or if it has different levels or unusual angles. Make sure the survey shows the exact sizes of both the lot and the house, and indicates precise grades of walks, steps, walls, drives, and the ground itself. The survey also should accurately pinpoint where all trees and other features lie on your property.

If your lot is small and level, or if you are especially determined, you can make your own site plan from scratch. Doing so will teach you much about your property.

To create your own plan, start with graph paper and let each square equal a foot or more. Tape pieces of the paper together. If you use separate sheets for sections of the yard, lay them out together to get the whole picture.

The best way to take your site's measurements is with a flexible 25- or 50-foot tape. On extremely large yards, you may want to measure your own average pace, then pace off distances.

First get everything down as it now stands. Start with the property lines, then indicate the exact position of the house. Show where the

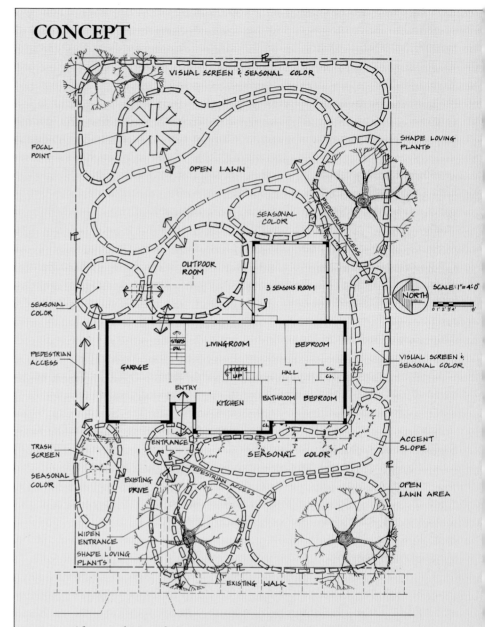

CONCEPT

After analyzing their property, the homeowners found that their main goals for the front yard were to make the entrance inviting all the way from the street to the door, and to add seasonal color. For the side yards, they needed to tame or take advantage of slopes. And in the backyard, they wanted to screen out a bad view, add a focal point, allow an open play area for their children, and establish an outdoor-living area for themselves and guests.

windows and outside doors are, and which rooms they lead into; that way you can plan views and accesses.

Next determine the location of other structures, drives, and walks. Plot your existing trees and their spread, both present and possible.

Mark slopes, overhead utility wires, hose outlets, downspouts, underground wires or pipes, and propane or septic tanks. Draw in the north point so you can consider sun and shade preferences and directions of cooling summer breezes or wicked winter winds.

Indicate good views you want to frame and poor views you want to screen. Mark vehicle traffic patterns. Get all family members involved, too. They can help you think of complications you should solve in the early stages. By considering everyone's wants and needs, you will ensure both appreciation and cooperation as the plan takes shape. The whole project will be less work, more fun, and more successful.

PROPOSED SITE

Next consider the changes you want to make. This can take some doing. On paper it is cheap and easy to try any variety of dreams, rearrange to your heart's content, and change your mind until you get it right.

The easiest way to do this is to make a drawing with all unchangeable features on it, then make as many photocopies as you need. Or spread tracing paper over the original and try different additions or variations.

Another option is to cut out paper shapes to indicate different structures or plantings and move these around until you find the combination that works best.

Don't restrict yourself to the bird's-eye view of your plan. Go outside often and imagine your drawing in various stages of growth and seasons of the year. Sit on the porch and conjure up the view to be, or walk around imagining your ideas bearing fruit. The main thing is to consider the pros and cons of all ideas.

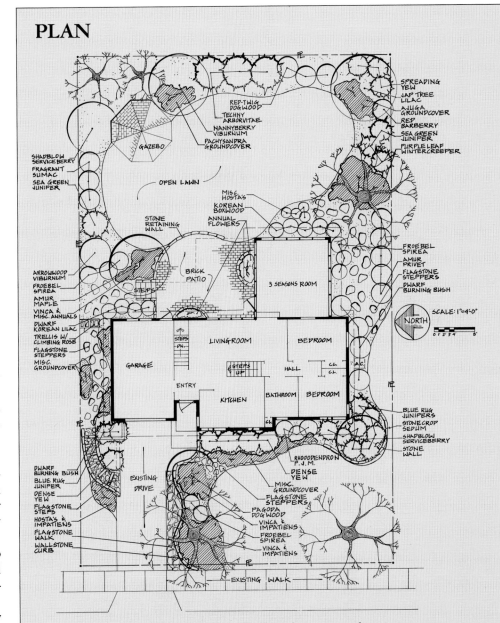

PLAN

For the front yard, a flagstone walk and a stone curb provide needed charm, and new plantings supply color. For the south side yard, a stone wall retains a now-level planting area. On the opposite side, flagstone steps and stepping-stones tame the slope and allow access. In the backyard—which will be a warm-weather retreat for the family—a brick patio replaces a concrete slab, and a gazebo adds an outdoor sitting room.

IMPLEMENTING THE PLAN

(Right) Once cold and colorless, the newly landscaped entry now welcomes visitors with bright borders of impatiens that bloom all summer after daffodils and crocus have faded. Interesting curves, shrubs for every season, and accent plants frame and focus the setting.

By the time all things are considered, the scope of your plan might frighten you a bit. But relax. You don't have to accomplish everything at once. After all, the key to successful landscaping often is to slice the overall objective into smaller tasks. Implementing these tasks in phases or stages over time—even a number of years, if desired—makes any project, no matter how involved, attainable.

FIRST, TREES

Yards with mature trees start out way ahead in a landscaping plan of action. If your yard isn't so blessed, however, and your landscaping plan calls for new trees, concentrate on them first. Trees take up to three years making initial root growth before they begin much topgrowth. Planting trees as soon as possible lets them settle in while you work on other landscaping phases.

For trees near the house and for framing views, get the largest trees you can afford. Larger trees let you achieve your landscaping goals years sooner.

For distant or less visible spots, start smaller trees and fill in around them with ground covers or flowers until the trees spread.

NEXT, DECIDE OTHER PRIORITIES

After taking care of the trees, you then need to decide what other area you want to concentrate on. Is it more important to you to landscape the front entry first, since it's the most visible to the public? Or, is adding a backyard deck or patio for private retreats and family get-togethers top priority? The choice is personal. But whatever area you concentrate on, as a general rule, build structures first, then do your smaller plantings.

Also, remember that no landscaping job ever is really finished. Even the best-laid plans—because they involve time, weather, and living material—need constant updating. New knowledge and varieties will dictate improvements over the years. So may changes in family needs. Even trees are cast in wood, not stone, so don't be afraid to change. It is *your* yard and *your* plan.

Gently curving and rising flagstone steps to the left of the garage lead to the back- and side yards. With a flared bed of shade-loving hostas and impatiens, this feature is attractive in itself, while promising added interest around the corner. Blue rug junipers soften the brick wall without obstructing the path. A dense yew in front of the garbage cans allows them to stay in a convenient spot without attracting attention.

At the side of the house opposite the garage, a rock wall levels the slope for a corner planting. Evergreen junipers give year-round substance. The serviceberry tree has white May blossoms, edible berries, and a yellow autumn color. Sedum and baby's-breath bask in spots of sun. Tubing buried beneath the bed drains water from the rainspout through the wall's square openings onto the lawn. For a final flourish, rock garden plants grow between the wall stones.

IMPLEMENTING THE PLAN *(continued)*

The focal and fun feature of the backyard is this freestanding gazebo. Background trees mark the edge of the property, filter noise, screen the neighboring apartment building from view, buffer winds, and assure privacy. Accent plants bring even more interest to the quiet getaway without adding the maintenance problems of a larger flower bed. New sodding lets healthy green turf act as a contrast to the light-colored gazebo, drawing attention to the structure.

PATIOS

This small, exposed backyard was seldom used. Now the family enjoys split-level living beneath the canopy of an ash tree. Outdoor living areas should remain in scale with indoor rooms. Making them too large is a common mistake.

Patios are perfect places to relax and enjoy the outdoors, cook meals on the grill, and visit in the twilight while the children chase lightning bugs.

Because patios are permanent structures, they require careful planning. Check local building codes and zoning ordinances first. Then determine the best place to fit your patio into your landscaping plan, preferably near the kitchen and family room for easy access.

Don't put your patio too far from the house, in the path of prevailing winds, or in full view of the neighbors, if you have other choices.

Use existing shade trees to full advantage. If your trees are still small, consider adding a trellis or arbor, and covering it with moonflower vine, morning-glory, or fragrant sweet autumn clematis. Or grow edible shade with grapes, kiwis, or white or scarlet runner beans. Other edible shrubs and container plants mix well with ornamentals to provide color, accent, and berries for your cereal.

Be sure your patio is large enough for your family and entertaining needs, yet small enough to feel intimate.

For ground-level interest, choose surfaces and patterns of concrete slab, flagstone, tile, brick, or wood slab, or loose material like wood chips and pebbles.

CONSTRUCTION TIPS

When building your patio, stake out the design and level the site. For the patio to be even with the surrounding yard or slightly above it, you'll need to excavate 6 to 8 inches. For good drainage, a patio adjacent to the house should slope away ⅛ to ¼ inch per foot.

Spread a 2- to 4-inch bed of fine gravel or sand in the excavated area. If you want to set material in mortar, pour an additional bed of concrete about 4 inches deep.

Roofs and walls over patios form barriers against the elements but cost a lot. Screen structures will keep out bugs, letting you enjoy outdoor air with the feel of indoor protection.

This elegant patio of patterned bricks overlooks a retaining wall and sloping yard. Trees, shrubs, and wildflowers screen the near end for privacy while adding shade, color, and fragrance.

In this desert oasis garden, a simple patio of flagstones and pebbles nestles under the canopy of a catalpa tree. Flagstone-and-pebble pathways wind between the surrounding flower beds for the feeling of a Mediterranean garden.

DECKS

A deck almost demands enjoyment as it sets you apart from the bustle of daily problems. And it gives you a chance to enjoy many indoor activities in the fresh air.

Besides providing family entertainment, a deck increases a home's property value, so think of it more as an investment than a luxury.

Decks are appropriate for any terrain or setting. They can frame a pleasant view or solve a landscaping problem in an odd-shaped yard. And they can offer easy access to the outdoors without stairs, making them great for the old or weary as well as the young and active.

A deck around an aboveground pool can tie the pool in with the landscape and help keep small children safely away from the water.

If you have a sloping yard, a deck will give you a much-needed level surface.

For unequaled enjoyment, embellish your deck with weatherproof furniture, wraparound benches, colorful cushions, or potted plants. Outdoor lighting, cleverly placed, can expand the uses of the deck, make for gala entertaining, and spotlight surrounding plantings.

CONSTRUCTION TIPS

Plan carefully, whether you design the deck yourself or call in a professional.

Check first for zoning restrictions, building codes, and easements. You may need a surveyor to specify exactly where you can begin to build in relation to property lines.

Keep an eye on the sun. The north and east sides of a home are pleasantly cool on a summer afternoon or evening. A deck facing west or south may get too warm.

If you are at all handy, decks are good projects to do yourself. Your local building supply store may help with material selection and ideas. Or hire a carpenter.

Be sure your deck blends with the color and design of your home.

(Left) This small deck combines a spa in latticed seclusion with shaded space for summer suppers.

(Opposite) This deck, cantilevered from a hillside, converts a problem slope into a relaxing living and entertaining space.

(Below) Multiple levels make decks dynamic. This one is far enough away from the house for peaceful entertaining, yet connected to the home's mainstream by stairs.

PRIVACY FENCES

Privacy doesn't mean "Keep Out," as this inviting entry shows. Artistic design and enticing cracks that tempt peeks from passersby suggest that the garden within must be enchanting and beckoning.

No longer are fences just for keeping children in and animals out. Today, they can turn the whole yard into a private park. This trend began in Sunbelt gardens where gentle seasons make the value of landscaping most apparent. It is increasing in popularity nationwide.

USES AND DESIGN

A privacy fence can surround all or part of a yard. It can be solid or have peekaboo openings, which lend a sense of mystery.

Fences can be elegant and expensive, or utilitarian chain link covered with English ivy or abloom with climbing roses.

A short stretch of fence or series of panels can separate parts of one yard from the next. Like walls in a house, fences help people to live close without closing in.

They also can support vines, give interesting backgrounds to plantings, protect from strong winds, create warm sunny nooks to shelter tender plants and winter-weary people, and unify a house and garden with material that harmonizes with both.

Garden gates, arches, and openings offer more possibilities for design and intrigue with their sense of welcome and promise. You may need a large gate to sometimes let vehicles through, and a smaller gate for easy daily opening. A gate or stile between neighbors allows for friendly visiting.

CONSTRUCTION TIPS

Check with the local building inspector to find out if the height of fences is regulated. It also is wise to build a minimum of 6 inches inside your property line just in case of a faulty survey.

Keep maintenance in mind, too. For example, you can leave redwood and cedar to weather to a natural gray and save the time of painting or staining. For security, make latches high and complicated enough to thwart toddlers.

Lacy lattice delicately shields those seeking solitude in this more formal garden. Fencing is like a frame—it sets the mood or garden theme. This one says elegant relaxation.

Hanging plants soften the expanse of this tall wood privacy fence. Such a wall might feel imprisoning if not made friendlier with plants.

SLOPE SOLUTIONS

Slopes well used can add fascination or privacy to your outdoor living, just as different levels in your home do. When poorly planned, however, they add only to maintenance problems.

If a slope is steep enough that it's difficult to establish grass or dangerous to mow, consider other treatments. Ground covers often are the best and easiest solution. Select them for beauty, as well as erosion control.

On long or steep slopes, a series of walls and terraces can differentiate living areas: a quiet cove at the top or bottom of the hill, for example; garden, orchard, or woodland plantings on the middle level; and turf near the house.

WALLS

Retaining walls are made from many materials to add architectural interest to a yard as well as hold its slopes in place.

Both dry walls and the stronger masonry walls require careful construction to withstand the tremendous pressure of the earth behind them. Because of that, hire a contractor for any wall over 3 feet high. For all retaining walls, set the foundations below the frost line; for a dry stone wall, slant the face toward the hill up to 2 inches for every foot of height so it won't bulge from the pressure.

Plan for drainage with small holes in the masonry near the base of the wall, or lay drain tile horizontally behind the wall.

Add interest with buttresses, panels, or plants cascading over the top. Set rock plants in the pockets of soil in a dry wall. Form raised beds at the tops of other walls.

STEPS

Steps dare you to imagine the beauty beyond and entice you to go exploring. Even the most rustic mulched path with railroad-tie risers adds undeniable charm to a slope.

Make steps less steep than those indoors and as wide as the walk leading to them. Use material that harmonizes with your yard and house.

(Opposite, above) Cut logs, set vertically, add interest and background to this spring garden, harmonizing with its natural feeling. Notice that this log wall is not used as an edging, but to divide levels.

(Opposite, below) A stucco wall billows with a bank of begonias and impatiens. Using the same material for both the wall and the house (not shown) results in a more formal feeling.

(Right) Walls of wood ties turn a steep bank into a bounteous vegetable garden. Weeding and picking are made hip-height easy. And climbing the stairs gives opportunity to notice new growth.

LAWNS AND GROUND COVERS

Thriving grass—green, lush, and trouble free—will carpet your yard with a surface suited especially for those hard at play or rest. Where growing grass is difficult or too extensive, turn to ground covers. They are easy to maintain and come in many inviting colors, textures, heights, and forms.

STARTING A LAWN

This lawn points the way for the foot as well as the eye, giving a definite sense of direction. For easy care, group lawn areas with plants of similar water needs. And be sure to keep other plantings from isolating islands of grass.

A lawn can last a hundred years, so plan and plant carefully—as shown on this page and the next—for a lawn that should thrive for generations.

■ **Grading**
Before starting a lawn, make sure the area is as level as possible and drains properly. For good drainage, slope the lawn gently away from your house. For severe grade, consider ground covers or a retaining wall. Mowing steep slopes is hard and can be dangerous.

Whenever building or drastically changing grades, remove the topsoil first, then respread it over the leveled surface. Big grading jobs may require professionals. For smaller jobs, a spade and rake or an old tire pulled by a rope will do.

■ **Improving the soil**
Test first. Buy a simple soil test kit from a local nursery, or contact your county extension agent and follow instructions. Most grasses thrive in a neutral or slightly acid environment with a pH level of 6 to 7. Add lime as needed to improve the structure and provide the best enrivonment (less acid, better chemical balance) for the soil bacteria.

Add organic matter, such as moist peat or weed-free compost, and additional topsoil, if needed, to increase growth and decrease maintenance. Also, broadcast a complete fertilizer (10–10–10, for example) using 10 to 20 pounds per 1,000 square feet, depending on the fertility of the soil. Till or spade 6 inches deep, making the soil pebbly, but not powdery. Remove any rocks or debris, then rake smooth, leaving shallow crevices to catch grass seeds.

■ **Choosing the kind of grass**
Choose from new, improved grasses according to how much sun the grass will get, and how you will use your yard. (See charts, pages 50–51.)

Mixtures give you the most benefits. In southern states, warm-season grasses turn brown after frost. Over-seed with a winter grass in the fall to keep weeds out and extend the lawn's color.

In the upper two-thirds of the country, cool-season grasses flourish in spring and fall. They turn brown in winter and often go almost dormant during a summer drought.

If starting a lawn from seed, always check the package label for percentage of germination, varieties included, and percent of inert ingredients. Better seed is worth the price; cheap seed is no bargain if you have to redo all the work.

■ **When to start**
The ideal time for sowing seed is early September, with very early spring second best. Sod,

WAYS TO START A LAWN

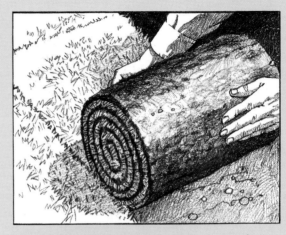

(Left) Using a mechanical spreader, apply half of the seed one way, the rest in a perpendicular direction over the same area.

(Right) When sodding, prepare the soil the same as for seeding. Lay sod soon after buying it, staggering the end seams. Roll and water as for seeding.

(Left) Sprigging or stolonizing buries starts of grass with only the top nodes above ground.

(Right) Use plugs to start grasses that spread by runners, such as zoysia or Bermuda grass. Most southern lawns are started this way and fill in quickly.

sprigs, and plugs can go in almost anytime, though spring or fall is preferred. If sowing seed, sow the amount called for on the package. Then rake lightly to cover the seed with about ⅛ inch of soil.

Roll the area after planting seed or sod, then, if seeding, cover with a mulch to conserve moisture. If you rent a drum roller with a surface of mesh fabric, you can roll the ground and apply a thin mulch of peat moss at the same time. Or spread straw about ⅛ inch thick over the seed after you've rolled the area. If you use burlap to retain moisture, remove it as soon as germination begins.

■ Watering and mowing

The main killer of all new lawns is dryness. To prevent this, water lightly several times a day for the first week; the next week, water at least once a day. Water less frequently but more deeply as grass grows.

Weeds may also germinate, but your new grass soon will crowd them out. Keep traffic off the grass until your lawn is well established.

When new growth is about 2 inches tall, mow the grass with sharp blades set about 1½ inches high. Fertilize lightly after mowing, as well as monthly for three or four months, giving thinner spots a bit more to equalize growth.

REJUVENATING A LAWN

No matter how thin and bedraggled wear and tear or the weather leaves your lawn, it has tremendous comeback power. Proper care will quickly improve an existing lawn.

NEW LIFE FOR AN OLD LAWN

Fall is normally the best time for repair in the North; early spring is best in the South.

First remove all litter and leaves. Then get rid of the weeds—by hand or, if necessary, by repeated applications of herbicide. At the same time, feed the remaining grasses.

To reseed individual areas of your lawn, wait as directed after using herbicide. Then loosen the soil 4 to 6 inches deep and work in some balanced fertilizer. Rake the ground to smooth it, spread good-quality seed, and tamp it down. Apply a light mulch to keep heavy rains from washing away seed and to conserve moisture.

If the entire lawn looks bad, check the thatch. Some is good. It recycles plant tissues, adds organic fertilizer, and helps control weed growth. But if the thatch is more than ¾ inch deep, it can harbor insects and diseases, prevent water and fertilizers from reaching the soil, and keep new grass from breaking through.

To make easy work of thatch removal, rent a power rake and set it deep enough to make small cuts in the soil. Otherwise, rake vigorously by hand. Add the thatch to your compost pile or use it as a mulch. Or use one of the thatch-removing fertilizers or sprays as directed on the product label. Soon your lawn will look new.

To give new life to your entire lawn, overseed right after removing thatch. Use good-quality seed, spreading it at about half the rate recommended for a new lawn—usually 1 or 2 pounds per 1,000 square feet.

In southern states you can plug warm-season grasses such as zoysia right into an existing lawn. They will eventually crowd out weeds and seeded grasses. Before plugging, water the lawn and mow low. After plugging, keep the soil just barely moist. The established grasses will shade

PERK UP YOUR LAWN

For extensive weeding, use weed killers, following instructions carefully—especially when using on a newly seeded lawn. Never spray on a windy day, and label the sprayer "For Herbicides Only." When weeds are few, weed with a long-handled asparagus cutter.

Apply lawn food to the entire lawn when growth resumes. For even greening, apply half in one direction, half in a second pass at right angles. If you are reseeding, wait a week after feeding to reseed, or delay feeding until you've mown the new grass at least once.

After seeding, water, using a fine spray so seeds don't wash away. Keep the soil moist until new grass becomes established. Also water after removing thatch to help the lawn recover.

the new grass and help retain moisture. Do not mow until the new grass is 2 inches tall. Continue as for a new lawn (see pages 46–47).

LEVELING HUMPS AND HOLLOWS

If unlevel parts of your yard—usually the result of earthworm activity or freezes and thaws—interfere with mowing or get boggy, it is time to take action.

In low spots, add a mix of weedless topsoil or sand and peat right on top of the grass to a depth of ¼ inch. Smooth it with an iron rake. Repeat twice a year until filled to the right level.

For deep depressions, slice back the existing sod in strips about 20 inches wide. Roll or fold the grass back, then fill the depressions with clean, rich soil. Smooth and tamp firmly, then replace the sod. Top-dress with ¼ inch of soil and water deeply.

To lower high spots, use a sharp, flat spade to remove inch-wide, 6-inch-deep wedges of turf the length of the mound. Repeat this at 10-inch-wide intervals. Soak the area thoroughly, then roll with a heavy roller to seal the spaces. Repeat in spring and fall until the hump disappears.

MAINTAINING A LAWN

Consistent care can become a pleasant habit and save extra work by preventing problems.

The nature of grass is to grow green at the top and turn brown at the base. By mowing often enough—usually at least weekly during active growth—you avoid cutting off all the existing green growth and encourage low, thick new growth. You also discourage weeds.

Check the charts on pages 50–51 for mowing heights for your kind of grass. As a general rule, do not cut the grass by more than one-third to one-half of its height. Get a mower you can handle and one with easy-to-change mowing levels. Keep the blades sharp. Mow a different direction every time. Mow shady spots less frequently and ½ inch higher. In heat or drought, cut the whole yard higher to save moisture.

Light clippings usually can stay on the lawn. They decompose quickly and add nutrients and humus. But if the grass gets too tall, remove the clippings to the compost pile or use them as a mulch. If you've used herbicide on the lawn in the last six weeks, let the clippings sit for six more before using them for mulch.

Watering is useless unless it gets deep into the soil, usually 6 to 12 inches. Sandy soils need less water but more often. When grass turns from rich green to a bluish tint, loses resiliency so footprints remain, and grows much slower, it needs watering. Water only when needed, though, because excess moisture is harmful, too.

Feeding in the spring and fall with a good, slow-release lawn food will keep growth strong enough to crowd out weeds. The spring feeding should contain nitrogen, phosphorus, and potassium in a ratio of 2:1:1 at a rate of about 4 pounds per 1,000 square feet. In the fall use a 1:2:2 mix to encourage healthy root growth during winter.

Edging and *trimming,* once endless chores, are now easy with power equipment. But you must use these tools carefully, especially around trees. Protect trees from damaging nicks by encircling them with mulch contained by edging.

Lawn care can be easy, with results that make outdoor living serene and luxurious. New grasses require fewer poisons and make better use of water. Too much grass, though, can drain natural resources and be tiresome to maintain, so grow grass only where you really want it.

49

COOL-SEASON GRASSES

Grass	Characteristics	Light	Mowing Ht. (In.)	Comments
BENT GRASSES *Agrostis* sp. **Colonial** 'Highland' 'Exeter'	Fine quality; fine-textured turf. Aggressive, usually dominant grass for well-kept small areas and golf-green appearance.	Sun	¾	Used mainly on golf greens; not suited to home lawns unless you wish to spend time watering, feeding, and mowing with a reel mower. Best in cool, humid climates or Northwest and Northeast. Many fine varieties.
Velvet	Tolerates low fertility.	Sun	¾	Sometimes used in seed mixes.
Redtop	Course-textured, stemmy.	Sun	1½–2	More adaptable. Doesn't bear much traffic; turns brown under heat stress. Best as temporary cover.
BLUEGRASSES *Poa* sp. 'Adelphi' 'America'	Dark green with V-shaped tips. Blades upright, fine-textured; soft growth. 3- to 4-foot root systems.	Sun	1½–2	Most popular choice for northern lawns in sun. Blends with other grasses. Green during cool, moist spring and fall. Goes dormant in hot, dry summers.
'Bonnieblue'	Quick spring green, dense, low.	Sun	1½–2	Hybrid standout from Rutgers.
'Eclipse'	Tolerates heat, drought.	Shade	1½–2	Top-rating hybrid from Rutgers.
'Glade'	Slow vertical growth. Resists smut, mildew.	Shade	1½–2	Can be used in sun, too.
'Merion'	Fast rooting as sod; slow from seed. Coarse texture.	Sun	1½–2	Original breakthrough variety. Wears well but needs much care. Not good in shade.
'Sydsport'	Dense, low, aggressive.	Sun	1½–2	Establishes fast and wears well. Resists disease.
FESCUES *Festuca* sp. **Coarse, tall**	Medium green, clumpy. Resists disease, drought. Best for play areas that get rough treatment.	Light shade	2–2½	Sow pure stand and at heavy rate for finer texture. 'Arid,' 'Falcon,' 'Galway,' 'Titan,' and 'Houndog' offer limited-care lawns.
Fine	Fine-textured grass; medium to dark green color. Mixes well. Needs little nitrogen.	Shade	2–2½	Often used for about 20 percent of mix with blue- and ryegrasses for shade and drought tolerance. Useful for over-seeding dormant Bermuda grass. Germinates faster than bluegrass, but compatible. More susceptible to disease than coarse fescues.
Red creeping	Spreads by underground rhizomes.	Shade	2–2½	'Ensylva,' 'Dawson,' 'Fortress,' and 'Pennlawn' are good varieties.
RYEGRASSES *Lolium* sp. **Annual, Italian**	Large seeds; germinates in a few days. Coarse. Dies out in winter in North, summer in South.	Sun	1½	Useful for temporary lawn or as green manure to turn under and improve soil. Also good for over-seeding dormant warm-season grasses in fall.
Perennial	Coarse; medium to dark green. Dense, fine-texture turf; almost equal to bluegrass but doesn't mow as neatly. Varieties such as 'Pennant' contain endophytic fungus, so they require less insecticide.	Sun or light shade	1½	Often sown in mixtures with bluegrass. Rye sprouts quicker, becomes established quicker. Makes a usable lawn in three weeks. Not as hardy in the North as in the southern two-thirds of the country. Use new cultivars: 'All-Star,' 'Derby,' 'Elka,' 'Fiesta II,' 'Pennant,' 'Pennfine,' 'Regal,' SR4000.

WARM-SEASON GRASSES

Grass	Characteristics	Light	Mowing Ht. (In.)	Comments
BAHIA GRASS *Paspalum notatum*	Very coarse, pasture grass; open habit; inexpensive to start but poorer quality. Erect and tough. Wide leaves. Seed heads unsightly in spring. Resists pests and diseases. Open to weeds.	Sun	2–3	Tolerates partial shade, neglect, drought or moist and humid conditions, acid or alkaline soil. Turns brown below 30 degrees. Start by seed or sod. Slow to germinate (20 days) and establish. Popular in Southeast. Improved varieties include 'Tifhi,' 'Wilmington,' 'Seaside,' 'Paraguay,' and 'Pensacola.'
BERMUDA GRASSES *Cynodon dactylon*	Tough, attractive lawn with care. 'Tif' series grasses are dwarf and fine textured, medium to dark green. Browns at 32 degrees. Over-seeding with fine fescues or rye gives year-round green and keeps out weeds when dormant.	Sun	½–1½	Does not like shade or cold, but resists drought, salt air, and wear fairly well. Needs frequent mowing and feeding, and can invade flower beds. Subject to nematodes in Southeast, eriophyid mite in Southwest. Named varieties must be started from sprigs, stolons, or plugs. Wears well; used for athletic fields. Easy walking.
'Santa Ana'	Medium texture, blue-green.	Sun	½–1½	Resists salt and smog. Tolerates pollution.
'Tifgreen'	Used on putting greens.	Sun	½–1½	Frequent feedings brighten color.
'Tifway'	One of the best 'Tifs'; used on fairways. Dark green; takes more cold.	Sun	½–1½	Stiffer; good for home lawns. Doesn't need as much mowing and care.
CENTIPEDE GRASS *Eremochloa ophiuroides* Chinese lawn grass	Medium green; medium texture, not as fine as Bermuda grass; takes less cold than Bermuda, but more than St. Augustine. Spreads by creeping stems. Mow infrequently.	Sun	1½	Not as tolerant of drought; discolors more readily. Well adapted to infertile, acid soils of Southeast from Carolinas south. Needs little feeding; give phosphorus and potassium only when dormant. Start by sprigs or plugs, 1 to 1½ feet apart. Water regularly. Not good on seashore.
ST. AUGUSTINE GRASSES *Stenotaphrum secundatum*	Broad flat stems, attractive blue-green nearly year-round. Thick, coarse stems; the best of the warm-season grasses for partial shade. Few seed heads.	Sun or light shade	1½–2	Almost as fast growing from plugs as Bermuda grass. Tends to build up spongy thatch that makes walking on it difficult. Invasive; will even climb shrubs. Subject to brown patch, gray leaf spot, nematodes, St. Augustine Decline (SAD) virus, and chinch bugs. Needs spraying for proper care.
'Bitter Blue'	Blue-green; frost tolerant.	Same	1½–2	Does not wear well.
'Floratam'	Dark green; resists virus and chinch bugs. Good in Texas.	Same	1½–2	Needs much sun. Poor tolerance to cold.
'Seville'	Most shade and cold tolerant.	Same	1½–2	Resists SAD and gray leaf spot, not chinch bugs.

ZOYSIA GRASSES
Zoysia sp.
Wide-leaf
  'Emerald'
  'Meyer'
  'Midwestern'
  'Belair'
  'El Toro'
	Dark green; hardiest of the warm-season grasses; slow growing but eventually dense. Grows as far north as Ohio but turns brown there from fall frost to last spring frost (six months). Can be overseeded with a grass such as rye for winter green. Good green all summer.	Sun	¾–2	Tolerates salt air, so used on both coasts. Very dense growth does not lend to over-seeding, though some success is developing with tall fescue mixes. Or use annual rye at one-fourth the recommended rate for new lawns. Start zoysia from named-variety sprigs or plugs set 6 to 12 inches apart in spring. May take two seasons to fill in completely. Water during drought. Remove thatch and spray as needed for pests and diseases.

Fine-leaf **'Cashmere'**	Looks like fine Bermuda grass but is less invasive.	Sun	¾–2	More tolerant of shade and grows considerably faster than other zoysias.

LAWN WEEDS

Name	Comments	Control
BLACK MEDIC *Medicago lupulina*	Low-growing annual or biennial with hairy stems. As with many weeds, it gains foothold where grass is thin or stressed, especially in dry times. Small, yellowish flowers from March to late fall. Pods are curved and black.	Thicken turf to choke out weeds by feeding, mowing high, and watering. Apply postemergence herbicide in early spring and in fall.
BUTTERCUP, CREEPING *Ranunculus repens*	A perennial with trailing stems. Yellow ½-inch flowers bloom from June to August. Likes cool, moist areas of Northeast and Northwest.	Dig out small infestations. For larger areas, apply a postemergence herbicide in spring.
CARPETWEED *Aizoaceae* family	Found across the country. Easy to recognize: many narrow stems, small leaves, and tiny white flowers. Forms thick, airy mat. Blooms from June to November. Self-sows.	Maintain thick turf with healthy grass to choke out weeds. Kill with postemergence herbicide. To increase effectiveness, spray first with soapy water or add a teaspoon of liquid soap to the spray.
CHICKWEED, COMMON *Stellaria media*	An annual with delicate, creeping stems that tear easily when pulled. Tangled stems root readily under cool, moist conditions. Found across the country. Has tiny white, starlike flowers from February to December. Self-sows.	Pull out early when infestation is small, before first seeds form. Use care to get all stems. For large area, apply postemergence herbicide in spring or fall.
CHICKWEED, MOUSE-EAR *Cerastium vulgatum*	A creeping perennial that forms dense matlike growth. Forms tiny white flowers with five petals from April to October. Prefers moist, cool conditions, in sun or shade. Grows almost everywhere.	Control by applying a postemergence herbicide. Difficult to pull because it entangles in the grass.
CLOVER, WHITE *Trifolium repens*	A perennial readily recognized by its typical cloverleaf shape and round white blooms. Self-sows. When bruised, leaves will stain clothing.	Dig out as soon as it appears. Spreads by creeping and rooting in. For a large area, use postemergence herbicide.
CRABGRASS, COMMON *Digitaria sanguinalis*	An annual bunchgrass found across the country, except in Southwest and southern Florida. Blooms from July to October. Doesn't grow in shade; likes moisture and sun. Seeds mature in late summer and early fall.	Choke out by keeping grass thick. Improve soil fertility and add humus. Don't overwater. Mow lawn high during spring to shade emerging seedlings. Use preemergence control in spring from forsythia to lilac time; postemergence after weeds appear.
CRABGRASS, SILVER **Goose grass** *Eleusine indica*	An annual bunchgrass. Likes warm, moist soil. Blooms from June to October. Seeds from July through October. Found across the country, except in Northeast.	Dig out small infestation with hand weeder. For large area, use a preemergence herbicide. After weeds appear, apply postemergence herbicide.

52

Name	Comments	Control
DAISY, OXEYE *Chrysanthemum leucanthemum*	A perennial that spreads by seeds and underground stems. Blooms from June to August. Found across the country, except in the Dakotas and parts of Wyoming and Montana.	Because they are hard to eradicate, dig weeds out as soon as they appear. Use strong concentration of a postemergence herbicide, but only on individual plants.
DALLIS GRASS *Paspalum dilatatum*	Narrow-leaf perennial bunchgrass that grows fast in low, wet areas of the East Coast, South, some of the Southwest, and the Oregon coast. Grows from May into fall. Spreads by seeds and underground stems.	Dig out small infestation. For larger problem, apply a postemergence herbicide. If necessary, apply treatment two or more times, seven days apart.
DANDELION *Taraxacum officinale*	Most-common perennial broadleaf weed, found across country, except in the Deep South. Has rosette of coarse-toothed, long leaves. Bright yellow blooms, mainly in the spring, develop into puffballs of seed heads easily blown by wind. Leaves and flowers are edible.	Dig out the entire taproot; otherwise, a new plant will grow. Or use a postemergence herbicide in the fall. Spot chemical applicators are available.
DOCK, CURLY *Rumex crispus*	Crinkly edged rosette of leaves, with two or more tall stems. 2- to 3-foot spikes of yellowish white flowers appear from June to September. Found across the country. Taproot goes down 2 feet. Many related species. Leaves are edible.	Dig out small infestation, being sure to get the entire root. On larger area, apply a postemergence herbicide. Spray into the center of each plant crown. May need two treatments, seven days apart.
GARLIC, WILD *Allium canadense*	One of the earliest perennial weeds to emerge in spring. Has tubular leaves and a distinctive odor. Likes wet, clay soils. Blooms from May to July. Spreads by bulbs or seeds in much of country. Edible.	Mow lawn regularly to prevent seed formation. Apply postemergence herbicide in late fall and early spring.
GERANIUM, WILD *Geranium masculatum*	A pink-flowered annual that blooms from February to June. Most likely a problem in dry, sandy soils on the West Coast and sometimes in the East.	Water the area to make weeds easier to pull. Control with a postemergence herbicide.
HAWKWEED Devil's paintbrush *Hieracium aurantiacum*	A creeping perennial that varies in height; has hairy, basal leaves; forms dense patches. Grows in moist, cool soil in northern half of country. Red-orange flowers cluster at tops of stalks from July to October.	Dig out if few. For many, use postemergence herbicide in spring or fall.

LAWN WEEDS (continued)

Name	Comments	Control
HEAL-ALL **Self-heal** *Prunella vulgaris*	Creeping perennial with clustered leaves, gangly stems, and purple or pink fingerlike flower spikes from May to fall. Likes rich, moist soil in most of the country.	Improve lawn care so grass crowds out weeds. Dig out single plants. Treat large areas with postemergence herbicide. May take two treatments, seven days apart.
IVY, GROUND **Gill over the ground** *Glechoma hederacea*	A creeping perennial that can quickly take over a lawn. Thrives mainly in damp, shaded areas in the eastern half of the country, except Florida. Scalloped, nickel-sized leaves on square stems. Purple flowers from April to June. Aromatic scent, more so when crushed.	Pull out small infestation. For larger area, apply postemergence herbicide in spring or fall. Treat twice, seven days apart.
KNOTWEED, PROSTRATE **Matgrass** *Polygonum aviculare*	Family of annual weeds that develops a mat of wiry stems and small, grasslike, bluish green leaves. Leaf joints are swollen and knotty. Inconspicuous greenish flowers from July to September.	Hard to pull because of stout taproot. Soak ground deeply before trying. Difficult to eradicate if allowed to mature. Use a postemergence herbicide.
LAMB'S-QUARTERS **White goosefoot** *Chenopodium album*	Common annual weed. Gray-green leaves with white undersides. Edible. Occurs most in newly seeded lawns or thin turf. Grows 40 inches tall. Plumelike, white flower and seed heads from June to October.	Mow lawn closely. Soak soil for easy pulling, or pull after rain. For large area, use postemergence herbicide.
NETTLE, DEAD *Lamium album*	Creeping annual or biennial that occurs on thin grass in rich, moist soil. Lavender flowers in spring and fall. Spreads by seeds and creeping stems.	Pull (be sure to wear gloves) if lawn is new. On established lawn with large infestation, control with postemergence herbicide.
NIMBLEWILL *Muhlenbergia schreberi*	A creeping perennial grass with long narrow stalks. Bears yellow or light green flower heads. Fine grayish green leaves. Found in eastern and central parts of country. Spreads by runners and seeds.	Pull during growing season. Difficult to eradicate, but solid colonies can be spot-treated with postemergence herbicide. Use care not to kill surrounding grass.
NUT GRASS, YELLOW **Nut sedge** *Cyperus esculentus*	A perennial in moist, sandy soils. Appears from July to September. Spreads by edible tubers and self-sows.	Control is difficult because of deeply rooted tubers. Carefully paint the weed grass with a glyphosate herbicide such as Roundup.

Name	Comments	Control
PENNYWORT *Hydrocotyle sibthorpioides*	A perennial that thrives in shady, moist areas from Massachusetts to Florida, west to Indiana and Texas, and in southern California. Produces small, round, white flower heads from July to October. Spreads by seeds and underground stems.	Apply a postemergence herbicide during active growth. May need two applications.
PLANTAIN, BROAD-LEAVED **Buckhorn** *Plantago major*	A perennial (sometimes an annual) with rosette of broad leaves, 3 to 6 inches long. Tall, slender, tough stalks bear pencil-shaped flowers and unsightly seed heads from June to October. Found across the country. Spreads by seed.	If infestation is small, dig out when soil is moist. For larger problems, use postemergence herbicide in early spring or fall.
QUACK GRASS **Couch grass** *Agropyron repens*	A hardy, rapidly spreading perennial bunchgrass. Forms a dense root structure by rooting at every joint of underground stems. Found across the country, except in parts of the Southwest and Deep South.	Cannot be eradicated without killing lawn grasses, too. Extend a black plastic cover over a patch to starve all growth. Or apply a vegetation killer; wait as directed before reseeding lawn.
SHEPHERD'S PURSE *Capsella bursa-pastoris*	A persistent annual that forms a circle of low leaves with white flowers on tall stems. Seedpods are flat and heart shaped.	Pull when soil is moist. Water well or pull after rain. For large area, use a postemergence herbicide.
SORREL, RED **Sheep sorrel** *Rumex acetosella*	A perennial that forms a matlike growth in early summer. Found across the country wherever soil and drainage are poor. Spreads by seeds and underground stems.	Use a postemergence control in early spring and early fall.
THISTLE, CANADA *Cirsium arvense*	Thrives in clay soils in the North. Long prickly leaves and lavender flowers up to 4 feet tall. Spreads by seeds and underground roots. Blooms from July to October.	Use knife to cut below ground and remove crown from roots. For larger infestation, apply a postemergence herbicide. May need two applications, seven days apart.
YARROW, COMMON **Milfoil** *Achillea millefolium*	Creeping perennial with very finely divided soft leaves and white cushiony blooms. Grows in poor soil in most regions, except in the Southwest. Spreads by seeds and underground stems.	Dig weed out as soon as it appears. For larger area, control with postemergence herbicide, applying twice, seven days apart, if needed.

LAWN DISEASES

Disease	Grasses Attacked	Infection Signs and Controls
Brown patch	All grasses in Midwest; rye-, bent, blue-, and St. Augustine grass in southern coastal areas.	Circular brown spots from 1 inch to several feet. Leaves first look brown and water soaked, then dry. Ryegrass appears slimy. Fungi live in plant debris. Symptoms appear suddenly when humidity and night temperatures are high. Disease thrives on excessive thatch and nitrogen. Use slow-release or reduced nitrogen in spring. Water mornings only. Apply lime if needed. Remove and discard clippings. Reduce shade; improve aeration and drainage.
Cottony blight, pythium blight	Lawn grasses in damp soil in hot, humid areas.	Check for masses of cottony fungi in the lawn. Fungi best seen in dampness of early morning. Reduce nitrogen, improve drainage, and increase air circulation by pruning or thinning surrounding shrubs. Reseed.
Dollar spot	Bent grasses are most susceptible. Also infects Kentucky bluegrass, fescues, and Bermuda, zoysia, and St. Augustine grasses.	Primary disease with spots the size of silver dollars, often running together to form irregular areas. Kills grass. Feed grass spring and fall. Give nitrogen in frequent, light applications. Destroy clippings. Avoid 'Nugget' and 'Sydsport' bluegrass cultivars. Fungicide may help.
Fairy rings	These fungi don't attack grass directly, but interfere with the roots' intake of water, oxygen, and nutrients.	A circular ring from a few inches to 50 feet in diameter, often with darker green grass inside and mushrooms around edges. Generally can be ignored in home lawns. To control, soak and feed the area with a garden root feeder. Removing thatch, aerating, or applying a wetting agent may help water penetrate. Replacing infested sod or fumigating are the only ways to eliminate and are expensive.
Fusarium blight	Common and often serious in bluegrass; less so in red fescue and bent grasses.	Most likely to occur in central states and Northeast, especially in hot, dry, windy weather. Small tan spots appear in early summer and may come together. Crown of dead plants can appear brown or black. Nematodes and other fungi may be involved. Use resistant seed or sod: 'Adelphi,' 'Parade,' or 'Sydsport.' Use 20-percent-improved perennial ryegrass. Water thoroughly. Apply a wetting agent to ensure deep soaking of root zone. Remove thatch and avoid excess nitrogen.
Leaf spots	Bermuda, St. Augustine, and bent grasses, and fescues.	Fungus spreads fast during warm, humid, rainy weather. Little brown spots show up on grass blades, then spread into long areas having gray centers with purple waterlogged edges. Grass looks scorched. Avoid quick-release nitrogen; use slow-release ureaform.
Melting out	Especially in bluegrass.	Small, round, gray, brown, or purplish black spots on leaf blades spread to kill leaves and roots. Most common during high temperatures and humidity, and on closely cropped lawns. Large areas seem to die almost overnight. Do not mow too low. Avoid excess spring nitrogen. Reduce shade; improve aeration and drainage. Use fungicides when disease first appears.
Red thread, pink patch, corticum	Weak, slow-growing, cool-season grasses.	Prevalent along northern coastal areas. Grass blades stick together with red threadlike strands of fungi. Infects in irregular patterns as grasses thin and die. Raise fertility level. If continues, check pH and adjust to 6 to 7 range. Use fungicide only if improved cultural practices fail.
Rust	Bluegrasses, ryegrasses; Bermuda, zoysia, St. Augustine grasses.	Rust-colored blisters on leaves cause plants to wither and die. When blisters burst, spores spread. Mow lawn weekly and catch and destroy clippings. Maintain adequate fertility.
Snow mold	Cool-season grasses. Snow is not required for pink snow mold. Affects low areas most.	Pink fungal strands can be seen in early morning at edges of patches 6 inches to several feet in diameter. Worse in wet, shaded areas where snow lingers. For last fall mowing, cut lawn shorter than usual, catching clippings. Do not feed late in the fall—after August 15 to September 15—to harden off or toughen the grass.

LAWN INSECTS

Insect	Description and Trouble Signs	Controls
Aphids, greenbugs	These tiny sap suckers develop in colonies, especially on bluegrass, causing a burnt orange color, particularly under trees.	Control with ladybugs, or soap and water with tobacco juice added (see control for leafhoppers). If those don't work, use chlorpyrifos or diazinon.
Armyworms, cutworms	Armyworms work in groups, grow to 1½ inches long, and have green, tan, or black stripes. Cutworms grow 2 inches long, are gray or brown and smooth. Both eat grass at the soil, leaving dead spots. Many forms eat at night from spring to late summer.	Keep lawn healthy by watering and feeding on schedule. Spray lawn at first sign with 1 cup liquid dish soap per 10 gallons of water. If damage persists, use *Bacillus thuringiensis.*
Billbugs	Billbugs are black or red-brown beetles, ¼ to ¾ inch long, with extended snouts. Do minor damage to leaves. White larvae that look like puffed rice eat roots and cause irregular dead patches; worst from mid-June through July. Spot adults on sidewalks in May or June. One of the four worst pests.	In lawns with a history of billbug damage or at first spotting, try soap first (see armyworms). It will at least remove surface tension and static barriers. If damage continues, use chlorpyrifos or diazinon.
Chinch bugs	Another least-wanted pest, these black and white bugs have reddish legs and grow at most ⅕ inch long. They attack cool-season grasses in early summer, with the worst attack by a second generation in September. Bad for St. Augustine grass, they inject a fluid that disrupts water conduction, causing wilt or death. Detect by pressing a bottomless can into the lawn and filling with water.	Discourage by keeping lawn well fed. Try gypsum and soapy water (see armyworms). Control thatch. Treat in June and August with bendiocarb, diazinon, ethoprop, or chlorpyrifos.
Grubs, white	One of the four most common pests, grubs are the larvae of several kinds of beetles. Thick, whitish, C-shaped worms grow from ¾ to 1½ inches long and eat grass roots underground. Infected turf feels spongy, and easily pulls up. Dead brown patches develop. Worst damage in April and May; some in September and October. Small animals tear up sod to feed on grubs.	Water area well, using a wetting agent if soil does not absorb quickly. Then apply diazinon or isofenphos as directed, watering thoroughly immediately afterward. Do not allow runoff. Treat grubs of Japanese beetle with milky spore disease.
Leafhoppers	Leafhoppers are yellow, brown, or green, slender, wedge-shaped insects less than ½ inch long that flit away as you pass. Especially active on East and West coasts, but found across the country. Suck juices from leaves, causing grass to turn white, yellow, then brown.	Treat with soapy water and tobacco juice (soak chewing tobacco in old stocking in a pint of hot water overnight). Use diazinon if needed. Seldom serious pests.
Mites	Clover mites are tiny red specks found in lawns across the country. Bermuda grass mites are pale green and microscopic, and attack Gulf Coast and western lawns. All spiderlike mites suck juices from foliage, which then wilts, yellows, and dies.	Avoid heavy fertilization. Control with diazinon at first sign of infestation.
Mole crickets	Mole crickets are brownish insects that come up from the soil at night. About 1½ inches long; prefer Bahia grass and warm, moist conditions. Eat roots, stems, other bugs, and earthworms, and leave irregular, brown patches.	Spread diatomaceous earth mixed with cheap laundry soap over turf. Or treat with diazinon.
Nematodes	Nematodes are tiny, often microscopic, transparent roundworms. Cause stunting and lack of vigor, sometimes bleached-out areas.	Keep lawn well fed and water on schedule. Shouldn't require further treatment.
Sod webworms	One of the most common and damaging lawn insects, sod webworms are buff white moths, about ¾ inch long, that fly zigzag patterns just above the grass at dusk, laying eggs. Gray, tan, or green larvae, up to 1 inch long, feed on shoots and crowns of blue-, bent-, and zoysia grasses, and fescues, causing irregular, close-clipped brown patches. May be as many as three generations a season: May, July, and September.	Discourage with soapy water treatment (see armyworms). If not, mow, then water well, a day before treating with *Bacillus thuringiensis*, bendiocarb, chlorpyrifos, diazinon, or ethoprop. Spray dry grass late in the day. Do not mow or water for 48 hours.

57

GROUND COVERS

(Right) Hostas thrive in shade with little care. Gardeners find them fascinating because of their many shades, sizes, and leaf forms. Some also have fragrant and showy blooms. All give the feeling of cool serenity on a summer day. Plant one to eight hostas per square yard.

(Right) English ivy forms a rich, textured, evergreen carpet that thrives in light or deep shade and lasts for years. It likes rich, moist soil but will tolerate less. It will climb up anything it reaches. Deciduous Boston ivy (not shown) has a flaming red fall color. Plant three per square yard.

(Right) Sheep or blue fescue, a dramatic ornamental grass, works well in sunny and dry, sandy locations.

(Opposite) Bugleweed or ajuga forms a low cover of dark green. This rapid grower thrives in any soil, and in sun, partial shade, or deep shade. Blue candles of bloom celebrate spring.

The step from building a yard with lawn grasses to building one with ground cover plants is like the step from painting with one color to painting with a paletteful. Once you get the feel, you'll find that the possibilities are wondrous.

Grass is basic and irreplaceable for ball games, picnics, playing, and softening the step in normal traffic areas. But grass uses more water and requires more maintenance than any other part of the landscape. Keep yours under control. Complement it with ground covers to add elegance and minimize maintenance.

CHOOSING GROUND COVERS

The secret to using ground covers successfully is to select the right ones. Learn about the plant you are considering and be sure it suits the purpose and the place.

Are you tired of adding mulch, trimming grass, or pulling weeds around trees and shrubs? Use a ground cover like ivy or pachysandra around them instead. The rich textures and colors will unify your landscaping.

Do you have an area under trees where the grass grows thin, or a slope where mowing is difficult? Plant ground huggers like bearberry, lamium, or vinca to prevent erosion.

Do you want low-growing plants among stepping stones? Use creeping thyme. Each step will send up waves of fragrance.

Can't keep children or dogs from cutting across a corner? Plant barberry, juniper, or low cotoneasters.

Some ground covers, such as acacia, bamboo, broom, and foamflower, will grow under adverse conditions. Many—including cress, candytuft, Irish moss, and santolina—are excellent in rock gardens. If you love certain rampant growers like mint or honeysuckle, use them in a contained area, such as a spot where mown grass or a sidewalk will keep them in bounds, or plant them in sunken pots.

Ground covers such as strawberries form an edible carpet, and many attract bees for pollination and birds for insect control.

GROUND COVERS *(continued)*

(Far left) Lily-of-the-valley, with its fragrant stalks of nodding bells, is a spring delight. Plant nine per square yard.

(Near left) Periwinkle or vinca has squared-off flowers of violet-blue or white, and small, dark leaves. Put in nine per square yard. Give more shade the farther south you live.

(Far left) Pachysandra is a reliable evergreen with light green leaves and, in spring, small, white flowers. Plant six to 12 per square yard.

(Near left) Tiny evergreen bearberry is a slow grower that produces red berries in fall. Plant four per square yard.

Plant and care requirements for ground covers are similar to those for a flower garden. Add lime, if needed, and as much organic matter as possible to the soil. In open areas, till the amendments into the soil. Under shrubs, however, avoid deep cultivation, which would disturb roots. Instead, add the humus into the planting holes and spread it between the new plants as mulch.

The distance to set plants apart varies with the plant habit. The closer you plant, the sooner the area will fill. The best way to economize is to start with the heart of an area and expand as the plants multiply, whether naturally or with a little help from you by root division, layering, or cuttings. Mulch between plants to reduce the need for watering and weeding, though some still will be necessary, especially the first season.

Most ground covers are best planted in spring or fall, whichever is the opposite of when they bloom. Shear off dead blossoms to keep plants neat and encourage blooming. Water and feed as you would any flower. Few ground covers have pest or disease problems.

Name	Zone	Description	Light	Comments
AFRICAN DAISY **Trailing freeway daisy** *Osteospermum* sp.	9	Profusion of 3-inch pink or lilac-fading-to-white daisies from November to March; sporadic bloom all year. Evergreen; 1 to 3 feet tall.	Sun	Excellent slope covering used mainly on West Coast. Set 2 feet apart. Will survive on one or two waterings a year. Mow or cut back every year or two in spring.
BELLFLOWER **Campanula, Serbian bellflower, Dalmation bellflower** *Campanula* sp.	3	Several campanula species are trailing and 6 to 10 inches tall. They have neat foliage and a profusion of blue to purple upright bells or star-shaped cups mainly in late spring and early summer.	Sun or light shade	Adaptable small-area ground covers that grow best in light shade and well-drained moist soil. Water regularly. Clip off dead heads, and divide clumps every three or four years. Treat for slugs and snails, if they chew the leaves.
BIRD'S-FOOT TREFOIL *Lotus corniculatus*	3	Evergreen in warm climates. Spreads rapidly; 1 to 2 feet tall. Three ½-inch leaflets per stem. Butter yellow, sweet-pealike blooms in summer; seedpods shaped like bird's foot. Coarse texture.	Sun or light shade	Originally a legume forage plant; tolerates poor soil but needs good drainage. Plant 2 pounds of seed per 1,000 square feet or set 20 plants per square yard. Mow as needed for neatness. Good bee plant.
BISHOP'S WEED **Goutweed** *Aegopodium podagraria* *'variegatum'*	3	Gray-green, compound leaves with white edges. Deciduous; 6 to 12 inches tall. White flower umbels best removed in early summer to control spread.	Shade or sun	Can become rampant. Easy to grow; thrives in dry, shaded soil. Set seven per square yard. Cut occasionally with mower at maximum height for neatness.
CANDYTUFT **Evergreen candytuft** *Iberis sempervirens*	3–8	Masses of white, 2-inch-tall flower spikes cover dense, little, dark green, foot-tall bushes in spring. Improved varieties bloom at intervals all season.	Sun	Attractive all year. Needs lots of humus. Tolerates seashore conditions. Starts easily from seed or plants set four to five per square yard. Cut back after bloom or severe winter.
CARMEL CREEPER *Ceanothus griseus* *'horizontalis'*	7	Called wild lilac; native to California coast. Deep green, glossy round leaves. Grows 1½ to 4 feet tall and spreads up to 12 feet. Violet-blue spring flowers.	Full sun	Tolerates salt spray and strong winds. Likes good drainage and sandy soil. Needs water, but not too much or it can get root rot. 'Yankee Point' one of best varieties.
CARPET BUGLE **Bugleweed** *Ajuga reptans*	3	Dark green, 6-inch-tall rosettes with bronze, purple, or rainbow overtones, or variegated with white edges and purple centers. Colors intensify in fall. Blue flower spikes bloom in spring.	Sun or light shade	One of the best low ground covers. Prefers moist, rich soil. Good as edging. Spreads quickly. Needs some feeding, watering, and light mulch in severe winters. Set 6 to 12 inches apart. Named varieties available.
CHAMOMILE, ENGLISH OR ROMAN *Chamaemelum nobile*	3	Fragrant herb with fernlike foliage. Delightful near walks, where crushing releases scent. Grows 3 to 10 inches tall. Small, button daisies in summer.	Sun	You can mow and walk on this as a lawn substitute. Spreads fast. Sections may die without reason. Fill from surrounding area. Start from seed or from plants set 6 to 12 inches apart. Survives drought well.
CORSICAN MINT **Creeping mint** *Mentha requieni*	6	2 inches tall or less; spreads to make fragrant, green carpet. Small, pale lavender spring blooms.	Sun or light shade	Shallow roots need constant moisture. Will take some traffic. Set plants 6 inches apart. Good as container or bonsai ground cover.
CORSICAN PEARLWORT **Irish moss** *Sagina subulata*	4	Tufted mosslike plant with 4-inch-tall needlelike leaves. Forms evergreen matting. Profusion of white flowers in summer.	Light shade	Good between stepping stones, among rocks, or under ferns. Likes rich soil and morning sun. 'Aurea' has golden leaves. Self-sows and can become a weed. Set 6 inches apart.

61

GROUND COVERS *(continued)*

Name	Zone	Description	Light	Comments
COTONEASTERS: **Rockspray** **Cranberry** **Bearberry** *Cotoneaster* sp.	5	Several low forms, 6 inches to 3 feet tall, that spread 4 to 15 feet. Small and thick, shiny green leaves, often in a fish-bone pattern. Little white or pinkish flowers bloom in summer; red berries and orange leaves in fall.	Sun	Tough, hardy shrubs that are easy to grow in not too acid soil. Most are deciduous; berries remain after leaves fall. *C. dammeri* is evergreen. None has thorns. Good covering for banks or retaining walls. Prune lightly. Do not shear. Spray to control mites or scale.
CROWN VETCH *Coronilla varia*	3	Masses of pink and white nodding stalks of sweet-pealike, fragrant flowers in summer. Plants grow 1 to 2 feet tall and up to 6 feet wide.	Sun	Widely used on highway banks; excellent for erosion control. Plant 1½ feet apart for quick cover. May be invasive. Mow, feed, and water in spring for low, bushy growth.
FERNS: **New York** *Thelypteris noveboracensis* **Resurrection** *Polypodium polypodioides*	7	Wide variety of familiar, long, gray-green fronds with many paired, notched leaflets; ½ to 3 feet tall. Rust-colored, seedlike spores.	Shade	Charming in natural settings or on shady sides of walls. Most are easy to grow and spread by root stalks. Thrive in moist, humus soil. Most die back for the winter.
FORGET-ME-NOT *Myosotis scorpioides* 'semperflorens' *M. sylvatica*	4	Pale blue flowers with pink, yellow, or white centers in spring and summer. *M. scorpioides* 'semperflorens' is a perennial, 8 to 18 inches tall. *M. sylvatica* is a 6- to 12-inch annual that self-sows yearly.	Shade	Especially good combined with tulips or used along stream banks. Likes rich, moist soil. Starts easily from seed or divisions; set nine per square yard. Varieties with pink or white blooms exist. Persistent but not invasive.
GAZANIAS: **Clumping gazania** *Gazania rigens* **Trailing gazania** *G. rigens* 'leucolaena'	8	Waves of bright daisies, each 1½ to 5 inches across, in spring, with scattered blooms throughout season. Foliage gray-green on underside; dark green on top. Grows to 1 foot tall.	Sun	Best in desert conditions. Runners root as they grow out. Good on banks or cascading over walls. Plant 1½ to 2 feet apart. Can be grown as an annual in cold-winter areas. Mass for best effect. Heat tolerant.
GERMANDER **Chamaedrys** **germander** *Teucrium chamaedrys*	5	Outstanding little shrubs that grow 8 to 18 inches tall and spread fast to make a 3-foot mat. Dark green, ¾-inch leaves. Evergreen in milder zones. Lavender spikes in spring.	Sun	Ideal for poor soils and hot, sunny locations. Plant 1 to 1½ feet apart. Shear back to 10 inches once a year. Mint family. 'Prostatum' grows only 4 to 6 inches tall. Bees love the blossoms. Good for edging.
GINGER, WILD *Asarum* sp.	4	Woodland plants, 6 to 10 inches tall, with heart-shaped, basal leaves, 2 to 6 inches across. Spreads by underground stems. Red-purple flowers hide at the base of the leaves in spring.	Sun or shade	Cold weather tints leaves purple. Strong root scent accounts for name. No relation to real ginger. Called snakeroot, its roots can be dried and used for flavoring. Plant 8 to 15 inches apart. 'Callaway' is mottled.
HEATH **Spring heath** *Erica* sp.	5	Similar to heather. Evergreen shrubs grow 7 inches to 3 feet tall, spreading 2 to 3 feet. Spring heath blooms in winter in mild areas for up to four months; February to May where cooler. *E. tetralix* hardier, naturalized on Massachusetts coast.	Sun or light shade	Tolerates alkaline soil. Treat as heather. Needs full sun in the North; light shade in Sunbelt. Tolerates sun and wind. Set plants 2 to 3 feet apart. Prune after flowering. Long season of bloom. Long-lasting cut flowers.
HEATHER **Scotch heather** *Calluna vulgaris*	4	Bushy little shrubs, 4 to 24 inches tall, with juniperlike needles in various colors. Bears masses of tiny white or pink to purple bells from midsummer to fall.	Sun or light shade	Does best in highly organic, moist, acidic soil. Adapted to Pacific Northwest and the Northeast. Use no lime and up to 50-percent acid compost, such as peat and oak leaf mold. Good cut flowers.

62

Name	Zone	Description	Light	Comments
HONEYSUCKLE, HALL'S *Lonicera japonica 'halliana'*	5–9	Vigorous vine, evergreen in mild areas. Grows 1½ to 2 feet tall. Fragrant white flowers turn yellow. Profusions in late spring, sporadic all summer. Children love to suck flowers for honey.	Sun or shade	Good to cover and hold soil quickly on steep banks, but rampant. Will choke trees in mid-Atlantic states. Plant 2 to 3 feet apart; shear every spring to contain and to prevent buildup of fire-susceptible undergrowth.
ICE PLANT, TRAILING Hottentot or sea fig 'Red Spike' *Lampranthus* sp. and others	9	Carpets of 2- to 3-inch daisies in brilliant colors. Grows 10 to 12 inches tall with succulent foliage of gray-green. Most bloom in late winter, some almost all year.	Sun	Breathtaking display, mostly on West Coast. Low-maintenance plant that includes several genera. Good for erosion control on slopes. Prefers sandy soil. Self-sow, or propagate with cuttings. Plant 1½ feet apart anytime. Water well.
INDIAN STRAWBERRY Mock strawberry *Duchesnea indica*	5	Leaves like wild strawberry form mat 2 to 3 inches thick. Yellow flowers, about ¾ inch across. Bright red berries held above foliage.	Sun or shade	Best used to cover large area. Spreads by runners. Can become a weed. Leaves stay green long into winter. Start seeds, then set six plants per square yard.
IVY GERANIUM *Pelargonium peltatum*	9	Bright green succulent leaves. Plants 1 to 2 feet tall, trailing 2 to 4 feet. Geranium flowers and colors abundant in late spring, sporadic all summer.	Sun or shade	Good on banks or balconies with English ivy. Plant 1½ feet apart in full sun. Blooms year-round along coasts, during warm months inland. Cut back after last frost for best new growth. Replant about every four years.
JASMINE, STAR Confederate jasmine *Trachelospermum* sp.	8	Luxurious, glossy evergreen foliage. Fragrant creamy white flowers, shaped like stars or pinwheels. Grows 8 to 18 inches tall and spreads 3 to 5 feet.	Sun or shade	Favorite where hardy. Shear tips of vine to encourage branching. Good to cover banks or tree roots, edge lawns, climb walls. Set 2 to 3 feet apart. Likes rich, moist soil.
JUNIPERS: Wilton carpet Chinese Creeping *Juniperus* sp.	2	Low-growing evergreen group with heights from 4 inches to 4 feet and many textures. Colors include silver, bluish and gray-green, bronze, gold laced, and purple tipped in winter.	Sun or light shade	Good for banks and slopes. Deters traffic. Full sun is best, and soil must be well drained. Slow growing, but will last years. Mulch heavily until established. Root rot, tip moth, tip blight, and bagworms can be problems.
LAMB'S-EARS Betony *Stachys byzantina*	4	Mulleinlike silvery leaves, soft and woolly, arching 1½ to 2 feet tall. Small, purplish flower spikes in summer. Spreads by underground roots.	Sun	Usually grown for unique foliage. Hardy for hot, well-drained areas. Plant seeds or set plants in spring, 1 to 1½ feet apart. Needs little water. Cut back and feed in spring.
LANTANA, TRAILING *Lantana montevidensis*	9	Spreading evergreen shrub, 1½ to 5 feet tall, in 3- to 6-foot-wide mounds. Clusters of 1-inch blooms all year in frost-free climates.	Sun	Delightful, strong odor when leaves are crushed. Good for erosion control on sun-drenched slopes. Named varieties are more compact. Cut back in spring for good bloom.
LEADWORT *Ceratostigma plumbaginoides*	5	Cobalt blue flowers in summer to early fall. Foliage has tints of bronze, and red, turning ruby red with cold weather. Grows 10 to 12 inches tall.	Sun or shade	Can be combined with vinca; good on banks or around shrubs. Mildly invasive. Set nine per square yard. Shear in spring. Flowers on tips of new growth. Mulch in Zone 5 in winter.
LILYTURF, CREEPING *Liriope spicata*	5	Fountainlike grassy clumps. Spreads by underground stems. Leaves to 1 foot tall. Lavender flower spikes in summer, ornamental black seeds.	Sun or shade	Used widely in South for borders or under trees. Tolerates moist soils or drought. Set plants 1 foot apart. Clip foliage in spring for neatness. Nice variegated kinds.

GROUND COVERS *(continued)*

Name	Zone	Description	Light	Comments
MAHONIA, CREEPING Dwarf holly-grape *Mahonia repens*	5	Hollylike leaflets: bluish green on top, powdery on underside. Often turn deep red in fall and winter. Fragrant yellow spring flowers in clusters. Grows 2 feet tall and wide.	Sun or shade	Spiny leaves deter traffic. Spreads by seeds or suckers. Protect from wind. Tolerates any soil and drought once established. Likes humus. Controls erosion. Use *Bacillus thuringiensis* if there is leaf damage. Birds love blue-black berries.
MAZUS, CREEPING *Mazus reptans*	5	Low (2-inch), fast grower with dark green leaves and many tiny spikes of blue or white spotted flowers in spring and summer. Foxglove family.	Sun or shade	Perennial; good between paving stones, over bulbs, or under trees or shrubs. Evergreen where there is no frost. Set nine per square yard. Does best in moist soil with lots of humus. Mulch in Zone 5.
MONDO GRASS Dwarf lilyturf *Ophiopogon* sp.	8	Similar to creeping liriope, but with blue rather than black fruit. *O. planiscapus 'arabicus,'* black mondo grass, has purple-black leaves up to 10 inches high, with pink or purple-black flowers.	Shade	*O. jaburan* grows 2 to 3 feet tall and has a variegated variety. Sod-forming ground cover. Cut back if foliage gets ragged in winter. Set ½ to 2 feet apart. Good under trees.
MONEYWORT Creeping jennie, creeping charlie *Lysimachia nummularia*	2	Bright yellow, buttercup flowers, 1 inch across; abundant flowering in spring, continuing all summer. Penny-shaped leaves. Plants 2 to 6 inches tall spread 2 feet.	Sun or shade	Grows anywhere; loves moisture. Good around rocks and pools. Can be rampant; may take over lawn. Bears some foot traffic. Plant 1 to 1½ feet apart. Most take full sun, but golden-leaved 'Aurea' needs some shade.
PHLOX, CREEPING Moss phlox, moss pink *Phlox subulata*	2	Waves of brilliant spring color: pink, white, or lavender to blue. Plants spread 1 foot and grow 6 inches tall. Moss-green foliage is evergreen and hardy.	Sun	Excellent for shrub or flower borders, sunny slopes, or rock walls. Plant six to nine per square yard in spring. Neutral to slightly alkaline soil, not overly rich, is best. Mow or shear after flowering. Fairly drought tolerant.
PINK Maiden pink, garden pink *Dianthus* sp. and hybrids	2	Hardy evergreen perennials with gray-green, grasslike leaves, 6 to 15 inches tall. Flat, showy red, pink, or white flowers in masses in early spring have spicy, clovelike scent.	Sun	Heavy-blooming cover for small areas; long favored for borders and edgings. Likes full sun, a little lime, and rich, moist soil. Set 6 to 8 inches apart. Shear seed heads for longer bloom.
SEDUM Stonecrop *Sedum* sp.	3	Creeping succulents in many forms, colors, and sizes from 2 to 10 inches tall. Leaves vary from light to dark green, silvery to bronze tipped. Flowers are yellow, white, and pink to rose.	Sun or light shade	Prefers poor soil and some drought; grows easily from plants set 9 to 12 inches apart in spring or fall. Moss stonecrop can cover an acre quickly with masses of yellow bloom. Short-lived near traffic or dogs.
'SILVER MOUND' ARTEMISIA Satiny wormwood *Artemisia schmidtiana*	3	Silvery leaves with woolly texture make attractive mounds. 'Silver Mound' gets 6 to 10 inches tall; related species, 3 inches to 2 feet. Tiny, inconspicuous yellow flowers. Leaves are aromatic when crushed.	Sun	Excellent accent; does well in any well-drained soil. Tolerates extremes of heat and drought, but not dampness or humidity. Space 12 to 15 inches apart in spring. Cut back severely in early spring to rejuvenate.
SNOW-IN-SUMMER *Cerastium tomentosum*	2	Tiny, silver-gray leaves form mat 3 to 6 inches tall. Abundance of delicate, white, dime-sized flowers in late spring. Spreads to 4 feet. Easy to start by seeds, cuttings, or divisions.	Sun	Good for rock gardens, as an edging in front of perennials, or over a bed of bulbs. Can be mildly weedy. Does well in desert, mountain, or coastal areas. Set nine per square yard. Divide every year or two. Clip dead heads.

Name	Zone	Description	Light	Comments
SPEEDWELLS: **Creeping** **Rock** **Woolly** *Veronica* sp.	4	Shiny, dark green foliage with blue, pink, or white flowers, mostly in spikes thickest in the middle. Grows 4 to 15 inches tall. Blooms late spring to September.	Sun or light shade	Vigorous creeper; good between paving stones or over bulbs. *V. repans* gives moss effect, can invade lawns. Tolerates some foot traffic. Full sun in north, some shade south.
STRAWBERRY, **WILD** **Sand strawberry** *Fragaria chiloensis*	5	Originally grown mostly for attractive foliage, 6 to 12 inches tall. Spreads 1 to 1½ feet in one year. White flowers in abundance in spring. Fruit edible; improved on Hybrid No. 25.	Sun or light shade	Tolerant and adaptable; will stand a little foot traffic. Remove blooms at first to promote runners. Mow in early spring, then feed. For best fruit, thin out some plants. If leaves yellow, apply iron.
SWEET **WOODRUFF** *Galium odoratum*	4	Dark green, sandpapery leaflets, like spokes, on square stems. Grows 6 to 8 inches tall. Clusters of tiny white flowers in early summer.	Shade	Long a favorite. Leaves give vanilla flavor for May wine. Good beneath high-branched conifer trees and rhododendrons, or over bulbs. Start seeds; space plants 1 foot apart.
THRIFT **Sea pink,** **common thrift** *Armeria maritima*	3	Tidy evergreens with stiff, 6-inch-tall, gray-green, grasslike leaves. Bears cloverlike clusters of 10-inch-tall white, pink, or rose flowers, from spring to fall (depending on climate).	Sun or light shade	Neat, billowing plant for rock gardens, fronts of borders, or between paving stones. Does well in sandy soil; may rot in rich moist soil. Shear faded flowers. Space 10 to 12 inches apart and divide as needed. Feed in fall.
THYMES: **Creeping** **Woolly** *Thymus* sp.	3	Creeping has tiny, dark green leaves on 2- to 6-inch stems. Wonderful aroma. Bears clusters of red, pink, white, or purple flowers in summer. Woolly is gray with fewer flowers.	Sun	Great between stepping stones because crushing releases fragrance. Can substitute for or be interplanted in lawn; plant in seat of outdoor bench. Many varieties available. Plant 6 to 10 inches apart. Likes poor soil.
VIOLET, SWEET *Viola odorata*	4–7	Hardy perennial with violet or white nodding flowers in early spring. Subtle scent. Dark green, heart-shaped leaves, 3 to 12 inches tall. 'Rosina' has pink blooms in spring and fall.	Sun or partial shade	Old-fashioned favorite. Likes woodsy soil and part shade. All parts are edible. Spreads by runners. Plant 8 to 12 inches apart. Mow or trim in fall and feed in spring for the most flowers. Can become a weed.
WINTER CREEPER, **PURPLE** *Euonymus fortunei* 'colorata'	5	One of hardiest evergreen vines, it creeps over the ground to form a 6-inch-tall mat. Dark green leaves turn purple-red in fall and winter.	Sun or shade	Very adaptable; full sun to full shade. Water regularly. Space 1 to 2 feet apart. Spray to control scale if it appears (likeliest in southern states). Mow in spring, every year or two.
YARROW, **WOOLLY** *Achillea tomentosa*	2	Flat, canary yellow flower heads cover olive, ferny foliage in spring. Six to 12 inches tall; evergreen; easy to grow.	Sun	Hardy, grows in any soil, and is fire retardant. Space 6 to 12 inches apart. Mow faded flowers or pick for dried bouquets.
YELLOW-ROOT *Xanthorhiza* *simplicissima*	4	Low, spreading deciduous shrub, about 2 feet tall. Uniform height; dark green compound leaflets and yellow stems. Feathery spikes of purple blooms in spring.	Sun or shade	Good in wet soils and to control mud and weeds near ponds and streams. Foliage turns orange in fall. Set nine plants per square yard in wild or natural settings.
YEW, SPREADING *Taxus* sp.	5	Low-growing, 1½- to 2-foot-tall form of popular evergreen. Needles dark green on top, lighter beneath, and 1 inch long. Cushion Japanese yew denser. Will spread 10 feet in diameter.	Sun or shade	Neat and formal in effect. Best used singly, in rich, moist, well-drained, not too acid soil. Leaf juices and berries can be poisonous. Slow growing. Bears pruning. Tolerates drought once established. Mulch.

TREES

From spectacular springtime shows of bloom and fiery fall foliage to wispy wintry images cast by deciduous specimens, trees are unequaled for adding drama to yards. The sheer size of trees—even ornamentals—commands our attention. Plant the right tree and provide proper care, and you will create a rewarding relationship that could outlast a lifetime.

SELECTING A TREE TO FIT YOUR NEEDS

When choosing a tree consider its winter hardiness and its adaptation to your yard's soil type and moisture level. Weigh, too, the exposure to the sun and wind the tree will receive. For help, look over pages 74–85 and visit your nursery.

Look for ease of maintenance (including a manageable size) and visual interest, too. And keep a tree's scale in mind: Choose a smaller tree for an intimate area, such as a patio. A large tree will do best farther from the house.

■ Evergreens
Coniferous evergreens can stand alone as specimens or serve as screens, windbreaks, or back-drops for flowering trees or shrubs. The dense foliage masses of broad-leaved evergreen trees make them effective as specimen groups, or as screens or borders.

■ Deciduous trees
Large deciduous trees, or shade trees, frame and canopy outdoor spaces. Cooling in summer and often colorful in autumn, they also can enliven the winter scene with the color, line, and texture of bark and branches. Medium and smaller deciduous trees often provide vivid autumn foliage and bear fruit. But since many of them greet spring or summer with bouquets of bloom, they're referred to as flowering trees.

(Above) Nestled among deciduous trees, this house benefits from the summer shade they cast. In winter, sunlight pours through the trees—then leafless—to warm and brighten the house.

(Opposite) Grouped conifers form a privacy screen and windbreak. Their year-round greenery also provides welcome shelter for birds.

FLOWERING TREES

Flowering trees are the most breathtaking ornamentals in any landscape. Their blooms flood the sky with color—and often fill the air with fragrance, too.

TREE SHAPES

Some flowering trees have wide-spreading or weeping umbrella shapes; others form densely branched ovals or mounds. Columnar trees can work as accents or hedges. Some flowering trees grow large enough to act as shade trees, especially if pruned to encourage upward branching. Smaller types, branching close to the ground, make good screens or specimen clusters.

Many flowering trees—such as cherry, crab apple, and plum—thrive best in open spaces with full sun. The purple-leaved plum and other trees with colored foliage demand full sun for maximum color. Other species—including serviceberry, sorrel tree, and flowering dogwood—tolerate or even prefer light shade. (The eastern flowering dogwood, *Cornus florida,* once a landscape mainstay, is now threatened by an anthracnose epidemic. But you may feel that the intrinsic beauty of this splendid tree outweighs the risk of an early loss.)

Although most flowering trees are spring bloomers, some—like Japanese pagoda tree, sorrel tree, and yellowwood—bloom in mid- to late summer. Many flowering trees also bear wildlife-attracting fruit. A number of them have interesting bark; consider the light gray bark of magnolia, the black trunk of redbud, or the cherrylike bark of tree lilac. (When searching for colorful, interesting trees to add to your garden, don't overlook the Japanese maple. Though not a flowering tree, the Japanese maple has many varieties of form, branch and leaf shape, and leaf color, making it a good candidate to serve as a specimen tree.)

Plant flowering trees in your lawn for viewing as sculptural elements. Or place them near enough to the house to enjoy at close range. Remember, however, to always consider the hues of surrounding plants, outdoor furniture, and buildings when choosing a flowering tree.

(Above) Hardy throughout the United States, flowering crab apples produce masses of fragrant bloom in spring.

(Left) Crab apple blossoms may be white, pink, or red. In autumn, the trees produce showy fruits in shades of yellow and red.

(Left and above) The crisp blooms of Japanese or Kousa dogwood are even more beautiful when viewed from above. The bracts, which form on horizontally spreading branches, give rise in late summer to strawberry-shaped scarlet fruits. An added bonus: The tree attracts songbirds.

(Near left) In early spring, 'Kwanzan' cherry produces spectacular double, 2½-inch flowers on its boughs.

(Left) Oriental cherries— such as this uplifting 'Kwanzan'—come in many varieties with white to deep pink flowers. Cherry trees are compact enough to be planted near the house.

71

AUTUMN COLOR

Shorter days and cooler nights bring on the annual tree extravaganza of fall colors. Use these colors to add dazzle to your landscape.

Many large trees sparkle in autumn. Beech, birch, sour gum, sweet gum, sugar and red maples, ash, and oak are just a sampling. Among smaller trees, autumn standouts are pear, sorrel tree, dogwood, and Japanese maple.

Plan the setting for these trees carefully. Provide autumn show-offs with a backdrop of evergreens, or create a counterpoint between their foliage and the color of your house, whether a pastel shade or a deep, dark tone.

Many trees offer more than one autumn asset, for even more dramatic effect. For example, beeches sport golden or bronze leaves and silvery bark. Birches have yellow leaves and textured white bark. Japanese maples combine fiery red or orange-yellow foliage with elegant, delicate texture and form. Many crab apples, after dropping their leaves, are covered with a spectacular fruit display.

(Left) The fan-shaped leaves of ginkgo turn a sunny yellow, then fall off all at once, making raking a one-time effort.

(Left) Though striking year-round, the beauty of Japanese maple foliage is at its height in autumn, when the tree combines exquisite texture with brilliant color. Here, a pair of Japanese maples frame a home's entrance.

(Opposite) The fall colors of sugar maples range from yellow to orange to red—sometimes with all three hues on one leaf.

TREES

Tree	Type	Fall Foliage	Shade Density	Height/ Width	Zone	Soil Preference	Comments
AMUR CORK TREE *Phellodendron amurense*	Deciduous	Yellow	Light	30' tall, 30' wide	5	Tolerant	Mature tree offers picturesque spread and corklike ridged bark. Tolerates pollution. Use as specimen in open area.
ARBORVITAE *Thuja* sp. **American** *T. occidentalis*	Coniferous	Ever-green	Dense	50' tall; width varies with variety.	3	Moist, well drained	Use as specimen tree or in hedge. Dense, scalelike foliage. Good cultivars are 'Techny,' 'Nigra,' 'Hetz Wintergreen.' Also called white cedar.
Western *T. plicata*	Coniferous	Ever-green	Dense	50' tall, 20' wide	6	Moist, well drained; pH adaptable	For screen, hedge, or group. Uniformly dark green foliage; attractive light brown to reddish shredding bark. Sun to partial shade.
ASH *Fraxinus* sp. **Green** *F. pennsylvanica*	Deciduous	Yellow, purple	Light	60' tall, 25' wide	2	Tolerant	Little care. Use as specimen tree. 'Marshall's Seedless' and 'Summit' are popular varieties.
White *F. americana*	Deciduous	Yellow, purple	Light	90' tall, 45' wide	4	Tolerant	Big, fast-growing, adaptable shade tree. Volunteer seedlings can be a problem. Good types are 'Autumn Purple,' 'Rose Hill,' and 'Autumn Applause.'
BALD CYPRESS *Taxodium distichum*	Deciduous	Reddish brown	Medium	70' tall, 30' wide	5	Well drained, moist, acid	Deciduous conifer with soft texture and slender pyramidal shape. Distinctive in a grove or by water's edge; adapts to wet or dry soil.
BAUHINIA *Bauhinia variegata*	Broad-leaved evergreen	Ever-green	Light	20' tall, 15' wide	10	Well drained, slightly acid	Specimen tree for small yard. Covered with pink, white, or purple blooms in late winter or early spring.
BEECH *Fagus* sp. **American** *F. grandifolia*	Deciduous	Golden yellow	Dense	50'–80' tall, 30'–50' wide	4	Tolerant, but prefers acid soil.	Spreading branches, silvery bark, occasional inedible nuts. Shallow root system—do not disturb.
European *F. sylvatica*	Deciduous	Golden yellow	Dense	90' tall, 50' wide	5	Tolerant, but prefers acid soil.	Magnificent specimen with bark resembling elephant skin; low-growing branches. Shallow roots must not be disturbed.

Tree	Type	Fall Foliage	Shade Density	Height/ Width	Zone	Soil Preference	Comments
BIRCH *Betula* sp. **Canoe or paper** *B. papyrifera*	Deciduous	Yellow	Medium to light	70' tall, 30' wide	2	Tolerant, but prefers moist areas.	Beautiful white bark peels naturally. Grow in clumps of two to four trunks.
European white or weeping *B. pendula*	Deciduous	Yellow	Medium	50' tall, 20' wide	2	Tolerant	Dramatic specimen with slightly drooping branches, delicate foliage. Somewhat short-lived; prone to borer attack.
River *B. nigra*	Deciduous	Yellow	Medium	40' tall, 30' wide	5	Moist, acid	Peeling bark with layers of gray and reddish brown. Resists birch borer; tolerates wet soil.
BUCKEYE, OHIO *Aesculus glabra*	Deciduous	Orange	Dense	30' tall, 30' wide	4	Moist, well drained	Specimen tree for spacious area. Rounded and low branched, with greenish white spike flowers in spring.
CALIFORNIA INCENSE CEDAR *Calocedrus decurrens*	Coniferous	Evergreen	Dense	30' tall, 10' wide	6	Moist, well drained	Columnar or conical, with dark green foliage in vertical fanlike sprays.
CAROLINA SILVER-BELL *Halesia carolina*	Deciduous	Yellow	Medium	40' tall, 30' wide	5	Moist, well drained, acid	Small tree, sometimes multistemmed, with bell-shaped white flowers, ridged bark.
CEDAR *Cedrus* sp. **Atlas or atlantic** *C. atlantica*	Coniferous	Evergreen	Medium to dense	60' tall, 35' wide	6	Rich, well drained, preferably acid	Picturesque, with bluish foliage and stiff branches that often droop slightly. Use as specimen.
Deodar *C. deodara*	Coniferous	Evergreen	Medium to dense	70' tall, 40' wide	7	Rich, well drained	Same as above, with graceful pendulous branches.
CHINABERRY *Melia azedarach*	Deciduous	Yellow-brown	Medium to dense	45' tall, 30' wide	7	Tolerant	Plant for quick shade. Fast growing, with compound leaves and fragrant blooms.
CRAB APPLE *Malus* sp.	Deciduous	Yellow, orange, brown	Light to medium	10'–50' tall, 10'–20' wide	Varies	Rich, well drained	Grows in almost any climate in U.S. Single, double, or semidouble white or pink spring flowers. Produces yellow or red fruits; good in jellies or for birds. Desirable choices are *M. x atrosanguinea*, *M. baccata*, *M.* 'Donald Wyman,' *M. floribunda*, *M. hupehensis*, *M.* 'Red Jade,' *M. sargenti*, *M. tschonoski*.

TREES *(continued)*

Tree	Type	Fall Foliage	Shade Density	Height/ Width	Zone	Soil Preference	Comments
CYPRESS, FALSE *Chamaecyparis* sp. **Atlantic white cedar** *C. thyoides*	Coniferous	Evergreen	Dense	30' tall, 10' wide	4	Moist to wet, humus rich	Useful as hedge or screen in wet soil, and in sun to light shade. Bluish green foliage, columnar form.
Sawara *C. pisifera*	Coniferous	Evergreen	Dense	Varies	4	Well drained	Numerous cultivars, many conical or pyramidal with feathery texture.
CYPRESS, ITALIAN *Cupressus sempervirens*	Coniferous	Evergreen	Dense	60' tall, 3' wide	8	Well drained, fairly dry	Use in hedges and windbreaks. Quick growing, but best where summers are long, hot, and dry. Bluish green, scalelike foliage.
DOGWOOD *Cornus* sp. **Cornelian cherry** *C. mas*	Deciduous	Not notable	Dense	20' tall, 20' wide	5	Tolerant; well drained	Multistemmed and rounded, with profuse yellow flowers in early spring. Red fruits in autumn appeal to birds.
Flowering *C. florida*	Deciduous	Orange, brown, red	Light	30' tall, 20' wide	5	Well drained	Best in light shade. Pink or white single flowers; most varieties bear red inedible berries. Vulnerable to anthracnose blight.
Japanese *C. kousa*	Deciduous	Orange, red, brown	Light	25' tall, 15' wide	6	Well drained	White flowers, occasionally tinged with pink, borne atop foliage in late spring. Attractive red fruits. Use as specimen.
Japanese cornel *C. officinalis*	Deciduous	Reddish	Medium	20' tall, 20' wide	5	Tolerant; well drained	Similar to cornelian cherry dogwood, but less compact. Yellow flowers; blooms early.
Pagoda *C. alternifolia*	Deciduous	Reddish purple	Medium	20' tall, 15' wide	4	Moist, well drained	Wide-spreading horizontal branches, with white flowers. Good substitute for flowering dogwood. Light shade.
DOVE TREE *Davidia involucrata*	Deciduous	Yellow-brown	Medium	50' tall, 40' wide	7	Well drained	Occasionally produces unusual spring flowers: two large white pendulous bracts surround yellow ball-like flower head.
FIG *Ficus carica*	Deciduous (evergreen in warm areas)	Yellow	Dense	20'–30' tall, 30'–40' wide	7	Tolerant. If soil is too rich, fruit production will be low.	Fast growing, with large, lobed leaves; fruits early in life. Most varieties self-fruit, so only one tree needed.

Tree	Type	Fall Foliage	Shade Density	Height/ Width	Zone	Soil Preference	Comments
FIR, DOUGLAS *Pseudotsuga menziesi*	Coniferous	Ever-green	Dense	100' tall	5	Moist, well drained	Hardy. Fast growing for a conifer. Can be sheared for hedge, or makes an impressive lawn specimen. Bluish green, soft, 1-inch needles.
FIR, WHITE *Abies concolor*	Coniferous	Ever-green	Dense	75' tall	4	Moist, well drained	Hardy, fast-growing conifer. Use as specimen. Often loses lower branches as it matures. Fragrant, blue-green needles; bristly overall texture.
FRINGE TREE *Chionanthus virginicus*	Deciduous	Gold, yellow	Light	12'–30' tall, 20' wide	5	Moist, well drained	Use as lawn tree or in group planting. After leaves appear, produces blizzard of fleecy, white flower tassels. Slow growing. Tolerates pollution.
GINKGO Maidenhair tree *Ginkgo biloba*	Deciduous	Yellow	Light	80' tall, variable widths	5	Tolerant	Slow growing. Pest and disease free; tolerates pollution. Fan-shaped leaves on stiffly diagonal, uplifted branches.
GOLDEN-RAIN TREE *Koelreuteria paniculata*	Deciduous	Yellow-brown	Light to medium	30' tall, 15' wide	6	Well drained	Use as specimen. Twelve- to 15-inch drooping clusters of small yellow flowers cover tree in early summer, followed by bladderlike seedpods. Tolerates soot; prefers full sun.
GUM, SOUR Black tupelo, pepperidge *Nyssa sylvatica*	Deciduous	Scarlet, orange, yellow	Medium	70' tall, 50' wide	5	Moist, well drained, slightly acid	Pest- and disease-resistant specimen tree. Glossy foliage; inedible black fruits relished by birds in fall. Good for wet-area plantings. Does not transplant well.
GUM, SWEET *Liquidambar styraciflua*	Deciduous	Yellow, red, purple	Medium to dense	70' tall, 50' wide	6	Tolerant, but best in moist, well drained	Fast growing in moist areas. Disease resistant, pest free. Silver-gray bark, star-shaped leaves. Mature trees have spiky seed clusters. Wide-reaching roots need ample space.
HAWTHORN *Crataegus* sp. **Paul's scarlet** *C. laevigata 'pauli'*	Deciduous	Not notable	Medium	25' tall, 10' wide	5	Tolerant	Double white flowers in spring. Scarlet fruits in fall.
Washington *C. phaenopyrum*	Deciduous	Not notable	Medium	25' tall, 20' wide	5	Tolerant	White flowers in spring; red fruits stay on tree through winter. Tolerates pollution and dry or clayey soil.

77

TREES *(continued)*

Tree	Type	Fall Foliage	Shade Density	Height/ Width	Zone	Soil Preference	Comments
HAWTHORN *(continued)* **'Winter King'** *C. viridis* 'Winter King'	Deciduous	Not notable	Medium	25' tall, 25' wide	5	Tolerant	Lovely vase-shaped tree with rounded crown. White flowers and long-lasting red fruit.
HEMLOCK *Tsuga canadensis*	Coniferous	Ever-green	Dense	50'–80' tall, 30'–50' wide	4	Moist, slightly acid	For sun or shade. Short, flat, dark green needles; slightly pendulous branches. Use as specimen, or clip for hedge or screen. Numerous varieties; some dwarf or weeping.
HOLLY *Ilex* sp. **American** *I. opaca*	Broad-leaved evergreen	Ever-green	Dense	40' tall, 20' wide	6	Moist, well drained, acid	Dense, pyramidal tree with branches low to ground; glossy foliage. Red berries on female tree, provided male is nearby. Tolerates salt and pollution.
English *I. aquifolium*	Broad-leaved evergreen	Ever-green	Dense	70' tall, 40' wide	7	Tolerant; prefers well drained, slightly acid.	Sharply pointed leaves; bright red berries. Some types variegated. Use as specimen. Best if both sexes planted.
Longstalk *I. pedunculosa*	Broad-leaved evergreen	Ever-green	Dense	20' tall, 15' wide	6	Moist, well drained, acid	Laurel-shaped leaves; abundant red fruits. Tolerates wind more than many hollies. Use as small tree or large shrub; works espaliered, as specimen or screen, or in massed plantings.
HONEY LOCUST, THORNLESS *Gleditsia triacanthos inermis*	Deciduous	Yellow	Light to medium	40'–70' tall, 30'–40' wide	5	Tolerant	Use in difficult seashore or city conditions. Does not have thorns or seedpods. Delicate, fernlike foliage. Plant for light shade.
HOP HORNBEAM *Ostrya virginiana*	Deciduous	Yellow	Medium	30' tall, 20' wide	5	Moist, well drained, acid	A graceful native tree with slightly shaggy bark. Slow growing. Plant in spring; full sun to heavy shade.
HORNBEAM, EUROPEAN *Carpinus betulus*	Deciduous	Yellow	Medium to dense	40' tall, 40' wide	5	Tolerant	Fluted gray bark; dense foliage. Very adaptable and easily sheared; use in hedge or windbreak.
HORSE CHESTNUT, RED *Aesculus x carnea*	Deciduous	Yellow-brown	Medium to dense	40' tall, 35' wide	4	Moist, well drained	Red, conical flower clusters in spring. Tolerates soot. Hardier, less messy than common horse chestnut. 'Brioti' is a striking variety.

Tree	Type	Fall Foliage	Shade Density	Height/ Width	Zone	Soil Preference	Comments
JAPANESE PAGODA TREE *Sophora japonica*	Deciduous	Red-gold	Light to medium	75' tall, 60' wide	5	Moist, well drained	Resists pests, soot, and diseases. Fast growing. Long clusters of white flowers in late summer. 'Regent' is recommended.
JUNIPER *Juniperus* sp. **Chinese** *J. chinensis*	Coniferous	Ever-green	Dense	15'–50' tall (depends on variety)	4	Well drained	Scalelike, prickly, blue-green to gray-green foliage. For specimen trees, choose 'Columnaris,' 'Keteleeri,' 'Hetzi.' (Other varieties available in shrub or ground-cover forms.)
Eastern red cedar *J. virginiana*	Coniferous	Ever-green	Dense	Varies with variety	3	Well drained	Slow-growing specimen or windbreak. Reddish peeling bark. Blue berries relished by birds. Easily sheared. 'Canaerti' and 'Glauca' are good varieties; many shrub and ground-cover types, too.
KATSURA TREE *Cercidiphyllum japonicum*	Deciduous	Yellow-orange to scarlet	Medium to dense	60' tall, 40' wide	5	Moist, well drained	Resists insects and diseases. Gives good shade, yet still allows air circulation. Use as specimen. Attractive peeling bark; small leaves.
KENTUCKY COFFEE TREE *Gymnocladus dioica*	Deciduous	Yellow	Light to medium	50' tall, 30' wide	5	Tolerant	For light shade in a roomy setting. Coarse texture and somewhat messy seedpods, but picturesque branching.
LARCH, EUROPEAN *Larix decidua*	Deciduous conifer	Yellow	Medium	60' tall, 25'–30' wide	2	Moist, slightly acid	Soft-textured foliage. Cones stay on year-round. Use as specimen in spacious setting. Branches slightly pendulous.
LARCH, GOLDEN *Pseudolarix kaempferi*	Deciduous conifer	Golden yellow	Light	30'–80' tall, 20'–30' wide	6	Moist, well drained, acid	Long, soft needles; in winter, a pyramid of fine brown twigs. Slow growing; suitable for modest space.
LEYLAND CYPRESS *Cupressocyparis leylandi*	Coniferous	Ever-green	Dense	50' tall, 15' wide	6	Well drained	Fast-growing evergreen with pyramidal form and fine-textured scalelike foliage, similar to that of false cypress.
LILAC, JAPANESE TREE *Syringa reticulata*	Deciduous	Not notable	Medium	20' tall, 15' wide	5	Moist, well drained	A true tree, with cherrylike bark and rounded crown. Creamy white flower clusters in June. Best in full sun.

TREES *(continued)*

Tree	Type	Fall Foliage	Shade Density	Height/Width	Zone	Soil Preference	Comments
LINDEN *Tilia* sp. **'Redmond'** *T. x euchlora* 'Redmond'	Deciduous	Not notable	Dense	40' tall, 30' wide	5	Tolerant	A vigorous, pyramidal shade tree with glossy foliage; endures city conditions. Full sun. Creamy yellow flowers in late spring.
Silver *T. tomentosa*	Deciduous	Not notable	Dense	60' tall, 40' wide	5	Tolerant	Highly ornamental shade tree with uplifted branches. In breeze, leaves reveal silver undersides. Fragrant flowers in early summer.
Small-leaved European *T. cordata*	Deciduous	Yellow	Medium to dense	70' tall, 30' wide	5	Moist, well drained	Fast, hardy growth. Tolerates soot. Tiny, fragrant white panicles in early summer. Tight pyramidal shape. 'Greenspire' is excellent choice.
LONDON PLANE TREE *Platanus x acerifolia*	Deciduous	Grayish green-brown	Medium to dense	100' tall, 80' wide	5	Moist, well drained	Fast-growing shade tree. Tolerates soot; resists diseases that affect the related sycamore. Maplelike leaves; round seedballs; unusual creamy olive bark that peels in patches.
MAGNOLIA *Magnolia* sp. **Cucumber tree** *M. acuminata*	Deciduous	Brown	Dense	85' tall, 30' wide	5	Rich, well drained	Grow for shade. Inconspicuous flowers; colorful cucumber-shaped seedpods. Branches often skirt ground.
'Merrill' *M. kobus x loebneri* 'Merrill'	Deciduous	Yellow-brown	Light to medium	30' tall, 30' wide	5	Moist, well drained	Transplant in spring. Grows faster and blooms at younger age than many magnolias. Fragrant, floppy-petaled, early-spring flowers.
Saucer *M. x soulangiana*	Deciduous	Brown	Light	25' tall, 25' wide	6	Moist, well drained	Large, white-purple, cup-shaped flowers in early spring before leaves appear. Attractive slate-gray bark.
Southern *M. grandiflora*	Broad-leaved evergreen	Ever-green	Medium to dense	80' tall, 50' wide	7	Moist, well drained, acid	Stately tree, available in many varieties. Use as large shade or street tree in the South. Old leaves replaced every two years. Saucer-size, creamy white flowers in spring and summer.
Yulan *M. heptapeta*	Deciduous	Brown	Medium	35' tall, 25' wide	6	Moist, well drained, acid	Large, white, cup-shaped flowers in April; smooth gray bark. Transplant in spring; give full sun.

Tree	Type	Fall Foliage	Shade Density	Height/ Width	Zone	Soil Preference	Comments
MAPLE *Acer* sp. **Hedge** *A. campestre*	Deciduous	Yellow	Dense	30' tall, 30' wide	5	Well drained	Dense with low branches. Makes attractive small specimen, or shear for hedge. Tolerates pollution; likes full sun to light shade.
Japanese *A. palmatum*	Deciduous	Scarlet	Light to medium	20' tall, 20' wide (many varieties smaller)	6	Moist, well drained	Specimen tree. Countless elegant varieties. Green, red, or red-green star-shaped to threadlike leaves. Partial shade or, for best color, sun.
Red *A. rubrum*	Deciduous	Red-orange	Medium	70' tall, 50' wide	4	Tolerant, if kept moist	Fast growing. Produces a haze of red flowers in very early spring.
Sugar *A. saccharum*	Deciduous	Yellow, orange, red	Medium to dense	75' tall, 50' wide	3	Moist, well drained	Grows more slowly than other maples. Not for city environments.
Sycamore *A. pseudoplatanus*	Deciduous	Brown	Dense	60' tall, 35' wide	6	Well drained; tolerates salt.	Use in seaside settings or where road salt is a problem. Attractive cultivar is 'Purpureum.'
Trident *A. buergeranum*	Deciduous	Yellow, red	Medium	25' tall, 20' wide	7	Well drained	Orange-brown scaly bark; lustrous foliage. A low, rounded tree; good for shade in small yard. Tolerates heat and drought.
MONKEY-PUZZLE *Araucaria araucana*	Broad-leaved evergreen	Ever-green	Light to medium	80' tall, 40' wide	7	Tolerant	Branches are weirdly twisted and whorled. Sharply pointed, scalelike leaves.
MOUNTAIN ASH, KOREAN *Sorbus alnifolia*	Deciduous	Orange, scarlet	Light to medium	50' tall, 30' wide	5	Well drained	White blossoms followed by red berries, which birds relish in fall. Smooth gray bark; fernlike foliage. Low branches often skirt ground.
OAK *Quercus* sp. **Cork** *Q. suber*	Broad-leaved evergreen	Ever-green	Medium to dense	60' tall, 50' wide	7	Well drained	Fast growing. Interesting bark; source of commercial cork. Use as specimen tree.
Holly *Q. ilex*	Broad-leaved evergreen	Ever-green	Medium to dense	60' tall, 50' wide	9	Well drained, loose	Use as specimen or clip for hedge. Small, hollylike leaves.
Live *Q. virginiana*	Broad-leaved evergreen	Ever-green	Dense	60' tall, 100' wide	7	Moist, well drained	Fast growing; easily transplanted. Specimen or shade tree. Massive trunk and branches.

81

TREES *(continued)*

Tree	Type	Fall Foliage	Shade Density	Height/ Width	Zone	Soil Preference	Comments
OAK *(continued)* **Pin** *Q. palustris*	Deciduous	Red to bronze	Medium	70' tall, 40' wide	5	Well drained, slightly acid	Use as specimen. Hardy; storm sturdy. Strong pyramidal form. Deeply lobed glossy leaves.
Scarlet *Q. coccinea*	Deciduous	Scarlet	Medium	75' tall, 60' wide	4	Well drained, slightly acid	Fast-growing shade or specimen tree. Does not transplant well.
Shingle *Q. imbricaria*	Deciduous	Russet red	Medium	75' tall, 60' wide	5	Well drained, slightly acid	Use as hedge or windbreak. Easily sheared. Laurellike leaves cling to tree into winter.
White *Q. alba*	Deciduous	Violet, purple-red	Medium to dense	90' tall, 80' wide	4	Well drained, slightly acid	Very slow growing; difficult to transplant. Majestic when mature. Leaves have rounded lobes.
Willow *Q. phellos*	Deciduous	Yellow	Medium	60' tall, 40' wide	6	Well drained, slightly acid	Fast growing; shallow roots make transplanting easy. Slender, willowlike leaves.
PEAR, 'BRADFORD' CALLERY *Pyrus calleryana* 'Bradford'	Deciduous	Reddish purple	Dense	35' tall, 20' wide	5	Tolerant	Resists blight and pests; symmetrical; adaptable. Upright branches covered with white blooms in spring; no pears, however.
PECAN *Carya illinoinensis*	Deciduous	Yellow	Light to medium	100' tall, 75' wide	6	Deep, moist, well drained	Use as lawn or specimen tree. Edible nuts produced where summers are long.
PINE *Pinus* sp. **Austrian** *P. nigra*	Coniferous	Ever-green	Dense	60' tall, 20' wide	4	Well drained	Dark green, 5-inch needles in bundles of two. Cones are 2 to 3 inches long. Use as specimen or in windbreak. Resists soot.
Japanese black *P. thunbergiana*	Coniferous	Ever-green	Medium	40' tall, 15' wide	6	Tolerant	Dark, lustrous, long-needled foliage and picturesque branches. Tolerates salt spray.
Monterey *P. radiata*	Coniferous	Ever-green	Dense	50' tall, 30' wide	7	Well drained	Needles in bundles of three. Plant as specimen. Most widely planted in southern California.
Scotch *P. sylvestris*	Coniferous	Ever-green	Medium to dense	75' tall, 30' wide	3	Well drained	Fast growing and picturesque, with twisted blue-green needles and red bark on mature trees. Hardy in seashore, city, or dry conditions. Many varieties.
White *P. strobus*	Coniferous	Ever-green	Medium to dense	100' tall, 40' wide	3	Well drained	Soft-textured, light green needles in bundles of five. Mature specimens stately.

Tree	Type	Fall Foliage	Shade Density	Height/ Width	Zone	Soil Preference	Comments
PRUNUS *Prunus* sp. **Almond** *P. dulcis*	Deciduous	Yellow	Medium	24' tall, 15' wide	7	Moist, well drained	Use as early-flowering specimen tree. Pink and white flowers cover tree in early spring.
Apricot *P. armeniaca*	Deciduous	Yellow	Medium	30' tall, 20' wide	6	Moist, well drained	Early flowering. Used especially in southern California. Bears tasty fruits.
Cherry, higan *P. subhirtella*	Deciduous	Yellow	Light to medium	30' tall, 30' wide	6	Moist, well drained	Use as specimen. Most popular is 'Pendula,' or weeping cherry. 'Autumnalis' blooms again in fall.
Cherry, okame *P. okame*	Deciduous	Bronze	Light	20' tall, 15' wide	6	Moist, well drained	Compact size and shape; fine texture. Pink flowers in April. Use as specimen, in masses, or in staggered rows for hedgelike effect.
Cherry, Oriental *P. serrulata*	Deciduous	Yellow	Light to medium	Most varieties 20'–25' tall, 20'–25' wide	6	Moist, well drained	Use as specimen. Many hybrids. Upright or vaselike form; pink or white single or double flowers. Fragrant. 'Kwanzan' is popular double-flowered type.
Cherry, sargent *P. sargenti*	Deciduous	Red-bronze	Medium to dense	50' tall, 50' wide	5	Moist, well drained	Use as combination specimen and shade tree. Pink flowers, followed by black fruit. Attractive bark.
Cherry, yoshino *P. yedoensis*	Deciduous	Yellow	Light to medium	40' tall, 40' wide	6	Moist, well drained	Tiers of white or pink single flowers in early spring. Famous for Washington, D.C., display.
Pissard plum *P. cerasifera* 'atropurpurea'	Deciduous	Purple	Light to medium	25' tall, 20' wide	4	Moist, well drained	Fine for small yards. Pink flowers, followed by purple foliage. Does best in full sun. Needs occasional pruning.
REDBUD **Judas tree** *Cercis canadensis*	Deciduous	Yellow	Light to medium	35' tall, 30' wide	5	Moist, well drained	Purple-pink blossoms along boughs in early spring. White and pure pink varieties also available. Large heart-shaped leaves. Mix with other flowering trees.
REDWOOD, DAWN *Metasequoia glyptostroboides*	Deciduous	Brown	Medium to dense	100' tall	6	Moist, well drained	Fast-growing, soft-textured deciduous conifer for large, sunny yard. Reddish, peeling bark; both trunk and overall form are conical.

TREES *(continued)*

Tree	Type	Fall Foliage	Shade Density	Height/ Width	Zone	Soil Preference	Comments
SERVICEBERRY *Amelanchier* sp. **Allegheny** *A. laevis*	Deciduous	Yellow, red	Light	30' tall, 15' wide	5	Moist, well drained; pH tolerant	White flowers, bird-attracting black fruit; good in naturalistic or woodland plantings.
Downy serviceberry, shadbush *A. arborea*	Deciduous	Yellow, apricot, red	Medium	25' tall, 15' wide	5	Moist, well drained; pH tolerant	Streaky, smooth-textured, gray bark; edible, purplish black fruit. Often multistemmed and shrubby; fleecy white blooms in early spring.
Shadblow *A. canadensis*	Deciduous	Yellow, red	Medium	20' tall, 15' wide	5	Moist, well drained	Trees covered with white flowers in spring, followed by edible maroon and purple berries, relished by birds.
SILK TREE Mimosa tree *Albizia julibrissin*	Deciduous	Yellow	Light	35' tall, 25' wide	7	Tolerant	Feathery, fernlike foliage. Pink, powder-pufflike flowers throughout the summer. Good near patio or porch, or on lawn. Not storm sturdy. Often multistemmed.
SMOKE TREE *Cotinus* sp. **American** *C. obovatus*	Deciduous	Scarlet	Medium	20' tall, 15' wide	6	Tolerant	Use as lawn or specimen tree. Excellent fall color.
Purple *C. coggygria* 'purpureus'	Deciduous	Purple	Medium	15' tall, 15' wide	6	Well drained	Purple leaves; pinkish gray midsummer flowers. Dramatic in grouped planting or shrub border, though not shapely enough for use as specimen. Requires little maintenance once established.
SORREL TREE *Oxydendrum arboreum*	Deciduous	Scarlet	Medium	30' tall, 20' wide	5	Moist, well drained, acid	A specimen plant for all seasons. Laurellike foliage, late-summer flowers, intense fall color, and handsome, gray, furrowed bark.
SPRUCE *Picea* sp. **Colorado** *P. pungens*	Coniferous	Ever-green	Dense	80' tall, 25' wide	3	Well drained	Dark green to pale blue foliage. Often used as specimen, but looks better in massed planting. 'Glauca' is a popular blue variety.
Serbian *P. omorika*	Coniferous	Ever-green	Dense	90' tall, 30' wide	5	Rich, moist, well drained	Slender pyramidal growth and glossy foliage. An excellent specimen; tolerates semishade, city conditions.

Tree	Type	Fall Foliage	Shade Density	Height/ Width	Zone	Soil Preference	Comments
STEWARTIA, KOREAN *Stewartia koreana*	Deciduous	Orange, scarlet	Dense	35'–45' tall, 15'–20' wide	6	Moist, well drained, slightly acid	Pyramidal form; glossy camellialike foliage; cup-shaped, white, July flowers; flaking bark. Shelter from strong sun. Often hard to find.
TULIP TREE *Liriodendron tulipifera*	Deciduous	Yellow	Dense	100' tall, 50' wide	5	Moist, well drained	Massive, pyramidal, impressive if given plenty of space. Greenish yellow, cup-shaped flowers in spring after leaves unfurl. Fast growing.
UMBRELLA PINE *Sciadopitys verticillata*	Coniferous	Ever-green	Dense	20' tall, 10' wide	6	Moist, well drained	Does well in full sun to light shade; tolerates salt spray. Lushly textured, with needles in whorls like umbrella ribs. Very slow grower.
WILLOW *Salix* sp. **Babylon weeping** *S. babylonica*	Deciduous	Yellow	Medium	40' tall, 40' wide	6	Moist, well drained; tolerates wet soil.	Fast growing. Graceful, refined specimen for wet areas. Weeping branches sweep the ground. Easily damaged by storm or insects. Needs frequent pruning.
Golden weeping *S. alba 'tristis'*	Deciduous	Yellow	Light	75'–100' tall, 50'–60' wide	3	Moist	Benefits from pruning and fertilizing; thrives in wet ground. Golden brown bark, golden twigs, silver green foliage.
Wisconsin or niobe weeping *S. x blanda*	Deciduous	Yellow	Medium	40' tall, 40' wide	4	Moist, well drained; tolerates wet soil.	Fast-growing hybrid for specimen use in wet location. Long pendulous branches. Needs frequent pruning; not sturdy in storms.
YELLOWWOOD *Cladrastis lutea*	Deciduous	Orange, yellow	Medium to dense	50' tall, 40' wide	3	Moist, well drained	Use as specimen, in grouping, or as shade tree. White flowers in long clusters. Smooth, gray bark. Brittle crotches.
ZELKOVA *Zelkova* sp. **Elm** *Z. carpinifolia*	Deciduous	Red, brown	Medium	75' tall, 60' wide	7	Tolerant	Slow growing. Use as specimen tree. Resists damage from drought and heavy winds.
Japanese *Z. serrata*	Deciduous	Yellow, orange, brown	Medium	50'–60' tall, 50'–60' wide	6	Tolerant	Small-leaved, vase-shaped, large shade tree. Sometimes promoted as replacement for American elm. 'Village Green' is recommended.

PLANTING AND ESTABLISHING TREES

Always start with the best-quality nursery stock possible. Investing a few dollars more at this stage could make a big difference in how sturdy your tree will be in a few years.

Work with a reliable nursery or garden center, and look for strong, straight trunks and well-spaced branches. There should be little (if any) breakage or bruising of the bark. Foliage should be lush and show no signs of wilting, disease, or insect activity.

TYPES OF STOCK

Trees from mail-order nurseries usually come bare root. They are harvested in the fall, over-wintered, then shipped in spring. Other nurseries may supply trees grown in 3- to 7-gallon (or larger) pots, boxes, or fiber containers.

Trees that are tricky to transplant, including many native species, do better if grown in containers. But make sure that the tree you select is not pot-bound, with its roots encircling the soil. Look for white root tips just showing inside the pot. These will continue rapid growth.

Perhaps most often, you'll find balled-and-burlapped, or "B&B," trees. The nursery digs the tree when it is dormant and wraps the root ball in jute or plastic burlap. Though hallowed by custom, this procedure can stress the tree because a good portion of the roots are lost. A balled-and-burlapped tree demands careful storage and transportation.

PLANTING AND WATERING

Plant bare-root trees while they're still dormant in spring as early as you can work the soil. You can plant container trees any time during the growing season, though some experts contend early fall planting gives container plants a head start on spring growth before the heat of summer. Plant balled-and-burlapped trees at almost any point in the growing season, but early spring and early fall are best times. This

PLANTING AND STAKING

(Far left) For a bare-root tree, dig a hole 2 feet wider than the roots; then build a mound for roots to rest on. Stake the tree with fabric ties.

(Near left) Leave jute burlap on a balled-and-burlapped tree, if you like, but remove any plastic, wire basket, wires, or cords. Stake or use guys.

SOLVING POOR DRAINAGE

(Far left) Elevate the grade if poorly drained soil or a high water table is a problem. Grade softly back to existing elevation to avoid bumps.

(Near left) Or, dig a trench leading down and away from the planting pit, then install perforated pipe. The pipe should drain into a dry well or similar opening.

gives the roots time to get established before the onset of very hot or cold weather.

For all tree types, dig a plant pit at least 2 feet wider than the root ball. Dig it wider still if the soil is compacted or otherwise in poor condition. Make the pit only as deep as the root ball, no deeper. If you're planting in your lawn, pile the soil on a tarp.

Plant your new trees in well-drained, fertile soil. To check drainage, fill your planting pit with water and let it stand overnight. If all the water hasn't drained, you'll need to plant the tree higher or provide drainage with perforated pipe (see illustrations, opposite, bottom).

Break up all clods in the excavated soil. If the soil is sandy or gravelly, mix about one-third fertile loam with the backfill soil. If your soil is high in clay, replace it with good topsoil. Recent research shows that adding any other amendments such as fertilizer, peat moss, manure, or sand is unnecessary.

At planting time, completely remove any plastic from the tree stock. You can leave jute burlap in place (it will rot away), but remove any cords. Take a container tree out of its pot only just before planting; exposing the tree even briefly to open air can damage its roots. If a container tree is at all pot-bound, take a sharp knife and score the tree's root ball vertically to a depth of about ⅛ inch at 2- or 3-inch intervals all the way around. This will help to encourage outward root growth.

Set the root ball in the pit. Partially backfill with soil, tamping gently to eliminate air pockets. Water thoroughly; let the water soak in, then backfill completely. Build a rim around the edge of the filled area to create a saucer. Fill the saucer with water and let it soak in overnight. Refill the saucer the following day.

After this initial watering, watch the tree's water supply carefully for the first year. In dry periods, water every five to seven days. A water lance or soaker hose (see illustrations, above right) conserves water.

CARE AFTER PLANTING

Depending on its type, size, and location, your tree may need some extra care until it is established. Use tree wrap or tape, available at garden centers, only during the first winter; remove it in summer. To ensure that the wind doesn't damage new roots by rocking the tree, fasten the tree to stakes. Drive a 2x2- or 2x3-inch stake vertically into the soil below the root

WATERING TREES

(Far left) Use a water lance to deliver water straight to the roots with minimum waste. Mulch around the tree's base to further reduce water loss.

(Near left) To prevent the topsoil from washing away, distribute water slowly and evenly with a canvas soaker hose.

ball, about 6 inches from the trunk on the side of the prevailing wind. Fasten the stake to the tree (see illustration, opposite, top left). Or, if the tree's trunk is more than 2 to 3 inches in diameter, stretch guy wires to three anchors or stakes spaced evenly around the tree (see illustration, opposite, top right). Protect the bark by running support wires through grommets made of 3-inch-wide pieces of carpet or webbing.

To prevent competition for nutrients from weeds or grass, and to conserve soil moisture, mulch around all newly planted trees. Use leaves, pine needles, bark chips, gravel, or stone chips. A porous barrier under the mulch helps reduce weeds, but avoid plastic. It reduces the amount of oxygen available to the roots. Spread the mulch at least 3 to 4 inches deep, starting 6 inches from the trunk and extending 2 to 3 feet in all directions.

Apply fertilizer to the mulch area two or three times during the first and second growing seasons. Use commercial fertilizer, manure, or any other high-nitrogen organic fertilizer. Aim for 2 ounces of nitrogen per tree.

A final note: There is no need to prune out one-third of the top growth, as used to be recommended. Do, however, remove dead or broken branches at planting time.

CARING FOR TREES

Though trees can flourish unattended in nature, a tree destined to beautify and live out its life in your yard should receive your attention and care. Grown under optimum conditions—which only you can ensure—a tree has a good chance to become the beauty you hope it will be.

TRAINING A YOUNG TREE

Training a tree from the whip stage promotes the development of a single leader and strong, evenly spaced branches. First, cut back the whip to stimulate branching. After the second growing season, select key branches to be the scaffolding of the tree's growth from then on. When removing unwanted branches, be sure not to leave stubs, which can become hosts to rot or disease.

Very young trees often need selective pruning to promote structural soundness. Remove branches that could form narrow or weak crotches once the trees mature. Such crotches are apt to split in wind- or ice storms. Eliminate double leaders (except on small ornamental trees) by removing one of the competing pair. Take out any branch that crosses and rubs against another, or any branch growing too close to another.

As a tree grows, you may wish to remove its low-growing limbs for appearance, to increase air circulation, and to make mowing around the tree easier.

PRUNING OLDER TREES

Sometimes an older tree requires trimming to stay within bounds. For example, limbs may begin to interfere with power lines. Or the branches of a shade tree may block light or obstruct views.

Certain types of trees, such as willows, will be sturdier and more attractive if given regular prunings. Other trees, such as cherries and crab

TRAINING A YOUNG TREE

1 Proper training assures that young trees planted as whips mature into beautifully shaped trees. Immediately after planting, make a cut at about a 6-foot height, above a bud, to force branching.

2 After the second growing season remove unwanted branches. This selective pruning leaves a strong, graceful foundation for later growth.

3 Growth in the third year forms the basis of the tree's ultimate shape. Well-spaced branches with strong crotches and a single leader will mature into a specimen tree.

apples, tend to develop long, straight, fast-growing shoots or water sprouts that need removing for the sake of the tree's health and appearance.

When you remove any branch, large or small, cut it back to a crotch. Make an angled cut that preserves the branch collar, if any, and the bark ridge at the base of the branch (see illustration, page 91). This will help to form a callus evenly around the edges of the cut and seal the wood against fungi and other organisms that could cause decay.

■ When to prune
The best time to prune is during a tree's dormant period, especially at the end of the period (late winter). Avoid pruning in spring when leaves are forming or in fall when they're dropping. Prune in summer only if it's essential to expose branches or improve sight lines.

■ Pruning evergreens
When pruning evergreens, follow the same guidelines as for other trees, except in the case of pines. Because pines grow only from their tips, removing a pine bough may create a gap until adjacent foliage fills in. To shape a pine, break off the tops of the spring shoots or candles when they snap easily—rather than just bend—in your fingers.

■ Pruning myths
Much traditional advice on pruning and wound treatment has been based on misconceptions. For example, tree professionals long recommended that you cut off branches flush with the trunk, paint wounds with tree paint, and fill large cavities with concrete. But now these practices are avoided.

Flush cutting delays healing and tends to cause uneven formation of a callus, thus encouraging the onset of decay.

Applying paint, shellac, or asphalt to tree wounds causes problems, too. The coating eventually cracks and allows moisture to accumulate underneath. The result is an ideal environment for rot.

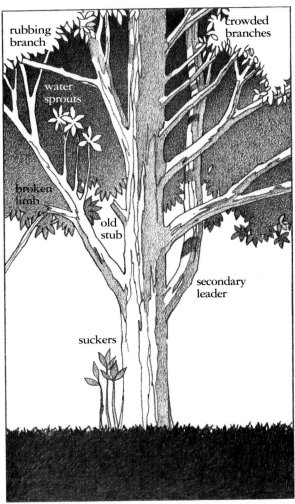

A tree will need your help a number of times during its life. Shown here are some situations a tree could encounter that may cause problems if unremedied. Rubbing branches, broken limbs, and old stubs can allow insects to enter. Water sprouts and suckers tax a tree's strength. Narrow crotches and crowded branches create weak growth and are unsightly. For detailed pruning drawings, see pages 90–91.

Scouring old cavities, filling them with concrete, drilling drainage holes—all these practices merely impede the tree's natural self-protective mechanisms. Research has shown that a tree naturally isolates, or compartmentalizes, a wound or cavity, in effect localizing decay. To disturb the compartment by scouring or drilling fosters additional decay. And concrete, like paint, traps moisture that could cause rot.

CARING FOR TREES *(continued)*

WHEN PRUNING IS NEEDED

(Left) Use pruning shears to snip off a small branch that crosses and rubs against another. Unless trimmed, the rubbing branches could cause a bark wound, which invites disease.

(Right) If two branches are too close together, use a pruning saw to remove the smaller branch.

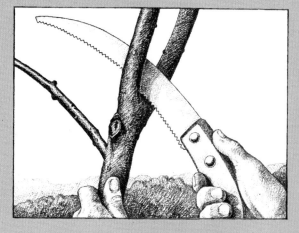

(Left) If a young tree has two competing leaders, remove one of them. Left uncut, the two branches, when mature, might form a weak crotch that could split.

(Right) Prune water sprouts, which tax the strength of a tree, with shears or long-handled loppers.

(Left) For clearance under a tree, remove the lower branches over several growing seasons, cutting off one or two branches a year. Make the cuts so the branch collars remain.

(Right) Clip off suckers from around the base of a tree. Trim flush with the trunk or root.

Besides training and pruning, you may need to provide other care for a tree. Storms can injure a tree. So can insects and diseases. Should any situation arise that could endanger a tree, it's time to take action.

REPAIRING INJURIES

For branches cracked or broken off by storms, follow the cutting recommendations on pages 88–89 and in the drawings opposite and at right. If a branch dies, remove the dead wood, making sure to cut *outside* the callus. Opening the callus exposes the tree to pest infestation.

When bark has been damaged, you may be able to promote healing if the bark is still intact—or cleanly broken off—and still moist. Nail the bark back in place, spread wet paper towels over the wound, then wrap the dressing securely in white plastic for about three weeks.

If that kind of first aid is unfeasible, wait one growing season to see how much bark loosens around the wound. Then carefully trim away the loose bark with a knife or chisel. Make the cut as smooth an oval or circle as possible; avoid cutting a sharp V at the top or bottom.

To reinforce a structurally weak tree, especially if a break would endanger people or property, call in professionals to stretch steel rods or cables between large branches.

TOPPING A TREE

Trimming the top of a tree is usually unadvisable. Ideally, you want to consider a tree's mature size and shape when you first select it and choose its location. If it does become necessary to top a tree, however, cut branches that are at least one-third smaller in diameter than adjacent ones, and try to keep the integrity of the tree's form. Cut each branch back to a crotch, leaving no stub beyond the branch collar.

INSECTS AND DISEASES

Opinions differ about how to control insects and diseases in trees. Some authorities contend that

CUTTING BIG LIMBS, STUBS

Never cut off a large branch with a single cut. Instead, use a three-cut sequence to remove the limb, making sure to leave the bark ridge and branch collar intact.

When removing a dead stub, cut outside the callus. This avoids exposing live wood to possible infection.

pesticides and fungicides do more harm than they do good. Others argue, however, that when a tree is severely stressed—by gypsy-moth caterpillars, for example—it's only sensible to eliminate the problem.

In any case, remember this general rule: Every tree has a better chance of shrugging off occasional problems if it's in vigorous health and given the soil, water, sun, and exposure it likes. (Refer to the charts on pages 74–85 for optimum conditions for each tree. See pages 92–93 for more information about controlling insects and diseases.)

TREE DISEASES

Disease	Description and Trouble Signs	Control
Anthracnose	A fungus infection, anthracnose attacks many species, including ash, birch, hickory, London plane, maple, and oak. Cool, moist conditions promote infection. Spores are airborne; fungi overwinter in fallen leaves and on trees. Signs are spotted, blotched, or distorted leaves; cankers on twigs; falling twigs.	Destroy or compost leaves; prune out infected tree parts. Fertilize fall and spring to promote vigor. Try Bordeaux mixture (copper sulfate with lime). Suggested fungicides include ferbam and thiram.
Anthracnose, dogwood	Caused by a fungus (*Glomerella cingulata*), this anthracnose infection is rapidly becoming a major threat to flowering dogwoods. Leaves wilt and twigs die back, first on lower branches. Infected leaves usually remain on tree during winter. Fungus may enter through bark wounds; wet weather, mild temperatures foster its growth. Trees are most vulnerable if old, inadequately nourished, or otherwise stressed.	Maintain vigor of healthy trees to prevent infection. Fungicide spraying in early spring and at two-week intervals may help control.
Cytospora canker	Cytospora (or leucostoma) canker is the most common disease of spruces; attacks hemlocks and some other conifers as well. Fungus causes bark lesions; foliage turns brown and falls off, usually starting on lower branches. Occurs where trees are stressed by wet weather, drought, or poor growing conditions.	Prune diseased branches in dry weather. Avoid injuring trees, as spores may enter through small breaks in bark.
Fire blight	A bacterial disease spread by insects, fire blight affects apple, hawthorn, and pear trees. Signs are black leaves on new shoots and branches, cankers on dead bark.	Fungicides have no effect; research on antibiotics is under way. If infection occurs, cut, destroy affected parts; disinfect tools.
Juniper blight	A fungus, juniper blight infects not only juniper but many needled evergreens. New growth turns light green, then brown, then gray. Hits lower branches first, moves up tree. Especially bad in wet spring.	Prune and destroy affected twigs and branches in late winter when tree is dry. Spray with copper sulfate weekly, starting in spring, for three or four weeks.
Rust	Rust fungi create unsightly orange growths on trees; many rusts get started on specific alternate host plants. (White pine blister rust moves from currant family plants to pines.) Cedar-apple, cedar-hawthorn, and cedar-quince rusts produce reddish galls (called cedar apples) or swellings on twigs of cedars (juniperus). In spring, sticky orange spore masses emerge. Carried by wind, spores infect crab apple, hawthorn, mountain ash, and serviceberry trees, among others.	Hand-pick cedar galls in spring. If necessary, destroy the less important of the two plant hosts to break the cycle. Try spraying in midsummer with ferbam or thiram.
Sphaeropsis tip blight	Sometimes called diplodia tip blight, sphaeropsis tip blight is a major problem of Austrian, Scotch, and other pines. Stunted new growth and brown needles cause lower branches to die. Usually worst in weak or older trees, or when trees are stressed by wet soil, drought, compacted soil, or other difficulties.	Prevent by providing good growing conditions. If necessary, use fungicide spray at bud break and again two weeks later.
Verticillium wilt	Soil-borne fungi can infect many maple species as well as Kentucky coffee tree, linden, redbud, smoke tree, and yellowwood. Foliage on all or part of tree yellows, wilts, dies back. In maples, extremely early fall color often is a sign of this disease.	Prevent by watering and fertilizing adequately. Remove affected branches. If whole tree is severely infected, remove and replace with resistant species such as beech, birch, oak, sweet gum, or willow.

TREE INSECTS

Insect	Description and Trouble Signs	Control
Aphids	These small, soft-bodied insects suck tree sap, causing foliage to wither. On pine or beech trunks, may appear as cottony masses. May cluster on new growth of crab apple or undersides of beech leaves.	Release commercially available predators such as ladybugs and lacewings. Insecticidal soap may be effective. Chemical controls include malathion and other insecticides.
Black vine or taxus weevils	Weak, dying branches and notched leaves on false cypress and other evergreens may indicate feeding by this beetle. (Yew or taxus is primary host.) Grubs eat roots; beetles feed on foliage.	Try to stop beetles from climbing tree by using Tanglefoot or other sticky barrier. Or, in late July or early August, treat soil with malathion, tree with diazinon or malathion.
Borers	Tunneling larvae of bronze birch borer start at tops of birches and can kill whole trees. Dogwood and peach borers also can kill trees. Early signs (leaf loss, rusty patches, or swellings on bark) often come too late for treatment. Young or weak trees or trees with damaged bark are especially susceptible.	Protect trees by wrapping when young and by practicing careful hygiene, mulching, fertilizing, and watering. If infestation occurs, cut off and destroy affected parts. For birch borer, spray with methoxychlor in early summer.
Caterpillars	Tent caterpillars feed on cherry, other ornamentals in early spring. Inchworms, cankerworms, gypsy-moth caterpillars eat leaves of oak, hickory, beech, others in late spring.	Use 3- to 4-percent dormant oil spray. Apply *Bacillus thuringiensis* once or twice early in infestation. Carbaryl is chemical control.
Lace bugs	These sucking insects infest sycamore, hawthorn, cherry, many broad-leaved evergreens. Whitish or yellowish spots appear on leaves; molasseslike excretions on undersides of leaves. Twigs and leaves may drop.	Try soap sprays; or spray or dust with pyrethrum. Or apply diazinon or malathion. Natural predators of some lace bugs include lacewings, assassin bugs, and spiders.
Leaf miners	Birch leaf miner and holly leaf miner are particularly damaging. Small flies lay eggs on new foliage; larvae then feed inside leaves, which turn brown, drop prematurely. In birches, reduced vitality then makes tree more susceptible to borers and other problems.	Because sanitation is key, destroy or compost fallen leaves, prune back new growth if possible, remove any water sprouts. Spray birch with methoxychlor or malathion; for holly, try diazinon or malathion.
Leaf-skeletonizing beetles	Japanese beetles and elm-leaf beetles reduce foliage to lacy skeletons.	Use milky spore disease (*Bacillus popilliae*) to kill Japanese beetle larvae in soil. Carbaryl may control these beetles.
Pine bark beetles	Larvae of several beetle species tunnel under pine bark, damaging bark and causing foliage at treetops to turn yellow or red, then die. Signs are holes dug in bark, exuded "pitch tubes," and reddish sawdust.	Avoid mechanical injury, soil compaction, water-table change, other stresses. Remove old or weakened trees. If tree becomes infested, remove it and destroy all debris.
Pine sawflies	Numerous species of sawflies lay eggs on pine foliage; larvae devour needles, may defoliate trees. Some consume old needles; some, young needles.	Remove plant debris under trees. Spray in May or June; rotenone or carbaryl may be effective.
Scales	White, gray, or brownish scale insects can encrust branches or twigs of oak, tulip tree, white pine, others. Scales suck sap, causing stunted, discolored, or wilted growth. Scales' honeydew also supports molds.	Apply dormant oil before buds open; or try insecticidal soap sprays. In growing season, 1- to 2-percent oil spray may help. Biological controls include ladybugs, scale parasites.
Spider mites	Spider mites, the size of grains of salt, damage hemlock, spruce, juniper, other evergreens. Lower foliage may fade to light or whitish green, then turn brown and die.	Prevent with dormant oil spray. Or spray in early July with diazinon. Ladybugs and lacewings are predators.

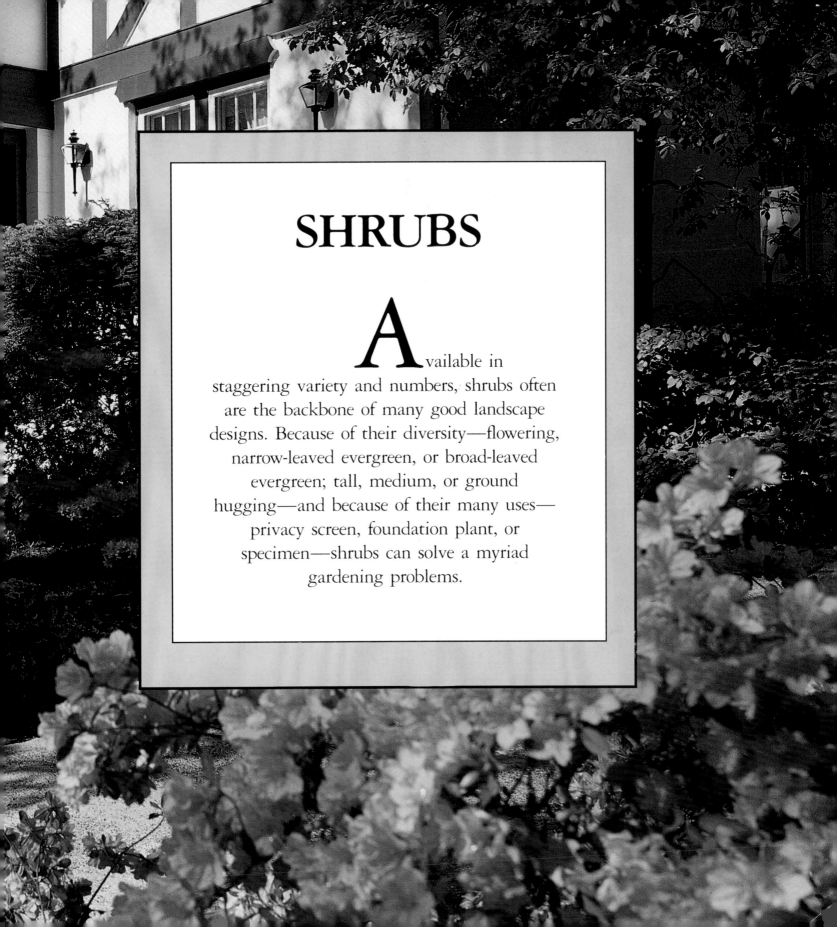

SHRUBS

Available in staggering variety and numbers, shrubs often are the backbone of many good landscape designs. Because of their diversity—flowering, narrow-leaved evergreen, or broad-leaved evergreen; tall, medium, or ground hugging—and because of their many uses—privacy screen, foundation plant, or specimen—shrubs can solve a myriad gardening problems.

CHOOSING SHRUBS

Versatile and valuable in landscapes, shrubs can dress up, cover up, or accent a home's features. Whether selected as the finishing touch to a landscape plan or as the first endeavor to soften the look of new construction, shrubs have earned a rightful place as a quick-and-easy answer to many landscaping problems: Quick, because most shrubs grow rapidly, promising good bloom and spreading in the first season after planting; easy, since many shrubs are hardy and can withstand minimal care and even drought.

SHRUB TYPES AND USES

Deciduous flowering shrubs, broad-leaved evergreens, and conifers—or narrow-leaved evergreens—are the three basic shrub types. Evergreens offer so much versatility in landscaping, they often are overused. A successful design combines shrubs of each group in a harmonious medley of sizes, textures, and shapes.

For low-maintenance landscaping, put your emphasis on the natural shapes of shrubs. Deciduous shrubs have four typical shapes: arching branches, erect, rounded, and spreading. The chart opposite lists many deciduous flowering shrubs according to their shapes. Evergreens, on the other hand, have five basic growth patterns: low and trailing, medium spreading, horizontal spreading, round compact, and upright.

Visualize your landscape with an artist's eye. For informal borders, use rounded shrubs. Vertical lines characterize erect or upright forms, making them perfect accents or specimens in the garden or in front of a home's windowless wall or garage. They also are useful as narrow hedges, but may need frequent pruning.

Graceful, fountainlike silhouettes of arching shrubs make them a restful sight in a yard. Use them in shrub borders or as specimens, or to highlight the ends of narrow hedges.

(Above) Junipers come in just about every plant shape imaginable. Here, a tall, lean variety teams with its short, squatty relative to soften the straight lines of a home.

(Left) Pendulous clusters of pearly white flowers adorn this andromeda by an entry. An attractive plant year-round, it offers showy bronze-colored new foliage.

Large spreading types, with branches extending in horizontal lines, make ideal foundation or front-of-the-yard plants.

In small gardens where you want to use a variety of plants, select upright, medium-size plants and only a few spreading varieties.

WHERE TO PLANT

Shrubs can accent the best architectural features of the home—or hide bare, boring spots, such as foundation walls. Shrubs also can help a home blend with its surroundings.

In general, plant shrubs wherever strong vertical architectural lines meet the ground.

At the front of the house, use a strong corner grouping. To emphasize the entrance, use tall, accent plantings at either side of the doorway. Evergreens with upright, rounded, or pointed shapes, such as pine or yew, are effective. For a special touch, add an accent plant, such as a flowering clematis. Place lower-growing plantings under windows. Use short hedges or dwarf shrubs in a front border to unify the house and site, creating a textured background for bedding flowers.

Keep plantings along the side of the house simple. For best effect, group three or more of the same kind of shrub together.

If your home has a high foundation, use large shrubs at the corners, then add vines or espaliered plants on one of the walls as an accent.

Informal shrub borders help frame a house, as well as separate it from neighbors.

Low-spreading and quick-growing species used on a steep slope help control soil erosion. Spreading evergreens, a hardy and handsome choice, can transform an eyesore into an easy-care asset.

Shrubs also can soften the stark look of walls. To make high walls appear lower, group shrubs of similar height at the base of the wall.

DECIDUOUS SHRUB SHAPES

Shrub	Height in Feet	Flower Color
ARCHING BRANCHES		
Beautybush	15	Pink
Butterfly bush	12	Lilac
Forsythia	10	Yellow
Lilac daphne	3	Blue
Slender deutzia	4	White
Spirea	6	White
ERECT		
Common lilac	20	Mixed
Hibiscus	10	Mixed
Highbush cranberry	15	Mixed
Lemoine mock orange	6	White
Red-osier dogwood	7	White
ROUNDED		
Flowering quince	6	Mixed
Hydrangea	4–9	Mixed
Kerria	6	Yellow
Persian lilac	10	Violet
Weigela	10	Red
Witch hazel	10	Yellow
SPREADING		
Dwarf ninebark	4	White
Fragrant viburnum	9	White
Japanese quince	3	Mixed
Sargent crab apple	6	White
Spreading cotoneaster	6	Pink
Staghorn sumac	20	Green

A blank fence offers a perfect backdrop for an artistic espaliered design. A trained berry-laden or blossoming shrub can convert a boring, unadorned fence into an attractive feature that will embellish any landscape.

CHOOSING SHRUBS *(continued)*

*Springtime show-offs,
azaleas provide a
spectacular display.
Wonderful border plants
in masses, or fine
specimens, azaleas grow
in most of the country
and are available in
many colors.*

Despite the rich variety of shrubs available, too many gardeners rely on a few tried-and-true favorites. Shrubs can offer as much color, shape, and texture as perennials, annuals, bulbs, or trees.

■ Add a splash of color

Like Cinderella dressed for the ball, many shrubs are transformed each spring into ravishing beauties, arrayed colorfully in blossoms that delight the senses. In selecting flowering varieties, give thought to their blooming sequence, as well as to the hue and size of blossoms.

You'll get the best results by massing together several shrubs of the same type and color. Planting one of everything just gives a polka-dot effect that forces the eye to jump from one color to the next.

■ Create mirages with shrubs

You can use all of the features of shrubs—color, height, spread, and form—to alter the proportions of your garden.

To make a view seem longer, place bold or broad-leaved plants in the front, with small-leaved, delicate shrubs placed farther away. Because light and bright colors advance and dark colors recede, you can give the illusion of less space and depth by placing light-foliaged shrubs—those with silver or bluish tinges, or yellow—in the background, with deeper tones—purples or dark greens—up front.

(Above left) Fragrant flowers and showy blossoms reward gardeners who favor an old standby, the lilac.

(Above right) The yellow blossoms of the forsythia herald the coming of spring. A bit of pruning and fertilization after flowering keeps the plant in prime shape.

(Left) French hydrangea makes a stunning specimen shrub, bursting with clouds of lilac-hued blossoms.

PRIVACY SCREENS

A private yard, like a tranquil island, has irresistible allure. And you can create your own outdoor sanctum without a chain-link, wood, or stone fence. Shrubbery screens can be more effective than any of these at blocking noise, wind, sun, and visual intrusion—and be more eye-catching, too.

FORM FOLLOWS FUNCTION

Define your objective before selecting the shrubs for your screen. Is your goal to divide or define an area, or to create an impenetrable screen? Plant evergreens for year-round protection and privacy; use flowering deciduous shrubs to create a temporary decorative and friendly screen.

Tall hedgelike shrubs, whether evergreen or dense deciduous varieties, create excellent background plantings. These upright forms also require less horizontal space in the garden.

Flowering shrubs make colorful accents in a garden each spring or summer, and can be intermingled with evergreens or massed together in a border for a hedgelike effect.

■ Creating your privacy screen

Whether used to divide one portion of a garden from another or to separate properties, living privacy screens offer the chance for beautiful combinations of texture, colors, and shrub sizes. They can become, in fact, seasonal focal points.

Start at the back with taller shrubs. Plants growing 7 feet high make good choices for most screens. They will undoubtedly be much smaller when you buy them, but leave generous

A mixed border featuring low-growing shrubs and taller trees creates a graceful and effective barrier between neighboring yards. Using the same type of shrub throughout the border gives the design cohesion.

space between them when planting so they'll have room to mature.

For best results with flowering screens, follow the basic principles of color theory. Deeply colored flowers recede when contrasted with dark foliage; when set against a light yellow-green background, they stand out. In shady areas, light-toned flowers look best. Brilliant flowers are striking in a sunny spot next to a pale or white-toned wall.

Mix hot red or scarlet with pink or pastels for a lively color combination. Strong yellow and pink hues are jarring, but a blend of yellow and yellow-orange tones works well. Red is at its best with white or dark green as the background color; rose and yellow-pink hues shine against white backdrops. Careful planning of colors can create a refreshing look to your landscape while offering the privacy you covet.

MAKING YOUR CHOICE

Although there are many ways to achieve privacy with plants, your shrubbery screen should reflect the special needs of your landscaping design, as well as your yard's soil and light conditions. A living privacy screen should reflect, too, your dedication to the upkeep demands of the plants you choose. Screens can be formal, clipped hedges of leafy green, or plantings set in a more random, natural fashion. Do you want to spend several weekends annually pruning a forsythia hedge or trimming back lilacs in the border? Or do you prefer an evergreen with slow growth patterns and self-maintaining habits? The choice—as well as the time—is yours.

Ficus shrubs, left to grow tall, form a lofty privacy screen that adds more elegance to an already stately setting.

101

PLANTING SHRUBS

A dazzling shower of white blossoms cascades over a bridal bouquet in full bloom. Nurturing an infant plant into a spectacular specimen like this begins with proper planting techniques.

Shrubs solve many landscaping problems, but when making your plant choices, carefully consider their needs first. Do they require sun or shade? Wet or dry soil? What are their pruning requirements, and do they need protection in winter?

SHRUB FORMS

You can buy shrubs from the nursery in three forms: bare root, balled and burlapped, or container grown.

■ Bare-root shrubs

Bare-root shrubs are best planted in winter or early spring. Keep the roots moist until you're ready to plant. Dig a hole somewhat larger than the root area. Plan to set the shrub slightly deeper than it was before. Lay a shovel handle across the hole to help determine proper planting depth. Mold a loose cone of soil in the bottom of the hole, then set the shrub in the hole and spread its roots over the cone. Backfill the hole halfway, tamping the soil slightly around the roots. Give the plant a good soaking, then fill with remaining soil.

■ Balled and container-grown shrubs

Although more expensive than bare-root plants, balled-and-burlapped shrubs and shrubs grown in containers are available during peak gardening seasons.

To plant balled or container shrubs, dig a hole a foot wider than the root ball and about as deep. Lower the root ball carefully and center it. If balled, loosen the burlap around the trunk, but you need not remove it. Burlap decays rapidly and will not interfere with root development. If the shrub is wrapped in plastic, or is in an asphalt or cardboard container, cut the wrap or container, then remove it after positioning the root ball in the hole. If the plant is in a metal container, ask the nursery to cut slits in the container before you take it home. Then remove it and place the plant in the hole. For both balled and container shrubs, backfill the hole as for bare-root shrubs.

CARING FOR NEW SHRUBS

To help catch water, form a shallow depression around the trunk of the newly planted shrub. Give the shrub a good soaking after planting. In a few days, water it deeply again. Trim the plant back to one-fourth its original height if you plan to keep it sheared, one-half for an informal look. Shear all evergreens to a uniform size and shape. Place mulch all the way around the base, to within an inch or two of the trunk.

MOVING MATURE SHRUBS

Spring and fall are the best times to safely move a shrub, but with a little caution you can shift an established shrub to a new home even in the summer, too.

Use a sharp spade to cut a circle about the plant's roots, then shape the roots and surrounding soil into a ball by undercutting lower roots. When the ball is free and can be rocked to one side, wrap it in burlap, then fasten with twine at the top. Because balled shrubs are heavy, you may need help moving the plant. Keep the roots moist. Remove the twine fastening but leave the burlap on the root ball. Plant as for new shrubs, then give it a good soaking of water.

For the next two weeks, cool the plant each day during hot weather with mist from the hose, but avoid overwatering. Watering once a week is ample for a newly transplanted shrub.

PLANTING A SHRUB

Dig the planting hole a little larger than the root area. To make refilling the hole and cleanup easier, put a tarp or piece of plastic next to where you'll dig the hole, then place the soil on it.

When planting a bare-root shrub, keep it moist until you set it in the ground. Plant the shrub a little deeper than it grew before being moved. Place a shovel across the hole to help determine planting depth.

If the plant is in an asphalt or cardboard container, place it in the hole before removing the container. Then cut away the sides.

CHOOSING AND PLANTING A HEDGE

Common boxwoods, which can reach a height of 20 feet, form a soft-looking hedge that separates neighboring properties, plus provides privacy. Box also shears well, if a more formal look is desired.

Like a decorative wall, a hedge marks a boundary, dividing the yard while giving it an orderly pattern, whether prim or playful. Hedges may be real barriers, or act as graceful guardians of paths or flower beds.

HEDGE HEIGHTS

Low, high, or in between, the height of a hedge depends on its purpose, the kind of shrub selected, and how often you trim it. As always with shrubs, choosing the best type for the soil, site, and landscape design is essential.

Low hedges—1 to 3 feet tall—must be slow growing and neat, and tolerate regular pruning. If you want to keep a hedge less than 2 feet tall, shearing is a must. To keep plants within bounds, begin training them the first year.

Formal hedges create beautiful backdrops for other garden plantings, plus lend to the good looks of a well-manicured garden. To maintain its natty appearance, a formal hedge requires periodic pruning.

Medium hedges—3 to 5 feet tall—include azaleas, many types of yews, and roses. Use a medium-tall hedge to screen unsightly areas in the yard, such as where you store trash containers. For an informal look, clip your hedge annually or semiannually to keep the plants compact.

A tall hedge, ranging anywhere from 5 feet to even higher, is an elegant background planting. For centuries, close-clipped hedges of boxwood, yew, cypress, and holly have bordered the beds and boundaries of formal gardens around the world.

PLANTING TECHNIQUES

To determine the position and spacing of shrubs in a hedge, you must first consider the mature height of the plants. The effect you want and just how fast you want it also will help you decide how to plant your hedge.

If you have space for a wider hedge, or if you want it to look full quickly, use the staggered-row method (see illustration, top right). Staggered planting also is a good way to disguise an unsightly wire fence; simply plant a row on each side of the fence to hide it.

For a hedge that will line up straight, with all the plants set close together, use the trench method (see illustration, bottom right).

For either method, generously lace the holes with compost or manure.

■ Caring for a hedge

The young hedge will need ample watering its first summer. Prune the sides of the new hedge frequently to help spur sprouting and denser branching. Let the top grow to the desired height, then trim along the sides as needed. Shear the hedge so it tapers in toward the top. This allows plenty of light to reach the sides.

Informal hedges, such as shrub roses, are romantic beauties in a more relaxed form. Well fed and well tended, a bank of roses in blossom is a breathtaking way to create an informal border, especially suitable in a country-style garden. Plant the same color and type for the most pleasing effect.

PLANTING A HEDGE

For a quick, dense hedge, use the staggered-row method of planting. This approach is ideal when you have space for a wider, informal hedge, or when you want to form a screen faster. Mark holes before digging to ensure even spacing.

If your hedge will be straight and the plants set close together, use the trench method. A trench dug the width of two shovel blades will accommodate most young plants. This method also makes pruning and watering easier.

SELECTING THE RIGHT SHRUB

Fast-growing hedges give almost instant results, but also need nearly incessant shearing later on. The rewards of labor eventually saved with slow-growing shrubs should be weighed against the advantages of planting quicker-growing screens. Yew, holly, and boxwood—classic hedge shrubs—are rather slow growing. Fast-growing shrubs, like bush honeysuckle, privet, and laurel, require lots of pruning.

Among the evergreens, hardy Leyland cypress is an old favorite, providing rapid early growth. A slower pace sets in as it matures.

PRUNING SHRUBS

The old saying that timing is everything holds doubly true for pruning shrubs. For best results, prune winter-hardy deciduous shrubs in winter or early spring, shaping plants before new leaves and flowers appear. (For advice on pruning winter-tender or evergreen shrubs, see pages 108–109.) Early pruning promotes healing and gives you an open-branch framework to study as you snip.

WHY PRUNE?

Most deciduous shrubs can survive—and some may even thrive—if never pruned. However, to control size, improve shape, or remove deadwood, pruning is necessary and desirable. Pruning also encourages flowering, coaxing a shrub to produce larger, if fewer, flowers.

Finally, pruning discourages disease and insect infestations by opening up the plant to better air circulation and more light.

HOW TO PRUNE

The first step when pruning either deciduous or evergreen shrubs is to remove deadwood, broken branches, and weak, spindly twigs. This will help ensure a plant's good health. It might even

---

PRUNING TECHNIQUES

(Left) To reduce size, increase bloom, and control shape of a mature plant, remove some of its branch tips, a process called heading back. Cut right above a strong bud.

(Right) To rejuvenate an old, bushy shrub with many limbs, cut out one-third of the older branches at the soil line each year.

(Left) To make a plant airier and less dense, thin it by trimming a few limbs back to the ground or main branch.

(Right) To help keep a plant symmetrical and accent its natural form, cut off new shoots as they appear.

be enough to please the eye. Prune further only to improve the shrub's shape, using one of the techniques shown on these two pages.

To keep deciduous shrubs sound and shapely, trim the plants back a little bit each year. Prune spring-flowering shrubs, too, when blossoms begin to fade.

For a light heading back, cut one-fourth of the top growth—over the crown and sides—from any type of shrub. This stimulates side branching and more compact growth. A shrub with a lot of twiggy branches benefits from a hard heading back, or heavy pruning, deep into the crown. To keep the plant well-groomed, re-move one-fourth of its branches each year, cutting back half their length. Some shrubs, such as hydrangea or red-osier dogwood, demand severe heading back each year to be at peak performance. For severe heading back, cut all the way to the ground.

To rejuvenate an old deciduous shrub, each year for three years cut out about one-third of the oldest canes flush with the base of the shrub. By the third year, your plant will be a more productive specimen with full new growth.

Shrubs pruned heavily each year will need a little extra care in the form of mulching and fertilization.

(Left) To increase flower size, trim all branches back. This stimulates production of a few strong stems and fewer, but larger, flowers.

(Right) Remove suckers unless the new growth is needed to rejuvenate the plant. Carefully dig away soil from around the suckers, then cut them off at the root.

(Left) To keep growth dense, clip shoots to help stimulate limbs to produce more growing points. Usually, two new points replace the one removed. Use a knife or hand pruners.

(Right) To keep plants small, head-back or thin, depending on the final shape you want the plant to have.

PRUNING SHRUBS *(continued)*

Winter-tender shrubs and evergreens both require special care when pruned: winter-tender shrubs to promote flowering and vigorous new growth, evergreens to keep from defacing otherwise unblemished profiles.

WINTER-TENDER SHRUBS

Shrubs like abelia, tamarisk, and butterfly bush die back to the ground each year in the coldest areas of the country.

Flowers on abelia form on new growth. Give this plant a pruning in April, cutting off all growth showing winter damage. Cut out one-third of the most crowded stems, taking them down to within an inch or so of the ground. Removing some of the oldest wood on mature shrubs helps stimulate new young wood, encouraging abundant flowers.

Buddleia alternifolia, or fountain butterfly bush, usually does not die down to the ground. Flowers occur on new growth, so cut off some of the oldest canes as soon as flowers fade. To keep an older plant vigorous, remove up to one-third of the oldest canes yearly. Leave 4- to 5-inch stubs with at least two buds on them.

The popular *Buddleia davidi* (orange-eye butterfly bush or summer lilac) tends in most winters to die back to the ground. Cut its canes after flowering to nearly soil level, keeping two buds on a stub. When new shoots are a couple of feet high, thin out the youngest, saving only the most vigorous. Then pinch the shoots remaining at the tips. In colder areas, mound soil 8 inches high around the base to protect the buds. Remove the mounds in spring, then cut back the tops several inches after the danger of frost has passed.

The ramosissima species of tamarisk flowers on growth from the current season, so prune this plant heavily to a few inches in early spring, while the shrub is still dormant. Head-back to keep the shrub in scale with the landscape and to avoid an open, bare-looking base. Clip flowers after they bloom.

SPECIAL PRUNING TIPS

Winter-tender shrubs—such as tamarisk, abelia, and butterfly bush—die back to the ground in some areas. Remove old tops. New sprouts will grow from the roots.

Some shrubs, such as hills-of-snow hydrangea, need severe pruning. Cut as desired for bloom. High cuts will give more, but smaller, flowers; low cuts will yield larger, but fewer, flowers.

Narrow-leaved evergreens of proper size and shape need only light shearing to keep them neat.

EVERGREENS

Pruning evergreens is more methodical and less creative than pruning other shrubs. You can trim a deciduous shrub and feel comfortable that you're stimulating growth, but an overly enthusiastic cut of the wrong evergreen branch could mean a huge hole in the shrub for years.

Once removed, branches are at best partially replaced. Only when plants become injured, scraggly, diseased, or suffer winterkill should you attempt to severely manicure evergreens.

Most conifers fall into two groups: those pruned after new growth starts (such as fir, pine, spruce, and hemlock), and those pruned before new growth (juniper, arborvitae, and yew). Regardless of the type, limit pruning conifers to correcting problems and cutting branch tips for compact shape and symmetry.

Begin when plants are young, then attend to them regularly—but lightly. Cut lower branches only if diseased or dead. Evergreens can look top-heavy if trunks are bare at the bottom, and they rarely fill in. To camouflage any necessary pruning of the lowest branches, fill in with annual and perennial flowers, ground covers, or shorter shrubs.

Prune yew and hemlock with hedge shears. Trim only to reinforce the natural contours of the plant. Spruce and fir form natural pyramidal shapes. Nip off the terminal buds on their branches as soon as they appear to help laterals grow and strengthen weak branches.

Of all the evergreens, pine needs the least pruning. Its informal nature doesn't demand shearing to look well kept. Prune vigorous new growths (called candles) before they harden. Cutting candles on the main branches to half their length forces laterals, encouraging a fuller plant. Juniper produces dense growth in the spring. Prune early, before this new growth appears. Prune lightly, too, using the "shingling" technique (that is, trim the upper branches of spreading juniper so they don't overhang the lower branches).

BASIC PRUNING TOOLS

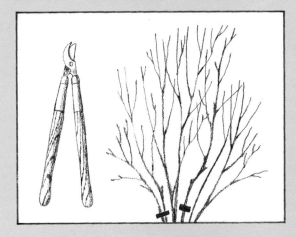

Loppers are the tool of choice for cutting out diseased, broken, or dead canes on shrubs like viburnum, lilac, forsythia, shrub roses, spirea, or mock orange. Cut as shown.

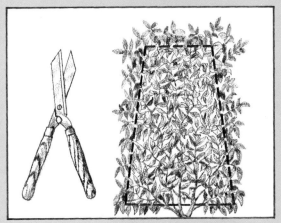

Hedge clippers keep formal hedge plants under control. Shrubs like honeysuckle, privet, boxwood, or alpine currant may need several yearly shearings. Clip out-of-place twigs as they appear.

Shears are ideal for the severe pruning required by bush roses, shrub althaea, red-osier dogwood, and peegee hydrangea, among others. Cut to side branches or buds to stimulate new growth.

DECIDUOUS SHRUBS

Shrub	Height	Foliage and Flowers	Zone	Exposure and Soil	Comments
ARALIA, FIVE-LEAVED *Acanthopanax sieboldianus*	3'–6'	Dark green, palmate-arranged leaves turn yellow in fall. Sharp spires at leaf base.	5	Tolerates most light and soil conditions.	Use as foliage plant or in hedge. Tolerates soot.
BARBERRY *Berberis* sp. **Japanese** *B. thunbergi*	5'	½-inch yellow flowers, bordered with red, hang on the plant in early spring. Bright red, oval berries follow. Foliage is bright green but red-leaved varieties exist. Twigs are thorny.	5	Full sun or partial shade. Tolerates most soils.	Use in hedge or alone as specimen. Easily sheared. Makes an attractive barrier planting. Birds like its winter berries. Dwarf form grows to 2 feet.
Korean *B. koreana*	4'	¼-inch yellow flowers in hanging clusters in spring, followed by bright red berries. Thorny twigs.	6	Full sun or partial shade. Tolerates most soils.	Use in hedge or alone as specimen. Easily sheared. Good barrier planting.
Mentor *B. x mentorensis*	3'	¼-inch yellow flowers hang on plants in early spring, followed by dark red berries. Thorny twigs.	7	Full sun or partial shade. Tolerates most soils.	Resists heat and drought better than other varieties. Evergreen in zones 6–10.
BEAUTYBUSH *Kolkwitzia amabilis*	15'	½-inch pink or pink-and-white flowers in spring, followed by unusual brown seedpods that cling until winter. Foliage turns red in fall. Bark peels attractively.	6	Full sun or partial shade; moist, well-drained soil	Use as specimen plant. Looks best grown singly. Needs no pruning or special care.
BLUEBERRY, HIGHBUSH *Vaccinium corymbosum*	15'	¼-inch white or pinkish blossoms in late spring, followed by tasty blue-black berries. Leaves turn brilliant scarlet in the fall; twigs stay bright red all winter.	3	Full sun or light shade; acid, well-drained soil	Use as specimen or in informal hedge. Shallow root system is easily damaged by hoeing. Keep mulched. Prune in spring.
BROOM *Cytisus* sp. **Kew** *C. x kewensis*	1'	Small, yellow, sweet-pealike flowers in early spring.	6	Full sun; well-drained soil	Quick, dense grower. Use in rock gardens.
Scotch *C. scoparius*	10'	Sweet-pealike flowers in spring. Mixed colors.	6	Full sun; well-drained soil	Quick growing. Use as specimen plant. Prune after flowering. Dwarf varieties grow to 2 feet.
Spike *C. nigricans*	6'	Yellow, sweet-pealike flowers on 6- to 12-inch-long spikes in midsummer.	5	Full sun; well-drained soil	Quick growing, hardy. Blooms in all situations.
BUCKEYE Dwarf horse chestnut *Aesculus parviflora*	15'	½-inch white flowers in 10- to 15-inch-long spike clusters in midsummer. Dark green, palmate-arranged leaves turn yellow in fall.	5	Full sun; moist, well-drained soil	Vigorous and attractive. Forms dense mound twice as wide as its height. Reproduces by underground suckers

Shrub	Height	Foliage and Flowers	Zone	Exposure and Soil	Comments
BUCKTHORN, ALDER *Rhamnus frangula*	12'	Small berries change from red to black in fall. Smooth branches.	3	Full sun or partial shade; moist, well-drained soil	Only 'Tallhedge' is widely grown. Use in hedge and as screen. Resists pests; vigorous.
BUTTERFLY BUSH *Buddleia* sp. **Fountain** *B. alternifolia*	12'	¼-inch, lilac-colored flowers on long spikes in early summer.	6	Full sun; well-drained soil	Vigorous and hardy. Use as specimen in large yards. Needs room to be showy.
Orange-eye, summer lilac *B. davidi*	15'	½-inch flowers cluster on spikes up to 1½ feet long. Attractive silver-gray foliage.	5	Full sun; well-drained soil	Vigorous and hardy. Open and shaggy in appearance. Plants die back to ground each winter in cold areas.
CINQUEFOIL, SHRUBBY *Potentilla fruticosa*	4'	½- to 1-inch, yellow or white, single flowers from midsummer until fall.	2	Full sun; well-drained soil	Hardy; resists pests. Low growing and dense; long periods of bloom. Use along foundation, in border.
COTONEASTER *Cotoneaster* sp. **Cranberry** *C. apiculatus*	4'	Very small, red-violet flowers in spring, followed by ½-inch, red-orange berries. Shiny leaves.	5	Full sun or partial shade; well-drained soil	Spreading, horizontal branches. Use on slope or along foundation; train on walls.
Creeping *C. adpressus*	10"	Very small, pinkish flowers in the spring, followed by ½-inch red berries. Shiny green leaves.	5	Full sun or partial shade; well-drained soil	Low growing; roots where branches touch ground. Use on slope or in rock garden. Needs no pruning.
Many-flowered *C. multiflorus*	12'	½- to 1-inch white flowers cover branches in spring, followed by large red berries.	6	Full sun or partial shade; well-drained soil	Very showy all seasons. Use as a specimen plant.
Spreading *C. divaricatus*	6'	Small, pink-violet flowers in spring, followed by ½-inch red berries. Shiny green leaves turn red in fall.	5	Full sun or partial shade; well-drained soil	Widely spreading branches in upright plants. Use in hedge or as specimen.
CRAPE MYRTLE *Lagerstroemia indica*	7'–20'	1½- to 2-inch flowers in 8- to 12-inch-long clusters in late summer. White, pink, red, and lavender blooms. Yellow or red leaves in fall. Bark peels.	7	Full sun; moist, rich, well-drained soil	Resists pests and diseases. Prune in early spring before flowering Use in informal hedge or as specimen plant.

111

DECIDUOUS SHRUBS *(continued)*

Shrub	Height	Foliage and Flowers	Zone	Exposure and Soil	Comments
DAPHNE *Daphne* sp. **February** *D. mezereum*	4'–5'	Small, pinkish, very fragrant flowers cluster along stems in early spring, followed by ½-inch, red, poisonous berries.	5	Full sun or partial shade. Does best in light, sandy soil.	Small and upright in growth habit. Needs some winter protection in cold areas. Keep roots cool in warm weather. Use as specimen.
Lilac *D. genkwa*	3'	½-inch, pale blue, lilaclike flowers in early spring, followed by small white berries. Not as fragrant as *D. mezereum.*	5	Full sun or partial shade. Does best in light, sandy soil.	Not always winter hardy. If frost damage occurs, trim back to ground level. Use as specimen plant.
DEUTZIA *Deutzia* sp. **Fuzzy** *D. scabra*	7'	Single or double, white or pink flowers cover branches in early spring. Light foliage.	6	Full sun or partial shade. Tolerates most soils.	Very showy plant; good as specimen. Prune old wood each year, new wood after flowering.
Slender *D. gracilis*	6'	½- to 1-inch, white blossoms cover branches in early spring. Light green foliage.	5	Full sun or partial shade. Tolerates most soils.	Use as specimen in border or bed. Wide-spreading, arching branches. Cut branches for early indoor forcing.
DOGWOOD *Cornus* sp. **Cornelian cherry** *C. mas*	20'	Small, yellow flowers in 1-inch clusters cover plant in early spring; followed by edible red berries in fall. Red leaves in fall, too.	5	Full sun or partial shade. Tolerates most soils.	Hardy; resists pests. Colorful all seasons. Use in hedge, as screen, or as specimen. Berries make tasty preserves. Flowers early.
Japanese *C. kousa*	25'	1- to 2-inch clusters of white flowers in later spring. Red berries and leaves in fall.	6	Full sun or partial shade. Tolerates most soils.	Use as a specimen plant. Very showy. Berries attract birds.
Red-osier *C. sericea*	7'–10'	White flowers in loose 2½- to 3-inch clusters appear intermittently from late spring to midsummer, followed by white inedible berries. Red leaves and twigs in fall.	2	Full sun or partial shade. Tolerates most soils.	Vigorous and hardy. Likes moist areas. Reproduces by underground stolons; plant where space is not limited. Use in hedge or as screen. Birds relish its berries.
Tatarian *C. alba*	10'	2-inch clusters of white blossoms in late spring, followed by ½-inch, bluish white berries. Reddish green leaves in fall; brilliant red twigs in winter.	3	Full sun or partial shade. Tolerates most soils.	Hardy; resists pests. Colorful twigs in winter. Use in informal hedge, as screen, or as specimen.

Shrub	Height	Foliage and Flowers	Zone	Exposure and Soil	Comments
ELAEAGNUS *Elaeagnus* sp. **Autumn olive** *E. umbellata*	18'	Tiny, yellowish white, fragrant flowers in spring; followed by scaly, inedible berries.	2	Full sun; well-drained soil	Vigorous and hardy. Use in hedge or as screen. Requires little care.
Cherry *E. multiflora*	6'	¾-inch fragrant flowers appear in late spring, followed by ½- to 1-inch, red, cherrylike berries.	5	Full sun; well-drained soil	Vigorous and hardy. Use in hedge or as screen. Edible berries attract birds. Resists soot.
Silverberry *E. commutata*	10'–12'	Tiny, silvery, yellow, fragrant flowers in spring, followed by ½- to 1-inch, silvery, rounded berries. Silvery leaves, too.	2	Full sun; well-drained, slightly alkaline soil	Vigorous and hardy. Use in hedge or as screen. Requires little care.
ELDERBERRY, AMERICAN OR SWEET *Sambucus canadensis*	8'	8- to 12-inch clusters of tiny white flowers in midsummer, followed by edible, blue-black or red berries. 'Aurea' has brilliant yellow foliage in summer.	4	Full sun or partial shade; rich, moist, well-drained soil	Large, vigorous, spreading plant. Use berries in wine and preserves. Birds enjoy fruit. Does best in wet area. Easily pruned.
EUONYMUS *Euonymus* sp. **European spindle tree** *E. europaea*	20'	Inconspicuous flowers in late spring, followed by bright pink seedpods in fall.	4	Full sun or partial shade. Tolerates most soils.	Very hardy and vigorous. Subject to scale infestation.
Strawberry bush *E. americana*	8'	Small, pinkish purple flowers in spring, followed by pinkish red fruit bearing bright orange seeds. Leaves turn dark red in fall.	7	Full sun or partial shade. Tolerates most soils.	Very hardy native shrub. Use in hard-to-plant moist areas.
Winged *E. alata*	8'	Subtle flowers in spring, followed by pinkish red seedpods in fall. Crimson leaves in fall; twigs lined with unusual bark ridges.	4	Full sun or partial shade. Tolerates most soils.	Very hardy and useful. Plant in hedge, as screen, or as specimen. Requires little pruning. Very showy year-round. The dwarf 'Compacta' reaches 4 feet.
FORSYTHIA *Forsythia* sp. **'Arnold Dwarf'** *F. x intermedia 'Arnold Dwarf'*	4'	Small, greenish yellow flowers appear randomly over the plant in early spring. Foliage is deep green.	5	Full sun or partial shade. Tolerates most soils.	Low growing with arching branches that root on contact with soil. Vigorous, dense foliage.
Border *F. x intermedia*	10'	2-inch, trumpetlike, yellow-gold flowers in early spring, followed by deep green foliage.	5	Full sun or partial shade. Tolerates most soils.	Vigorous and hardy with graceful, arching branches. Give plenty of room. Prune after flowering.

DECIDUOUS SHRUBS *(continued)*

Shrub	Height	Foliage and Flowers	Zone	Exposure and Soil	Comments
FORSYTHIA *(continued)* **Korean golden-bells, early forsythia** *F. ovata*	5'	1- to 1½-inch, trumpetlike, yellow-gold flowers in early spring, followed by deep green foliage.	5	Full sun or partial shade. Tolerates most soils.	Graceful, arching branches. Most cold hardy of the forsythias. Blooms before other varieties.
HIBISCUS Rose-of-sharon, shrub althaea *Hibiscus syriacus*	6'–10'	2- to 4-inch, single, double, or semidouble flowers in late summer. Flower colors include white, red, pink, blue, and violet bicolors. Light green foliage.	6	Full sun or partial shade; moist, well-drained soil	Resists soot. Can be trained to tree form. Use in narrow, hard-to-plant areas, in hedge, as screen, or as specimen.
HONEYSUCKLE *Lonicera* sp. **Amur** *L. maacki*	15'	Small, whitish yellow, very fragrant flowers in late spring, with small, scarlet, inedible berries.	3	Full sun or partial shade; well-drained soil	Tolerates cold. Late-flowering variety. Use in hedge, as screen, or as specimen.
Morrow *L. morrowi*	8'	Small, whitish yellow flowers in late spring, followed by deep purple-red, inedible berries. 'Xanthocarpa' has yellow fruits.	4	Full or partial shade; well-drained soil	Dense, mound shaped. Berries relished by birds. Use in hedge, as screen, or as specimen.
Winter, fragrant *L. fragrantissima*	8'	Tiny, white, very fragrant flowers cover the plant in early spring, followed by small, inedible, red berries.	6	Full sun or partial shade; well-drained soil	Flowers early; very spreading. Use in hedge, as screen, or as specimen.
HYDRANGEA *Hydrangea* sp. **Bigleaf, garden** *H. macrophylla*	5'–8'	5- to 10-inch, rounded clusters of tiny flowers cover the plant in summer. Flowers blue, white, or pink, depending on soil acidity.	6–7	Full sun or partial shade; rich, moist, well-drained soil	Very showy in flower. Use in foundation planting or border. Dies back in cold areas.
Hills-of-snow *H. arborescens* 'grandiflora'	4'	6-inch clusters of tiny white flowers in rounded heads cover plant midsummer. Bright green leaves.	4	Full sun or partial shade; rich, moist, well-drained soil	Dense; globular. Very showy in flower. May die back in cold-winter areas. Prune in early spring.
Peegee *H. paniculata* 'grandiflora'	30'	12-inch, pyramidal clusters of flowers midsummer. Blossoms are white, then fade to pink or purple; cling well into winter.	4	Full sun or partial shade; rich, moist, well-drained soil	Use as specimen plant; can be trained to tree form. Cut flowers for dried bouquets. Prune for vigor.
Oak-leaved *H. quercifolia*	6'	6-inch, conical clusters of tiny white flowers midsummer. Oak-shaped leaves turn red in fall.	5	Full sun or partial shade; rich, moist, well-drained soil	Showy all seasons. Very spreading; best planted alone as specimen.

Shrub	Height	Foliage and Flowers	Zone	Exposure and Soil	Comments
KERRIA *Kerria japonica*	8′	2-inch yellow flowers bloom in mid-May. Popular for its green twigs in winter.	5	Full sun or partial shade. Prefers well-drained soil.	Use as shrub border or specimen. Prune after blooms fade.
LILAC *Syringa* sp. **Chinese** *S. x chinensis*	15′	Clusters of ½-inch, red-purple, fragrant flowers in spring.	3	Full sun; well-drained soil	Upright, spreading growth. Use as specimen plant.
Common *S. vulgaris*	20′	½-inch fragrant flowers in 6- to 8-inch-long clusters. Colors include violet, blue, pink, white, yellow, and magenta.	4	Full sun; well-drained soil	Dense, vigorous, upright growth. Use in hedge or as specimen. Tolerates cold. Prune dormant old wood yearly. Over 400 varieties.
Hungarian *S. josikaea*	12′	¼-inch, red-purple, fragrant flowers on 4- to 6-inch clusters in late spring. Foliage is shiny green.	4	Full sun; well-drained soil	Valued for its late blooms. Use as specimen plant in large yards, or as screen or hedge.
Late *S. villosa*	10′	8-inch clusters of ¼-inch, rose to white flowers in late spring.	2	Full sun; well-drained soil	Tolerates cold; vigorous. Dense, spreading. Cut off dying flowers and seed clusters to promote growth.
Persian *S. x persica*	6′–10′	¼-inch, violet, fragrant flowers in 3-inch-long clusters in late spring. Small leaves. 'Alba' has white flowers.	5	Full sun; well-drained soil	Valued for its small size. Use as specimen or accent. Prune dormant old wood yearly.
MOCK ORANGE *Philadelphus* sp. **Lemoine** *P. x lemoinei*	4′–8′	1- to 2-inch, single or double, fragrant, white flowers in early summer.	5	Full sun or partial shade; moist soil	Use as specimen plant or in shrub border. Needs little pruning, except of deadwood.
Sweet *P. coronarius*	10′	Single, white, very fragrant flowers in early summer. In fall, foliage turns yellow. 'Aureus' has yellow leaves, turning green later.	5	Full sun or partial shade. Tolerates most soils.	Tolerates drier conditions than most shrubs. Use as specimen or in shrub border.
Virginalis *P. x virginalis*	5′–9′	1- to 2-inch, single or double, fragrant, white flowers in early summer.	5	Full sun or partial shade; moist, rich, well-drained soil	Very showy with delicate flowers. Needs little pruning.
NINEBARK *Physocarpus opulifolius*	10′	¼-inch, whitish pink flowers in early spring, followed by greenish brown seedpods that cling through midwinter.	2	Full sun or partial shade; well-drained soil	Cold hardy. Needs no pruning. Very dense. Use in border, as screen, and as windbreak.

DECIDUOUS SHRUBS *(continued)*

Shrub	Height	Foliage and Flowers	Zone	Exposure and Soil	Comments
PEARLBUSH *Exochorda racemosa*	10'–12'	Strings of white buds open into 2-inch, single, white flowers in mid-spring.	5	Full sun. Tolerates most soils.	Use as specimen in large yards.
PEONY, TREE *Paeonia suffruticosa*	7'	6- to 12-inch single, semidouble, or double flowers in late spring. Many colors.	5	Prefers partial shade; can tolerate full sun. Rich, moist, well-drained soil.	Very showy. Use as specimen or in beds. Protect in cold-winter areas.
PHOTINIA, ORIENTAL *Photinia villosa*	15'	Small white flowers in 1- to 2-inch-wide clusters in late spring, followed by ½-inch red berries and red fall foliage.	5	Full sun or partial shade; well-drained soil	Use as an unusual specimen plant. Showy all seasons. Birds relish its berries.
PRIVET *Ligustrum* sp. **Amur** *L. amurense*	15'	¼-inch white flowers in 1- to 3-inch-wide clusters in early summer, followed by small berries.	4	Full sun or partial shade. Tolerates most soils.	Quick growing; tolerates cold. Hardy, very dense. Use in hedge.
Border *L. obtusifolium*	9'	¼-inch white flowers in 1- to 3-inch-wide clusters in early summer, followed by small black berries in fall. Leathery green foliage.	4	Full sun or partial shade. Tolerates most soils.	Attractive and quick growing. Very dense. Use in clipped or unclipped hedge, as screen, or as specimen.
California *L. ovalifolium*	15'	¼-inch white flowers in 1- to 3-inch-wide clusters in early summer, followed by small black berries in fall.	6	Full sun or partial shade. Tolerates most soils.	Attractive, quick growing, and very dense. Semievergreen in warm-climate areas.
Ibolium *L. x ibolium*	12'	¼-inch white flowers in 1- to 3-inch-wide clusters in early summer, followed by small black berries in fall.	4	Full sun or partial shade. Tolerates most soils.	Quick growing, more attractive than amur privet. Tolerates soot. Birds relish its berries.
PUSSY WILLOW *Salix* sp. **Goat willow, French** *S. caprea*	25'	Twigs are covered with 1- to 2-inch-long, silver-pink catkins in early spring that gradually turn yellow with pollen.	5	Full sun; moist, well-drained soil	Quick growing. Use as specimen or screen. Cut twigs in late winter for indoor bouquets.
Korea rose gold, rose gold *S. gracilistyla*	10'	Twigs are covered with 1- to 2-inch-long, rose catkins in early spring that gradually turn yellow with pollen. Foliage is gray-green.	6	Full sun; moist, well-drained soil	Quick growing. Is bushier and blooms earlier than other pussy willows. Use as screen or in border.
Pussy willow *S. discolor*	20'	Twigs are covered with 1-inch white catkins in early spring that gradually turn yellow with pollen. Foliage is gray-green.	2	Full sun; moist, well-drained soil	Quick growing. Smaller, hardier; blooms later than goat willow. Prune after catkins disappear.

Shrub	Height	Foliage and Flowers	Zone	Exposure and Soil	Comments
QUINCE *Chaenomeles* sp. **Flowering** *C. speciosa*	6'	1- to 2-inch, single or double, pink, red, white, and bicolored flowers cluster on branches in mid-spring.	5	Full sun; well-drained soil	Very showy. Use fruits in jellies and jams. Use as specimen or in hedge.
Lesser *C. japonica*	3'–4'	1- to 2-inch, reddish orange, single flowers cluster on branches in mid-spring. No fruit of consequence. 'Alpina' grows to only 15 inches and has orange flowers.	5	Full sun; well-drained soil	Use in low border and along foundation. Little pruning required.
REDBUD, CHINESE *Cercis chinensis*	8'	½- to 1-inch, red-purple, sweet-pealike flowers cover branches in mid-spring. Leaves are large, turn yellow in fall.	8	Partial shade; well-drained soil	Use as specimen plant, on lawn, or along foundation. Needs no pruning. Requires some wind protection.
RHODODEN-DRON, AZALEA *Rhododendron* sp.		(For broad-leaved evergreen rhododendrons, see pages 124–125.)			
Albrecht *R. albrechti*	5'	2-inch, rose-colored blossoms cover plant in spring.	6	Full sun or partial shade; moist, acid soil	Hardy and fragrant.
Coast, dwarf *R. atlanticum*	2'	1¼-inch white blossoms, tinged with crimson, cover plant in spring.	6	Full sun or partial shade; acid, moist soil	Hardy and fragrant.
Mollis hybrid, Chinese *R. molle*	5'	2- to 3-inch flowers cover plants in late spring. Colors are pink, salmon, yellow, and white.	6	Full sun or partial shade; moist, acid soil	Vigorous, showy hybrid. Use in beds or foundation plantings, or as an accent.
STEWARTIA Showy, mountain camellia *Stewartia ovata* 'grandiflora'	15'	2- to 4-inch, cup-shaped, white blossoms with purple centers open in midsummer. Foliage turns red-orange in fall. Bark is variegated and peels on mature shrubs.	7	Full sun or partial shade; rich, moist, acid soil	Use as specimen plant. Needs little pruning.
SUMAC *Rhus* sp. **Fragrant** *R. aromatica*	8'	Inconspicuous, yellow flowers in mid-spring. Red berrylike fruit; red and yellow fall foliage.	3	Full sun; light, well-drained soil	Quick growing. Use as ground cover or foundation plant. Attractive in fall.

DECIDUOUS SHRUBS *(continued)*

Shrub	Height	Foliage and Flowers	Zone	Exposure and Soil	Comments
SUMAC *(continued)* **Shining, dwarf** *R. copallina*	20'	Tiny, greenish yellow flowers on 4- to 5-inch spikes. Red berrylike fruits. Scarlet fall foliage.	5	Full sun. Tolerates most soils.	Quick growing. Use as specimen or as backdrop in border. Pruning encourages growth.
SYMPHORI-CARPOS *Symphoricarpos* sp. **Indian currant, coralberry** *S. x chenaulti*	7'	Inconspicuous, greenish white flowers in midsummer, followed by small red-violet berries.	3	Full sun or partial shade. Tolerates most soils.	Berries are attractive in fall. Use on hard-to-plant slope. Prune in early spring.
Snowberry *S. albus 'laevigatus'*	3'	Inconspicuous pink flowers in midsummer, followed by ½-inch, white, waxy berries in fall.	3	Full sun or partial shade. Tolerates most soils.	Berries attractive in fall. Use as specimen or in hedge or shrub border. Arching form.
TAMARISK, KASHGAR *Tamarix hispida*	15'	Tiny pink flowers in late summer. Feathery, light green foliage.	7	Full sun; well-drained soil	Thrives in dry areas. Use as specimen or in shrub border.
VIBURNUM *Viburnum* sp. **Arrowwood** *V. dentatum*	15'	Tiny white flowers in 1- to 3-inch-wide clusters in early summer. Blue berries and scarlet foliage in fall.	3	Full sun or partial shade; well-drained soil	Use as specimen or in border. Birds relish its berries. Needs little pruning.
European cranberry bush *V. opulus*	12'	Tiny white flowers in 2- to 4-inch-wide clusters, surrounded by a margin of ½-inch blossoms in late spring. Red berries in fall.	3	Full sun or partial shade; well-drained soil	Dense and vigorous. Use tall forms in shrub border, low forms in rock garden.
Sargent cranberry bush *V. sargenti*	12'	Tiny white flowers in 2- to 3-inch-wide clusters mid-spring, followed by red berries in fall.	6	Full sun or partial shade; well-drained soil	Very vigorous and hardy. Use in border, as screen, or as specimen.
WEIGELA, OLD-FASHIONED *Weigela florida*	8'–10'	1-inch, pink, trumpetlike flowers cover plant in late spring. Foliage is deep green.	5	Full sun or partial shade. Tolerates most soils.	Use as specimen plant or in shrub border. Graceful, arching branches.
WITCH HAZEL *Hamamelis* sp. **Chinese** *H. mollis*	30'	1- to 2-inch-long yellow, ribbonlike, fragrant flowers cover plant in early spring.	5	Full sun or partial shade; rich, moist, well-drained soil	Grown for very early bloom. Use as specimen or border plant.
Common *H. virginiana*	15'	½- to 1-inch yellow, ribbonlike flowers in late fall. Foliage turns yellow at same time.	5	Full sun; rich, moist, well-drained soil	Grown for late bloom. Use as shrub backdrop. Often open and loose in growth. Tolerates soot.

CONIFEROUS SHRUBS

Shrub	Height	Shape and Foliage	Zone	Soil	Comments
ARBORVITAE, AMERICAN *Thuja occidentalis*	7'–10' (avg.)	Most are compact, pyramidal. Foliage is green or blue-green, scalelike, fan shaped.	3	Rich, moist, well-drained soil	Slow growing. Use as foundation plant or in hedge. Does not tolerate heat. Prune early spring.
CEPHALOTAXUS Japanese plum yew *Cephalotaxus harringtonia*	30'	Multistemmed. Wide spreading, but 'Fastigiata' is columnar in habit. Dark green with 1½-inch needles.	6	Moist, well-drained, acid soil	Similar to yews but not as dense. Use in hedge or as screen. Bears 1-inch, purple-green, plum-shaped fruits. Shear in spring before new growth.
CRYPTOMERIA Japanese cedar *Cryptomeria japonica 'nana'*	3'	Dwarf variety. Broad, mound shaped. Dark green, needlelike foliage.	5	Moist, well-drained soil	Use along foundation. Handsome in patio tubs.
CUPRESSO-CYPARIS *Cupressocyparis leylandi*	To 50'	Narrow; columnar. Scalelike foliage.	5	Moist, well-drained soil	Very fast growing. Easily sheared to any dimensions. Prune in early spring before new growth shows.
CYPRESS, FALSE *Chamaecyparis* sp. **Dwarf hinoki** *C. obtusa 'nana aurea'*	4'	Broad, flattened foliage that's scalelike and fan shaped. Spreads to 3 feet.	5	Moist, well-drained, slightly acid soil	Slow growing. Use in rock garden or along foundation. Prune any time.
Moss sawara *C. pisifera 'squarrosa'*	To 30'	Dense, conical. Feathery soft, scalelike foliage.	4	Moist, well-drained, slightly acid soil	Slow growing. Needs thinning as it ages to enhance character. Prune any time.
Plume *C. pisifera 'plumosa'*	To 100'	Dense, fluffy, scalelike, feathery green foliage. Gold variety also available. Upright branches. Compact.	4	Moist, well-drained, slightly acid soil	Slow growing. Use as specimen. Can get unsightly when mature. Can be pruned at any time.
Slender hinoki *C. obtusa 'gracilis'*	20'	Very dark, glossy green color. Slender, weeping shape. Tip and branch buds droop slightly.	4	Moist, well-drained, slightly acid soil	Slow growing. Choice specimen for entryways.
Thread leaf *C. pisifera 'filifera'*	To 100' (6'–8' avg.)	Dense, long, threadlike, dark green foliage. Some varieties are yellow. Loose mound shape.	4	Moist, well-drained, slightly acid soil	Slow growing. Unusual foundation or specimen plant. Can be unsightly when mature.

CONIFEROUS SHRUBS *(continued)*

Shrub	Height	Shape and Foliage	Zone	Soil	Comments
JUNIPER *Juniperus* sp. **Creeping, creeping cedar** *J. horizontalis*	1′	Dense; low spreading. Blue-green or steel blue needles.	3	Well-drained soil	Excellent ground cover, especially on slope. Blue berries in fall. Color intensifies in winter.
Dwarf common *J. communis* 'compressa'	4′	Broadly spreading. Foliage is grayish green with ¼-inch needles.	3	Well-drained soil	Good foundation plant. Prune any time. Plant in rock garden.
Hollywood *J. chinensis* 'torulosa'	20′	Broad conical. Tufted needles and scales.	4	Well-drained soil	Interesting, twisted branching habit. Do not prune.
Pfitzer *J. chinensis* 'pfitzerana'	6′	Dense; broad; flat topped. Scalelike, feathery foliage and needles.	4	Well-drained soil	Fast growing. Tolerates partial shade. Needs constant pruning.
Shore *J. conferta*	1′	Dense; low spreading. ¼-inch, green needles.	6	Prefers sandy, seashore locations.	Use as ground cover in sandy, hard-to-plant areas. Prune any time.
PINE *Pinus* sp. **Bristle-cone, hickory** *P. aristata*	10′–40′	Variable shape. Dark blue-green, 1- to 1¾-inch needles in clusters of five.	6	Well-drained soil	Slow growing. Picturesque branching habit. Use as specimen or in patio tub.
Dwarf white *P. strobus* 'nana'	6′	Dense; rounded to conical. Soft, green, 4-inch needles in bundles of five.	4	Well-drained soil	Slow growing. Use in rock garden or along foundation.
Mugo, mountain *P. mugo*	30′	Dense; rounded, low spreading. Bright green, 1½- to 3-inch needles in pairs.	4	Well-drained soil	Slow growing. Use in foundation planting. Subject to scale infestation.
SPRUCE, DWARF WHITE *Picea glauca* 'conica'	8′	Dense; pyramidal. Single trunk. Tufted, ½-inch-long, light green needles.	5	Well-drained soil	Slow growing. Use as specimen or with low-growing shrubs.
YEW *Taxus* sp. **Irish** *T. baccata* 'stricta'	15′	Dense; narrow columnar or rounded. Dark green, lustrous, 1-inch needles. A golden variety also available.	7	Well-drained, slightly alkaline soil	Upright, picturesque branching. Use in hedge. Fleshy red berries in fall.
Japanese *T. cuspidata*	20′	Shape depends on variety. Green, lustrous, 1-inch needles.	5	Well-drained, slightly alkaline soil	Ideal foundation, hedge, or specimen plant. Easy to shear.
Spreading English *T. baccata* 'repandens'	3′	Dense, low spreading, flat. Green, lustrous, 1-inch needles.	6	Well-drained, slightly alkaline soil	Branches slightly pendulous. Use in foundation planting or as a ground cover.

BROAD-LEAVED EVERGREEN SHRUBS

Shrub	Height	Foliage and Flowers	Zone	Exposure and Soil	Comments
ABELIA, GLOSSY *Abelia x grandiflora* 'Edward Goucher'	6'	½- to 1-inch pink flowers in clusters of one to four appear in midsummer, continue until frost. Glossy green leaves turn bronze in autumn.	6	Full sun or partial shade; well-drained soil	Dense, rounded shape. May die back in cold-winter areas, but quickly resprouts in spring. Use along foundation, or in border or hedge.
ANDROMEDA *Pieris* sp. **Mountain, fetterbush** *P. floribunda*	6'	Small, white, fragrant flowers in drooping, 4-inch clusters of three to five in early spring. Shrub is attractive year-round.	5	Full sun or partial shade; well-drained, slightly acid soil	Very showy. Use in border or along foundation. Needs some protection in cold-winter areas.
Japanese, lily-of-the-valley bush *P. japonica*	10'	Small, white, fragrant flowers in drooping, 5-inch clusters of three to five in mid-spring. New foliage is bronze; when mature, bright green.	6	Full sun or partial shade; well-drained, slightly acid soil	Showy ornamental shrub. Use in border, along foundation, or as specimen.
AUCUBA **Japanese laurel** *Aucuba japonica*	15'	Tiny violet flowers appear in early March, followed by red berries in fall. Foliage is large and variegated with bright yellow markings.	8	Partial or deep shade; moist, well-drained soil	Plant both sexes for berry production. Needs little pruning. Resists smog, so does well in urban area.
BARBERRY *Berberis* sp. **Black** *B. gagnepaini*	6'	Small yellow flowers cover plant in late spring, followed by blue-black berries in fall. Small, sharp thorns.	6	Full sun or partial shade; moist, well-drained soil	Dense branching habit. Showy all seasons. Use in hedge or border.
Darwin's *B. darwini*	8'	Yellow-red flowers cover shrub in mid-spring. Purple berries in fall. Glossy green leaves turn green-violet in fall. Thorny twigs.	7	Full sun or partial shade; moist, well-drained soil	Dense branching habit. Needs little pruning. Effective all year.
Mentor *B. x mentorensis*	3'	Tiny yellow clusters of flowers in mid-spring. Red berries in fall. Glossy green leaves on stems armed with small thorns.	6	Full sun or partial shade; moist, well-drained soil	Tolerates cold and heat. Dense branching habit makes it good for screening.
BOTTLEBRUSH, CRIMSON *Callistemon citrinus*	25'	4- to 8-inch, brushlike clusters of long red stamens appear in late winter and continue through the summer.	9	Full sun; well-drained soil	Quick growing. Use as specimen or screen. Prune after flowers fade for vigorous growth.
BOXWOOD *Buxus* sp. **Common box** *B. sempervirens*	To 15'	Small, glossy green leaves. 'Argenteo-variegata' has leaves spotted with white.	6	Full sun or partial shade; moist, well-drained soil	Many varieties. Use as specimen or in shrub border. Easily sheared.

BROAD-LEAVED EVERGREEN SHRUBS *(continued)*

Shrub	Height	Foliage and Flowers	Zone	Exposure and Soil	Comments
BOXWOOD *(continued)* **Littleleaf box** *B. microphylla*	3′	Small, glossy green leaves. 'Compacta' and 'Nana' are dwarf cultivars averaging 15 inches tall.	6	Full sun or partial shade; moist, well-drained soil	Easily sheared. Use as hedge plants. More cold hardy than sempervirens.
CAMELLIA *Camellia* sp. **Common** *C. japonica*	45′	Showy, 3- to 6-inch, single or double flowers mid-fall through spring. Many flower colors.	8	Partial shade; moist, rich, acid, well-drained soil	Many varieties. Use as specimen or in border. Needs little pruning.
Sasanqua *C. sasanqua*	15′	Showy, 2- to 4-inch, single or double flowers early fall through midwinter. White, rose, and pink flowers.	7	Partial shade; moist, rich, acid, well-drained soil	Several varieties. Use as specimen or in border. Valued for early bloom.
COTONEASTER, ROCK *Cotoneaster horizontalis*	3′	Small pink flowers appear in early summer, with bright red berries in fall. Glossy green leaves.	6	Full sun; well-drained, slightly alkaline soil kept on the dry side	Low branches. Use in rock gardens or on slopes as ground cover.
DAPHNE *Daphne* sp. **Burkwood** *D. x burkwoodi*	4′	½-inch, whitish, fragrant flowers appear in mid-spring, followed by small red berries in summer. Gray-green leaves.	6	Partial shade; moist, well-drained soil	Dense, moundlike growth habit. Does not like wet soil; touchy about growing conditions. Poisonous.
Winter *D. odora*	4′	Tiny, red-violet, fragrant flowers appear in early spring. Foliage is glossy green.	7	Partial shade; moist, well-drained soil	Dense, moundlike growth. Most fragrant of daphnes.
EUONYMUS *Euonymus* sp. **Big leaf winter creeper** *E. fortunei 'sarcoxie'*	4′	Tiny, inconspicuous flowers in the spring, followed by pinkish seedpods with orange berries inside.	6	Full sun or partial shade. Tolerates most soils.	Loses leaves in cold-winter areas. Rambling; can be trained on wall or used as ground cover.
Evergreen, Japanese spindle tree *E. japonica*	15′	Tiny flowers in spring, followed by pinkish seedpods opening to orange berries inside. Foliage is glossy green.	8	Full sun or partial shade. Tolerates most soils.	Easily sheared to any dimension. Use in foundation planting or border, or as specimen.
Spreading *E. kiautschovica*	10′	Tiny, inconspicuous flowers in spring; pinkish seedpods with orange berries inside follow.	7	Full sun or partial shade. Tolerates most soils.	Hardier than japonica species in cold-winter areas.
FATSIA **Japanese aralia** *Fatsia japonica*	20′	1- to 2-inch clusters of white flowers on stalks in midwinter; small black berries follow.	8	Partial to heavy shade; rich, well-drained, moist soil	Use in foundation planting, border, or tub, or as specimen.

Shrub	Height	Foliage and Flowers	Zone	Exposure and Soil	Comments
FIRE THORN *Pyracantha* sp. **Gibbs** *P. atalantioides*	15'	Small white flower clusters in spring, followed by scarlet berries.	7	Full sun. Tolerates most soils.	Use in border or as specimen.
Scarlet *P. coccinea*	6'	Small white flower clusters in spring, followed by scarlet berries. Thorny.	7	Full sun. Tolerates most soils.	Colorful. Use in border or espalier on a wall.
GARDENIA **Cape jasmine** *Gardenia jasminoides*	6'	2- to 4-inch, very fragrant, double or single, waxy, white flowers in mid-spring through fall. Dark green, glossy, leathery leaves.	8	Full sun or partial shade; rich, moist, acid soil	Use as specimen, in tub or border, or as houseplant in North. Not as hardy as camellia.
HEATH *Erica* sp. **Spring** *E. carnea*	1'	Small, rose-colored flowers in early spring. Also in pink, red, or white.	5	Full sun; moist, acid soil	Use in beds, borders, or rock gardens. Mulch.
Twisted *E. cinerea*	2'	Small flowers in early summer in rose, pink, white, or purple.	5	Full sun; moist, well-drained soil	Prune after flowers fade. Mulch. Use in beds.
HEATHER *Calluna vulgaris*	2½'	Small flowers in midsummer in 1- to 4-inch clusters. Many varieties. Rose, white, pink, or purple flowers.	4	Full sun or light shade; acid, well-drained, highly organic soil	Use in beds, borders, or rock gardens. Mulch. Prune in early spring.
HIBISCUS, CHINESE *Hibiscus rosa-sinensis*	8'	3- to 6-inch, single or double flowers in midsummer, continuing for several months. Colors include red, white, pink, or yellow.	9	Full sun or partial shade. Tolerates most soils.	Very showy and quick growing. Needs protection from severe weather. Use as specimen or screen.
HOLLY *Ilex* sp. **Chinese** *I. cornuta*	9'	Tiny inconspicuous flowers in early summer; bright red berries in fall and winter. Glossy pointed leaves.	7	Full sun or partial shade; well-drained, slightly acid soil	Female plant produces fruit without pollen. Needs little pruning.
Japanese *I. crenata*	15'	Tiny flowers in early summer; black berries in winter. Small, glossy, green leaves.	6	Full sun or partial shade; well-drained, slightly acid soil	Sexes are separate. Varieties for almost every garden use.
HOLLY GRAPE **Oregon grape** *Mahonia aquifolium*	3'	Small clusters of yellow flowers in mid-spring. Blue-black, grapelike fruits in midsummer. Hollylike leaves are glossy green.	6	Partial shade; well-drained, moist soil	Hardy and attractive. Use in border, along foundation, or as tall ground cover.
LAUREL, CHERRY OR ENGLISH *Prunus laurocerasus*	18'	Small white flowers in 2- to 5-inch clusters appear in late spring; blue-black berries in fall.	7	Full sun or partial shade; moist, well-drained soil	Quick growing. Use as windbreak or screen, or in hedge. Easily sheared in early spring.
MYRTLE *Myrtus communis*	15'	½- to 1-inch white flowers during summer, followed by blue-black berries in fall. Leaves are deep green and aromatic.	9	Full sun or partial shade; well-drained soil	Use in hot, dry areas as specimen, or in border or hedge. Easily sheared to any dimension.

123

BROAD-LEAVED EVERGREEN SHRUBS *(continued)*

Shrub	Height	Foliage and Flowers	Zone	Exposure and Soil	Comments
NANDINA **Sacred bamboo** *Nandina domestica*	8'	Small white flowers in 4- to 8-inch clusters appear in midsummer, followed by many bright red berries. Leaves turn red in cold-winter areas. 'Alba' has white berries.	7	Full sun or partial shade; rich, well-drained, moist soil	Cut off old stems in early spring each year. Use along foundation or in border. Plant two or more plants to increase berry production.
OLEANDER *Nerium oleander*	20'	2- to 3-inch, single or double, fragrant flowers in early spring through summer. Colors are red, yellow, white, rose, or pink. Leaves are narrow, glossy green.	8	Full sun; rich, moist, well-drained soil	Tolerates hot, dry conditions. Resists soot. All parts of plant are poisonous. Use in tub or border, or as specimen or screen.
PHOTINIA *Photinia serrulata*	40'	Small white flowers in 4- to 7-inch-wide clusters open in mid-spring. Red berries in winter. Young bronze foliage turns glossy green.	7	Full sun or partial shade; well-drained soil	Very vigorous and hardy. Keep dry during summer. Prune back occasionally.
PITTOSPORUM, JAPANESE *Pittosporum tobira*	18'	Small, white, fragrant flowers appear in mid-spring. Leaves are leathery and green. 'Variegata' has leaves variegated with white.	8	Full sun or partial shade. Tolerates most soils.	Very hardy; resists pests. Use as screen, or in hedge or border. Prune after new growth begins; again later.
PRIVET *Ligustrum* sp. **Chinese** *L. sinense*	12'	Small white flowers in 2- to 4-inch clusters in midsummer.	7	Full sun or partial shade. Tolerates most soils.	Very hardy; resists pests. Slow growing.
Glossy *L. lucidum*	30'	Small white flowers in 4- to 8-inch clusters in late summer, followed by blue-black berries.	8	Full sun or partial shade. Tolerates most soils.	Very hardy; resists pests. Use as screen, or in hedge or border. Prune after new growth begins; again later.
RAPHIOLEPIS **Indian** **hawthorn** *Raphiolepis indica*	5'	Dark green leaves, 3½ inches long. Pinkish ½-inch in loose clusters in April, followed by blue-black berries.	9	Tolerates most light and soil conditions.	Slow growing, so select plants that are flat or upright according to your landscaping needs.
RHODODEN-DRON, AZALEA *Rhododendron* sp.		(For deciduous rhododendrons, see page 117.)			
'Glen Dale' *R. 'Glen Dale Hybrid'*	5'	1- to 3-inch single or double flowers cover the plant in spring. Glossy, green foliage. Many colors.	7	Partial shade; well-drained, acid soil	Dense, spreading. Use in bed or mass display, or along foundation.
Indica *R. indicum*	6'	2- to 4-inch clusters of pink to violet flowers cover plant in early summer.	6	Partial shade; well-drained, acid soil	Many varieties. Dense, spreading. Cut off fading flowers for more vigorous flowering the next year. Mulch for best results.

Shrub	Height	Foliage and Flowers	Zone	Exposure and Soil	Comments
'Kaempferi' *R. 'Kaempferi Hybrid'*	6'	2- to 3-inch single flowers cover plant in spring. Glossy, green foliage. All colors. Many varieties.	7	Partial shade; well-drained, acid soil	Dense, spreading. Use in beds, borders, or mass plantings for colorful display. Keep mulched.
'Kurume' *R. 'Kurume Hybrid'*	3'	Clusters of ½- to 1-inch single or double flowers cover plant in spring; many colors.	7	Partial shade; well-drained, acid soil	Many varieties. Bushy, low grower. Use in beds, borders, or rock gardens.
RHODODEN-DRON, RHODO-DENDRON *Rhododendron* sp.		(For deciduous rhododendrons, see page 117.)			
Carolina *R. carolinianum*	6'	3-inch clusters of rose-violet flowers cover plant in mid-spring. Many varieties.	6	Full sun or partial shade; rich, acid, well-drained soil	Many varieties. Dense and moundlike. Blooms earlier than most species.
Catawba *R. catawbiense*	10'	4- to 6-inch clusters of lilac-colored flowers, spotted with green in early summer. Many varieties.	5	Partial shade; rich, moist, well-drained, acid soil	Many varieties. Dense, spreading. Best hybrids. Very hardy and showy. Cut fading flowers.
Fortune's *R. fortunei*	12'	3- to 4-inch clusters of rose-violet flowers in late spring. Many hybrid varieties with red and pink shades.	6	Partial shade; rich, moist, well-drained, acid soil	Very showy. Use in beds, borders, or mass plantings. May need winter protection. Cut fading flowers.
ROSEMARY *Rosmarinus officinalis*	4'	½- to 1-inch, fragrant, pale lavender-blue flowers cover the plant in late winter to early spring. Glossy leaves with pleasant aroma.	7	Full sun. Tolerates most well-drained soils.	Use in beds, borders, and hedges. Needs little pruning. Keep dry to prevent spindly growth.
SKIMMIA, JAPANESE *Skimmia japonica*	5'	Tiny, fragrant, white flowers in 2- to 4-inch clusters appear in mid-spring; bright red berries cling through winter.	8	Partial shade; rich, moist, well-drained soil	Use in foundation planting or border. Plant two or more for berry production. Needs little pruning.
VIBURNUM *Viburnum* sp. **David** *V. davidi*	3'	Dark green, deeply veined leaves; 3-inch-wide clusters of white flowers. Blue berries attract birds.	9	Partial shade; well-drained, acid soil	Attractive form and foliage, but not showy. Use as foundation shrub, in beds, or as foreground plant.
Laurustinus *V. tinus*	10'	Small pinkish flowers in late winter, followed by shiny, blue berries in midsummer, later turning black.	7	Partial shade; well-drained soil kept dry	Use in hedge or as screen. Prune in early spring. Attracts birds.
XYLOSMA, SHINY *Xylosma congestum*	15'	Small, yellow-green leaves are bronze when young.	8	Full sun or partial shade. Tolerates most soils.	Can train to tree form. Useful in hot, dry areas. Easily sheared to any size. Use in border.

VINES

Whether
grown as earth-hugging ground covers or
skyward climbers, vines can delight gardeners
in surprising ways. A flowering vine allowed
to climb an aging tree, for example, can bring
new glory to a faltering frame. Or, a leafy
vine on a well-placed arbor can shade a sun-
drenched patio. The only difficulty is choosing
just the right vine.

SELECTING A VINE

Your greatest problem in selecting a vine may be too many choices. To narrow the possibilities, look first at what kind of soil, light, space, and temperature your garden can provide. Also, study neighborhood plantings, and find out the names of vines that thrive in your area.

Learn, too, how different vines hold themselves up—by twining stems, curling tendrils, aerial rooting, or small suction disks (see page 131). Roses, for example, climb with beauty but assume you will supply the necessary support. The same goes for climbing annuals. If your garden lacks good support for vines, consider adding some. Trellises, gazebos, fences, and wire cages extend nice handholds for vines. You can even tie vines to other plant stems.

Look for container-grown stock at local nurseries or order from mail-order houses.

VERSATILE VINES

Vines can do wonders enhancing just about any garden setting—or solving any problem. One strong vine with vivid bloom can add drama to your sitting terrace, obscure an unpleasant view, or engulf an old shed. A brilliant, fast-growing wisteria can cover a homely wall.

A batch of climbing roses gives sudden beauty to a bald terrace. Honeysuckle vines, which offer delicate blooms and sweet fragrances through summer and decorative berries in fall, do well along fence tops.

Hybrid clematis vines produce magnificent flowers that tend to bloom near eye level. Their colors range from deep purple to golden yellow, from large sculptured whites to urn-shaped scarlet flowers and plumed fruit. Any of these, properly supported, makes a fine display beside a garden gate or front entry.

Leafy vines do well as vertical backdrops for floral displays or to hide vegetable patches. A climbing euonymus might scale a brick wall beside an entry door. Boston ivy fills a narrow space where flowers won't grow, or elbows its way around the corner of a house to lead you to a back garden.

When garden space is limited, use vines to clothe and unify the walled areas. Grape vines need little space, and yield food as a bonus. Evergreen vines, which provide year-round visual interest, can grow in shade if enough reflected light bounces their way.

Wisteria requires root and stem pruning after it blooms to reduce its weight and protect adjacent plants.

Bougainvillea needs a mild climate, full sun, and good, moist soil. In colder climates, grow it in containers so you can take it indoors for a winter bloom.

CARING FOR VINES

Because of their floating state, vines—and their supports—need care. High winds and icy winters can damage them. Careful attention during planting and frequent inspections later on will go a long way toward ensuring that your plants always look their best.

STARTING VINES

Vines are easy to start. Perennial vines usually begin as transplants or as cuttings. Quick-growing annuals, on the other hand, generally start from seed, although more and more gardeners are buying seedlings.

■ Perennial vines

Perennial vines are offered commercially in garden centers or through mail-order catalogs, most often in late spring for immediate planting. Usually, they come in plastic pots or paper cartons.

These hardy plants grow slower than annual vines but will reward you with fine foliage and beautiful blooms for years. Keep your garden's color scheme in mind when making selections.

Before you buy, read all labels and catalog information for hardiness predictions. You want to make sure the plants you buy will grow in your climate.

If you feel adventurous, try starting new seedlings from cuttings taken with a sharp knife. (Ask friends with vines you're fond of if you can take cuttings from their plants.) Make the cuttings just below leaf nodes; roots develop best there. Remove any leaves up a few inches and set the stems upright into pots containing a non-organic rooting medium. Place each pot in a plastic bag, water, then tie the bag closed to prevent leaf wilt. Roots should form in three to six weeks.

Whether your young vine is a transplant or root cutting, use the same procedure for setting it into your garden. Dig an 8-inch hole and add

STARTING FROM CUTTINGS

1 Use a sharp knife to take cuttings 4 to 6 inches long. Cut just below the point where the leaf joins the stem. Roots grow best there. Strip away all lower leaves before potting.

2 Fill a pot with evenly moistened vermiculite, perlite, or sand. Insert bare stem ends in the pot. After three or four weeks, pull a cutting to check root growth. If enough roots are present, harden the young plants, then transplant outdoors.

amendments if necessary (for example, if the soil is clayey). Carefully knock the plant out of its container and set it into the hole. Fill the hole, pat the soil lightly, and water. Tie the main stem to a stake or tape it to a wall. Apply plant food after new growth starts.

■ Annual vines

Whether to start seeds for annual vines indoors or out depends on how long they take to mature. You'll find this information on most seed packets. If you live in a warm zone or the vine matures quickly, you can sow the seeds directly into the ground. Otherwise, start the seeds indoors by pressing them barely under soil in little pots or paper cups. When the danger of frost passes, move the seedlings outside several hours a day to harden before transplanting them.

If you buy seedlings at a garden store, hardening is unnecessary. Plant these robust seedlings outside after the danger of frost has passed.

TRAINING VINES

First decide what you want each vine to do: provide shade, offer screening, add color, or serve as a major garden feature. Determine, too, how each plant can be trained. Annual vines are light, so they don't need a lot of support. Perennial vines, however, become woody and heavy, and require good support. Build trellises, ladders, and stilt supports—whatever each vine requires. Rely as little as possible on wire attachments screwed into wooden walls. In time, the attachments will damage the walls.

Consider instead hanging chicken wire panels 1 or 2 feet from the walls. Just thread metal rods through the tops and bottoms of the wire panels, then anchor the rods to screw hooks in the eaves and to stakes below at ground level.

MAINTAINING VINES

When your vines become rampant enough to need pruning, curb the upper stems but encourage bottom branching by interweaving and supporting the smaller stems. The aim should be a robust pillar of green, top to bottom.

Prune perennial vines annually. In early spring, cut away all dead wood. Prune live vines on nonflowering types any time. For flowering perennial vines, prune live growth in early spring if the vine flowers on new wood (this year's growth) or after flowering if the vine blooms on old wood (last year's growth).

Because of their short life spans, annual vines seldom need pruning. Simply arrange vining stems for maximum color effect.

HOLDING ACTIONS

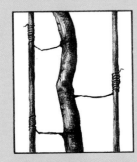

Clinging tendrils
lend strong support to grapes, and more delicate assistance to clematis, bittersweet, and passionflower. The strength of support matches the plant's need.

Twining varieties
wind their stems around nearby stakes and trellises. This is the means of support for honeysuckle, wisteria, silver-lace vine, and fast-growing actinidia.

Adhesive disks
or suction cups perform the magic that holds Boston ivy to a brick wall, Virginia creeper to a wooden fence, and trumpet creeper to anything it can reach.

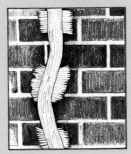

Rootlike holdfasts
reach into dry crevices. To hold securely as the vine's weight increases, they grow longer. They prefer rock walls and creviced brick.

ANNUAL VINES

Annual vines are fast-growing beauties that offer good solutions to your immediate garden plans. Their vivid colors and tall, climbing strands come in a variety of forms. And given a sunny place, they can, in one season, grow from seed to bud to flower, and still find time to produce new seeds in fall for winter storage and spring planting.

Each year hybridizers introduce new vining temptations. Morning-glory, once offered only in delicate lavenders, now comes in heavenly blues, scarlet and chocolate hues, and pearly whites. Lisianthus wins favor with roselike blooms in pink to purple through midsummer. Moon vines bloom on summer evenings with dramatic, hurried unfoldings that take less than a minute. Vine-type vegetables are winning attention for their decorative attributes. Lablab, the hyacinth bean, has glossy foliage, lilac blossoms, and shiny pods, all ascending together. Red-stemmed spinach climbs on a tower, offering leaves for summer salads.

Climbing nasturtiums are eager to go just about anywhere, whether it's up a flight of stone steps or up and over a wire trellis in a garden.

This soft-stemmed herb has a fragrance that pleases many, including cooks who use it to garnish salads. Its flowers are bright orange and long lasting.

Plant the seeds indoors in spring and move the seedlings outside as the weather warms. Or take 4-inch cuttings in fall for overwintering indoors.

Nasturtiums climb to 12 feet.

(Far left) Black-eyed susan vines are a surprise to gardeners who know the freestanding black-eyed wilding better. The vine can creep up to 6 feet. In mild climates, it blooms from seed in one year.

(Near left) Cypress vine offers delicate scarlet flowers 1½ inches long. A tropical native and a member of the morning-glory family, it grows in California and the South, and is considered a tender annual.

Vine	Fruit and Flower Habit	Comments
BALLOON VINE *Cardiospermum halicacabum*	Inconspicuous white flowers; balloon-shaped seedpods.	Ideal for trellises; needs sun. Annual in North, perennial in South. Grows from seed.
BALSAM PEAR *Momordica charantia*	Small yellow blossoms; gourdlike fruit.	Has large, deeply lobed leaves. Can grow 30 feet in one season. Needs rich, moist soil. Quick-growing cover for porches.
BEACH PEA *Lathyrus japonicus*	Rose to purple flowers in clusters.	At home along the shores of seas and lakes, it sprawls on sandy soil and has tough, long, sand-binding roots.
BLACK-EYED SUSAN *Thunbergia alata*	Yellow or orange, daisylike flowers with purple throats. Blooms through summer.	A twining, summertime vine that grows in sun or shade. Temperatures below 50 degrees can kill. Needs long growing season.
CANARY-BIRD FLOWER *Tropaeolum peregrinum*	Small, feathery, yellow flowers in summer.	Thrives in poor soil but needs moisture and shade. Prefers cool nights. Will grow 10 feet, over a trellis, quickly.
CARDINAL CLIMBER *Ipomoea x multifida*	2-inch, crimson, morning-glorylike flowers all summer.	Can grow 20 feet long in sun or shade. A twining vine, it needs well-drained, sandy soil.
CATHEDRAL BELLS **Cup-and-saucer vine** *Cobaea scandens*	Purple, bell-shaped flowers 2 inches across. Blooms spring into summer, for six months.	A southern favorite, it grows rapidly and clings by tendrils.
CYPRESS VINE *Ipomoea quamoclit*	Star-shaped, red or white flowers; blossoms all summer.	Has delicate foliage that grows 20 feet long. Prefers full sun but can take partial shade.
DUTCHMAN'S-PIPE **Pipe vine** *Aristolochia durior*	Inconspicuous pipelike flowers.	Grows fast to 30 feet. Needs space or will crowd other plants.
HYACINTH BEAN **Indian, Egyptian bean** *Dolichos lablab*	Purple or white flowers in summer; black or white seeds; oval leaves.	Grows rapidly up to 15 to 30 feet. Good for climbing a fence or trellis. In colder climates, plant in a sunny place.
JAPANESE HOP VINE *Humulus japonicus*	Fruit resembles hops used to make beer. 'Variegatus' has leaves splashed with white.	Will twine up porches, fences, and trellises. Prefers sun and ample moisture. It can become a pest with self-seeding.
MOONFLOWER *Ipomoea alba*	Fragrant white flowers that open at dusk and close by noon the next day.	Ideal screening vine. Grows rapidly in sun with large, heart-shaped leaves. If soil is too rich, it blooms less.
MORNING-GLORY *Ipomoea purpurea*	Purple, blue, scarlet, pink, and white flower varieties bloom from dawn till noon.	Very popular annual vine with many blooms. Good on fences and porches. Thrives in almost any soil. Considered a weed by some.
NASTURTIUM, GARDEN *Tropaeolum majus*	Brilliant and fragrant flowers all through summer. Scent is pungent.	Covers old tree stumps, fences, or porches. Can grow in poor soil with little sun. Thrives on neglect. Sow seeds after frost.
SCARLET RUNNER BEAN *Phaseolus coccineus*	Small red flowers, resembling sweet pea blossoms, in profusion.	Tall and twining, but still needs tying. Good summer screen for west-facing porch. Plant in well-drained soil. Grows quickly.

PERENNIAL VINES

Perennial vines are a charming family of plants, each with a great deal of individuality. Although some varieties prefer certain geographic locations—preferences you should keep in mind when making your selections—you'll find it hard to exhaust the choices no matter where you live.

■ Geography matters

There are southern vines that can't stand northern winters, and northern vines that wilt in southern heat. In between are vines like wisteria and passionflower that prosper as long as you protect them from bitter winds. Each vine reacts differently to an environment.

Northern perennial vines, for example, are generally leafless through the bitter days of winter and look lifeless. In fact, their tops may actually die back. But when spring comes, their stems leaf out, and they show signs that they soon will flower and produce fragrances. Put a southern variety in the same setting and you're probably going to have a plant that's really dead the following spring.

One way to increase your chances of making successful selections is to buy your perennial vines at a local garden center. There you are likely to find vines suitable to your climate. If you order through a catalog, be sure to read closely about the hardiness of any vine you're interested in.

■ A clematis for almost every location

The clematis vine offers splendor in many hues and seasons. Considered the most beautiful of northern climbers, its many hybrid and species vines make it almost mandatory to include in your garden plans.

Seek out *C. montana* in pale pink for spring bloom, *C. henryi* in sculptured white for early summer, and *C. x jackmani* in blues to purple plus vivid variations. For late summer, try *C. tangutica*, with its golden yellow nodding blooms that in turn become silver-gold plumed fruit. With 270 species in this genus, your selection potential is almost infinite.

(Above) Sweet autumn clematis is a hardy, vigorous grower offering festoons of white flowers in leafy clusters. Of Japanese origin, its fragrant flowers are 1½ inches wide.

(Left) Trumpet vine can provide shade, create privacy, and project beauty. It is of the campsis species.

Vine	Zone	Fruit and Flower Habit	Comments
ACTINIDIA **Chinese gooseberry** *Actinidia chinensis*	8	White and yellow fragrant flowers in early summer.	Flowers appear on previous year's wood; leave plenty when pruning for maximum bloom. Prune after flowering. Good twining vine.
BITTERSWEET *Celastrus* sp.			
American *C. scandens*	4	Yellow capsules with red berries in fall.	Very hardy twining vine; good for a sunny wall.
Oriental *C. orbiculatus*	5	Inconspicuous flowers, but red and yellow berries in clusters along sides of twigs.	One of the best twining vines. Grows rapidly; has rounded leaves.
BOUGAINVILLEA *Bougainvillea* hybrids	9	Large clusters of red, pink, orange, and purple blooms.	Twining climber. Grows best in the South in full sun. In the North, grow as houseplant, move outside in summer.
CAROLINA JESSAMINE **Evening trumpet flower** *Gelsemium sempervirens*	7	Fragrant yellow flowers all summer.	Evergreen twining shrub. Needs support. Good on fences or as ground cover. Start new plants from cuttings or seed.
CLEMATIS *Clematis* sp.			All grow best facing away from the sun.
Armand *C. armandi*	7	White flowers in spring.	Blooms on previous year's wood. Prune after flowering. Evergreen or semievergreen.
'Big Petal' *C. macropetala*	6	Large blue flowers with many sepals in spring.	Prune after flowering.
Curly *C. crispa*	6	Long, purple, bell-shaped flowers all summer.	Blooms on current year's wood.
'Duchess of Edinburgh' *C. florida* hybrid	6	Pure white double flowers that resemble gardenias.	Blooms on previous year's wood.
Golden *C. tangutica*	5	A woody vine with bright yellow flowers in late spring; plumed seed heads in early fall.	Soft gray-green leaves form a good background for masses of flowers. Needs full sun. Long-lasting blooms.
Henryi *C. henryi*	5	Large ivory petals with sculptural markings; blooms up to 7 inches across.	A showy climbing vine; does best in light, loamy, and well-drained soil.
Jackmani *C. x jackmani*	6	Has large purple flowers in profusion in midsummer; seed heads in fall.	A popular hybrid that blooms on current year's woody stems.
'Nelly Moser' *C. patens* hybrid	6	Pale mauve petals; profuse blooms.	Popular hybrid.
Pink anemone *C. montana* 'Rubens'	6	Red and pink flowers in late spring; decorative seed heads in summer.	Long-lasting flowers on previous year's wood. New foliage is bronze colored. Grows rapidly.
Scarlet *C. texensis*	6	Many urn-shaped scarlet flowers in midsummer; plumed seed heads in fall.	Excellent ornamental native. Grows rapidly. Evergreen or semievergreen.
Sweet autumn *C. paniculata*	5	Many fragrant white flowers in midsummer; seed heads in fall.	One of the easiest vines to grow. Has dense foliage. Resists disease and insects. Evergreen or semievergreen. Good for bank or slope.

PERENNIAL VINES *(continued)*

Vine	Zone	Fruit and Flower Habit	Comments
CLEMATIS *(continued)*			
Virgin's bower *C. virginiana*	5	Small, white flowers in late summer; seed heads in fall.	Good in a wildflower garden. A native that grows rapidly and tolerates wet soil.
CORAL VINE **Queen's-wreath** *Antigonon leptopus*	9	Pink flowers from late summer to fall.	Tolerates hot, dry conditions. Climbs by tendrils. Heart-shaped leaves.
CREEPER, VIRGINIA **Woodbine** *Parthenocissus quinquefolia*	4	Dark blue berries in fall.	Ideal for covering brick or stone walls, or as a ground cover. Produces bright scarlet coloring in fall. Tolerates dry soil; grows rapidly.
CROSS VINE *Bignonia capreolata*	6	Orange-red flowers in late spring.	Vigorous vine. Grows well on a screen. Climbs by adhesive disks.
FIVE-LEAF AKEBIA *Akebia quinata*	5	Clusters of purple flowers in late spring. Graceful twinings.	Vigorously twining vine. Can go rampant if not controlled. Will grow in shade. Prefers well-drained soil.
GRAPE *Vitis* sp.			
Amur *V. amurensis*	5	Black grapes in fall.	Vigorous and hardy. Leaves turn purple-crimson in fall.
Glory vine *V. coignetiae*	5	8-inch-long fruit clusters.	Grows vigorously, holding on by clinging tendrils. Leaves turn red in fall.
River-bank *V. riparia*	3	Inconspicuous but fragrant flowers; purple and black grapes in fall.	A hardy plant with lustrous foliage.
HONEYSUCKLE *Lonicera* sp.			
Chinese woodbine *L. tragophylla*	6	Bright yellow flowers through summer; red berries in fall.	Prefers shade and limestone soil. Twines.
Everblooming *L. heckrotti*	4	Trumpet-shaped flowers with purple outsides, yellow insides. Blooms all summer.	One of the best climbing honeysuckles.
Henryi *L. henryi*	6	Red, purple, or yellow flowers in early summer; black berries in fall.	Good ground cover. Semievergreen in the North; evergreen in the South. Twines.
Trumpet *L. sempervirens*	4	Orange-scarlet flowers all summer; red berries in fall.	Hardy; grows rapidly and tolerates dry soil. Semi- to evergreen.
HYDRANGEA, CLIMBING *Hydrangea anomala petiolaris*	5	Large clusters of white flowers in early summer.	One of the best climbing vines. Will grow in shade but best in sun. Prune in fall or early spring. Clings to brick or stone.
IVY			
Algerian *Hedera canariensis*	8	Black berries in fall.	Fast grower. Thick, dark green leaves. Evergreen. Will grow in shade.

Vine	Zone	Fruit and Flower Habit	Comments
Boston, Japanese creeper *Parthenocissus tricuspidata*	5	Dark blue berries in fall.	Clings to stonework. Ideal for city conditions. Turns scarlet in the fall.
English *Hedera helix*	6	Black berries in fall.	Many varieties. All cling well to walls and stone. Grows rapidly and will grow in shade. Good as ground cover for embankments.
JASMINE **Common white** *Jasminum officinale*	7	Fragrant white flowers all summer.	Popular vine. Ideal for trellises or arbors.
Japanese *Jasminum mesnyi*	8	Small, yellow flowers in spring and summer.	Needs moist soil. Beautiful; not as hardy as other varieties.
Yellow Star *Trachelospermum asiaticum*	8	Fragrant ivory flowers from early spring to midsummer.	Hardy jasmine. Evergreen. Tolerates wet soil.
MATRIMONY VINE, COMMON *Lycium halimifolium*	5	Small, light purple flowers in early summer; orange to red berries in fall.	Ideal for poor soil; good for embankments. Can become a rambling shrub, so keep pruned.
PASSIONFLOWER *Passiflora caerulea*	8	White and pink petals. Purple corona. Flowers summer to fall.	Beautiful; popular in southern gardens. Will grow in sheltered Midwest conditions.
RAMBLER ROSE *Rosa* sp.	4	Large clusters of red, pink, and white flowers in late spring.	Needs support. Prune old canes immediately after flowering. Shelter from north winds.
SCARLET KADSURA *Kadsura japonica*	7	Small, ivory flowers all summer. Scarlet berries in fall.	Twining evergreen shrub good for embankments. Leaves turn reddish in fall.
SILVER-LACE *Polygonum auberti*	4	White to greenish flowers in panicles in late summer.	Vigorous twining vine. Dense foliage. Tolerates dry soil.
SKY VINE **Bengal clock vine** *Thunbergia grandiflora*	8	Blue on white tubular flowers in pendulous clusters. Blooms in mid-spring.	Evergreen. Popular on arbors or porches.
TRUMPET VINE *Campsis* sp. **Chinese trumpet creeper** *C. grandiflora*	8	Large, showy scarlet flowers in midsummer.	Vine needs support.
Trumpet vine *C. radicans*	5	Orange, yellow, or scarlet flowers in midsummer.	Will cling to stone or brick (needs additional support because of its weight). Tolerates wet or dry soil.
WINTER CREEPER *Euonymus fortunei*	6	Handsome green foliage bears orange berries in fall.	Evergreen. Clings well to stone; otherwise, needs wire support.
WISTERIA *Wisteria* sp. **Chinese** *W. sinensis*	5	Blue and purple flowers in dense clusters in spring.	Grows rapidly. Popular vine; makes beautiful specimen.
Japanese *W. floribunda*	5	Violet, pink, red, and white flowers in racemes in spring.	Flowers bloom from top to bottom of the racemes. Many varieties. Grows rapidly; needs pruning.

PERENNIALS AND BIENNIALS

Look at any
flower garden and you're almost sure to see
lots of perennials. And for good reason. They
come back year after year, providing a
pleasing variety of colors, textures, shapes,
and heights. Colorful biennials, on the other
hand, are shorter lived, but add a special
charm all their own.

CONSTANT COLOR

Blue forget-me-nots, English daisies, Iceland poppies, felicia, and coralbells splash this spring garden with vibrant color.

A flower garden that blooms from end to end spring to frost, or perhaps even year-round, doesn't just happen. Getting each plant to present its colors at a specific time and place is the result of skillful planning, as the garden on these two pages shows.

For color early in the growing season, turn to plants that begin blooming as the weather warms. Follow their color with plants that bloom later. This constant flow of changing color will shift the garden's focal points of attention as the seasons change, yielding a garden alive with color both bold and always moving.

For added design features in your garden, make sure that, in addition to flower color and season of bloom, you consider the heights of plants when full-grown and the texture and color of their foliage.

Planning a garden for constant color using only perennials is difficult because many peren-

In summer, the garden opposite assumes a different hue. Perennial sedum, rudbeckias, and campanulas team with annuals—including petunias, marigolds, and zinnias—for the show.

nials bloom for a short period, often just a few weeks. That's why gardeners who love colorful gardens plant annuals and biennials among their perennials.

Interplanting is a big reason for the success of the garden shown here. Perennials are generously distributed throughout, with blocks of annuals and biennials planted between them.

When the perennials finish blooming, their foliage will furnish background texture and color.

With experience and study, the strategy of getting color during each season comes naturally. When the foliage of spring bulbs fades, fill in with young annual plants. Then replant areas once filled with cool-season bedding plants, such as violas, using tender bulbs or more annuals for warm weather.

PERENNIAL BASICS

Successful gardening often is just a matter of following good basics. Getting your perennials to perform well is no different.

■ Preparing the soil

Cover the soil with 2 to 4 inches of organic matter: well-rotted manure, compost, or peat moss, or a combination of these. Spade in or power-till a foot deep, then rake smooth.

■ Planting

Dig a hole several inches larger in diameter than the spread of the roots. With bare-root plants, space the roots in all directions so they become firmly established.

Set plants at the proper depth (the same level they grew before). You can see the marks of the original depth on bare-root stems and most divisions. Place container-grown plants so their soil is level with the surrounding area. Add soil, pressing it down so it's level with the surrounding area. Form a shallow saucer with soil, then water thoroughly. Level the soil saucer after a couple of weeks.

■ Labeling and staking

Using short stakes and a waterproof pen, label the locations of newly planted perennials, especially those you plant in the fall. Also, make a master plan showing where you placed your plants, when you planted them, and where you obtained them.

Keep the soil moist, but don't overwater. Avoid overfeeding, too. Plants will be stronger if they are fed just enough to produce normal yearly growth. Provide support early for tall plants such as delphinium, lupine, and foxglove. Keep plants tied or trained to stakes or wire-frame supports.

■ Winter protection

Prepare the perennial garden for winter after the first hard frost. Cut and remove all dead stalks, trimming stems to within 4 inches of the ground. In cold-winter areas, after the soil freezes, apply a mulch of straw, holding it in place with branches or chicken wire.

PLANTING

1 Set the root ball at its original depth. For bare-root and divided plants, look for the original soil line. Place container-grown plants so the soil is level with the surrounding area. Double-check with a board or straightedge.

2 After positioning the plant, fill the hole with amended soil or topsoil, then gently press down to eliminate air pockets around the roots.

3 Follow with a deep, thorough watering. Then apply a few inches of mulch. Shredded bark, compost, or grass clippings work well.

PROPAGATING PERENNIALS

Increasing your supply of perennials usually is simple, once you know the process for each type of plant. The four commonly used methods of propagating perennials are seeds, stem cuttings, root cuttings, and division. Check "Perennials Portfolio" (starting on page 150) for which methods to use with individual plants.

■ Seeds

Plant perennial seeds in spring or summer. Sow them in nursery flats or a cold frame, or make a seedbed in an out-of-the-way spot of your garden. Keep seedlings watered and lightly fed. Thin and space them out when they are about 2 inches tall.

Use a cold frame to harden young plants before transplanting them, and to overwinter recently propagated perennials and biennials.

■ Stem cuttings

Begin by taking 3- to 4-inch lengths of healthy, leafy stems from just below the tips of recent growth. Remove the leaves from the bottom 1½ inches. Treat with a rooting compound and insert the bottoms an inch or so into a flat of moist vermiculite. Cover with plastic, then set the flat where it gets bright light but no direct sun. Shift to individual containers of soil or transplant to the garden when well rooted.

■ Root cuttings

Take root cuttings just before active growth begins in early spring. Carefully expose a portion of the root system and cut the thickest roots into 3-inch sections. Plant these pieces horizontally, either in individual containers of soil or directly in the garden. Cover with an inch of soil.

■ Plant divisions

Dividing the crown of a perennial produces several good-size plants quickly. Dig up the entire plant and wash or shake off enough soil to expose the crown. Separate the clump into individual plants, each with a growth point and leaves, a portion of stem, and a mass of roots. Some plants pull apart; others require a sharp knife for cutting through the fleshy crown.

DIVIDING PLANTS

1 Begin plant division by digging and lifting the entire clump. This is best done during cool, overcast weather.

2 Remove enough soil to expose the growth points, or crowns. Some plants can be broken into divisions by hand. Others must be sectioned with a knife.

3 Make sure each division contains a mass of healthy roots, the joining stem (crown), and leaves.

PERENNIALS FOR SPECIAL CONDITIONS

Because of their diversity, you can find perennials suited to nearly every garden situation. Use types such as daylily in soil with low fertility and little organic matter. Where soil is moist or boggy, pick types such as astilbe. In dry soils, use plants such as Oriental poppy. Pick plants such as hosta for areas with half-day shade or dappled shade all day. Most plants listed under poor soil grow better in well-prepared and properly fertilized soils. Those listed under dry soil also grow well in moister conditions, especially if given good drainage.

POOR SOIL
Daylily

DRY SOIL
Oriental poppy

WET SOIL
Astilbe

SHADE TOLERANT
Hosta

Poor Soil

Ageratum, hardy
Aloe
Baby's-breath
Candytuft
Catnip
Cerastium
Daylily
Geranium,
   cranesbill
Globe thistle
Leadwort
Moss phlox
Oenothera
Rudbeckia
Sedum (most
   types)
Stachys
Swamp saxifrage
Thyme
Verbascum
Virginia bluebells
Yarrow

Wet Soil

Astilbe
Bee balm
Bergenia
Blue flag
Eupatorium
Ferns (most types)
Forget-me-not
Galax
Globeflower
Helenium
Japanese iris
Lobelia
Loosestrife
Lungwort
Marsh marigold
Swamp milkweed
Swamp saxifrage
Sweet woodruff
Spiderwort
Violet
Yellow flag

Dry Soil

Aloe
Anthemis
Baby's-breath
Baptisia
Butterfly weed
Coreopsis
Gaillardia
Helianthus
Leadwort
Oriental poppy
Poker plant
Rudbeckia
Santolina
Sedum
Spurge
Thrift
Yarrow
Yucca

Shade Tolerant

Anemone, Japanese
Astilbe
Bergenia
Bee balm
Bleeding-heart
Columbine
Coralbells
Ferns
Forget-me-not
Galax
Globeflower
Helleborus
Hosta
Hypericum
Jacob's-ladder
Lily-of-the-valley
Lobelia
Loosestrife
Physostegia
Primrose
Spiderwort
Swamp rose
   mallow
Thalictrum
Virginia bluebells

DESCRIPTIONS & PREFERRED LOCATIONS

Name	Colors	Time of Bloom	Plant Height	Spacing	Comments
ERECT					
Delphinium	Blue, white, violet, pink, purple	Early summer; early fall	2½'–6'	12" (small) 2' (large)	Use for vertical accent. Stake and tie tall kinds. Cut flower spikes before seeds set to encourage rebloom in autumn.
Iris, tall bearded	White, blue, red, pink, yellow, others	Late spring to early summer	2'–3'	8"–10"	Needs full sun and well-drained soil. Divide about every fifth year. Set rhizomes shallow.
Liatris	Rose, purple, white, bluish purple	Summer to fall	1½'–6'	12"–20"	Endures partial shade. Good for vertical accent. Blooms open from top of the spike down.
Loosestrife	Purple, rose, pink	Summer	2'–4'	1'–2'	Prefers a moist, shady location. Long flower spikes give accent to garden.
BUSH					
Aster, hardy	White, pink, red, blue, purple	Late summer to fall	3'–4'	10"–2½'	Plant in full sun. Encourage bushiness by pinching off shoot tips when plant is 12 inches tall. Support tall varieties.
Bleeding-heart	White, pink, rose	Spring	1½'–2'	15"–2'	Endures partial shade. Remove yellow foliage after flowers bloom.
Chrysanthemum	Yellow, red, white, pink, bronze, others	Fall	1'–4'	15"–2'	Give full sun. Divide and transplant every other spring (yearly in warm-winter areas). For bushiness, pinch off shoot tips when plants are 4 inches tall.
Oriental poppy	White, pink, orange, red	Late spring to early summer	2'–4'	1½'–2'	Produces bold, dramatic flowers. Propagate in late summer using root cuttings.
Peony	White, pink, maroon, red	Late spring to early summer	2'–4'	2½'–4'	Grows in full sun or partial shade, in well-drained soil. Seldom needs dividing. Plant buds 1 to 2 inches below soil surface.
Phlox	White, pink, blue, red, others	Summer to early fall	2'–4'	1'–2'	Best in fertile soil with lots of moisture; use mulch. Do not allow seeds to set. Divide every third year.
Shasta daisy	White	Summer	1'–4'	12"–20"	Excellent cut flower. Low maintenance. Divide every other spring (yearly in warm-winter areas).
CUSHION					
Moss phlox	White, pink, blue, red, lavender	Spring	6"	6"–12"	Useful in rock gardens and on banks. Combines well with spring bulbs.
Thrift	Pink, white, crimson, purple	Spring to early summer	6"–12"	10"–15"	Grown for its grassy foliage and globe-shaped flowers. Valuable as an edging and in rock gardens.
Viola	White, yellow, pink, purple, blue, bicolors	Spring; all year in mild climates	6"–8"	8"–12"	Best in moist soil. Tolerates partial shade during summer heat. Good in rock gardens and with wildflowers.

PLANNING PERENNIAL BORDERS

A successful perennial garden should be carefully planned, yet have an unplanned look that provides an attractive show throughout the season. Such a look is possible when you arrange compatible plants informally and space them to show off their best features in your garden.

The plans below and opposite are designed to give such a look. The lists of plants accompanying each plan are only suggestions. Many other plants would work as well. If you want a longer or shorter garden, or one in a shape other than rectangular, simply repeat or decrease plant groupings to fit the desired size and shape.

When choosing one of these plans, or when developing one of your own, first consider the amount of sun your garden receives during most of the season. If it gets direct sun only a couple of hours each day, or gets dappled shade most of the day, use plants suited to shade or partial-shade areas. Areas receiving at least six hours of direct sun every day are suited for full-sun plants.

Choosing plants for season-long display is one of your most important design tasks. If all the flowers bloom at the same time, the garden is drab much of the year. Keep the garden bright all season by including annuals and bulbs in the

PARTIAL-SHADE PERENNIAL BORDER

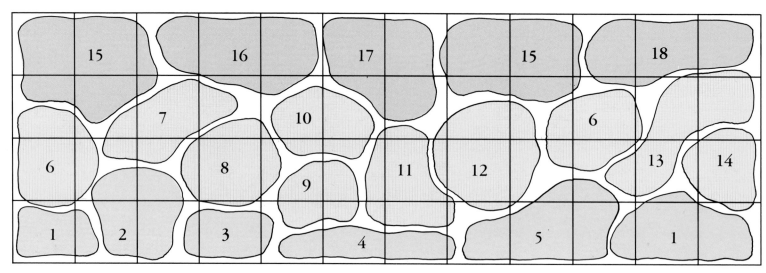

1 square = 1 foot

Front of the Border

1. Species tulip (8*);
   wax begonia later (3)
2. *Hosta decorata* (3)
3. Dwarf fern (3)
4. Mixed crocus (24);
   dwarf impatiens later (5)
5. Wild ginger (3)

Mid-Border

6. Astilbe (3)
7. Daffodil (10)
8. Tulip (10);
   tall impatiens later (4)
9. Hosta 'Kabitan' (3)
10. Bleeding-heart (1)
11. Daffodil (12)
12. *Hosta fortunei*
    'albomarginata' (3)
13. Tulip (12); tall
    impatiens later
14. *Hosta lancifolia* (1)

Back of the Border

15. Lady fern (*Athyrium
    filix-femina*) (3)
16. Monarda (3)
17. *Hosta sieboldiana* (1)
18. Loosestrife (3)

Numbers refer to the quantity of plants or bulbs to set out.

plan, as shown below and opposite. Get early color by planting spring-flowering bulbs in areas you'll later plant with annuals. Plant the bulbs near perennials with arching stems, such as peonies, so the perennial foliage can hide the yellowing bulb foliage in late spring.

Because most perennials bloom for just a few weeks, consider foliage textures and colors, blends of colors, and distribution of colors across the garden throughout the season. Emphasize the informal nature of the garden by planning masses of plants, rather than single plants scattered throughout. For best effect, group three to five plants of a variety. And don't set plants in rows. Put them in the shape of a triangle or in no particular shape at all. Of course, you can plant some plants that grow large, such as peonies, singly.

Space plants so the garden looks full but not crowded. Each plant or grouping should have room to display itself naturally, without a squeezed look.

The depth of your flower bed is important, too. If you will be able to tend it from just one side, a depth of 4 feet, as shown on these plans, is about right. With this size, you'll have enough space to taper plant heights from back to front and to work from one side.

SUNNY PERENNIAL BORDER

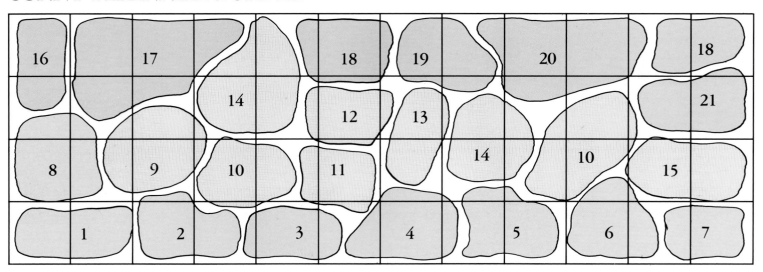

1 square = 1 foot

Front of the Border
1. Species tulip (8*);
   dwarf zinnia later (8)
2. Basket-of-gold (3)
3. Crocus (12);
   petunia later (4)
4. 'Silver Mound' artemisia (3)
5. English daisy (5)
6. Creeping phlox (3)
7. Daffodil (8); .
   dwarf marigold later (5)
8. Daffodil (10);
   tall marigold later (8)

Mid-Border
9. Peony (1)
10. Tulip (10);
    tall zinnia later (8)
11. Cushion mum (1)
12. Phlox (3)
13. Yarrow (3)
14. Daylily (3)
15. Aster (2)

Back of the Border
16. Solidago (3)
17. Delphinium (6)
18. Lily, imperial
    strain (3)
19. Rudbeckia (4)
20. Hollyhock (8)
21. Globe thistle (3)

*Numbers refer to the quantity of plants or bulbs to set out.

STARTING WITH PERENNIALS

After picking plants based on their tolerance of the amount of sun or shade in your garden, next consider plant height. Perennials range in height from low creepers such as cerastium and moss phlox to towering spires such as delphinium. For ease of planning, it's simplest to group perennials into three major height categories: front of the border, mid-border, and back of the border.

The chart below lists perennials in each category. Some plants may end up slightly higher or lower than the height range indicated for each category, and there are many additional choices besides those listed. As you read "Perennials Portfolio" (beginning on page 150), you'll notice some plants have several species or varieties of differing heights, and some are available as dwarf selections.

PERENNIAL HEIGHTS

Front of the Border (Dwarf to 15 inches)	Mid-Border (15 to 30 inches)	Back of the Border (Over 30 inches)
Adonis	Agapanthus (bulb)	Aster, hardy
Arabis	Astilbe	Baby's-breath
Artemisia ('Silver Mound')	Balloon flower	(Gypsophila paniculata)
Baby's-breath (Gypsophila repens)	Bee balm	Baptisia
Basket-of-gold	Bleeding-heart	Bear's-breech
Bellflower (Campanula carpatica)	Blue marguerite	Daylily (some varieties)
	Butterfly weed	Delphinium
Candytuft	Chrysanthemum (many varieties)	Foxglove* (some varieties)
Cerastium	Columbine	Globe thistle
Chrysanthemum (cushion types)	Coralbells	Helenium
Crocus (bulb)	Coreopsis	Helianthus
Dianthus	Erigeron	Heliopsis
English daisy*	Foxglove* (some varieties)	Hibiscus
Flax	Gaillardia	Hollyhock*
Gentian	Gas plant	Iris (spuria and Japanese)
Geranium, cranesbill	Geum	Japanese anemone
Grape hyacinth (bulb)	Hosta (many types)	Liatris
Hyacinth (bulb)	Iris (some types)	Ligularia
Iris (dwarf)	Jacob's-ladder	Lily (many hybrids; bulb)
Leadwort (dwarf)	Jupiter's-beard	Matilija poppy
Moss phlox (Phlox subulata)	Lavender	Phlox (Phlox paniculata)
Narcissus (bulb)	Lobelia	Purple coneflower
Oenothera	Mountain bluet	Queen-of-the-prairie
Potentilla (some varieties)	Painted daisy	Snakeroot
Primrose	Penstemon	Solidago
Stokesia	Peony	Thermopsis
Thrift	Physostegia	Verbascum
Tulip (botanic varieties; bulb)	Poppy	Yarrow (most varieties)
Veronica (some varieties)	Rudbeckia	Yucca
Viola*	Shasta daisy	
	Spiderwort	
	Tulip (bulb)	
	Virginia bluebells	

*Biennial

SHORT PERENNIALS
Variegated arabis

MEDIUM PERENNIALS
Hosta

TALL PERENNIALS
Liatris

Mixing and matching perennials by height, color, and texture yields a garden that will truly delight the eye. Here baby's-breath softens the look of its neighbors—lythrum, delphinium, and malva.

APPROXIMATE PERENNIAL BLOOM DATES

Season of bloom is as important as plant height when you plan your perennial garden. For best show, choose plants from each of the three major blooming seasons for all height categories. Expect some variation, depending on your climate and cultural practices. After some refinement, your garden will produce a stunning show of color and textures from front to back, from season to season.

Spring	**Summer**	**Fall**
February through early May	*Mid-May through mid-August*	*Late August to frost*
Adonis	Astilbe	Aster, hardy
Arabis	Baby's-breath	Chrysanthemum
Basket-of-gold	Bee balm	Daylily (late-season types)
Bergenia	Campanula	Delphinium (rebloom)
Bleeding-heart	Columbine	Felicia
Buttercup	Coralbells	Goldenrod
Candytuft	Coreopsis	Helenium
Crocus (bulb)	Daylily (early and	Helianthus
Dianthus	mid-season types)	*Helleborus niger*
(*Dianthus x allwoodi*)	Delphinium	Hosta
Doronicum	Globe thistle	Japanese anemone
Grape hyacinth (bulb)	Heliopsis	Penstemon
Hyacinth (bulb)	Iris	Physostegia
Iris (dwarf)	Liatris	Pincushion flower
Narcissus (bulb)	Lily (bulb)	(*Scabiosa caucasica*)
Phlox subulata	Loosestrife	Sedum
Primrose	Oriental poppy	Spiderwort
Scilla siberica	Peony	('Blue Stone')
Thrift	*Phlox paniculata*	
Tulip (bulb)	Shasta daisy	
Viola	Veronica	
Virginia bluebells	Yarrow	

PERENNIALS PORTFOLIO

ANCHUSA

ARTEMISIA

ALYSSUM

Also called basket-of-gold
Aurinia saxatilis
- ■ **Zone:** 3
- ■ **Height:** 8 to 15 inches
- ■ **Bloom time:** Spring
- ■ **Comments:** Basket-of-gold, or goldentuft alyssum, is grown primarily for its deep yellow flowers set against soft-textured, gray foliage. Its low-growing nature makes it useful in rock gardens, on slopes, as an edging, or combined with spring-flowering bulbs. Plants grow well in full sun or partial shade, but must have excellent drainage. Shear plants to half of their height after flowering.

Start from seeds sown in late summer or spring, or take stem cuttings anytime in summer. In cold-winter areas, overwinter young plants in a cold frame or sheltered garden spot. Divide every three years to renew old plants.

A. saxatilis 'compacta' has similar growth habits but is shorter. 'Citrina' has pale yellow flowers, and 'Plena' produces double yellow flowers.

ANCHUSA

Also called summer forget-me-not
Anchusa azurea
- ■ **Zone:** 4
- ■ **Height:** 3 to 4 feet
- ■ **Bloom time:** Summer
- ■ **Comments:** Summer forget-me-not is known for its beautiful, bright blue flowers. For blooms all summer long, remove dead flower clusters regularly. Plant in full sun and well-drained soil. Provide partial shade in areas subject to hot temperatures. Keep watered during dry periods; provide support in windy areas.

Anchusa grows easily from seeds sown in spring, and will reseed in many areas. To reproduce named varieties, take root cuttings in spring or propagate by division in spring or fall.

A. azurea 'Dropmore' has deep blue flowers on plants up to 4 feet tall; 'Little John' grows only 12 to 15 inches tall; 'Loddon Royalist' is 3 feet tall with intense blue flowers.

ANTHEMIS

Also called golden marguerite
Anthemis tinctoria
- ■ **Zone:** 3
- ■ **Height:** 2½ to 3 feet
- ■ **Bloom time:** Summer
- ■ **Comments:** Anthemis is perfect for the middle of the garden. It produces golden yellow, daisylike flowers throughout summer atop finely cut, aromatic foliage. Plants tolerate dry, hot locations and infertile soil, but need a well-drained site and full sun.

Keep flowers cut to encourage rebloom, and support the floppy stems.

Plant seeds outdoors in spring. Spring-sown plants often flower the first year. Encourage vigorous plants by dividing at least every two years (annually in warm-winter areas).

A. tinctoria 'Kelwayi' has deep yellow flowers and very finely cut foliage. 'Moonlight' produces pale yellow flowers.

ARTEMISIA

Also called wormwood
Artemisia species
- ■ **Zone:** 3
- ■ **Height:** Varies with variety
- ■ **Bloom time:** Spring through summer
- ■ **Comments:** Wormwoods are grown for their attractive, fine-textured, gray-green foliage, rather than for their flowers. Many have a delicate scent of lemon or camphor. They are attractive set against dark-foliaged plants, and provide a soft visual barrier between plants with sharply contrasting flower colors.

Artemisia grows well in infertile soils, but needs good drainage and full sun. It propagates easily when divided in the spring or from stem cuttings taken during early summer. Keep stem cuttings slightly dry to prevent rot.

A. absinthium 'Lambrook Silver' grows 3 to 4 feet tall with fine-textured leaves. *A. ludoviciana* 'albula,' the 'Silver-King' artemisia, reaches 3 feet. *A. schmidtiana 'nana'* is the 'Silver Mound' artemisia and grows only 8 to 12 inches high.

ASTER, HARDY

Also called michaelmas daisy
Aster species
- **Zone:** 4
- **Height:** 3 to 4 feet
- **Bloom time:** Late summer to fall
- **Comments:** Asters are a sure bet if you want reliable color in late summer and fall. They require full sun and thrive in moist, well-drained, fertilized soil. Provide support for tall types. Remove faded flowers to keep plants tidy and prevent self-sowing.

Plants are best propagated by division in the spring or fall. Replant only the most vigorous divisions from around the outside of the clump. Except in mild-winter areas, division every third or fourth year is sufficient.

Some of the most popular asters are hybrids of *A. novae-angliae* and *A. novi-belgi.* These are the michaelmas daisies and include varieties with white, pink, red, blue, and purple flowers. Several dwarf varieties also are available.

ASTILBE

Also called false spirea
Astilbe x arendsi
- **Zone:** 4
- **Height:** 15 to 30 inches
- **Bloom time:** Early summer
- **Comments:** Astilbes are ideal for areas of partial shade or full morning sun and afternoon shade. During late spring and early summer, they produce fluffy flower spikes—in white, cream, and shades of pink, salmon, and red—atop glossy, fernlike mounds of foliage. Water regularly, especially during hot, dry spells, and fertilize at least once just after flowering. Avoid cultivation, which damages the shallow roots.

Division, best done in spring just before the start of new growth, is the easiest propagation method. Many named varieties are available.

BABY'S-BREATH

Gypsophila paniculata
- **Zone:** 3
- **Height:** To 4 feet
- **Bloom time:** Early summer
- **Comments:** Few plants can equal the cloudlike display of a group of baby's-breath, with their dainty masses of white or light pink flowers held above small foliage on wiry stems. Flowering is heaviest in early to midsummer, but continues lightly for the rest of the season if you cut the flowers off before they go to seed.

Plant in full sun, and in well-drained, but not too fertile, soil. Because baby's-breath doesn't transplant well, start from seeds sown directly in the garden in spring; or use compressed peat moss pots and sow a small group of seeds in each. Thin all but the strongest seedlings. Or, use stem cuttings taken in midsummer.

G. paniculata 'Bristol Fairy' and 'Perfecta' produce double white flowers; 'Pink Fairy' produces double light pink flowers.

G. repens, creeping baby's-breath, grows about 8 inches tall. It flowers in early summer, and comes in white, pale purple, and pink varieties.

BALLOON FLOWER

Platycodon grandiflorus
- **Zone:** 3
- **Height:** 20 to 30 inches
- **Bloom time:** Summer
- **Comments:** Balloon flower's striking, star-shaped blue, pink, or white flowers make this old favorite a must-include plant for every perennial garden. Flowers develop from balloon-like buds, and are borne on arching stems throughout summer.

Protect plants from intense afternoon sun. This prevents fading, especially of the pink varieties. Soil should be moist, but loose and well drained, and enriched with organic matter.

Division in the spring is the quickest and simplest way to produce more plants. Or sow seeds, also in the spring. Seedlings, though, often require at least two years to reach flowering size.

HARDY ASTER

ASTILBE

BABY'S-BREATH

PERENNIALS PORTFOLIO (continued)

BLEEDING-HEART

CAMPANULA

BEE BALM

Also called bergamot or Oswego tea
Monarda didyma
- **Zone:** 4
- **Height:** 2 to 3 feet
- **Bloom time:** Summer to early fall
- **Comments:** Quick growing and attractive, bee balm is ideal for mid- to back-of-the-border locations. Tall stalks bear clusters of flowers, usually red, but also white, pink, and lavender. Bee balm attracts bees and butterflies.

Bee balm is an aromatic herb in the mint family, growing best in slightly shaded spots. It grows and spreads rapidly in moist, rich soil; poor or dry soil usually will make it shorter and more confined. Avoid planting bee balm where it might crowd nearby weaker plants. Good for naturalizing in woodland and bog gardens.

Propagate by division in the spring, or root newly cut, stocky stem cuttings in late spring.

BLEEDING-HEART

Dicentra spectabilis
- **Zone:** 4
- **Height:** 1½ to 2 feet
- **Bloom time:** Spring
- **Comments:** Every year, reliable and long-favored bleeding-heart brightens the spring garden with its gracefully arching stems of pink to rose, heart-shaped flowers. Bleeding-heart needs moist soil enriched with organic matter, and a partially shaded location. It combines well with ferns and other shade plants, and naturalizes nicely in woodland settings. Its finely cut, fernlike foliage works well with many spring-flowering bulbs.

In hot or arid areas, cut the foliage after the plant flowers because it yellows and becomes ragged. Propagate by division in early spring (in mild-winter areas, in either spring or fall). Take root cuttings in spring.

D. spectabilis 'alba' has pure white flowers. 'Luxuriant' is a hybrid with parentage of other species. It has reddish pink flowers, grows well in mild-winter areas, and tolerates more sun.

BUTTERFLY WEED

Asclepias tuberosa
- **Zone:** 4
- **Height:** 1½ to 3 feet
- **Bloom time:** Summer
- **Comments:** Durable butterfly weed covers itself with bright orange flowers—which butterflies love—all summer long. Attractive ornamental pods cover the plant following flowering.

Given full sun, it grows in nearly any soil, including dry, sandy locations. Propagate in spring by taking root cuttings or by sowing seeds directly in the garden.

Its young shoots are slow to emerge in the spring, so mark their location to avoid damaging them during early spring cultivation.

CAMPANULA

Also called bellflower
Campanula species
- **Zone:** 3
- **Height:** 6 inches to 3 feet
- **Bloom time:** Early summer
- **Comments:** A mainstay plant in almost every perennial garden, campanula comes in a nearly endless array of growth habits. Species range from low, sprawling types suited for edgings and rock gardens to upright types that produce vertical, spirelike flower stalks.

Plant in full sun (in hot climates, in partial shade) in moist, well-drained soil amended with organic matter. Remove faded flowers to encourage continued blooming. Divide every three or four years, replanting strong divisions from the outer portion of the clump. Strong-growing types may require division every other year in mild-winter areas. Mulch after the ground freezes where winter is severe. Many types grow easily and quickly from seeds.

C. carpatica produces compact mounds about 8 to 12 inches tall and is excellent for edgings and rock gardens. It flowers heavily in summer, lightly afterward. Most are light blue, although 'Alba' has white flowers.

Clusters of erect 2-foot stems carry the deep blue to purple flowers of *C. glomerata*. These grow well in moist soils, and flower most of the summer. A white-flowered variety is available.

Peach-leaved bellflower, *C. persicifolia*, produces stems up to 3 feet tall, and is a good choice for the back of the border. The graceful, nodding flowers are available in blue or white. 'Grandiflora Alba' produces especially large white flowers.

CANDYTUFT

Also called evergreen candytuft
Iberis sempervirens

- ■ **Zone:** 3
- ■ **Height:** 6 to 12 inches
- ■ **Bloom time:** Late spring
- ■ **Comments:** Candytuft produces a low compact mound of dark green foliage smothered with snow-white flowers in spring. If sheared after flowering, it often reblooms in fall in areas with a long growing season. Because it grows low, candytuft is ideal for edgings, in rock gardens, as an underplanting with late-flowering tulips, or in combination with other low plants.

Plant in full sun (in hot, arid climates, in partial shade). Candytuft does best with regular watering, and in fertile, amended soil. Candytuft is evergreen in mild-winter climates, but does not grow well in the Gulf Coast areas. In cold areas, it may die back to the ground. There, mulch it after the ground freezes.

Divide in early spring (in mild-winter areas, in fall). You also can root it by taking stem cuttings after its spring growth matures slightly.

CERASTIUM

Also called snow-in-summer
Cerastium tomentosum

- ■ **Zone:** 2
- ■ **Height:** 6 inches
- ■ **Bloom time:** Late spring to early summer
- ■ **Comments:** Snow-in-summer is a widely used creeping plant that rarely grows more than 6 inches tall. Its leaves are woolly gray; its flow-

ers, snow-white. Use it in rock gardens, on slopes, or as an edging in the front of mixed-flower gardens. Plants grow vigorously and can become invasive.

Plant in full sun and well-drained soil. Increase by seeds, by division, or by taking stem cuttings just after flowering stops.

CHRYSANTHEMUM

Also called mum or garden mum
Chrysanthemum x morifolium

- ■ **Zone:** 4
- ■ **Height:** 1 to 4 feet
- ■ **Bloom time:** Fall
- ■ **Comments:** For reliable flowering from late summer to hard frost, and for ease of growth, chrysanthemums are hard to beat. Most popular garden varieties are offered as cushion mums, and produce dense, compact low mounds smothered with flowers. Other types grow to 4 feet, and are sometimes trained to a single stem with one bloom. Flowers come in all colors but blue, and a wide range of forms, including single, anemone, semidouble, and double.

Plant in moist, well-drained soil, in a full-sun location. Use low-growing types in the front of perennial gardens or as an edging elsewhere. Taller types are excellent suppliers of cut flowers. All types grow well in containers.

Some varieties aren't winter hardy in coldest climates. In those areas, mulch after the soil freezes, or lift clumps and overwinter in a cold frame. Propagate by stem cuttings or by dividing clumps in spring when new shoots are 2 inches tall. Plant the most vigorous portions.

In mild-winter areas, divide yearly.

Pinch the stem tips to encourage compact, stout growth and lots of flowers. Start pinching after spring growth reaches 4 inches tall. Continue pinching every couple of weeks, but stop by mid-July so flower buds can form.

CANDYTUFT

CERASTIUM

CHRYSANTHEMUM

153

PERENNIALS PORTFOLIO *(continued)*

CORALBELLS

COREOPSIS

DAYLILY

COLUMBINE

Aquilegia species
- **Zone:** 4
- **Height:** 15 inches to 2½ feet
- **Bloom time:** Late spring
- **Comments:** Columbine is a colorful, spring-flowering perennial at home in several garden locations. It's widely used in the middle of perennial gardens, in rock gardens, in wildflower gardens, and mingled among late-flowering tulips. The graceful plants produce arching sprays of white, yellow, pink, red, blue, or bicolored crown-shaped flowers. Many types have long spurs projecting backward from the flower.

Plant in full sun in areas with cool summers; otherwise, partial shade. Soil must be well drained. Propagation is easiest using seeds sown either in spring or late summer. Only vigorous-growing types produce enough crowns to make division practical.

'Biedermeier' strain grows about 15 inches tall. The long-spurred 'McKana's Giant' mix produces plants up to 2½ feet tall in a variety of bold colors; 'Spring Song' is double flowered.

A. caerulea, or Rocky Mountain columbine, grows 2 to 3 feet tall and has flowers with bluish purple sepals and white petals.

CORALBELLS

Also called alumroot
Heuchera sanguinea
- **Zone:** 3
- **Height:** 1½ to 2 feet
- **Bloom time:** Late spring through summer
- **Comments:** Coralbells' trademark is mounded foliage, 8 to 12 inches tall, topped with slender stems of small, bell-shaped flowers. Coral, white, pink, or red flowers are available. Use in perennial gardens, woodland areas, rock gardens, or any area of full sun to partial shade that calls for a reliable early summer flower. Soil must be moist, well drained, and amended with organic matter.

Divide old, established clumps in early spring every four or five years. Where winters are mild, divide in early spring or fall. You also can sow seeds in spring. Coralbells don't perform well in the warmest portions of the Gulf States.

COREOPSIS

Also called perennial tickseed
Coreopsis species
- **Zone:** 4
- **Height:** 8 inches to 2½ feet
- **Bloom time:** June to frost
- **Comments:** A dependable and easy-to-grow perennial, coreopsis is known for its long flowering season. The golden yellow, daisylike flowers—either single or semidouble—are excellent for summer bouquets. Plant in full sun, in nearly any well-drained soil.

Sow seeds in late summer or divide plants in early spring every three or four years.

C. auriculata 'nana' produces golden orange flowers on plants only about 8 inches tall. *C. lanceolata* 'Sunray' grows about 20 inches tall and produces deep yellow, mostly double flowers. 'Moonbeam,' a variety of *C. verticillata,* is 2 feet tall with light yellow, star-shaped flowers.

DAYLILY

Hemerocallis hybrids
- **Zone:** 3
- **Height:** 1½ to 3½ feet
- **Bloom time:** Late spring to fall
- **Comments:** No perennial garden would be complete without daylilies. They are reliable, easy to grow, and nearly maintenance free. Although individual flowers usually last only one day, each plant blooms for several weeks. By planting an early, a mid-season, and a late variety, you'll have flowers all summer and into fall. Some varieties are repeat bloomers.

Daylilies produce clusters of trumpet-shaped flowers atop strong stocks from 1 to 6 feet tall. Flowers are available in all colors except blue and pure white; some are bicolored.

Plant in full sun or partial afternoon shade, in moist, well-drained soil. Propagate by division after flowering is completed in late summer or fall. Vigorous-growing varieties may require dividing every four or five years.

Plant daylilies in gardens according to their heights. Use in the filtered shade of high-branched trees, in sunny spots in woodland gardens, on gentle slopes, or in broad drifts in lawn areas. Short varieties are ideal in containers.

DELPHINIUM

Delphinium species
- **Zone:** 4
- **Height:** 2½ to 6 feet
- **Bloom time:** Early summer; rebloom in fall
- **Comments:** Delphiniums have few rivals for producing a bold display of tall flowers with a strong vertical accent. Most varieties fit best in the back of a perennial garden, but some grow only about 2½ feet tall and work well in the middle of a garden. Delphiniums are usually most effective planted in groups of three or more. Flowers are predominantly blue, but also are available in white, pink, lavender, violet, and purple.

Plant in full sun, in moist, well-drained amended soil. Protect from wind, and provide support as flower stalks develop. Most types rebloom in fall if you cut off the flower stalks just above ground level right after they fade.

Delphiniums do best in cool-summer areas, often failing to grow more than one season in the warmest parts of the Gulf States. They thrive along the Pacific Coast, including the warmest portions, but not in inland, arid locations.

Propagate from seeds sown in spring or midsummer. Spring-sown dwarf varieties often flower the same year. In cold-winter climates, protect young seedlings by mulching after the soil freezes, or by overwintering in a cold frame. Divide established clumps in early spring (in mild-winter climates, in fall).

The 'Pacific Giant' hybrid group, which includes the popular 'Round Table' mix, grows 6 feet tall in a full range of colors. 'Magic Fountains' and 'Fantasia' mixes reach 2½ to 3 feet. *D. x belladonna* varieties grow 3 to 4 feet tall.

DIANTHUS

Also called pink
Dianthus species
- **Zone:** 4
- **Height:** 6 to 15 inches
- **Bloom time:** Spring and early summer
- **Comments:** The dianthus, or pink, genus includes several popular perennials grown for their pink, white, or red flowers borne above mats or clumps of grayish blue, grassy leaves. Most are fragrant; some blend two colors.

Plant in full sun, in well-drained soil amended with organic matter. Most species don't tolerate hot, arid conditions. Some species are not winter hardy in all areas and must have special attention. Begin in the late fall by shearing off one-third of the top growth of mat-forming types. After the soil freezes, apply a loose mulch such as evergreen branches. Because most pinks rot easily, avoid a mulch that packs tightly.

Rejuvenate clumps about every third year by division, replanting only the vigorous outer growth. Or root recently formed, stocky stem cuttings in early summer.

D. x allwoodi, the Allwood pink, grows up to 15 inches tall and has extremely fragrant flowers of white, pink, red, or a combination. 'Alpinus' grows only about 6 inches tall and is a good addition to rock gardens and dry walls.

The maiden pink, *D. deltoides,* produces a low, dense mound of foliage. Fragrant flowers are mostly red or pink and are carried on stalks 8 to 12 inches tall.

D. gratianopolitanus is the cheddar pink. It grows only 6 to 8 inches tall and is topped with single, pink flowers. 'Tiny Rubies' is double flowering.

D. plumarius is called cottage pink or grass pink. It produces low mounds of blue-gray foliage and flowers of white, pink, purplish rose, and red on stems 12 to 15 inches tall. Flowers may be single or double, and are fragrant.

DELPHINIUM

DIANTHUS

PERENNIALS PORTFOLIO *(continued)*

FELICIA

FEVERFEW

FLAX

FELICIA

Also called blue marguerite
Felicia amelloides

- **Zone:** 9
- **Height:** 1 to 2 feet
- **Bloom time:** Early summer to frost
- **Comments:** Felicia is grown mainly for its long-season production of blue-petaled, yellow-centered, daisylike flowers. The foliage mound reaches a height of about 1½ feet, with flowers borne well above on thin, strong stems, making them suitable as cut flowers. Use in the middle of a perennial garden, in front of a gray or other light-colored background, and in containers.

If you remove faded blooms, flower production is nearly continuous from late spring until frost and almost year-round in mild-winter areas. Cut plants back to a height of 6 to 8 inches after each bloom cycle to force new growth.

Plant in full sun and moist soil for best growth. Too much shade or dryness reduces the number of flowers.

Propagate by taking slightly firm stem cuttings in late spring or summer. Seeds are sometimes available and plants occasionally self-sow.

Treat as a summer annual in all but zones 9 and 10. A few varieties are available, varying mostly in flower size and intensity of flower color. *F. amelloides 'variegata'* has leaves marked with white.

FEVERFEW

Chrysanthemum parthenium

- **Zone:** 4
- **Height:** To 2½ feet
- **Bloom time:** Summer
- **Comments:** Often listed as matricaria in garden catalogs, feverfew produces masses of inch-wide flowers all summer long. Typical flowers on this old-fashioned perennial are single and daisylike, with white petals and a yellow center. 'Golden Ball' has all-yellow, buttonlike flowers, and 'White Star' produces all-white flowers. To keep plants blooming and to prevent reseeding, cut off flowers as they fade.

Feverfew is useful for filling voids in the summer garden, and combines well with most brightly colored flowers. Both its foliage and flowers are scented. Plant in full sun, in nearly any soil. Propagate by division in early spring every three or four years, by stem cuttings taken in midsummer, or by seed.

FLAX

Linum species

- **Zone:** 5
- **Height:** 1 to 1½ feet
- **Bloom time:** Summer
- **Comments:** Both the blue and bright yellow varieties produce delicate, saucer-shaped flowers on wiry stems. Flax is ideal for the front of a perennial garden, or for use in rock gardens.

Plant in full sun and well-drained fertile soil. Propagate by taking nonflowering stem cuttings in midsummer, or by sowing seeds in early spring. Division usually is unproductive because most plants produce few crowns.

The blue species, *L. perenne,* is especially useful because of its soft, sky blue flowers and fine, graceful habit. Golden flax, *L. flavum,* produces golden yellow flowers in early summer on plants up to 15 inches tall. 'Compactum' reaches only 6 inches.

GAILLARDIA

Also called blanket flower
Gaillardia x grandiflora

- **Zone:** 4
- **Height:** 1 to 3 feet
- **Bloom time:** Summer to early fall
- **Comments:** Grown primarily for its attractive two-toned flowers in shades of gold, red, and brown, gaillardia adds lots of warm color to the middle of a garden. Flowers are perfect for cutting, blooming all summer and into early fall.

Plant in full sun, in well-drained soil. Blanket flower does well in adverse conditions and in average soil. As flower stalks emerge, give taller varieties support. Remove faded blooms to keep plants vigorous and productive. Propagate by division in spring (in warm-winter areas, also in fall). Or sow seeds in spring or midsummer.

The center of the plant may rot over winter in poorly drained soil. If this happens, dig and replant vigorous plantlets from the outside in early spring.

Several color selections are available. 'Goblin' grows only about 1 foot tall, producing flowers with predominantly orange-red petals tipped with yellow.

GAS PLANT

Dictamnus albus
- **Zone:** 3
- **Height:** 2 to 3 feet
- **Bloom time:** Summer
- **Comments:** Gas plant, an old-fashioned favorite, blooms faithfully every year with no special care. Because plants grow up to 3 feet tall with an equal spread, use in the middle to rear of the garden.

Gas plant gets its common name from the fact that on a hot evening, when the air is still, you can produce a small burst of flame by holding a lighted match near an open bloom.

Plant in full sun or light shade, in well-drained soil enriched with organic matter. If soil preparation is adequate, plants will last several years without requiring replacement. Propagate from seeds, but expect to wait two or three years for the first flowers to form.

The flowers of *D. albus* are white; those of 'Rubrus,' purplish red; and those of 'Purpureus,' purplish pink.

GENTIAN

Gentiana species
- **Zone:** 4
- **Height:** 4 inches to 1½ feet
- **Bloom time:** Late summer to early fall
- **Comments:** Gentians descend from mountain wildflowers, and, characteristic of many alpine plants, prefer cool, moist, but well-drained locations. Many are low growing, making them perfect for use in rock gardens, in the front of

cool, shaded perennial gardens, or blended with other shade-tolerant plants in woodland gardens. Gentians are hard to grow in hot or arid regions.

Most gentians are started from seed, although they germinate and grow with some difficulty. They also are slow to bloom. Purchasing started plants from a nursery is the easiest way to acquire plants.

Gentians are known for their intense blue flowers. Of the commonly planted species, *G. andrewsi,* bottle gentian, and *G. asclepiadea,* willow gentian, grow about 2 feet high. The soapwort gentian, *G. saponaria,* grows 1½ feet high.

GERANIUM

Also called cranesbill geranium
Geranium species
- **Zone:** 4
- **Height:** 6 inches to 1½ feet
- **Bloom time:** Spring and summer
- **Comments:** Often confused with the genus pelargonium (also commonly called geranium), cranesbill geranium is a hardy perennial that forms low mounds of color in late spring and summer. Where summers are mild, some species flower all season long. Flowers are pink, magenta, and purple, with deeply cut, attractive foliage. All are used as edging plants; some are used in rock and wall gardens.

Cranesbill geraniums require no special care. They flower well in full sun or partial shade, and do well in poor soil. In fact, a soil too fertile causes spindly growth and sparse flowering. Established clumps need dividing every fourth or fifth year in early spring. (In mild-winter areas, you can divide them in fall.)

Popular *G. himalayense* produces pale lilac flowers on plants up to 15 inches high and blooms all summer. *G. sanguineum* is perhaps the most widely adapted cranesbill. It produces a flood of reddish purple flowers all summer (in mild climates, into fall). *G. cinereum* and *G. dalmaticum* are reliable dwarf species.

GAS PLANT

GERANIUM

157

PERENNIALS PORTFOLIO *(continued)*

GEUM

HELIANTHUS

GEUM

Also called avens
Geum species
- **Zone:** 6
- **Height:** To 2 feet
- **Bloom time:** Summer
- **Comments:** Geums produce ruffled flowers in brilliant yellows, reds, and oranges, as well as white. Blooms are single or double on erect stems above mounds of attractive, lobed foliage. Use as a cut flower or as a reliable addition to a perennial garden.

Plant in full sun (in areas with very hot summers, plant in partial shade), and in well-drained soil amended with organic matter. Mulch during the heat of summer to keep the shallow roots cool and moist. In areas with very cold winters, add more mulch after the ground freezes to provide protection. Increase by division of clumps every three or four years.

'Lady Strathedon,' a popular variety of *G. quellyon,* produces yellow, double flowers on 2-foot stems. 'Mrs. Bradshaw' has intense scarlet, semidouble flowers, also on 2-foot stems. Both bloom in June and July, and usually rebloom in fall in areas with a long growing season.

G. reptans grows 6 to 8 inches tall and produces yellow or orange flowers. It spreads by runners and makes a good rock garden subject.

GLOBE THISTLE

Echinops ritro
- **Zone:** 4
- **Height:** 4 feet
- **Bloom time:** Summer
- **Comments:** Globe thistle is an attractive, reliable, and unusual back-of-the-garden plant. Metallic blue, spherical flowers are carried on strong stems above a mound of silvery, woolly leaves. The flowers attract bees, and are good for cutting and drying. Because plants have a coarse texture and make a strong color accent in the garden, place them carefully.

Plant in full sun and well-drained soil. Plants are fairly drought tolerant, and soil of average fertility is suitable. Give plants plenty of space, and provide support in windy locations.

Divide globe thistle when the center of the clump begins to open. In warm-winter areas, the clump may require dividing every two years; in cold-winter areas, less often.

'Taplow Blue' produces deep blue flowers and makes a perfect companion for yellow summer flowers.

HELENIUM

Also called false sunflower or sneezeweed
Helenium autumnale
- **Zone:** 3
- **Height:** 4 to 5 feet
- **Bloom time:** Late summer into fall
- **Comments:** Helenium is valued in the perennial garden for its late-season flower color when few other perennials bloom. The daisylike flowers are good for cutting, and come in warm tones of orange, mahogany, and deep yellow.

Use in the back of a flower garden, in naturalized areas, or alone as a small hedge. Taller varieties get rangy and require support. Pinch off shoot tips in late spring and early summer to encourage more flowers. Plant in full sun, in moist but not rich soil. Propagate every three or four years by dividing in spring. Control plant spread by cutting off and removing new plants that form around the edge of the plant's clump.

H. autumnale 'Brilliant' grows only about 3 feet tall. 'Butterpat' produces deep golden yellow flowers, also on 3-foot plants. 'Moorheim Beauty' features dazzling bronze-red flowers on 4-foot plants.

HELIANTHUS

Also called perennial sunflower
Helianthus species
- **Zone:** 4
- **Height:** To 6 feet
- **Bloom time:** Late summer into fall
- **Comments:** Because of its height, helianthus is a perfect choice for the back of a garden or the center of a large island bed. It provides masses

of color, usually deep yellow, from late summer to the end of fall. Flowers may be single and daisylike, or double and frilly.

Plant in full sun; otherwise, they develop weak, floppy stems with few flowers. Soil should be well drained. Propagate by dividing in the spring every three or four years.

H. angustifolius, the swamp sunflower, grows to 6 feet tall. Flowers are single daisy types, generally with dark, purplish brown centers surrounded by yellow petals. Swamp sunflower does best where the soil is kept moist, but will tolerate some drought.

Hybrid perennial sunflowers, *H. x multiflorus,* begin flowering in midsummer, and produce flowers up to 5 inches across on plants from 3 to 6 feet tall. The hybrid perennial sunflower is less drought tolerant than the swamp sunflower. Popular 'Flore Pleno' grows 4 feet tall with masses of double, shaggy-petaled yellow flowers. 'Morning Sun' produces double, golden yellow flowers on 5- to 6-foot plants.

HELIOPSIS

Also called oxeye
Heliopsis helianthoides

- **Zone:** 3
- **Height:** To 5 feet
- **Bloom time:** Summer
- **Comments:** The overall garden effect of heliopsis is similar to that of helianthus, but plants of oxeye are usually stouter, begin flowering earlier in the summer, and tolerate poor, dry soil and partial shade better. Several varieties are available, most producing either semidouble or full-double flowers in the yellow to orange-yellow range. All are good as cut flowers.

Propagate by sowing seeds in early to midsummer, or by division. In mild-winter areas, divide clumps in spring or fall; in cold-winter areas, divide in spring.

Most oxeyes are horticultural selections of *H. helianthoides 'scabra.'* Popular types include 'Golden Plume,' with double flowers on 3-foot

plants; 'Incomparabilis,' which produces bushy plants with semidouble, golden flowers; and 'Summer Sun' with orange-yellow flowers on 3-foot plants.

HELLEBORUS

Also called Christmas rose
Helleborus niger
Also called Lenten rose
H. orientalis

- **Zone:** 4
- **Height:** 1 to 1½ feet
- **Bloom time:** Late fall to spring
- **Comments:** Christmas and Lenten roses are unusual because their blooming season extends from late fall to spring, providing flowers at a time when most other plants are dormant. Depending on locality, Christmas rose can flower any time from November to spring, producing pinkish green or white flowers on 12-inch stalks. Lenten rose usually blooms later in a wider range of colors, including cream, green, purple, and pink. Flowers of both are cup shaped and borne on stalks up to 1½ feet tall.

Both plants thrive in a partially shaded location with rich, moist, but well-drained soil. Use helleborus in a shaded portion of a perennial garden, in front of a shrub border, or naturalized in a woodland garden. Its attractive evergreen foliage combines well with most early-flowering bulbs.

In areas where autumn is long, cool, and damp, flowering may begin in the fall. Be sure to protect the plants if you live in an area that has cold winters but no snow cover. An unused storm window provides good protection when used as a cold frame.

Propagate by dividing established clumps as soon as possible in the spring after flowering. Handle the brittle roots carefully to avoid losses. Neither type requires frequent division. You can start the plants from seeds, but production of flowering-size plants is slow. The Lenten rose often reseeds naturally. Seedlings can be dug up in spring and moved if done carefully.

HELIOPSIS

HELLEBORUS

PERENNIALS PORTFOLIO *(continued)*

HOSTA

IRIS

HOSTA

Also called plantain lily or funkia
Hosta species
■ **Zone:** 4
■ **Height:** To 3 feet
■ **Bloom time:** Summer to early fall
■ **Comments:** Hostas are among the most useful and decorative perennials for areas of shade to partial shade. They range from 4-inch miniatures to 3-foot giants, and have both attractive foliage and showy flowers.

Foliage is available in an array of colors and patterns from solid deep green to blue-gray or yellow-gold; some have colorful stripes of white or other contrasting colors. Leaf textures vary from smooth and shiny to heavily quilted to soft and lustrous. Leaf shapes also vary: long and narrow, wide and blunt, or almost round.

Showy spikes of trumpet-shaped, often fragrant flowers rise above the foliage mound in summer or early fall. Colors include white, lavender, and pale violet.

Use hostas as a ground cover under trees; in perennial beds; as edgings for paths, walks, and drives; in woodland shade gardens; or in separate beds of several varieties planted to display a pleasing contrast of size, leaf shape, and hue.

Plant in partial to deep shade, in soil that is rich, moist, and well drained. Hostas survive hot, dry spells, and will perform adequately in poor soils as long as drainage is good. If watered well, many will survive in full sun, although the sun may bleach the foliage color, especially of variegated forms.

Propagate by division from spring to early summer (in mild-winter areas, you also can divide in fall just after flowering). Hundreds of hosta varieties exist, including several recent introductions with hefty price tags. Plenty of less expensive, more common varieties, though, are quite capable of giving a full range of colors, sizes, and textures. Hostas are a good investment because they are nearly foolproof and last a lifetime if properly located.

ICELAND POPPY

Papaver nudicaule
■ **Zone:** 5
■ **Height:** 12 to 15 inches
■ **Bloom time:** Spring; in mild areas, also in winter
■ **Comments:** Few plants rival Iceland poppies for their show of crepe-paperlike flowers up to 4 inches across in a wide array of colors. Most are sold as a color mix and include warm tones such as gold and red, along with lighter colors such as cream and yellow. Flowers emerge from puffy, drooping buds, and are carried atop strong, wiry stalks.

Iceland poppies are short-lived perennials and need replanting every few years. They originated in arctic areas but survive and perform best as perennials where winters are mild and summers are fairly cool and moist. In areas of severe winters or hot summers, and in all arid locations, handle them as a cool-season annual.

Start plants using seeds sown in late summer. Provide winter protection, such as a cold frame, in harsh-winter areas. Overwintered plants begin flowering in early spring, and make perfect companions for spring-flowering bulbs. Where winter temperatures are mild, Iceland poppies flower all winter and spring.

IRIS

Iris species
■ **Zone:** 4 (most species)
■ **Height:** 6 to 50 inches
■ **Bloom time:** Spring to early summer
■ **Comments:** Whether you're planting a new perennial garden or just brightening up an old one, you certainly should consider giving top billing to the plants of the iris group. These easy-to-grow plants are available in at least six major classifications: tall bearded, dwarf bearded, Dutch, Japanese, Siberian, and spuria. All come in an array of colors, sizes, and varieties.

Tall bearded iris (sometimes listed as German iris) come from an old-fashioned and widely planted group, and provide some of the most magnificent plants in the perennial garden. They usually grow from 2 to 3 feet tall. If given some winter protection, they are hardy to Zone 3. Plant in full sun, in moist, well-drained soil.

Dwarf bearded iris grow from 8 to 16 inches tall. They are available in fewer colors than their tall counterparts, but their flowers often are sweetly scented.

Both types of bearded iris grow from thick fleshy stems called rhizomes. Plant the rhizomes in late summer by placing them horizontally with the fan of foliage above the soil. The rhizome's top surface should be at or just below the soil surface. Avoid deep planting. Lift clumps, divide, and replant every four or five years. Rhizomes dislike too much moisture, so be sure the bed drains well.

Dutch iris grow from bulbs and are available in white, yellow, blue, violet, and bicolors. They are hardy to Zone 5. In mild-winter areas, many begin flowering in December and continue into spring. Plant the bulbs 3 inches deep, 4 inches apart.

Japanese iris are sold either as *I. ensata* or *I. kaempferi.* They flower in midsummer on sturdy stalks up to 4 feet high. Colors include white, pink, violet, purple, and blue, many with yellow markings. Like bearded iris, Japanese iris grow from rhizomes. Japanese iris need constantly moist conditions and slightly acid soil.

Siberian iris produce white, blue, lavender, or purple flowers. Flower stems grow from 2 to 4 feet tall out of clumps of fibrous roots and have slender, grassy foliage. Siberian iris require conditions similar to Japanese iris.

Spuria iris often grow up to 5 feet tall, blooming about the time the tall bearded iris begin to fade. Plant in a sunny, well-drained location, rich in organic matter. Divide whenever the plants become too crowded, about every three to five years.

JACOB'S-LADDER

Polemonium caeruleum

- **Zone:** 4
- **Height:** 2 to 2½ feet
- **Bloom time:** Spring to early summer
- **Comments:** Jacob's-ladder is superb for supplying deep blue color to shady portions of a perennial garden during late spring and early summer. Flower stalks rise above a ferny foliage mound, producing nodding flowers of deep blue to purple. Jacob's-ladder is effective with narcissus and late-flowering yellow tulips. It combines well, too, with shade plants, making it a good addition to woodland gardens.

Plant in partial shade, in moist but well-drained soil. Before planting, add a generous amount of organic matter to the soil. To propagate, sow seeds in summer or divide established clumps in late summer, after flowering.

P. caeruleum is available in a white-flowered form, too. A relative, *P. reptans,* grows only 12 inches tall and has pale violet flowers.

JUPITER'S-BEARD

Centranthus ruber

- **Zone:** 4
- **Height:** 3 feet
- **Bloom time:** Spring to early summer
- **Comments:** Perfect for the middle or back of a perennial garden, jupiter's-beard has masses of white, pink, crimson, or red flowers. Blooms are sweet scented and long lasting, so do well in cut arrangements. In mild-winter areas, flowering begins in early spring; otherwise, expect flowers from late spring to early summer.

No matter whether planted in sun or partial shade or what the soil type, jupiter's-beard will take off and rarely need attention, making it perfect for out-of-the-way or neglected areas.

Start new plants by dividing established clumps in early spring or just after flowering. You also can dig young seedlings from around mother plants, but expect some color variation. Jupiter's-beard self-sows, and may need controlling to keep it from taking over the garden.

JACOB'S-LADDER

JUPITER'S-BEARD

PERENNIALS PORTFOLIO *(continued)*

LAVENDER

LEADWORT

LIRIOPE

LAVENDER

Lavandula angustifolia
- **Zone:** 6
- **Height:** 1 to 2½ feet
- **Bloom time:** Mid- to late summer
- **Comments:** Lavender, an herb-garden favorite, also is at home in a sunny perennial bed where you can feature both its gray-green, woolly leaves and its spikes of fragrant, blue-violet flowers. Use it in the middle to front of the perennial garden, or in rock gardens and herb plantings. It also makes an unusual low hedge, and attracts bees.

Plant in full sun, in well-drained soil enriched with organic matter. Lavender does best in moist soil, but survives drought fairly well. Because lavender tolerates reflected light and heat from paving, it makes a good edging along walks. In cold-winter areas, mulch well after the soil freezes. Prune off half of the top growth just before growth begins in spring.

'Hidcote' produces rich purple flowers on compact plants. 'Munstead Dwarf' grows only about 12 inches tall, producing lavender flowers nearly all summer.

LEADWORT

Also called plumbago
Ceratostigma plumbaginoides
- **Zone:** 5
- **Height:** 12 inches
- **Bloom time:** Midsummer to fall
- **Comments:** Leadwort's glossy foliage and deep blue, phloxlike flowers make it an asset in any garden. As an added feature, the foliage turns reddish purple in the fall. Because it grows only about 12 inches tall, leadwort is perfect in the front of a perennial garden or shrub border, in a rock garden, or as a ground cover.

Plant in full sun or partial shade, in nearly any soil as long as it is well drained. To start new plants, divide established clumps or take firm, stocky stem cuttings in midsummer.

Leadwort is marginal for winterhardiness in the northern portions of Zone 5, especially in exposed spots. Protect by applying several inches of loose mulch after the soil freezes. Because leadwort is slow to emerge in spring, be careful not to cut into plants during early cultivation.

LIATRIS

Also called gay-feather
Liatris spicata
- **Zone:** 4
- **Height:** 2 to 6 feet
- **Bloom time:** Summer to fall
- **Comments:** Although often overlooked and underrated, liatris, with its spires of colorful flowers, adds a distinct vertical accent to almost any perennial garden. Plants bear white, rose, or purple flowers on tall, spiky stems. Flowers are ideal for cutting, and dry well for use in winter bouquets. An interesting feature of the plant is that its flowers open from the top down, instead of from the bottom up, as with many other plants.

Gay-feather thrives in sun or partial sun. Most any well-drained soils will do, although light, almost sandy soil is best. Avoid planting where water stands, especially during winter.

To increase plants, divide established clumps in spring (in mild-winter areas, divide in fall, too). Divide established clumps every three or four years to keep them vigorous. Liatris also can be started from seeds sown in spring to produce blooming plants the following year.

Liatris is especially effective planted in groups or clumps. Use the taller types in the back of the garden. Dark-purple-flowered 'Kobold' grows only 1½ to 2 feet tall and is nice near the front of a garden. 'White Spires' grows 3 feet tall.

LIRIOPE

Also called lilyturf
Liriope muscari
- **Zone:** 6
- **Height:** 12 to 20 inches
- **Bloom time:** Midsummer to fall
- **Comments:** Lilyturf forms attractive mounds of gracefully arching leaves, then sends

up tightly clustered, stout flower spikes beginning in midsummer. Flowers usually are lilac purple, sometimes white; a variegated foliage form is available.

Use alone or in groups near the front of a perennial garden, as an edging along walks, and as a ground cover beneath shrubs and trees. Plant in partial shade, in moist, fertile, well-drained soil. Forms with white flowers or variegated foliage need fairly deep shade. All tolerate more sun in cool regions. Winter weather may damage foliage in Zone 6, but shearing off ragged tops in early spring won't hurt the plants, which will regrow from the roots. Propagate by dividing established clumps in early spring.

Foliage of 'Variegata' has creamy yellow stripes and violet flowers. 'Monroe's White' produces white flowers.

LOBELIA

Also called cardinal flower
Lobelia cardinalis
■ **Zone:** 2
■ **Height:** 2 to 3 feet
■ **Bloom time:** Summer to fall
■ **Comments:** Cardinal flower is excellent for a cool, shady, moist location such as a woodland garden, a moist meadow area, a bog garden, or along a stream. Where summers are cool, lobelia tolerates nearly full sun. The bright red flowers are borne on spires above the foliage.

Plants reseed freely. Or propagate by digging and replanting offsets that develop around established clumps. Digging offsets helps confine plants, and encourages productive new growth.

LOOSESTRIFE

Lythrum salicaria
■ **Zone:** 4
■ **Height:** To 4 feet
■ **Bloom time:** Summer
■ **Comments:** Loosestrife is a good choice for moist, mid- to back-of-the-border locations in full sun or light shade. It produces slender spires

of pink, purple, or rosy red flowers from June to September. Remove faded flowers to keep plants tidy and encourage longer blooming. Propagate by division every three or four years. Divide in the spring in cold-winter areas; elsewhere, in spring or fall. Root slightly firm, stocky stem cuttings in early summer.

One of the most popular varieties is 'Morden's Pink,' which grows 3 to 4 feet tall and produces rich pink flowers. 'Robert' features rosy pink flowers on plants 2 feet high; its foliage develops a purplish red color in the fall. The shortest variety, 'Happy,' grows only about 1½ feet tall with deep pink flowers. None of these varieties reseeds freely, and none becomes aggressive or weedy.

LUPINE

Lupinus species
■ **Zone:** 4
■ **Height:** 3 to 4 feet
■ **Bloom time:** Spring through summer, if cool
■ **Comments:** Although native varieties of lupine are numerous, the only strain lending itself to use in most garden situations is the group called Russell hybrids. Plants grow 3 to 4 feet tall and produce spectacularly large spikes of flowers in cream, yellow, pink, purple, red, blue, and bicolors. Foliage is deeply cut and attractive. Because of their tall, stately manner, lupines are best planted in masses in back-of-the-border locations. Support may be necessary in windy locations

Start lupines from seed sown in midsummer. In areas with a long growing season, lupines usually flower the following year; otherwise, two years may be required before flowering. Plants develop deep taproots, making them difficult to transplant.

Lupines grow best when the weather is cool, making them well suited to the Pacific Coast and to most high-elevation gardens. Intense heat and unsuitable soil types limit their summertime performance in other areas.

LOBELIA

LUPINE

PERENNIALS PORTFOLIO (continued)

LYCHNIS

ORIENTAL POPPY

LYCHNIS

Also called catchfly or Maltese-cross
Lychnis species

- ■ **Zone:** 4
- ■ **Height:** 1 to 3 feet
- ■ **Bloom time:** May through July
- ■ **Comments:** Lychnis is a reliable and easy-to-grow source of summertime flowers in white, pink, purple, or red. All the commonly available species do well in full sun and well-drained soil. Propagate by sowing seeds in midsummer, or by dividing established clumps in spring.

L. x arkwrighti grows about 15 inches tall with brilliant red flowers. The Maltese-cross, *L. chalcedonica,* grows taller, up to 3 feet, also with bright red flowers. Varieties are available in white, pink, and salmon, too. Both these species do better in rich, moist soil, and tolerate light shade.

L. coronaria is a real standout because of its bright red-pink flowers on 30-inch stems atop gray, woolly foliage. Also called mullein pink, *L. coronaria* is most easily propagated from seed, and usually flowers the year after sowing.

German catchfly, or *L. viscaria,* grows 12 to 15 inches tall and produces flowers of brilliant purplish red or purplish pink. Flowers of the variety 'Zulu' are nearly pure red, and a white form also is available. Portions of the stalk below the catchfly flower are sticky, hence the plant's common name. Both of the latter species, *L. coronaria* and *L. viscaria,* perform better and last longer when planted in full sun and light, sandy soil.

OENOTHERA

Also called evening primrose or sundrops
Oenothera species

- ■ **Zone:** 4
- ■ **Height:** 1 to 1½ feet
- ■ **Bloom time:** Summer
- ■ **Comments:** Few plants are more suited to the rock garden or a location in the front of a perennial garden than oenothera. It thrives in full sun and light, sandy soil, producing masses of open, cup-shaped flowers of yellow, pink, or white. Propagate by sowing in midsummer, or by dividing established clumps.

O. missourensis is known as Ozark sundrops or Missouri primrose. It grows only about 12 inches tall and has a trailing or slightly sprawling habit. Foliage is gray-green, and the bright yellow flowers often open to 5 inches across.

The showy primrose, *O. speciosa,* produces smaller flowers of about 2 inches across, either white or pink. Plants grow 1 to 1½ feet tall, and spread aggressively by slender underground rhizomes. Plant *O. speciosa* only where it won't crowd nearby plants. Showy primrose is sometimes sold as *O. berlandieri,* a related species with similar growth habits and requirements.

O. tetragona, the common sundrop, is a somewhat variable species, but usually grows 1½ to 2 feet tall. Flowers are lemon yellow. This species, sometimes sold as *O. tetragona 'youngi,'* may perform as a biennial in some locations.

ORIENTAL POPPY

Papaver orientale

- ■ **Zone:** 3
- ■ **Height:** 2 to 4 feet
- ■ **Bloom time:** Late spring to early summer
- ■ **Comments:** Oriental poppies supply breathtaking, flamboyant color to springtime and early-summer gardens. Colors include white, pink, orange, and various shades of red, each with a dark contrasting center. Flowers open from large, nodding buds atop stems carried well above the gray-green, dissected foliage. Blooms may grow as large as 6 inches across.

Most varieties grow from 3 to 4 feet tall and require support. A few dwarf varieties are available, reaching no more than 2 feet high. Use Oriental poppies in the middle to back of a garden, in wildflower gardens, or in naturalized areas. After flowering, plant tops die, but new growth emerges by early fall. Try to surround Oriental poppies with plants that will fill the void during the summer dormant period. In areas with a long growing season, they may bloom again in fall.

Flowers are spectacular in arrangements, but need special treatment. Just as the bud begins to open and show the petals, harvest by making a clean cut on the stem with shears or a sharp knife. Immediately sear the stem cut in an open flame, then plunge the stem into cool water.

Grow in full sun, in nearly any rich, well-drained soil. Poor drainage often causes crown rot, especially during winter.

Oriental poppies grow best undisturbed, but to increase plant numbers, divide them or take root cuttings in August or early September, just as plants emerge from their summer dormancy. This gives young plants enough time to establish before winter, ready to flower the following spring. Plant container-grown plants, sometimes available from nurseries, in spring.

During the growing season, apply a mulch around the roots to keep soil temperature cool and to reduce moisture loss. In cold-winter areas, pull mulch up around the crown after the soil freezes.

PAINTED DAISY

Also called pyrethrum
Chrysanthemum coccineum

■ **Zone:** 4
■ **Height:** 1½ to 2 feet
■ **Bloom time:** Summer
■ **Comments:** Painted daisies are somewhat unusual members of the chrysanthemum genus because they flower early in the season rather than in the fall. Beginning in early summer, expect masses of white, pink, or red flowers, either single or double, on graceful stems rising from mounds of ferny foliage. Painted daisies are excellent cut flowers, and are perfect for use in the middle of a garden. Most require support to prevent flower stalks from falling over. Cut plants nearly to the ground after flowering to encourage a second bloom.

Plant in full sun, in rich, moist, well-drained soil. Any amount of shade leads to weak, floppy stems. During periods of drought, water paint-

ed daisies and maintain a mulch over the roots to conserve moisture. Increase plants by sowing seeds in midsummer for flowering the following year. Established clumps can be divided in spring in cold-winter areas (in spring or fall in mild-winter areas).

PENSTEMON

Also called beard-tongue
Penstemon species

■ **Zone:** 3 to 5 depending on the species
■ **Height:** 1 to 3 feet
■ **Bloom time:** Late spring through fall
■ **Comments:** Penstemon is known for its spikes of attractive flowers, some in soft pastels of pink, blue, lavender, or white, others in hot reds or scarlets. The foliage usually is glossy dark green. Most penstemons begin flowering in late spring and continue through summer. If cut back after flowering, they usually rebloom, sometimes into early winter in mild areas.

Plant in full sun or partial shade, in moist, well-drained soil. Soil does not have to be rich or heavily fertilized for satisfactory growth. Propagate from seeds sown in midsummer. Division of established clumps works, but is sometimes difficult because the clumps may be woody. Stem cuttings root easily and quickly. Take stocky, leafy stem portions from a few inches below the tip anytime from mid- to late summer.

P. barbatus is the hardiest of the commonly available beard-tongues, handling winters in Zone 3. Several varieties are available, providing a choice of heights and flower colors.

P. x gloxinioides is hardy only into mild portions of Zone 8. Most varieties grow 2 to 3 feet tall. 'Firebird' produces bright red flowers; 'Midnight' has deep purple flowers.

Most forms of *P. heterophyllus* grow only 15 to 18 inches tall. One variety, 'Blue Bedder,' has blue flowers, but other colors of this species are available, including white and pink.

PAINTED DAISY

PENSTEMON

PERENNIALS PORTFOLIO *(continued)*

PEONY

PHLOX

PEONY

Paeonia species
- **Zone:** 3
- **Height:** 2 to 4 feet
- **Bloom time:** Late spring to early summer
- **Comments:** Peonies are legendary for their colorfully showy flowers, their reliability, and easy care. The flowers are mostly white, pink, maroon, or red, and are favorites for cutting. They may be single, semidouble, double, or one of a few other special forms. Although tree peonies exist (actually shrubs usually bare-stemmed at the base), the common peony is the herbaceous type that dies to ground each winter, then produces springtime growth as tall as 4 feet. Install stakes or peony ring supports early to avoid damage from wind and driving rains.

Most are hybrids sold by variety name; some are sold just by color. No single variety flowers for more than about 10 days, but you can extend the season by selecting early, midseason, and late bloomers. Flowering season begins about the time tulips open and ends about two months later.

Use peonies in mixed perennial gardens, in front of hedges and evergreen plantings, in large drifts in lawn areas, bordering walks and driveways, along fences or walls, and as single specimens. Peonies produce beautiful flowers for cutting.

Plant peonies in full sun or light shade; heavy shade produces weak stems and few flowers. Peonies require moist, enriched, well-drained soil. Mulching is helpful in summer and winter.

Propagate by division, usually only once every six to 10 years. Some plants may produce well for up to 20 years before requiring division and replanting. Early September is the best time for division in Zone 6 and colder zones; October elsewhere. Before dividing, cut stems back to a height of 4 inches. Carefully lift the entire clump after loosening the soil all around. Shake the soil off the roots or wash it off with a jet of water, avoiding injury to the fragile pink buds, or eyes. Cut away any damaged roots and separate into sections, each with five to eight buds, if possible. Keep divisions moist and out of direct sunlight. Replant eyes 1 to 2 inches below ground level. Deeper planting may result in fewer blooms. Shallower planting risks winterkill. Be careful not to damage the eyes as you backfill with soil. Water thoroughly.

PHLOX

Phlox species
- **Zone:** 3
- **Height:** To 4 feet
- **Bloom time:** Spring, summer, or early fall
- **Comments:** Phlox is one of the most versatile and colorful groups of flowering perennials, ranging from the low, spreading moss phlox to the familiar tall garden phlox. Flower colors include many soft pastels (pink, blue, or lavender) and white, as well as darker tones of red and orange. Many have a contrasting center.

Plant in full sun or partial shade, and, except where noted below, in moist, humus-enriched soil. Garden phlox is especially susceptible to powdery mildew fungus and needs a location with good air circulation. Add a thick mulch during summer to keep its roots cool.

Propagate by sowing seeds in midsummer, by dividing established clumps just after flowering, or by taking firm, leafy stem cuttings in summer.

Wild sweet william, *P. divaricata,* is a creeper, growing 12 to 15 inches tall with lavender-blue flowers in the spring. It is ideal for rock gardens, at the front of perennial gardens, or for naturalizing in woodland areas. A white-flowered variety is available.

P. paniculata (or *P. decussata*) is known as garden phlox or border phlox. It grows 3 to 4 feet tall, producing large trusses of fragrant flowers from summer to early fall. Use it at the back of perennial gardens. Many varieties are available, mostly in pastels. For other colors, plant salmon-orange 'Orange Perfection,' deep red 'Starfire,' and white 'Mt. Fujiyama.' Remove faded flowers to keep plants tidy and prevent reseeding.

Moss phlox, *P. subulata,* forms a dense, creeping mat, 6 inches high and 2 feet wide. The small leaves are slightly prickly, and the entire plant is covered with flowers in the spring. Colors include white, pink, blue, lavender, and red. Moss phlox performs well in average, well-drained soil not heavily amended with organic matter. It is hardy to Zone 2. Use in rock gardens, as a ground cover, or at the front of perennial gardens.

PHYSOSTEGIA

Also called false dragonhead or obedience
Physostegia virginiana

■ **Zone:** 3
■ **Height:** 2 to 4 feet
■ **Bloom time:** Late summer into fall
■ **Comments:** Obedience is the perfect choice when you need an easy-to-grow plant that produces tall, spikelike flowers in late summer. The square stems are stiff and rarely need support. Use in perennial gardens or let it run free in naturalized meadow gardens. Plants spread aggressively from underground stems, especially in rich, moist soil. Control the spread by lifting and dividing clumps every two or three years. In addition to division, you can propagate plants using seeds or stem cuttings.

Plant in full sun if soil is moist; otherwise, partial shade is better. Keep plants a little dry to make them less invasive.

Plants of the species grow to 4 feet tall and produce rose-pink flowers. 'Vivid' grows only about 2 feet tall with a similar flower color. For white flowers on plants about 2½ feet tall, plant 'Summer Snow.'

Obedience sometimes is listed as *Dracocephalum virginianum.*

POKER PLANT

Also called torch lily or red-hot-poker
Kniphofia species

■ **Zone:** 5
■ **Height:** 3 to 5 feet
■ **Bloom time:** Midsummer through fall
■ **Comments:** Poker plant is known for its tall, impressive flower spikes, often with a vivid blend of scarlet and yellow blooms, but also available as hybrids in separate colors of white, yellow, orange, and scarlet. The clumps of grassy, gray-green leaves grow 3 feet high.

Use singly as a specimen plant or in small groupings in the back of a garden. Flowers attract hummingbirds and are suitable for arrangements. Plant in full sun, but protect from heavy wind. A sandy, well-drained soil is ideal.

In the northern part of Zone 5, provide winter protection by tying the foliage together to shed water. A mulch helps, too. If possible, slope soil away from the plant so moisture doesn't accumulate at the crown.

To propagate, divide established clumps in spring in cold-winter areas; spring or fall in mild-winter areas. You also can replant small rooted plants, known as offsets, that develop around the crown. Cut them away carefully.

Kniphofia often is listed in nursery catalogs and older books as tritoma.

POTENTILLA

Also called cinquefoil
Potentilla species

■ **Zone:** 4
■ **Height:** 3 inches to 2 feet
■ **Bloom time:** June to frost
■ **Comments:** Often thought of as just a low-growing shrub, potentilla also is invaluable as a bright edging plant for walks or flower gardens. Its attractive flowers, much like small rose blossoms, may be white, yellow, orange, or red.

Plant in full sun (in very hot locations, in partial shade). A sandy, well-drained soil is best. Increase by seeds or by dividing in the spring.

P. nepalensis grows 15 to 18 inches tall, and its several varieties produce flowers of yellow, orange, or red. *P. recta,* the sulphur cinquefoil, features yellow flowers on plants 2 feet tall. Low, mat-forming *P. tabernaemontani,* or spring cinquefoil, grows only 3 inches high, producing yellow flowers. A good addition to rock gardens, this species can be invasive.

PHYSOSTEGIA

POKER PLANT

POTENTILLA

PERENNIALS PORTFOLIO *(continued)*

PRIMROSE

PURPLE CONEFLOWER

RUDBECKIA

PRIMROSE

Primula species
- **Zone:** 3 to 5 (depending on variety)
- **Height:** To 15 inches
- **Bloom time:** Early spring
- **Comments:** Primroses are a large group of popular garden plants noted for their flower show, mostly in early spring. In mild-winter areas, they often begin flowering in fall and continue through winter and into spring. Virtually every color but green is available in this genus. Many are bicolored, and some are available with frilled or sculpted petal edges.

Plant in partial shade and moist, rich soil. Some types grow well in boggy locations. Primulas do best where summer and winter temperatures are mild, and where the air is never too dry. Ideal conditions usually exist in high-altitude gardens in the western mountains, and along most of the U.S. Pacific Coast. In other areas, you'll have to develop a garden niche for primroses, even if it's less than ideal. Most will adapt to growing as potted plants.

Propagate by sowing seeds in midsummer. Where winters are extreme, protect young seedlings in a cold frame during the first winter. After clumps establish, you can divide them, preferably just after flowering finishes. Early-autumn division is suitable in mild-winter areas.

One group of primroses, the polyanthus (*P. x polyantha*), is popular because it's widely adaptable and produces large, impressive blooms on 9- to 15-inch stalks. Several varieties are available that produce flowers in all colors, many quite bright and with contrasting centers.

In areas not perfectly suited to primroses, the Japanese star primrose, *P. sieboldi,* is worth a try. It is better suited to dry conditions than most primroses because it becomes leafless and dormant during summer. Flower stalks are about 12 inches tall, and are borne above crinkly leaves. Colors include white, pink, rose, lavender, and purple.

Three species adapted to boggy areas are *P. bulleyana, P. helodoxa,* and *P. japonica.* These are hardy only to Zone 5.

PURPLE CONEFLOWER

Echinacea purpurea
- **Zone:** 3
- **Height:** 3 to 4 feet
- **Bloom time:** Summer
- **Comments:** Purple coneflower is an easy-to-grow, reliable perennial that returns loads of flowers with little care. Strong stems from 3 to 4 feet tall produce daisylike flowers all summer, most with drooping purple petals surrounding a distinct raised central cone. White and pink varieties are available, too. The flowers—up to 6 inches across—attract butterflies and are excellent for cutting.

Use near the middle to back of a flower garden, and in sunny portions of a wildflower garden. Plant in full sun or light shade, in well-drained, sandy-loam soil. Plants are fairly drought tolerant, but respond favorably to watering. Propagate by sowing seeds in summer, or by dividing established clumps. Divide in spring in cold-winter areas; in spring or fall elsewhere. Apply a protective winter mulch in zones 3 and 4 after the soil freezes.

RUDBECKIA

Also called black-eyed susan
Rudbeckia species
- **Zone:** 4
- **Height:** To 3 feet
- **Bloom time:** Summer through fall
- **Comments:** Rudbeckias produce masses of golden yellow, daisylike flowers with contrasting centers from midsummer till frost. Plants are rugged and easy to grow, and provide superb cut flowers. They are ideally suited to the middle portion of a sunny perennial garden, and tolerate nearly any soil type, as long as it is well drained. Soggy soil conditions, especially during winter, cause crown rot. Rudbeckias grow and flower best when watered, but will tolerate drought. Propagate by seeds or division. Where the growing season is short, sow seeds in midsummer for flowering the following year.

Some of the best selections are compact forms; 'Goldsturm,' for example, grows 2 feet tall. The 3-foot-tall 'Gloriosa Daisy' mix extends the color range to include combinations of red, bronze, orange, and yellow.

SALVIA

Also called sage
Salvia species
- ■ **Zone:** 4
- ■ **Height:** 2 to 5 feet
- ■ **Bloom time:** Summer to fall
- ■ **Comments:** Often thought of as only an annual flower, salvia has several perennial species, including the type used as a cooking herb, and types grown for their showy flowers, mostly blue or violet. Perennial salvias do best in full sun or partial afternoon shade, and grow in almost any well-drained soil. Some tolerate drought well.

Propagation is easy by division or from stem cuttings. Seeds of some types are available, and grow easily.

Mealy-cup sage, *S. farinacea,* is one of the most popular species and is readily grown from seeds. It grows 2 to 3 feet tall, with silvery gray leaves and blue, purple, or white flowers. Treat mealy-cup sage as an annual north of Zone 8. *S. officinalis* is the sage used for seasoning. It grows about 2 feet tall and produces gray-green, textured leaves and white or purple flowers. Other foliage colors are available.

The hybrid *S. x superba* has several varieties, including 'May Night' and 'East Friesland.' Both grow about 2 feet tall with dark violet to purple flowers. They are hardy only to Zone 5.

SEDUM

Also called stonecrop
Sedum species
- ■ **Zone:** 3
- ■ **Height:** 4 inches to 2 feet
- ■ **Bloom time:** Spring to late summer
- ■ **Comments:** Commonly used in rock gardens or wall gardens, many sedums also make first-rate ground covers and edging plants in perennial gardens. Most also are perfectly suited to containers. Sedum flowers are small, but are borne in large, showy clusters of red, pink, cream, white, yellow, or rust. Bees and butterflies flock to them.

All sedums are fleshy leaved and quite drought tolerant. Plant them in full sun or partial shade, in well-drained soil.

Propagation is simplest and fastest using divisions or stem or leaf cuttings. Seeds are available for some types. *S. x 'Autumn Joy'* is one of the most popular for garden use. It grows 2 feet tall with gray-green leaves. In late summer, huge flat clusters of pink flowers that will darken in autumn and last into early winter top off the plant. Showy stonecrop, *S. spectabile,* is similar in habit and size to 'Autumn Joy,' but flower colors are rose to deep red.

Two good low-growing choices are *S. kamtschaticum* and *S. spurium.* The first, known as orange stonecrop, grows 6 to 10 inches tall and produces orange-yellow flowers. The latter grows about 4 inches high and has pink or red flowers. 'Dragon's Blood' has crimson flowers all summer; its green leaves turn bronze in fall.

SHASTA DAISY

Chrysanthemum x superbum
Sometimes listed as *C. maximum*

- ■ **Zone:** 4
- ■ **Height:** 1 to 4 feet
- ■ **Bloom time:** Summer
- ■ **Comments:** Shastas are unparalleled for producing a summer-long supply of flowers to enjoy in the garden or in flower arrangements. Single types have a yellow center surrounded by snow-white petals; the doubles are all white and sometimes frilly. All are borne on strong stems.

Plant in full sun or partial shade, in moist, well-drained soil. Propagate by division or by seeds. In cold-winter areas, divide in the spring every two or three years. In mild-winter areas, divide in spring or early fall, and as often as yearly. Many recently introduced varieties come true from seeds.

SALVIA

SEDUM

SHASTA DAISY

PERENNIALS PORTFOLIO *(continued)*

SPURGE

THALICTRUM

SPURGE

Euphorbia species
- **Zone:** 4
- **Height:** 1 to 4 feet
- **Bloom time:** Spring to early summer
- **Comments:** If you want low-maintenance perennials that thrive in hot, dry, sunny locations, give spurges a try. Related to the poinsettia, these plants are showy, not because of their flowers, but because of the colorful leaflike bracts surrounding and below the small flowers. Most of the bracts are white, green, or yellowish green.

Many types are commonly grown in rock gardens and wall gardens, or used in mass as a ground cover. They also make interesting additions to perennial gardens. Spurges are not fussy about soil, as long as it is well drained. Seeding is the normal propagation method, but division works if young plants are handled carefully.

E. characias grows from 3 to 4 feet tall with chartreuse bracts and blue-gray leaves. It is hardy only to Zone 7. The cushion spurge, *E. epithymoides,* forms a low, cushion mound about 12 inches high with showy, bright chartreuse bracts. It is hardy to Zone 4, but does poorly in humid climates. *E. griffithi* 'Fire Glow' has spectacular red-orange bracts atop 30-inch tall plants. It is hardy to Zone 5.

STACHYS

Also called lamb's-ears or betony
Stachys species
- **Zone:** 4
- **Height:** 8 to 18 inches
- **Bloom time:** Summer
- **Comments:** Lamb's-ears, or *S. byzantina* (sometimes sold as *S. olympica*), is grown primarily for its low mounds of soft, gray, woolly leaves. It makes a perfect edging in perennial gardens or alongside dark paving that accents its foliage. Use it in rock gardens and as a gray ground cover, too. Its pinkish purple flowers are insignificant. Remove old leaves; thin out annually to keep plants tidy and productive.

Big betony, or *S. macrantha,* has purple flowers on stalks 1 to 1½ feet tall. Use it in the front of the garden. 'Robusta' has rosy pink flowers.

Grow both species in full sun and well-drained soil. Big betony tolerates some shade. Propagate by dividing established clumps.

THALICTRUM

Also called meadow rue
Thalictrum aquilegifolium
- **Zone:** 3
- **Height:** 3 to 4 feet
- **Bloom time:** Summer
- **Comments:** Meadow rue is known for its delicate, airy flowers and fine, lacy foliage. Flowers usually are lavender, but are available in white, pink, and reddish purple; leaves are gray-green.

Plant in full sun or partial shade, in moist, rich, well-drained soil. Some afternoon shade is best in hot summer areas. Divide plants in spring or sow seeds in spring to early summer.

THRIFT

Also called sea pink or armeria
Armeria maritima
- **Zone:** 3
- **Height:** 6 to 12 inches
- **Bloom time:** Spring to early summer
- **Comments:** Thrift forms low mounds of light green grassy foliage that send up 8- to 12-inch stalks topped with globe-shaped flowers.

Blooms usually are deep pink, but may be white, crimson, or purple. Flower production is heaviest in late spring and early summer (in mild-winter areas, flowering begins again in mid-autumn and continues during winter).

Use thrift as an edging along the front of a perennial garden, between stepping stones, and in rock gardens and wall gardens. Plant in full sun, in well-drained soil. Choose soil with average fertility; rich soils produce loose, open plants that often do not overwinter successfully. Propagate by dividing established clumps in spring or late summer.

A. maritima 'alba' has white flowers on stems only about 6 inches tall; 'Laucheana' produces deep crimson flowers.

VERONICA

Also called speedwell
Veronica species
- **Zone:** 4
- **Height:** 6 inches to 3 feet
- **Bloom time:** June to September
- **Comments:** The veronica genus has several species in a range of sizes, some suitable for use in rock gardens, as ground covers, or as low edgings, and others for use in mid- to back-of-the-garden locations. Most have blue, spikelike flowers, but pink and white forms are available.

Plant veronica in a sunny, well-drained location. Veronica grows well in heat and is fairly drought tolerant. Divide established clumps after flowering but before mid-autumn. Divide every four or five years to keep plants vigorous.

V. grandis 'holophylla' grows 2 to 3 feet tall with blue flowers. *V. latifolia* grows from 1 to 1½ feet tall, but the popular 'Crater Lake Blue' selection is more compact. Spike speedwell, *V. spicata,* grows from 15 to 20 inches high and produces flowers in white, pink, or blue.

YARROW

Achillea species
- **Zone:** 3
- **Height:** 8 inches to 5 feet
- **Bloom time:** June to September
- **Comments:** Yarrow is known for its ferny foliage and showy flat flowers, its ease of growth, and its range of heights. Flowers may be white, yellow, or pink, or shades in between. Heights range from the 8-inch woolly yarrow, a ground cover, to the 5-foot fern-leaf yarrow.

Plant in full sun because even a small amount of shade reduces flowering and makes tall plants floppy. Achillea tolerates rugged conditions, and average soil is suitable as long as it is well drained. Propagate by division in spring or in early fall after flowering.

Fern-leaf yarrow, *A. filipendulina,* is perhaps the most familiar species. It grows 3 to 5 feet tall, with yellow flowers and gray-green fernlike leaves with a spicy fragrance. Even in full sun, it requires support. The several available varieties vary mostly in intensity of flower color.

Common yarrow, *A. millefolium,* has flowers of white, pink, or rose-red. Plants grow about 2 feet tall and are very invasive. Locate where they won't crowd nearby plants.

A. x 'Moonshine' also grows about 2 feet tall, but produces yellow flowers and silvery green leaves. It is an excellent garden plant and is a good source of cut flowers from late spring to early fall.

Woolly yarrow, *A. tomentosa,* grows about 8 inches tall and produces yellow flower heads that are nearly 2 inches across, set against fragrant, gray, woolly leaves. Use as a ground cover, in rock gardens, and as an edging in the front of perennial gardens.

YUCCA

Also called Adam's-needle or soapweed
Yucca species
- **Zone:** 4
- **Height:** 3 to 10 feet
- **Bloom time:** Summer
- **Comments:** With rosettes of stiff, sword-shaped leaves and striking flower stalks often reaching 10 feet in height, yuccas are breathtaking. Their waxy flowers are white, cream white, or greenish white, usually fragrant, and borne in a large cluster atop the flower stalk.

Plant in full sun or light shade, in well-drained soil. For easiest propagation, carefully dig and transplant the offsets, or young plants, that develop around the crown. Or use seeds.

Yuccas are associated with desert landscapes, but are useful in more temperate climates. Use as a specimen, at the corners of perennial gardens, or in small groups in island plantings.

Y. filamentosa is Adam's-needle yucca, and *Y. glauca* is soapweed. Both are planted extensively, but soapweed is the hardier of the two, surviving winters in Zone 4.

VERONICA

YUCCA

171

BIENNIALS PORTFOLIO

CANTERBURY-BELLS

ENGLISH DAISY

ALPINE FORGET-ME-NOT

BIENNIALS BASICS

To a botanist, biennials are seed-grown plants that produce foliage the first year, then flower, set seed, and die the second year. To a gardener, however, biennials are that plus much more. Colorful, reliable, old-fashioned, and reminiscent of grandmother's day, biennials produce some of the best garden flowers.

Biennials grow easily from seed, but their two-year life cycle requires that gardeners pay careful attention to when they do the seeding. In areas with a very short growing season, sow near mid-July. August is ideal in most climates, and early September is fine where winters are mild and short. Spring sowing will work, but plants usually won't flower until the next spring.

Sow outdoors directly in the garden or in shallow seed flats. Keep seedbeds and young plants watered. Thin young seedlings, then later, if necessary, transplant into the garden or individual pots. Unless winters are mild, protect first-year plants in a cold frame or with mulch.

CANTERBURY-BELLS

Campanula medium
■ **Zone:** 4
■ **Height:** 1½ to 4 feet
■ **Bloom time:** May to July
■ **Comments:** Canterbury-bells produce spectacular spikes of cuplike flowers, some with attached petals in the form of a saucer. Colors include white, pink, blue, purple, and rose. Most varieties grow between 2 and 4 feet tall, making them perfect for the middle to rear of a garden. They look best when planted in small groups, rather than singly. All canterbury-bells make good cut flowers. The tall-growing types require support.

Plant in full sun, in rich, moist, well-drained soil. The 'Cup-and-Saucer' mix produces plants about 3 feet tall; each flower has a cup and attached showy saucer. 'Musical Bells' is a dwarf mix that reaches about 20 inches tall.

ENGLISH DAISY

Bellis perennis
■ **Zone:** 4
■ **Height:** 4 to 8 inches
■ **Bloom time:** Spring to early summer
■ **Comments:** Popular in rock gardens, as an edging plant, or with spring bulbs, English daisy produces asterlike blooms above low foliage clumps. Colors include white, pink, rose, and red. English daisy's flowers may be single, semi-double, or double.

Plant in partial shade, especially if summer heat comes early. Soil should be moist, rich, and well drained. English daisy naturalizes in shady portions of woodland gardens and in high-mowed lawns.

English daisy is really a perennial, but is usually handled as a biennial. In areas with a long growing season, it may even perform as an annual if sown in very early spring. It reseeds freely where well adapted, becoming established. Flowers from these seeded plants, however, are usually dull in color and single.

FORGET-ME-NOT, ALPINE

Myosotis sylvatica (often listed as *M. alpestris*)
■ **Zone:** 3
■ **Height:** 8 inches to 2 feet
■ **Bloom time:** Spring
■ **Comments:** Planted with spring-flowering bulbs, alpine forget-me-not creates an almost unforgettable sight. Its azure flowers easily team with the subtle colors of most spring bulbs. It also is a perfect choice for naturalizing in woodland settings, or for color in rock gardens.

Myosotis prefers cool weather and is a good choice for areas that stay moist and are shaded from the direct rays of the sun. It reseeds easily and can become weedy if uncontrolled. When planted in a hot sunny spot, it quickly wilts.

Flowers of most varieties are blue, but other colors are available. 'Carmine King' produces rosy carmine flowers, and 'White Ball' has large, pure white flowers. 'Victoria' is a mix of white, pink, rose, and blue.

FOXGLOVE

Digitalis purpurea

- **Zone:** 4
- **Height:** 2½ to 5 feet
- **Bloom time:** Late spring to midsummer
- **Comments:** *Caution: Poisonous if eaten.*

Few plants rival foxglove for production of spectacular flower spikes in colors of white, cream, yellow, pink, rose, and purple. The individual flowers along the spike are thimble shaped and spotted inside.

Except for the short variety 'Foxy,' plant foxglove in a wind-sheltered area in the back of the garden. Full sun is best only if summer temperatures are mild; otherwise, some afternoon shade is necessary. Soil should be rich, moist, and well drained. Where conditions are ideal, plants self-sow and establish themselves as perennials.

'Excelsior' grows 5 feet tall with blooms all around the stem rather than on just three sides, as is usual. 'Foxy'—actually a cool-season annual—grows just 30 to 40 inches tall. It will flower the first year if sown in very early spring.

HOLLYHOCK

Alcea rosea (sometimes listed as *Althaea rosea*)

- **Zone:** 4
- **Height:** 3 to 8 feet
- **Bloom time:** Summer
- **Comments:** No garden, especially one featuring old-fashioned flowers, would be complete without hollyhocks. Known for dramatically tall flower spikes, hollyhocks are useful at the back of gardens, along fences and walls, and for screening unwanted views. Flowers may be as large as 4 inches across, single or double. Colors include white, yellow, pink, rose, red, or purple.

Plant in full sun, in deep, rich, well-drained soil. Once established, hollyhocks tolerate dry conditions, although they grow better when watered. Established plantings grow year after year, acting as perennials.

Popular 'Chater's Double,' grows 6 feet tall, with large, fully double flowers. 'Pinafore' produces frilly, ruffled flowers, both singles and doubles, on plants 3 to 4 feet tall.

PANSY

Viola x wittrockiana
(sometimes listed as *Viola tricolor*)

- **Zone:** 4
- **Height:** 8 inches
- **Bloom time:** Spring to fall
- **Comments:** Popular for their charming flowers in a wide range of colors, pansies are well suited for many uses. They're perfect for beds and edgings, in rock gardens and wall gardens, in pots and window boxes, mixed with spring-flowering bulbs, and as cut flowers.

Available in all colors except green, pansy flowers traditionally have had contrasting "face" markings, but many recent varieties have solid colors. Some produce flowers up to 4 inches across. To encourage more and larger flowers, keep faded flowers picked.

Plant in full sun only where weather is cool all summer; otherwise, plant in partial shade. Soil must be rich, moist, and well drained.

SWEET WILLIAM

Dianthus barbatus

- **Zone:** 4
- **Height:** 6 inches to 2 feet
- **Bloom time:** May to July
- **Comments:** Sweet william provides low to medium mounds of colorful flowers suitable for cutting. Its strong stems bear large, flat flower heads in a variety of colors, including white, pink, rose, red, deep violet, and bicolors.

Use in the front to middle of a flower garden, as a source of cut flowers, naturalized in woodland settings, and in rock gardens.

Plant in full sun and in nearly any soil as long as it is well drained. Many sweet williams self-sow under ideal conditions. Most varieties grow 15 to 24 inches high, but dwarf selections, such as 'Indian Carpet,' grow only 6 to 8 inches tall.

FOXGLOVE

HOLLYHOCK

SWEET WILLIAM

ANNUALS

Gardeners love annuals, and for good reason. These plants quickly go blooming crazy, producing a grand and glorious, season-long display of cheerful color. Add to that their versatility—they're as much at home in big, bold beds as they are in window boxes—and it's no wonder almost every type of flower garden contains annuals.

USES FOR ANNUALS

Annuals come in an endless array of colors, textures, habits, and sizes. They are just as diverse in function, too, playing a variety of garden roles—major and minor—quickly, easily, and successfully.

IN MASS PLANTINGS

Because annuals are inexpensive, many gardeners fill an area with dozens—even hundreds—of a single type of annual to create a mass planting.

The effect of mass planting is eye-catching, and perhaps deliberately extravagant. Massing calls for plants with strong visual effects: bright colors, prominent lines, and attention-grabbing textures. Use mixes with a wide range of colors, such as the many warm tones of marigold or zinnia. Or work with a single color, such as hot pink impatiens or petunia. For good verticals, use larkspur or tall snapdragon, and, for striking effect, go with big plants such as castor bean or sunflower.

Large areas are naturals for massing. Bold beds in a lawn, wide sweeps along the driveway or property line, shady swaths beneath the canopy of a big tree—all are good candidates for mass plantings.

Massed plantings don't have to be massive, though. Smaller areas—such as between the curb and sidewalk, or along either side of the front steps or garden gate—work well, too. Mass plantings, in fact, often make small areas appear larger.

Large or small, mass plantings fill an area with quick, inexpensive color and add a dramatic, seasonal flair to the landscape.

AS EDGINGS AND HEDGES

Trimming the edge of a flower garden with a row of compact, low-growing annuals gives the entire planting a sense of continuity, adds a finishing touch, and visually ties the garden to the lawn or other surroundings. Edgings are equally useful along driveways, patios, and walkways where they not only add color, but also help soften harsh, straight lines.

Naturally tidy, compact plants that have a long flowering season are best in edgings. Some excellent choices include ageratum, alyssum, wax begonia, and French marigold.

Mass plantings of annuals—here, wax begonia edged with ageratum—have a bold, dramatic effect. With quick-to-flower annuals, results come fast and last for months.

At the other extreme are tall, dense-growing annuals that make perfect temporary hedges or screens. Plants such as burning bush, cleome, and tithonia are good hedge choices. Use them to screen a view, mark a boundary, or act as a windbreak.

FOR CUTTING

Whether you're a serious flower arranger or someone who just likes to cheer up a room with fresh-cut flowers, you'll reap rewards from annuals planted for cutting. A separate cutting garden is ideal if your property is large, but well-planned mass plantings and small beds of mixed flowers can double for snipping. Choose annuals with long, stiff stems and durable blooms. Top-notch choices are aster, cosmos, dahlia, marigold, snapdragon, and zinnia. If you plan to harvest often, plant more than just a few, being sure to give them plenty of space so their stems will grow strong. Harvest regularly to keep more flowers coming.

FOR FRAGRANCE

Don't overlook annuals as a great source of garden fragrance. Few plants can top the delicate sweet scents of alyssum, mignonette, pink, stock, or sweet pea. Place these plants where you'll have the most opportunities to enjoy their fragrance: on the porch, deck, or patio; under a window; near the door or garden gate; or at a spot in your yard you often walk by.

IN ROCK GARDENS

Rock gardens and dry rock walls often lack color. Annuals can fill bare spots quickly, and supply seasonal color. Choose from low-growing, spreading annuals such as alyssum, lobelia, and portulaca. If watering will be a problem, pick types that can survive with little water.

Annuals work in almost any situation. Here, impatiens in a window box and along a foundation—where they team with coleus—add color to a shady spot.

Annuals work their magic even in small areas. Salvia, marigold, alyssum, and lobelia provide a festival of color for all who stop at this garden bench. The alyssum and lobelia scent the surroundings, too.

MIXING ANNUALS

Bring together four or five annuals in one bed, using enough of each to create irregular swatches, swirls, and drifts, and you've made a mixed garden. Or work several types of annuals in among perennials and spring-flowering bulbs to fill the gaps and extend the flowering period, and you've also made a mixed garden. Using annuals in either of these two ways is referred to as bedding.

MAKING YOUR BED

Think first of using annuals for their flower colors, but also use them to introduce variety of form and texture, or perhaps to create a foil between nearby clashing plants. The goal in a mixed bed should be a harmonious flow, rather than a disjointed collection of forms and colors.

Mixed beds can be formal or informal, large or small, with straight or curved edges. Unless the architecture of your house (or your preference) dictates a formal garden, an informal approach usually pleases the eye more and is easier to care for. Regardless of the formality of your approach, arrange annual plants within the bed in clumps or drifts rather than in stiff rows.

You can make the mixed bed as long as you want, but keep it only as deep as you can reach comfortably without stepping on the plants. If you place the bed where you can reach it from two sides, you can make it twice as deep.

Nearly every annual flower is suitable for bedding someplace in the garden. Consider the amount of sun an area receives, then give thought to plant height. A mixed bed with a building or fence behind it should have the tallest plants at the rear, working down in stages to low edging plants in front. When the bed is an island, which allows viewing from several sides, place the tallest plants at or near the center, then scale down to the edges.

Mixing annuals in your garden can have immediate effect, as this garden shows. Nearly all of its color comes from annuals, which are skillfully blended with each other, and carefully woven in among shrubs, perennials, and other permanent plants.

CONSIDER NEARBY COLORS

Where colors from surrounding plants are neutral, such as with evergreens, joining a palette of mixed colors and a jumble of textures can create a carefree look. When annuals are bedded near plants that have pronounced colors—such as flowering shrubs, perennials, or bulbs—harmony of color, size, texture, and design should be the goal.

A mixed bed can take a monochromatic approach, using various shades and tints of one dominant color. Or, when one or two colors dominate, add complementary colors to heighten the appeal.

To increase interest and relieve monotony, combine plants of different growth habits. Back a carpet of low-growing lobelia with the mounded form of impatiens and the vertical accent of larkspur. Think also of flower forms, such as the daisylike shapes of gaillardia, flaring trumpets of petunia, clusters of tubular nicotiana flowers, and plumes of celosia.

When designing beds of mixed annuals, however, don't stop with flower color or form. Choose some plants mainly for their foliage color or texture. Consider, for example, how the splotched leaves of coleus can color nearly any shady spot, or how adding dusty-miller, with its fine-textured gray leaves, can make a sunny location shine even brighter.

To keep a mixed garden from having a patchwork appearance, group each plant in numbers of at least three. A staggered or triangular arrangement is usually more attractive than straight-line planting. Repeat favorites or accent plants, so the eye moves along smoothly.

Finally, properly space the plants to give a full but uncrowded look. Generally, set mounded plants as far apart as their height at maturity; separate erect or linear growers by half their mature height. By skillfully mixing annuals with other plants, you can turn what would be an otherwise drab area into a delightful, colorful, flowing garden scene.

PORTABLE COLOR

Plant annuals in containers to enjoy color in nearly any outdoor location, not only in a garden. Just a few square feet of any outdoor space will do.

Annuals in containers are perfect for use on the patio, deck, or porch, where you can treat them like furniture, moving and rearranging to suit your needs. Or consider using large pots of sun-loving annuals near the pool, where their color and charm help break the monotony of large areas of bright paving. Even apartment, condominium, and town-house dwellers can grow a colorful garden if they have access to a balcony, windowsill, or rooftop.

ANNUALS FOR CONTAINERS

For containers, medium-size, low-growing, and trailing annuals usually look best. As a rule, mature plant height should be no more than 1½ times the container height. For greatest effect in small containers, fill them with one type of annual. For mixed plantings, use large, wide containers. Fill out your minigarden just as you would a flower bed, with taller plants in the center or behind low growers. Soften the edges by allowing trailers such as lobelia or verbena to spill over.

For best growth, place containers of annuals in full sun or partial shade. Few annuals grow and flower well in deep shade, but you can take advantage of the portability of containers to produce blooms for deeply shaded areas. Start by choosing shade-tolerant plants. Grow them in a partially shaded spot until flowering begins, then move them to deeper shade. After a couple of weeks, move the plants back to partial shade to encourage them to rebloom.

■ Choosing the right containers

Adequate drainage is the only absolute requirement for containers. Use containers with drainage holes in the bottoms or sides. Never use a container without a hole; even if you add a layer of gravel to its bottom, excess water will collect, causing the soil to become waterlogged.

Containers flowing with bright annuals are ideal for softening strong architectural lines. Sun-loving annuals—including marigold and lobelia—thrive in these portable containers.

Good planters are made of clay, ceramic, concrete, plastic, or weather-resistant wood such as cedar or redwood. But let your imagination go wild when selecting a container. Use sawed-off wooden barrels, old wheelbarrows, flue tiles, strawberry jars, or any other container that provides good drainage.

■ Growing mix and fertilizers

A blend of lightweight components is the only practical growing mix for containers. Other-

Enliven dull spots with groups of containers filled with colorful flowering annuals. Here, several sizes of containers house shade-tolerant New Guinea impatiens.

wise, the containers will be too heavy and won't drain adequately.

Prepared packaged mixes, often sold as planter mixes, usually work well. Try to use the coarse-textured types that don't puddle after watering. Or prepare your own mix by blending one-third peat moss or fine-textured composted bark, one-third coarse-grade perlite, one-sixth sifted compost, and one-sixth good garden soil. Substitute locally available components as long as the mix remains lightweight and drains well. Moisten the components as you mix them.

Before planting, be sure to add dry fertilizer to the mix according to package instructions. This is key to successful container gardening. A controlled-release fertilizer such as Osmocote is ideal. One application lasts at least four months, automatically metering out as the crop grows. Add 2 ounces of Osmocote 14–14–14 to each cubic foot (about 8 gallons) of homemade potting mix. For commercially prepared mixes, add Osmocote at half that rate.

If a drainage hole is large, cover it with screen or other material that will keep the soil from washing out, yet not plug the hole.

Fill the container with growing mix to within about 1 inch of its top, pushing down to eliminate air pockets. Plant as you would in the garden, except reduce normal spacing between plants by about one-third. (For example, if normal spacing in the garden is 12 inches, decrease it to about 8 inches.)

Immediately after planting, water thoroughly enough so some moisture comes out the drainage hole. Keep the upper soil moist with frequent, light waterings until plants are established, then water when the soil dries beyond 2 inches deep. For easy, accurate watering, use an automated drip-irrigation system controlled by a timer.

Avoid placing containers where heat becomes intense, such as against a west wall, or in windy locations. You'll find that most plants don't thrive in these conditions.

■ Care after planting

Provide container annuals all the care you normally would give annuals in the garden: pinch to induce branching, remove faded flowers, and control pests. If you didn't add a controlled-release fertilizer to the soil mix, apply liquid fertilizer every two to three weeks.

After flowering a few months, many annuals in containers get leggy and overcrowded. Shear them back, leaving healthy stems 4 to 6 inches long. If the growing season in your area is long, expect a repeat performance of growth and bloom. Even if you get just three or four months of color from your container plantings, you'll find that they add greatly to your surroundings.

HANGING BASKETS

Hanging baskets let you elevate garden displays to eye level or above, providing seasonal color and interest to porch and patio overhangs, lampposts, arbors, tree limbs, and other strong structures.

Growing plants in hanging baskets is much like growing them in other containers. In fact, you can convert a conventional container such as a wooden planter or a clay or plastic pot into a hanging basket simply by suspending it with supports. The classic hanging basket, however, is made of stout wire, usually formed in the shape of a half sphere.

Hanging baskets are viewed mostly from the sides or from below, so low-growing and trailing plants are good choices. Consider using alyssum, lobelia, French marigold, vinca, petunia, ageratum, and impatiens. Combine plants that have the same sun requirements.

BASKET PREPARATION

To prepare a wire basket for planting, soak coarse sphagnum moss (green moss) in water long enough to become thoroughly wet. Wring the excess moisture from a fistful of moss and begin stuffing the moss tightly into the wire openings, working from the inside and beginning at the bottom. Continue up the sides until you've lined the entire basket with a layer about 1 inch thick. Fill any gaps and make sure the top rim is firm.

Use the same lightweight, well-drained planting mix as for other containers (see pages 180–181). For best results, mix in a controlled-release fertilizer before planting.

Begin planting by putting an inch or two of soil mix in the basket. Working from the outside of the basket, carefully poke a hole in the moss just above the soil level and insert a transplant, pushing it in far enough so its root ball passes entirely through the moss lining. Insert other plants elsewhere at the same level, then add 2 more inches of soil. Continue adding plants and soil until you've almost reached the top. Gently

pack the soil so it's about 1 inch below the top rim. Plant the top as you would any container. Hang the finished basket in a slightly shaded spot; water thoroughly. For sun-loving plants, move the basket into full sun after a few days.

Hanging baskets, especially those lined with moss, dry more quickly than other containers, so be prepared to water daily during hot, dry weather. Never let the soil dry more than 1 inch below the surface. If you didn't incorporate a controlled-release fertilizer into the soil mix, apply a liquid fertilizer every two to three weeks.

STARTING ANNUALS

Y ou can grow most annuals from seed easily. Seed size and sprouting time generally dictate whether you should sow seeds indoors or outdoors.

SEEDING INDOORS

Sow seeds less than ⅛ inch across indoors in flats. Later, move the seedlings to small pots, and finally transplant them to the garden. Use the shallow flats professional growers use, or trim a milk carton to make your own. Flats should be at least 2 inches deep and must have drainage holes.

The germinating medium must be moist, well drained, and sterile. Packaged ready-to-use media meet these needs and are fairly inexpensive since a little goes a long way. A moistened homemade mix of half fine peat moss and half fine perlite or vermiculite is suitable. Don't use garden soil or reuse a germinating medium.

■ Sanitation is key

Clean the flat, then soak it for 30 minutes in a mix of 10 percent household bleach and 90 percent water. After the flat dries, fill it with moistened medium to within ¼ inch of its top. Tap to remove air pockets; refill if needed.

Make rows ¼ inch deep, 2 inches apart. Drop seeds in a row, spacing them so they almost touch. Cover the seeds to twice their thickness with sowing medium or clean, coarse sand. (For tiny seeds, such as those of begonia and impatiens, simply press them into the medium without covering.) Label the rows and water gently.

To keep the humidity high, slip the flat into a plastic bag, or cover it with a sheet of plastic or a pane of glass. Place it in a warm spot, preferably where it will get heat from beneath (the top of the refrigerator is a good spot). Unless the seeds need darkness for germination, place the flat in a bright spot. As long as condensation forms, don't water.

When the first seedlings sprout, remove the cover and place the flat in an indoor spot that receives full sun, keeping the soil slightly moist. Apply liquid fertilizer at one-fourth strength

STARTING ANNUALS INSIDE

Sow small seeds indoors in flats of sterilized mix. Drop seeds into shallow rows without crowding, then cover lightly. Keep the flat moist and warm, moving it to bright light when first seedlings pop through the mix.

Shift seedlings to individual small pots after two sets of true leaves form. Carefully remove a seedling with plenty of roots and soil, then plant deep enough so it doesn't fall over. Use sanitized pots and soil.

when seedlings are ½ inch tall. After two sets of true leaves form, shift the seedlings to individual pots of compressed peat-moss or sanitized small flower pots. Plant deep enough in germinating medium so the small seedlings don't fall over. Water gently; place in a cool, shady spot (still indoors). After a couple of days, move back to full sun. Apply half-strength liquid fertilizer after two weeks.

Try a fluorescent light for germinating and growing seedlings. Keep the lights on 24 hours until the seeds germinate, then cut back to 14 to 16 hours. As seedlings grow, adjust the bulb height to keep it 6 inches above the top leaves.

STARTING ANNUALS *(continued)*

Before moving your seedlings to the garden, you must introduce them to their new world slowly. They need to adjust to the rigors of outdoors through a process known as hardening off before settling in their final location.

MOVING INDOOR SEEDLINGS OUT

Four to six weeks after shifting seedlings to individual pots, move them out into full sun on mild days but bring them in at night. Give the seedlings a half day of sun the first three or four days, then increase the exposure gradually. After seven to 10 days, leave seedlings outside full-time in a frost-free, sunny location. Continue watering as usual. After hardening off the seedlings about a total of two weeks, transplant them to the garden. A cold frame is especially helpful for hardening off seedlings.

SEEDING OUTDOORS

Sowing seeds directly in the garden is useful for large seeds that usually sprout and grow quickly and for types that don't transplant well. Sowing in the garden also works well later in the year when the soil is warm.

Prepare the soil by incorporating fertilizer at half rate and adding plenty of organic matter. Spade or till, then rake to a smooth seedbed.

■ Sow in rows or scatter?

For annuals that don't transplant well, or for a natural look, scatter seeds over the entire planting area, sowing four or five seeds for every plant you want. Or drop small groups of seeds randomly around the prepared area.

Sowing in rows works well for plants that transplant easily, such as dahlia, marigold, and zinnia. Watering the plants and pulling weeds are easier when you work in rows. Make the planting row by opening a shallow trough deep enough for the seed and the covering. Follow spacing directions found on the seed packet: about 1 inch apart for large seeds, ½ inch for smaller seeds.

Whether you scatter or sow seeds in rows, cover them to a depth of four times their thickness with seedbed soil or a mix of half sand and half sifted compost. Label each row or area, then water gently. You must keep the seedbed moist, so be prepared to water once a day or more often. Place a piece of burlap or cheesecloth directly on the seedbed to hold moisture and reduce crusting.

■ Thinning seedlings

Thin seedlings after they develop two sets of true leaves. Thin so the remaining plants are separated by the distance indicated on the seed packet. If you don't want to discard good plants, carefully dig them, taking as much soil as possible with the roots, then set them in a new location. Water thoroughly.

PURCHASING TRANSPLANTS

Purchased transplants, sold as bedding plants, are especially valuable for annuals that are hard to germinate and those that grow best only in the special environment of a commercial nursery. You'll probably want to buy transplants of wax begonia, impatiens, petunia, torenia, and vinca.

■ What qualities to look for

As you shop, look for what professionals call "green" transplants. These haven't opened any flowers; instead, they've put their energy into producing strong stems, healthy green foliage, and flower buds. The best transplants also are short, stocky, and, if appropriate, branched.

Don't hesitate to knock a few transplants out of their containers to check the roots. There should be enough white roots at the edge of the soil ball to hold it together. Stay away from pot-bound or straggly plants, and avoid any with yellow, wilted, or damaged leaves.

■ Transplanting techniques

Before setting transplants, prepare the soil by adding preplant fertilizer and generous amounts of organic amendment such as peat moss, composted bark, or rotted manure. Thoroughly blend these into the soil. If the soil is dry, water, then wait a day before planting.

Make a planting hole wider and slightly deeper than the root ball. Slip a transplant from its container (except those in peat-moss pots) and check the root system. If the root ball is tightly knotted, use a knife or trowel to make two or three vertical slices about ¼ inch deep down the full length of the root ball. Carefully set the root ball in the hole ¼ to ½ inch deeper than it was before. Fill the hole with loose soil, then pack it gently with your fingers. Water thoroughly after you have planted all of the transplants.

Try to transplant in the evening or on a cloudy day, if possible. The cooler weather will be easier on the plants—and you. Be prepared to put up a temporary device to provide shade or protection if hot or windy weather follows.

Pinch the top ½ inch off each upright shoot about one week after transplanting if you want plants to branch and be more compact. Don't pinch naturally low-growing plants such as alyssum and lobelia. Keep the area free of weeds but avoid deep cultivation. Wait two to three weeks for the plant to grow a bit and its stem to firm up, then apply a mulch to help control weeds and keep the soil cool and moist.

■ Feeding transplants

Keep annuals in top shape and full color by feeding every six weeks with a dry fertilizer designed for flowers, or by applying a liquid fertilizer every two to three weeks. To make feeding easier, add a controlled-release fertilizer to the soil before planting. Controlled-release fertilizer needs to be applied only once because the food meters out automatically during the growing season.

When shopping for bedding plants, look for short, stocky, deep green plants such as those on the right. The others are stretched and poorly branched, and their light color indicates starvation.

Here also, the shorter plants are the better choice. They have lots of basal shoots to produce bushy, compact plants. The tall plants are probably root-bound and will grow poorly after planting.

■ Water requirements

Annual beds should receive an inch of water every week, even more during very hot weather. If rain doesn't fall, water the entire bed until the soil is wet at least 8 inches deep. If possible, water in the morning on a sunny day so the foliage won't stay wet too long. This helps reduce the chance of disease.

ANNUALS PORTFOLIO

ACROCLINIUM

AGERATUM

SWEET ALYSSUM

ACROCLINIUM

Also called strawflower
Helipterum roseum

■ **Height:** 1½ to 2 feet
■ **Comments:** One of several plants commonly called strawflower, acroclinium produces beautiful flowers in fresh-cut or dried arrangements. The cut flowers dry easily, holding their color well.

The mostly semidouble flowers open about 2 inches across and are daisylike, with yellow centers surrounded by white, cream, pink, or rose. They're borne on narrow, stout stems well above gray-green foliage.

Locate in full sun and well-drained soil. Once established, plants tolerate dry conditions. Overwatering often causes rot, especially in heavy clay soil. Where the growing season is long, sow seeds directly in the garden after the last frost. Sow monthly to extend bloom season. In short-season areas, sow seeds indoors eight weeks before the last frost. To transplant, use peat-moss pots and handle seedlings carefully.

AGERATUM

Also called flossflower
Ageratum houstonianum

■ **Height:** 4 to 10 inches
■ **Comments:** Ageratum produces low, dense mounds covered with small fluffy flowers. The compact tidy plants are favorites in edgings, window boxes, and other containers. Most varieties have lavender-blue flowers, but pink and white types are available, too.

Seeds are small and difficult to sprout when sown directly in the garden. Experienced gardeners usually purchase transplants, but seedlings can be started indoors seven to eight weeks before the last frost. Delay setting plants in the garden until after the last frost.

Locate in rich, well-drained soil and in full sun. Partial shade is better in very hot, long-season areas. White varieties have better flower color in light shade. In too much shade, plants stretch and open up.

'Blue Danube' always is uniform in habit and flower production. Other popular varieties include 'Blue Mink,' 'Pink Powderpuffs,' 'Summer Snow,' and the bluish mauve 'Blue Blazer.'

ALYSSUM, SWEET

Lobularia maritima

■ **Height:** 3 to 6 inches
■ **Comments:** An easy-to-grow, low-care annual, sweet alyssum is widely known for its sweet-fragrant flowers borne on low, spreading plants.

Flower color can be white, rose, lavender, or purple. Most newer varieties grow no more than 6 inches tall and spread about 1 foot. Some older varieties, or plants growing in too much shade, stretch to a foot or more in height. Use in edgings, beds, rock gardens, hanging baskets, and window boxes.

Locate in full sun or partial shade. Plants grow in nearly any soil but do best in moderately fertile, well-drained soil. Because it adapts to most conditions and reseeds freely, alyssum is common in some wildflower mixes.

Sow directly in the garden a few weeks before the last frost, or set small, vigorous transplants after the last possible hard frost. Plants flower quickly, so planting even into late summer is feasible in most areas. In mild areas of the Pacific Coast, alyssum grows and flowers year-round. Intense summer heat sometimes halts flowering, but cooler weather brings a new round of flowers. Cut back overgrown plants to encourage new growth.

Popular varieties include 'Snow Cloth,' 'Carpet of Snow,' rose-pink 'Rosie O'Day,' deep rose 'Wonderland,' 'Royal Carpet' (predominantly violet, with a white center), 'Violet Queen,' and the deep purple 'Oriental Night.'

AMARANTH

Also called tassel flower or love-lies-bleeding
Amaranthus caudatus

■ **Height:** 3 to 6 feet
■ **Comments:** Given full sun and plenty of

warmth, amaranth grows fast to near shrublike proportions, making it perfect for the rear of the flower bed or along a fence or wall. Foliage is usually blood red, and its long, ropelike flower clusters may be either golden green or maroon.

Locate in full sun and nearly any soil. Where the growing season is long, seed outside after frost danger passes. For an earlier start, especially in short-season areas, start seedlings indoors three to four weeks before transplanting. Starting too early is no advantage because plants require warmth to grow well. Once established, amaranth tolerates drought well.

A. tricolor produces highly colored leaves but insignificant flowers. The young leaves of 'Early Splendor' are crimson, later turning to deep chocolate, and maturing to brilliant cherry red at the top. Leaves of 'Joseph's Coat' are a mix of green, yellow, chocolate, gold, and crimson. Other varieties include 'Molten Fire' and 'Illumination.' All grow to about 3 feet tall.

AMMOBIUM

Also called winged everlasting
Ammobium alatum

■ **Height:** To 3 feet

■ **Comments:** An Australian native, ammobium produces daisylike flowers atop stiff stems with projections that resemble wings. Flowers have raised, yellow, button-shaped centers surrounded by several rows of white bracts. Stems are long, up to 2 feet, making the flowers good in fresh-cut or dried arrangements.

Plants thrive in heat and require full sun; locate in well-drained, preferably sandy, soil. Seed directly in the garden six weeks before the last frost, or start transplants indoors a few weeks earlier. Seedlings will tolerate light frosts. In Zone 10 and mild portions of Zone 9, seeding in fall produces flowers early the next spring.

ASTER

Also called China aster
Callistephus chinensis

■ **Height:** 6 inches to 2½ feet

■ **Comments:** Aster is known for its showy flowers in a variety of forms and colors. Flower types include single, double, pompon, and frilled or plumed. Colors are predominantly white, pink, red, blue, and purple. Dwarf types produce compact 6- to 12-inch-tall plants appropriate in edgings, beds, window boxes, and containers. Taller forms are used for mass plantings, supplying armloads of cut flowers.

Locate in full sun and rich, well-drained soil. Partial shade is preferable in very hot locations. Apply a mulch once plants are established; water regularly during dry spells. To reduce the risk of disease, plant in a location not occupied by asters during the previous three years. As a further precaution, spray to control disease-spreading aphids and leafhoppers.

Start seeds indoors six to eight weeks before the last spring frost. Asters can't tolerate cold weather, so shift transplants to the garden only after frost danger has passed. Sow directly into the garden after the weather has warmed. Repeat sowing every three weeks until midsummer for continuous flowering into fall.

BACHELOR'S-BUTTON

Also called cornflower
Centaurea cyanus

■ **Height:** To 3 feet

■ **Comments:** Though old-fashioned, this annual is popular today because it's easy to grow, is adaptable, and has beautiful white, blue, pink, rose, or purple flowers. The frilly flowers are semidouble and buttonlike, or fully double, and are superb when cut for fresh use or for drying. Bachelor's-button usually is available as a mix of colors, most growing to 2½ to 3 feet tall.

Because bachelor's-button withstands heavy frost, sow it as early in the spring as you can work the soil. In mild-winter areas, sow in late summer or fall for early spring bloom. Flowering is best during mild weather. For continuous bloom, repeat sowings every three weeks. Locate in full sun or partial shade, in nearly any well-drained soil.

AMARANTH

BACHELOR'S-BUTTON

187

ANNUALS PORTFOLIO *(continued)*

BALSAM

WAX BEGONIA

BELLS-OF-IRELAND

BALSAM

Impatiens balsamina

■ **Height:** 1 to 2½ feet
■ **Comments:** Widely used in Victorian gardens, balsam is just as useful today, especially when a colorful, carefree plant is needed in partial shade. The frilly flowers are semidouble or fully double, with some resembling camellia blossoms; colors include white, cream, pink, rose, scarlet, or purple. Most varieties are sold as a color mix and grow 2 to 2½ feet tall. 'Tom Thumb' mix produces very compact bushes 10 to 15 inches tall.

Locate in partial shade (in cool-summer areas, in full sun). Soil should be moist, rich, and well drained. Use tall types in mass plantings and mixed flower beds; short types in edgings and containers. Since balsam seeds germinate easily once the soil warms in late spring, sow directly in the garden when danger of frost has passed. For earlier flowering, start seeds indoors four to five weeks before the last frost. Plants grow best only after the weather warms.

BEGONIA, WAX

Also called bedding begonia
Begonia x semperflorens-cultorum

■ **Height:** 6 to 12 inches
■ **Comments:** Few plants are more reliable than wax begonias for producing nonstop flowers on easy-care plants in bright or shady locations. Numerous varieties produce white, pink, rose, red, or scarlet flowers. Their attractive waxy leaves may be green, bronze, or brownish. Most varieties produce weather-resistant, compact plants, making them perfect in edgings, mass plantings, window boxes, and other containers. They also grow as indoor plants.

Most wax begonias do best in partial shade; in deep shade, they stretch and flower poorly. In mild coastal areas and other locations where temperatures normally stay below 90 degrees, they tolerate full sun. Bronze-leaved varieties tolerate heat and sun best. Soil should be rich, moist, and well drained.

Experienced gardeners usually plant purchased transplants after danger of frost has passed. Seeds are tiny and germinate slowly, making it difficult to produce a good stand of plants even in ideal conditions. If seeds are used, sow them indoors three to four months before the last frost. Wax begonias actually are tender perennials, and grow and flower year-round in frost-free locations.

BELLS-OF-IRELAND

Also called shellflower
Moluccella laevis

■ **Height:** To 2½ feet
■ **Comments:** Bells-of-Ireland produces spikes of crisp, green, bell-shaped structures that actually are calyxes surrounding tiny white flowers. The spikes make good cut flowers, either fresh or dried, when the green bells turn creamy white. Blend bells-of-Ireland with other garden flowers, taking advantage of its distinct vertical habit and green color.

Sow seeds directly in the garden as soon as you can work the soil in spring. Sow again in fall in mild-winter areas. Give seeds only a shallow covering because they require light for germination. Plants often self-sow. Locate in full sun or partial shade, in nearly any well-drained soil. Growth is best in cool locations. For straight stems, protect plants against wind and rain.

BROWALLIA

Also called amethyst flower
Browallia speciosa

■ **Height:** 12 to 15 inches
■ **Comments:** Browallia produces masses of small, star-shaped, bell-like flowers in white, blue, or purple. Locate in a warm, partially shaded spot where the soil is rich, moist, and well drained. Flowering is heaviest during the warmest part of the year, but continues intermittently year-round in mild-winter locations. Dig up, pot, and bring plants indoors for winter enjoyment. Use browallia for mass plantings, to fill

voids in the shade garden or rock garden, and in hanging baskets and other containers.

If available, purchase bedding plants in late spring. Otherwise, sow seeds indoors six to seven weeks before the last frost. Germination requires soil temperatures near 70 degrees and may take up to three weeks.

Varieties include 'Blue Bells,' with violet blue flowers, 'Heavenly Bells' and 'Sky Bells' (both light blue), and the white-flowered 'Silver Bells.' 'Jingle Bells' is a mix of all these colors.

BURNING BUSH

Also called summer cypress
Kochia scoparia trichophylla

■ **Height:** 2 to 3 feet
■ **Comments:** Burning bush is planted for its growth habit and foliage color, rather than for its flowers. Plants grow into dense, upright bushes with light green, fine foliage (somewhat like a cypress) that turns intense purplish red in the fall. Use as a temporary hedge, and as a background to summer flower gardens.

Sow directly in the garden after all frost danger has passed, or start transplants indoors four to five weeks earlier. Use peat-moss pots to improve transplanting success. Plants self-sow and can become a nuisance in mild climates. Locate in full sun and nearly any well-drained soil. Best growth comes only in areas with warm nights. Summer foliage of the variety 'Acapulco Silver' is a mix of lime green and white, turning ruby red in autumn.

CALENDULA

Also called pot marigold
Calendula officinalis

■ **Height:** 10 to 20 inches
■ **Comments:** Calendula, excellent for flower gardens and containers, produces flowers that are mostly bright yellow or orange, though some are cream or apricot colored. The flower petals make an attractive, edible garnish and can be made into tea. 'Pacific Beauty' mix and 'Kablouna' mix grow to about 20 inches tall. Dwarf types, growing only about 12 inches tall, include 'Fiesta Gitana' mix and 'Dwarf Gem' mix.

Calendula is ideally suited to mild, coastal climates—where it will flower during winter, spring, and early summer—and to high-elevation gardens with mild summer temperatures. In hot-summer locations, plant in early spring for flowering before the onset of intense summer heat. Sow directly in the garden or set transplants in mid-spring in zones 1–5. Elsewhere, plant in fall. Remove faded flowers to foster reblooming.

Locate in full sun or partial shade, in rich, well-drained soil. Established plants grow in fairly dry conditions, but produce much better in moist soil. To discourage powdery mildew disease, locate where air circulation is good, and avoid crowding.

CALIFORNIA POPPY

Eschscholzia californica

■ **Height:** 1 to 1½ feet
■ **Comments:** A West Coast wildflower, the California poppy is popular for its silky, cup-shaped flowers. Colors include white, cream, yellow, gold, scarlet, red, and bright orange. Single, semidouble, and double forms are sold. Flowers sit atop slender stems above a compact mound of gray-green, carrotlike foliage.

Use with other wildflowers and to fill sunny garden spots, meadows, orchards, and other areas not mowed often. California poppy does best during cool weather, flowering from late fall through early summer in many areas of the Pacific Coast. Where summer temperatures normally exceed 80 degrees, plant in very early spring for spring and early-summer flowering. In high-elevation gardens, plants usually continue flowering through summer.

Sow directly in the garden as soon as the soil can be worked in the spring. Sow also in the fall in mild-winter areas of the West. Locate in full sun or partial shade, and in nearly any well-drained soil. Very rich soil or too much fertilizer promotes overgrowth and few flowers. Plants tolerate drought and reseed readily.

BROWALLIA

CALENDULA

189

ANNUALS PORTFOLIO *(continued)*

CANDYTUFT

CELOSIA

CALLIOPSIS

Coreopsis tinctoria

■ **Height:** 1 to 3 feet

■ **Comments:** The daisy-form flowers of calliopsis have dark reddish brown or purple centers surrounded by yellow, brown, purplish, or sometimes two-tone petals. Flowers on wiry stalks are borne above finely cut foliage over a long season. Use as cut flowers, in mixed flower beds, and in wildflower plantings.

Locate in full sun, in nearly any soil. Plants adapt to sites where many other annuals don't grow well, including infertile soil. Seeds germinate easily so growing transplants is unnecessary. In all locations, sow directly in the garden early in the spring (in mild-winter areas, also in fall). Don't bother thinning seedlings in naturalized and wildflower settings. Reseeds readily.

Most forms grow 2 to 3 feet tall, but 10- to 15-inch-tall dwarf varieties are available.

CANDYTUFT

Iberis species

■ **Height:** 10 to 20 inches

■ **Comments:** Hyacinth-flowered or rocket candytuft, *I. amara,* produces delightfully fragrant white flowers on spikes 18 to 20 inches tall. The blooms are excellent for cutting. Globe candytuft, *I. umbellata,* grows as a mound 10 to 12 inches tall, and is covered with white, pink, rose, crimson, or lavender nonaromatic flowers. Globe candytuft is ideal for edgings along walkways, for the fronts of flower gardens, and in rock gardens or containers.

Sow directly in the garden in mid-spring, or start seedlings indoors five to six weeks earlier. Hardened transplants will tolerate mild frost; in areas that have mild winters, sow seeds in fall for early-spring bloom. New plants do best in cool weather. Locate in full sun (in very-hot-summer areas, in partial shade) and in rich, moist, well-drained soil.

CASTOR BEAN

Ricinus communis

■ **Height:** 4 to 10 feet

■ **Comments:** *Caution: Seeds are poisonous.*
Castor bean produces a bold, tropical-looking plant with palmlike leaves up to 3 feet across. Leaves may be green, bluish green, or purplish red. Flowers are white, pink, or red, but are small and insignificant compared to the foliage. Use as a bold accent, a background, or a screen, or for tropical effect.

Sow directly in the garden in late spring, or start seeds indoors in peat-moss pots six to seven weeks before the last frost. Plants grow best in warm, humid locations, quickly developing large size and broad leaves. Locate in full sun or partial shade and, for best growth, in rich, well-drained soil. Castor bean is a perennial in mild-winter areas, usually becoming shrublike and sometimes growing 20 feet tall. It adapts to dry locations, although leaf size usually is reduced.

CELOSIA

Also called cockscomb
Celosia cristata

■ **Height:** 6 inches to 2½ feet

■ **Comments:** Celosia has two flower types. The plumed form produces loose, feathery flowers; the crested form produces tightly clustered, fanlike flower heads resembling a rooster's comb. Both come in a wide range of mostly warm colors including red, orange, gold, yellow, pink, and cream. The shorter varieties are ideal in edgings; taller varieties work best in mid- to back portions of gardens and as fresh-cut or dried flowers. Both short and tall varieties work well for mass bedding and in containers.

Locate in a warm garden spot in full sun and in rich, moist, well-drained soil. For earliest flowering, sow seeds indoors four to five weeks before the last frost. Handle seedlings carefully, preferably in peat-moss pots, to avoid transplant shock. Delay shifting to the garden until the weather warms. Or, in areas with a long growing season, sow celosia directly in the garden·

after all danger of frost has passed. Plants thrive on heat, often languish in cool-summer climates.

Celosia usually is sold as mixed colors, but some separate flower colors are available.

CHRYSANTHEMUM

Also called tricolor chrysanthemum
Chrysanthemum carinatum
■ **Height:** 2 to 3 feet
■ **Comments:** Not to be confused with the perennial, fall-flowering garden mum, tricolor chrysanthemum is an annual that grows easily from seed. Its showy, daisylike flowers have petals of white, yellow, gold, red, or maroon surrounding slightly raised, dark centers. Petal bases often are ringed with one or more contrasting color bands. Flowers are borne just above the finely divided foliage.

Use in the mid- to back portions of flower gardens, as cut flowers, and in naturalized areas. Locate in full sun, in moist, well-drained soil. Flower production is best in cool-summer areas and when faded blooms are removed.

Sow directly in the garden in both mid-spring and midsummer. Except in areas with a short growing season, transplants are unnecessary.

Other annual chrysanthemums include *C. multicaule,* with masses of small yellow flowers, and *C. paludosum,* which produces loads of white, daisylike flowers with yellow centers. Both reseed freely in mild-winter climates and grow to only about 6 inches tall.

CLEOME

Also called spider flower
Cleome hasslerana (sometimes listed as *C. spinosa)*
■ **Height:** To 5 feet
■ **Comments:** Massive, spidery, flower trusses of white, pink, or rose top cleome's tall stems all summer and into fall. Long slender seedpods follow, adding another attractive feature. Use in the backs of flower beds, along fences and walls, and as a quick-growing summer hedge. Shorter types are useful in large containers.

Cleome requires extended warmth. Locate in full sun and in average to rich, well-drained soil. Once established, plants tolerate heat and drought, but do better with frequent waterings. In areas with a long growing season, sow directly in the garden two weeks before the last expected frost. Elsewhere, start plants indoors six to seven weeks before the last frost date.

Three readily available varieties are 'Rose Queen,' 'Ruby Queen,' and white-flowered 'Helen Campbell.'

COLEUS

Coleus x hybridus
■ **Height:** 8 to 18 inches
■ **Comments:** With its wide range of foliage colors and shapes, and its tolerance of shade, coleus is a favorite to brighten shady garden locations. Locate in rich, moist, well-drained soil, in areas of partial to deep shade. Plants tolerate full sun in humid locations and when watered frequently. Use in mass garden beds; in edgings; with ferns and other shade plants; in pots, tubs, hanging baskets, and other containers; and as easy-care houseplants.

Pinch soft stem tips of tall types to encourage branching and compact growth. The light blue to purple flower spikes are almost incidental, and removing them encourages branching.

Coleus won't tolerate frost, so delay garden planting until all frost danger passes. In the spring, purchase transplants, root cuttings of overwintered plants, or start your own seedlings. Sow seeds indoors eight to 10 weeks before the last frost date. Cover very lightly with soil, then keep soil temperature between 75 and 80 degrees. Sowing directly in the garden usually is unproductive. Coleus roots easily using stem cuttings placed in water, or in containers of moist vermiculite or other rooting mix. Dig up and pot plants before fall frost for use as houseplants through the winter.

Numerous varieties are available. Some grow only 8 to 10 inches tall, many are in the 1- to 1½-foot range, and some older types grow as high as 2½ to 3 feet.

CHRYSANTHEMUM

CLEOME

COLEUS

ANNUALS PORTFOLIO *(continued)*

CYNOGLOSSUM

DAHLIA

DIMORPHOTHECA

COSMOS

Cosmos species

■ **Height:** 2 to 6 feet
■ **Comments:** Of the two cosmos species used in gardens, the more common is *C. bipinnatus,* or garden cosmos. Its attractive daisylike flowers of white, pink, maroon, or lavender are borne above delicate foliage on plants 4 to 6 feet tall. 'Sensation' mix, the variety planted most often, has single flowers up to 5 inches across. 'Candy Stripe' has striped petals; 'Sea Shells' has cone-shaped, fluted petals.

The other species, *C. sulphureus,* often is listed as yellow cosmos, although its flowers also can be orange, gold, or reddish orange. Compared with garden cosmos, the foliage of yellow cosmos is not as delicate, its flowers (at least those of most varieties) are smaller across but semi-double, and its plants usually are shorter and denser. The shortest varieties are in the 'Sunny' series: 'Sunny Red,' about 2 feet tall, and 'Sunny Gold,' about 2½ feet. 'Diablo,' with scarlet-orange flowers, grows to 2½ feet tall; 'Bright Lights' mix reaches 3 feet.

In addition to their use in mixed flower gardens, both species provide cut flowers, and the shorter varieties of *C. sulphureus* grow well in containers. Locate all in full sun or light shade. Growth and flowering is best in rich, moist soil, but any well-drained soil will do. Sow directly in the garden after frost danger passes, or start transplants indoors four to five weeks earlier. Tall varieties may need support.

CYNOGLOSSUM

Also called Chinese forget-me-not
Cynoglossum amabile

■ **Height:** 1½ to 2 feet
■ **Comments:** Although actually a biennial, cynoglossum flowers the first year from seed and usually is grown as a cool-season annual. The small, star-shaped flowers may be white, pink, or blue. 'Firmament,' the common variety, has sky blue flowers. Cynoglossum grows best during cool weather and combines well with late-spring bulbs. Use it in mass plantings, in edgings, and for cut sprays of flowers.

Sow directly in the garden in early spring in all locations (in mild-winter areas, also in fall). Set out seedlings started indoors about six weeks later. Plants reseed and can become a nuisance. Locate in full sun (in hot-summer areas, in partial shade). Soil should be well drained and moist, but it doesn't have to be rich.

DAHLIA

Dahlia hybrids

■ **Height:** 1 to 6 feet
■ **Comments:** Dahlias grown from seed and handled as annuals might best be called bedding dahlias to separate them from dahlias grown from tuberous roots. Dozens of bedding dahlia varieties are available, ranging from dwarfs no more than a foot tall to giants 5 to 6 feet tall. Except for blue and green, they come in nearly every color; most are solid, but some are bicolored. Flower forms include single, semidouble, double, pompon, anemone, and cactus-flowered with quilled and frilled petals.

Use dwarfs in edgings, in the niches of rock gardens, and in containers. Midsize types are perfect for setting in large containers, skirting the driveway, edging a raised deck, or blending with foundation plants across the front of the house. Tall forms are perfect background plants. All sizes have a place in mixed flower beds and, except for the shortest types, are a great source of cut flowers.

Locate in full sun, in well-drained, rich, moist soil. Choose an area with good air circulation to prevent powdery mildew fungus.

Sow directly in the garden after all chance of frost passes, or start transplants indoors six to seven weeks earlier. Pinch shoot tips of midsize and tall types to encourage bushiness. Tall types need support. Remove faded flowers to keep plants tidy and encourage continuous blooming. After foliage fades in fall, dig up swollen tuberous root clumps and store them through the winter to start more plants next spring.

DIMORPHOTHECA

Also called cape daisy or cape marigold
Dimorphotheca species

■ **Height:** 1 to 1½ feet

■ **Comments:** Two species of dimorphotheca are available, both producing daisylike, mostly single flowers. One species, *D. pluvialis,* grows to 1½ feet tall, producing white, pink, rose, and carmine flowers, all with yellow centers. Another species, *D. sinuata,* grows only about 1 foot tall, with satin-looking petals of white, cream, yellow, or apricot, all with dark centers. Petals of both are purplish on the underside. Flowers open only on sunny days, then close at night. Use in beds, edgings, containers, rock gardens, and wildflower gardens.

Sow directly in the garden one to two weeks before the last expected frost (in mild-winter areas, also in fall). Locate in full sun, in poor, well-drained soil; do not water heavily. Dimorphotheca performs best during cool weather.

DUSTY-MILLER

Centaurea cineraria

■ **Height:** 1 to 1½ feet

■ **Comments:** Dusty-miller is grown for its mounded clumps of silvery gray, feltlike foliage. Use as an accent, to provide texture and color contrast, or as a foil to soften the effects of nearby brightly colored plants.

Start seedlings indoors eight to 10 weeks before the last frost. Most gardeners, however, purchase transplants in spring. Locate in full sun. Soil needs good drainage but doesn't have to be rich. Shear tall, leggy plants in midsummer. Dusty-miller actually is a tender perennial that overwinters in mild climates.

The popular 'Silverdust' has deeply lobed leaves. Several other plants of similar use and culture are known as dusty-miller, including 'Silver-Lace' of the chrysanthemum genus.

GAILLARDIA

Also called blanket flower
Gaillardia pulchella (sometimes listed as *G. picta*)

■ **Height:** 1 to 2 feet

■ **Comments:** Most popular varieties of blanket flower produce semidouble or double pompon or daisylike flowers. Petals often are fringed and frilly, and colors include white, cream, yellow, orange, gold, red, and many bicolors. Use in garden beds and for cut flowers.

Plant in full sun and a warm location. Soil must be well drained, but need not be rich. Once established, plants endure drought and heat, growing where many other annuals suffer.

Sow directly in the garden in mid-spring in all areas (in mild-winter areas, also in the fall). Where summers are short, start seedlings indoors four to six weeks before the last frost. Growth in the garden is quick, and flowers come early. Remove faded flowers.

GAZANIA

Also called treasure flower
Gazania rigens

■ **Height:** 1 to 1½ feet

■ **Comments:** Gazania is grown for its daisylike flowers borne on short stalks above a low foliage mound. Colors usually are cream, yellow, gold, orange, pink, and red with contrasting centers. Some varieties are bicolored or striped. Flowers close at night and on cloudy days. Use in the fronts of flower beds, in edgings, in containers, and as a ground cover. Plants are perennial in mild-winter areas.

Gazania does best in hot, arid locations. Locate in full sun and well-drained soil. Plants often die early in humid areas, especially if overwatered. Remove faded flowers to keep plants tidy and encourage flowering.

Sow seeds indoors seven weeks before the last spring frost. Transplants often are found in nurseries, especially in mild-winter areas. Most gazanias are sold as a color mix, but separate colors are sometimes available. The 'Mini Star' series has 3-inch flowers on 8-inch-tall plants.

DUSTY-MILLER

GAILLARDIA

GAZANIA

ANNUALS PORTFOLIO *(continued)*

GLOBE AMARANTH

GYPSOPHILA

GERANIUM

Pelargonium species
■ **Height:** To 2 feet
■ **Comments:** The common garden geranium, *P. x hortorum,* often is listed as a bedding geranium or zonal geranium. Regardless of the name, varieties produce spectacular clustered flowers of white, pink, scarlet, orangish red, red, and salmon, some with contrasting centers or eyes. Foliage of most varieties is green, but also may be marked with a dark band or zone of color, or may be variegated. Plants grow 1½ to 2 feet tall, and are used in mass plantings, with other summer annuals, and in window boxes and other containers. In mild-winter areas, plants are perennial, becoming semiwoody and tall.

The stems of *P. peltatum,* the hanging or ivy geranium, trail to about 3 feet, making this species ideal for hanging baskets, window boxes, and rock gardens, or as a ground cover. Flowers usually are white, pink, red, burgundy, and lavender, with dark markings on the upper petals.

Locate both types in full sun or partial shade. Nearly any soil is suitable, but a rich, moist, well-drained soil produces best growth. Remove faded flowers to keep plants tidy and prevent seed formation. Propagate using stem cuttings rooted in moist vermiculite or other rooting mix. Or sow seeds indoors three to four months before the last frost. Overwinter both types indoors in pots.

Numerous other geraniums are available, including miniatures, tree types, and several species grown for their scented leaves.

GLOBE AMARANTH

Gomphrena globosa
■ **Height:** To 1½ feet
■ **Comments:** The globular flower heads of gomphrena look like clover blossoms, and come in white, pink, rose, lavender, and purple. They make excellent fresh-cut or dried flowers. 'Buddy' reaches 8 inches tall with deep purple flowers, and is perfect in edgings and containers.

Locate in full sun and nearly any well-drained soil. Established plants tolerate some drought, and thrive on heat and humidity. Sow seeds indoors six to seven weeks before the last frost, or, in areas with a long growing season, sow directly in the garden after frost.

G. haageana has reddish orange flowers shaped like small pinecones.

GODETIA

Also called farewell-to-spring
Clarkia amoena
(sometimes listed as *Godetia amoena*)
■ **Height:** 1½ to 3 feet
■ **Comments:** Godetia flowers look like those of azaleas, with satiny petals of white, pink, salmon, crimson, red, or lilac-crimson. Most are single, but some are semidouble, and many have dark blotches. Flowers are excellent for cutting gardens, mixed flower beds, and wildflower gardens.

Locate in full sun, in nearly any well-drained soil. Plants do best in areas with cool summers. In hot-summer areas, time for late-spring flowering. Transplanting is difficult, so sow directly in the garden as early in spring as you can work the soil. Seed in the fall in mild-winter areas.

C. unguiculata has erect, vertical stems growing 2 to 3 feet tall. Flowers are whitish, pink, rose, or lavender.

GYPSOPHILA

Also called baby's-breath
Gypsophila elegans
■ **Height:** 1 to 1½ feet
■ **Comments:** Baby's-breath produces clouds of dainty white, pink, or rose-colored flowers on wiry stems. Traditionally, it's grown for use as a delicate filler in fresh and dried bouquets. In flower beds, tuck baby's-breath into voids in the front to mid-portion, or use it in rock gardens.

Where summers are very hot, locate in partial shade; otherwise, in full sun. Soil must be well drained and not too fertile. Because baby's-breath tolerates moderate frost, sow directly in the garden in early spring (in mild-winter areas, also in late summer). Sow every few weeks for a continuous flower supply. Grow indoor transplants in peat-moss pots, allowing five to six weeks before shifting to the garden.

IMPATIENS

Also called busy lizzy or patience plant
Impatiens wallerana

■ **Height:** To 1½ feet
■ **Comments:** Impatiens is a top-rated annual because of its uniform habit, ease of growth, tolerance of shade, dependability, and dazzling blooms from early summer until fall. Flowers are mostly single, but doubles are available. Colors include white, pink, rose, red, scarlet, violet, salmon, and orange. Some have white centers. 'Accent' gets no more than 8 inches tall, 'Super Elfin' grows from 6 to 12 inches tall, and 'Blitz' reaches 1½ feet. These varieties come in separate colors and in color mixes. Use in mass plantings, with other plants, and in hanging baskets, window boxes, and other containers.

Where summers are hot, impatiens do best in partial shade, tolerating sun only if well watered. Don't be alarmed if foliage wilts during afternoon heat, as long as it perks up by evening. Plant in full sun or partial shade in cool-summer areas. Soil must be well drained and should be moderately rich. Avoid excessive fertilizer, which encourages leafy growth at the expense of flowers. Faded flowers are self-cleaning, and plants seldom require pinching.

Impatiens are sensitive to frost and should not be planted until weather warms. Most gardeners buy transplants. To produce seedlings, sow indoors 10 to 12 weeks before the last frost, keeping the soil temperature between 70 and 75 degrees. Sowing directly in the garden usually is unproductive. Root stem cuttings from plants overwintered indoors.

A separate group called New Guinea impatiens features attractive foliage that often is maroon or green variegated, with large cream or yellow, usually luminescent, flowers. Plants grow to 2 feet tall and tolerate the sun more than other impatiens. Most are propagated using stem cuttings.

LARKSPUR

Also called rocket larkspur, annual delphinium
Consolida ambigua
(sometimes listed as *Delphinium ajacis*)

■ **Height:** 3 to 4 feet
■ **Comments:** The vertical spikes of larkspur are clothed with flowers in white, pink, blue, purple, or maroon. Flowers are good for cutting. Foliage is lacy green. Use in the backs of gardens and along fences and walls. Tallest types may need support.

Plants are moderately frost hardy, and perform best during cool weather. Time planting to avoid hot weather. Sow directly in the garden in early spring (in mild-winter areas, also in fall). Because transplanting is difficult, place indoor-grown seedlings in peat-moss pots. Locate in full sun, in rich, moist, well-drained soil. Mulching and watering help pull plants through hot spells. Plants reseed freely.

LINARIA

Also called toadflax or baby snapdragon
Linaria maroccana

■ **Height:** 8 to 15 inches
■ **Comments:** Linaria, with its short spikes of small flowers, is like a miniature snapdragon. Colors are white, yellow, lavender, red, or carmine; many varieties are bicolored. Plants do best in cool-summer areas; where summers are hot, plant in time for spring flowering. Sow directly in the garden in early spring (in mild-winter areas, also in fall). For transplants, sow indoors five to six weeks before setting in garden. Keep seedling soil cool—near 60 degrees.

Plant in full sun or partial shade, in moist, well-drained soil. Growth is best in rich soil, but nearly any soil will do. Water and mulch during hot weather. Plants reseed freely.

Use in mass plantings, containers, or rock gardens, or with bulbs and other spring flowers in the fronts of gardens.

IMPATIENS

IMPATIENS—New Guinea

LARKSPUR

ANNUALS PORTFOLIO *(continued)*

LOBELIA

MARIGOLD

MIGNONETTE

LISIANTHUS

Also called prairie gentian
Eustoma grandiflorum
(sometimes listed as *Lisianthus russellianus*)
■ **Height:** To 3 feet
■ **Comments:** The beautiful poppylike or cup-shaped flowers of lisianthus open from long, pointed buds above silvery green foliage. The 2-inch flowers are white, pink, blue, or lavender; singles predominate, but double forms are available. Use in beds and in pots and other containers. Cut flowers are long lasting.

Because production of flowering-size seedlings requires six to seven months, purchase transplants right after the last frost in spring. Locate in full sun in cool-summer areas; otherwise, in partial shade. Plants grow and produce best in warm weather, and must be in well-drained, moist, and rich soil. To encourage bushiness and avoid the need for support, pinch off stem tips when young plants are transplanted, and again after 3 to 4 inches of growth occurs. In mild-winter areas, plant in fall and treat as a biennial.

LOBELIA

Lobelia erinus
■ **Height:** 4 to 6 inches
■ **Comments:** Lobelia is ideal in edgings, rock gardens, and containers. Blanketing the compact, spreading plants are small flowers in white, blue, magenta, rosy lilac, or purple; some have white centers or eyes.

Locate in full sun in cool-summer areas; otherwise, in partial shade. Soil must be moist, rich, and well drained. Flowering may stop during periods of intense summer heat, but plants will survive and rebloom if watered. Cut back after first bloom to keep growth compact and to encourage more flowering.

Sow seeds indoors eight to 10 weeks before last frost. Avoid overwatering seedlings. Established plants are moderately frost hardy, so early fall planting is safe in mild-winter areas.

Several varieties are available as separate colors and in mixes. Use the trailing or cascade types in hanging baskets and rock gardens.

MARIGOLD

Tagetes species
■ **Height:** 6 inches to 4 feet
■ **Comments:** Few annuals rival the popular marigold for its warm colors, quick growth, easy care, and wide range of heights and flower types. *T. patula,* the French marigold, and *T. erecta,* the American or African marigold, are the most widely planted.

T. patula grows from 6 to about 12 inches tall, forming a compact mound covered with flowers from 1 to 2 inches across. Colors include yellow, gold, orange, near red, and mahogany (which is unique to this species). Many varieties are bicolored. Flower form may be single, anemone, double, or crested with a raised center. Use in window boxes and other containers, in edgings, and in the fronts of gardens.

T. erecta grows 2 to 3 feet tall, but shorter and taller varieties are available. The semidouble or double flowers are large—3 to 4 inches across. Most have long stems good for cutting. Colors are primrose, yellow, gold, orange, and white; none is bicolored. Use in the mid- to back portions of flower gardens, for mass plantings, as a low hedge, in containers, and for cut flowers. Tall types may need support.

Locate all marigolds in full sun, in well-drained, moist soil of average fertility. Start seeds indoors four to six weeks before the last frost, and harden transplants before setting out. Sow directly in the garden after frost has passed and when soil is warm. French types often begin flowering within two months of seeding. Several days of temperatures above 90 degrees may slow flowering, but blooming will resume as temperatures cool. Remove faded flowers.

The triploid or mule marigold is a hybrid of *T. patula* and *T. erecta.* Growth habit and flower size and type usually fall somewhere between those of both parents. Triploids are unique because they are sterile and cannot reproduce.

They bloom continuously, even through intense heat, and are not weakened if left to go to seed. Sow indoors in warm soil because the germination rate is low.

MIGNONETTE

Reseda odorata

■ **Height:** 12 to 15 inches
■ **Comments:** Mignonette is an old-fashioned plant still prized today for its delightfully fragrant flowers. Bloom spikes are mostly lime yellow, often shaded toward brown, red, or white. Use where you can appreciate its fragrance: near a gate or doorway, in containers on the patio or deck, and in window boxes.

Locate in full sun in cool-summer areas; otherwise, in partial shade. Soil should be moist and well drained. Because it is hard to transplant, mignonette is best when sown directly in the garden. Sow in early spring in all areas (in mild-winter areas, also sow in late summer). Plants prefer cool weather and tolerate frost moderately well.

MIMULUS

Also called monkey flower
Mimulus x hybridus

■ **Height:** 10 to 12 inches
■ **Comments:** Monkey flower is known for its tubular, two-lipped blooms of yellow, gold, or red, usually splotched with a contrasting color. Flowers resemble large snapdragon blooms. They do best in a cool-summer climate, and combine well with ferns and other shade plants.

Locate in partial shade, in soil that is rich, moist, and well-drained. Where summer temperatures are moderate, plants tolerate more sun. Use also in pots and other containers in shaded locations and as indoor plants.

Because plants tolerate mild frosts, set in the garden in mid-spring. Start seedlings indoors seven to eight weeks earlier. Cover lightly with soil because seeds require light for germination. Where winters are mild, fall transplants will overwinter and begin flowering in early spring.

MORNING-GLORY

Ipomoea species

■ **Height:** To 10 feet
■ **Comments:** Long-favored as an easy-to-grow summer vine, morning-glory covers itself with tubular flowers of white, pink, red, blue, purple, or chocolate brown; some varieties produce multiple colors. Flowers open in the morning, fade by mid-afternoon, then open again the next morning. Because plants climb, they are excellent for covering fences and trellises, and also are useful in hanging baskets.

Before sowing, soak seeds in water for 10 hours, or nick the hard seed coat with a file. Sow directly in the garden after all frost danger passes, or start seedlings indoors four to five weeks earlier.

Locate in full sun, in well-drained soil. Avoid overwatering or overfertilizing, which produces vine at the expense of flowers. Some varieties need coaxing to begin climbing.

NASTURTIUM

Tropaeolum majus

■ **Height:** 8 inches to 6 feet
■ **Comments:** Most nasturtiums grow 12 to 15 inches tall and are used in mixed flower beds, edgings, and window boxes and other containers. Dwarf varieties are shorter; others climb to 6 feet if given support and tied when young. All are planted for their colorful, usually spurred flowers available in nearly every color but blue, purple, and green. Blooms are sometimes bicolored and may be single, semidouble, or double. Both the distinctly round-shaped, spicy leaves and the flowers are used in salads.

Sow directly in the garden after all danger of frost passes. Because plants grow quickly, little is gained by using transplants except in areas with very short seasons. Locate in full sun where summers are moderate; otherwise, in partial shade. Soil must be well drained and not heavily fertilized. Growth is best in cool weather; established plants tolerate drought and neglect.

MIMULUS

MORNING-GLORY

NASTURTIUM

ANNUALS PORTFOLIO *(continued)*

ORNAMENTAL CABBAGE

ORNAMENTAL KALE

NICOTIANA

Also called flowering tobacco
Nicotiana alata
■ **Height:** 1 to 3 feet
■ **Comments:** A relative of commercial tobacco, nicotiana is grown for its tubular, sweet-scented flowers. Colors include white, pink, rose, red, crimson, and lime green. Fragrance peaks during calm, warm evenings, and is most intense with old-fashioned varieties such as *N. alata 'grandiflora.'* Newer varieties lack strong fragrance, but are shorter, more compact, more weather resistant, and more floriferous. Plants in the 'Nicki' series grow 15 to 18 inches tall; in the 'Domino' series, 12 to 14 inches. The 'Sensation' mix has heavily scented flowers on plants 2 to 3 feet tall.

Sow directly in the garden after weather warms and frost danger passes, or start transplants indoors six to seven weeks earlier. Locate in full sun or partial shade, in well-drained, rich, moist soil. Plants thrive in heat and humidity, but need watering during dry spells. Remove faded flowers, and shear leggy plants in midsummer to encourage flowering into fall.

NIGELLA

Also called love-in-a-mist
Nigella damascena
■ **Height:** 1 to 1½ feet
■ **Comments:** The lacy foliage of nigella is topped with beautiful flowers of white, pink, blue, rose, lavender, or purple. The unusual seedpods that follow are ideal for use in dried arrangements. Growing about 1½ feet tall are 'Persian Jewels' mix, 'Miss Jekyll' with bright blue flowers, and white-flowered 'Miss Jekyll Alba.' Miniature 'Dwarf Moody Blue' grows only 8 inches tall.

Plant in full sun. Soil must be well drained but need not be rich. Established plants tolerate some drought. Nigella resents transplanting, so sowing directly in the garden is better. Because plants tolerate mild frosts, seed in early spring (in mild-winter areas, also in fall). For constant blooming, repeat every three to four weeks except during intense hot spells. Allow seedpods to develop on the plants for dry use. Plants reseed freely.

ORNAMENTAL CABBAGE AND KALE

Brassica oleracea acephala group
■ **Height:** 8 to 18 inches
■ **Comments:** Like their vegetable cousins, ornamental cabbage and kale are grown for their foliage—in this case, colorful and decorative. They develop large rosettes of gray-green foliage richly variegated with cream, pink, rose, and purple. Ornamental kale leaves are frilly edged and sometimes deeply lobed; those of ornamental cabbage usually are ruffled but don't form a tight head. Both are edible, but you'll enjoy the real vegetables far more.

Plants are striking and especially useful in mass plantings, edgings, and containers. Foliage color develops best during the cool weather of fall. Locate in full sun, in well-drained, rich, moist soil. Sow seeds in late summer, timing transplanting for four to five weeks before the first fall frost. Where winter temperatures don't drop much below 20 degrees, plants continue to grow until spring. Both types are less colorful in spring, but transplants can be set in early to midspring for a few weeks of show before the onset of hot weather.

ORNAMENTAL PEPPER

Also called Christmas pepper
Capsicum annuum
■ **Height:** To 2 feet
■ **Comments:** Ornamental peppers are related to bell peppers and other summer garden peppers, but are grown for ornament, especially for the small colorful fruits displayed above the foliage mound. Fruits may be short and puffy, conical, or long and slender. They usually ripen through colors of yellow, cream, lime green, orange, and purple, finally maturing red. The peppers are edible, but fiery hot. Use in mass plantings, edgings, and containers. Potted

plants brought indoors before frost continue their colorful display through Christmas.

Set transplants two to three weeks after last frost, starting seeds indoors eight to 10 weeks earlier. Because the seeds require light for germination, cover lightly with soil. Locate in full sun or light shade, in well-drained, average soil. Avoid overfertilizing. Established plants thrive on heat and humidity, and tolerate moderate drought. Mixes and named varieties are sold.

PETUNIA

Petunia x hybrida

■ **Height:** 10 to 18 inches

■ **Comments:** Few plants rival petunias for their display of eye-catching color, ease of growth, and variety of garden uses. Flowers come in all colors but green and orange; many are starred, zoned, striped, or otherwise marked with contrasting colors. The trumpet-shaped flowers often have frilly edges; most are singles, some are doubles, and a few are quite fragrant. The grandifloras produce large flowers—up to 4 inches across—and usually are wavy; multifloras produce more but smaller blooms, and tolerate summer heat better.

Plants form low mounds, usually 12 to 15 inches across, and are excellent in mixed beds, mass plantings, edgings, hanging baskets, window boxes, and other containers.

Start seeds indoors eight to nine weeks before the last spring frost, or buy transplants (which is more successful), setting transplants after all frost danger passes. Because they establish more quickly and perform better, use transplants that have healthy green leaves but no flowers.

Locate in full sun or very light shade, in well-drained soil of average fertility. Growth is best when soil is kept moist, but established plants tolerate moderate drought. Shear overgrown plants in midsummer to encourage fresh growth and flowering. Several mixes and dozens of named varieties are available.

PHLOX, ANNUAL

Also called drummond phlox
Phlox drummondi

■ **Height:** To 1½ feet

■ **Comments:** Low-spreading or mounded annual phlox is covered with flower clusters of white, creamy yellow, pink, blue, red, and lavender. 'Twinkle' has star-shaped flowers with centers of contrasting colors. Use mixed with late spring bulbs, in garden flower fronts, or in mass plantings, edgings, and containers.

Growth is best during cool weather (flowering may even stop during summer's heat). Time transplanting for two to three weeks before the last spring frost. Sow seeds indoors eight to nine weeks earlier. Keep seedlings cool and avoid overwatering to discourage diseases. Where winters are mild, transplant in early fall and early spring for nearly year-round flowering.

Locate in full sun or partial shade, in well-drained, rich, moist soil. Remove faded flowers. Shear and water plants during summer so they will rebloom as the weather cools.

PINK

Dianthus species

■ **Height:** 6 to 15 inches

■ **Comments:** The dianthus genus includes perennial carnation, biennial sweet william, and several species grown as annuals and referred to as pinks or China pinks. The frilly edged, slightly fragrant flowers may be white, red, scarlet, coral, pink, or bicolored. They are borne on stout stems above gray-green, grasslike foliage. Plants are low, often mounded, and are used in edgings, mass plantings, the fronts of flower beds, and window boxes and other containers.

Locate in full sun, in rich, moist, well-drained soil. Plants do best in cool, humid weather, and tolerate some frost. Set hardened transplants in the garden in mid-spring. Sow seeds indoors seven to eight weeks earlier. Cut back after flowering to encourage repeat blooms. Where winter temperatures stay above 10 degrees, plant in early fall for growth year-round.

ORNAMENTAL PEPPER

PETUNIA

ANNUAL PHLOX

ANNUALS PORTFOLIO *(continued)*

PORTULACA

RUDBECKIA

SALPIGLOSSIS

POPPY, SHIRLEY

Also called Flanders poppy and corn poppy
Papaver rhoeas

■ **Height:** To 3 feet
■ **Comments:** Shirley poppy, a longtime garden favorite, produces spectacular cup-shaped flowers textured like crepe paper atop tall stems. Blooms—from single to double—open from nodding, puffy buds and come in white, pink, salmon, brilliant red, and bicolored. Use in the mid- to back parts of flower gardens, in mass plantings, and in naturalized areas. Plants reseed in mild-winter areas.

Because transplanting is difficult, sow directly in the garden as early as you can work the soil in spring (in mild-winter areas, also in fall). Repeat spring sowings every few weeks for continuous bloom. Plant in full sun in well-drained, moist soil. Avoid fertilizing heavily.

PORTULACA

Also called moss rose
Portulaca grandiflora

■ **Height:** To 6 inches
■ **Comments:** Portulaca is ideal in edgings, beds, rock gardens, and containers. From early summer until fall frost, the low, mat-forming plants are covered with showy, ruffled flowers in all colors but green and blue. Blooms, which may be single, semidouble, or double, usually open fully only on sunny days.

Locate in full sun, in nearly any well-drained soil. Avoid heavy fertilizing. Plants thrive on heat and, once established, are fairly drought tolerant. Watering during dry spells yields best growth and flowering. If plants get leggy, shear to 2 inches tall in late summer. They'll quickly return to full bloom in fall. Plants reseed freely, but are seldom a nuisance.

P. oleracea produces trailing stems to 1½ feet and is ideal for hanging baskets and rock and wall gardens. 'Wildfire' mix has a wide range of brightly colored, mostly single flowers.

RUDBECKIA

Also called gloriosa daisy
Rudbeckia hirta

■ **Height:** To 3 feet
■ **Comments:** Gloriosa daisies are specially developed forms of the wild perennial black-eyed susan. Breeding introduced extra vigor and the ability to flower early the first year from seed. Plants thrive in heat, producing masses of strong-stemmed, daisylike flowers from midsummer until fall frost. Colors are predominantly golden yellow, but many mixes include yellow, orange, bronze, and mahogany; most have contrasting centers. Flowers, from 3 to 6 inches across, are excellent for cutting.

Locate in full sun or very light shade, in nearly any well-drained, moderately rich soil. Established plants tolerate drought. Sow directly in the garden after danger of frost passes, or use transplants started indoors six to seven weeks earlier. Tall varieties may require support. Gloriosa daisies reseed freely, and many are short-lived perennials in mild-winter areas.

Varieties include semidouble and double flowering forms, and plants only 2 feet tall.

SALPIGLOSSIS

Also called painted-tongue
Salpiglossis sinuata

■ **Height:** To 3 feet
■ **Comments:** Salpiglossis is ideal for the mid- to back portion of the garden, growing upright and showing off colorful, velvety flowers. Blooms are shaped like petunias, but have more unusual and richer color. Colors include yellow, gold, rose, red, pink, crimson, and purple; most varieties have contrasting colored veins. Use in beds and containers, and for cut flowers.

Plants do best during cool weather, and tolerate mild frosts. Set hardened transplants in midspring. Sow seeds indoors seven to eight weeks earlier, potting into peat-moss pots. Sowing directly in the garden usually is unsuccessful. Encourage branching by pinching tips of young plants when 6 inches tall. Locate in a spot that receives full sun but is protected from the wind. Soil must be very well drained, and should be rich and moist. Mulching and regular watering help plants endure hot spells.

'Bolero' mix grows to 2½ feet tall with a full range of colors. 'Splash' mix is bushier and more compact, reaching only 2 feet. Growing to only 15 inches tall is the more heat-resistant 'Dwarf Friendship' mix.

SALVIA

Also called scarlet sage
Salvia splendens

■ **Height:** To 3 feet

■ **Comments:** Easy-to-grow salvia is known for its showy flower spikes—usually brilliant red, but also white, pink, rose, scarlet, violet, and purple. Foliage is dark green. Plants are tidy, and all but the tallest withstand rain and weather. Use in beds, edgings, mass plantings, and containers.

At its best in areas of warm nights and high humidity, salvia needs partial shade in the Deep South and inland areas of the Southwest; otherwise, full sun. Soil must be well drained, moist, and rich. Because plants are sensitive to excess fertilizer, apply light doses only, once a month.

Sow seeds indoors eight to nine weeks before last frost, or buy transplants not yet in flower. Set plants only after the last frost when the soil is warm. Planting too early or using flowered transplants causes stunting.

The 'Hotline' series is early flowering and compact, growing only 8 to 10 inches tall. 'Carabiniere' series is available in several colors, growing 12 to 14 inches tall. 'Early Bonfire' reaches 2 feet and has brilliant scarlet-red flowers. 'Tall Splendens' grows to 3 feet with bright red flowers. 'Laser Purple' grows to about 1 foot; 'Purple Blaze,' to 16 inches.

SCABIOSA

Also called pincushion flower
Scabiosa atropurpurea

■ **Height:** 1½ to 3 feet

■ **Comments:** Fragrant, colorful pincushion-shaped flowers atop strong stems make scabiosa a favorite cut flower, for use either fresh or dried. The double blooms range from 2 to 4 inches across and come in white, blue, rose, lavender, and dark purple. Use in mixed beds and mass plantings, and for cut flowers.

Set transplants after the chance of frost passes. Sow seeds indoors four to five weeks earlier. In areas with a long growing season, sow directly in the garden in late summer for a fall crop. Locate in full sun, in well-drained, moist, average-to-rich soil. Keep flowers cut for continuous bloom.

Most types grow to 3 feet tall, but 'Dwarf Double' mix reaches only 1½ feet.

S. stellata—which is also known as drumstick, paper moon, and starflower—has blue to violet flowers that produce fascinating, golf-ball-shaped heads useful in dried arrangements. Plants grow to 1½ feet tall.

SCHIZANTHUS

Also called butterfly flower
Schizanthus pinnatus

■ **Height:** 12 to 15 inches

■ **Comments:** In areas with a long, cool growing season, schizanthus is a favorite in mixed flower beds, mass plantings, and window boxes and other containers. In all climates, it's a perfect pot plant for a cool greenhouse or sunroom. Plants have lacy, fernlike foliage and delicate bicolored flowers in pink, rose, red, yellow, white, and purple. Several mixes are available.

Sow seeds indoors eight to 10 weeks before transplanting. Because hardened plants tolerate mild frosts, transplant by mid-spring. For best results, flowers should peak before the onset of summer's heat. Where winters are mild, transplant in early fall, too. Locate in full sun in cool-weather areas; otherwise, in partial shade. Soil must be very well drained, moist, and rich. To produce wintertime potted plants in a cool greenhouse or sun-room, sow seeds in fall.

SALVIA

SCABIOSA

ANNUALS PORTFOLIO *(continued)*

SNAPDRAGON

STOCK

SNAPDRAGON

Antirrhinum majus
■ **Height:** To 3 feet
■ **Comments:** With their wide range of heights, snapdragons are suited to nearly every garden situation. Dwarfs—such as 'Floral Carpet' mix at just 7 inches high or 'Kolibri' mix at 8 inches tall—are perfect in rock gardens, edgings, and window boxes and other containers. For the middle of the garden, mass plantings, large containers, and cuttings, choose from the several medium (14- to 20-inch) varieties, including 'Coronette,' 'Little Darling,' 'Monarch,' and 'Sprite.' All are mixes with a wide range of colors. In the middle to back of the garden, in mass plantings, and for superb cut flowers, use the tall types—including the popular mixes 'Bright Butterflies,' 'Madame Butterfly,' 'Rocket,' and 'Topper'—which grow from 2 to 3 feet or slightly higher. Individual colors are available from many series.

Snapdragons come in all colors except green and blue, and in many bicolors. The pouched, tubular flowers on dense upright spikes can be "snapped" open and closed. Petals of some varieties are open, rather than pouched, flaring into a ruffled, butterflylike display.

Because hardened seedlings can tolerate moderate frost, transplant to the garden three to four weeks before last spring frost. Sow seeds indoors six to seven weeks earlier. Snapdragons thrive in cool weather and often are better timed for fall bloom by sowing seeds in midsummer. In mild-winter areas, set out transplants in fall for winter and spring bloom.

Locate in full sun or partial shade, in rich, moist, well-drained soil. Discourage disease by spacing adequately and providing good air circulation. Pinch young plants to encourage branching, and remove all faded flowers.

SNOW-ON-THE-MOUNTAIN

Also called ghostweed
Euphorbia marginata
(sometimes listed as *E. variegata*)

■ **Height:** 1½ to 2½ feet
■ **Comments:** For an easy-to-grow and refreshing accent among the colors of summer and fall flowers, few plants top snow-on-the-mountain. The bottom leaves are green; those farther up are edged in white; and the bracts (just below the small flowers) are snow-white. All combine to make an eye-catching break from colorful flowers.

Sow directly in the garden in late spring, or sow seeds indoors five to six weeks earlier. Aside from requiring full sun, plants have few demands, growing in nearly any well-drained soil. They need little fertilizer, and, once established, tolerate heat and drought well. Plants reseed, but seedlings are easy to remove. Handle plants carefully because the milky sap may irritate your eyes and skin.

STATICE

Limonium sinuatum
■ **Height:** To 2½ feet
■ **Comments:** Productive, easy-to-grow statice yields some of the most colorful and durable dried flowers. Dense, flattened sprays of crisp blossoms top stiff, winged stems. Colors include white, yellow, pink, rose, lavender, blue, and purple; many varieties have contrasting centers. Foliage forms a low, ground-hugging rosette.

Sow seeds indoors eight weeks before the last frost, using peat-moss pots to reduce transplant shock. Set seedlings in the garden after frost danger passes. Sow directly in the garden in areas with a long growing season. If seeds are still encased in husks, break before sowing.

Locate in full sun, in well-drained soil. Statice tolerates seaside conditions, heat, and drought.

STOCK

Matthiola incana
■ **Height:** 10 to 30 inches
■ **Comments:** Long favored for its delightfully fragrant, colorful cut flowers, stock looks best when timed to flower during cool weather.

Set transplants three to four weeks before the last spring frost in all areas and again in mid-fall in mild-winter areas. Start seedlings indoors six to seven weeks before transplanting. For the highest percentage of double flowers, select only the palest, light green seedlings from the seed flat. Others will be mostly singles.

Flowers may be white, creamy yellow, pink, crimson, lavender, purple, and purplish blue. For compact plants, seldom over 1½ feet tall, and for earliest flowering, choose from the dwarf seven-week and 10-week varieties (the numbers refer to the time between germination and flowering under ideal conditions). Taller and later-flowering varieties include 'Beauty of Nice,' growing to 20 inches tall, and 'Giant Imperial' mix, reaching 2½ feet tall. Those described as column stock produce only one strong spike per plant and are normally grown commercially for the cut-flower market.

Use all sizes in mixed flower beds and mass plantings; use shorter types in edgings and containers. Plant where you can enjoy the fragrance. Give plants full sun where temperatures are cool; part shade otherwise. Soil must be rich, moist, and well drained. Water during dry spells.

STRAWFLOWER

Also called everlasting
Helichrysum bracteatum

■ **Height:** To 3 feet
■ **Comments:** The pompon or buttonlike blooms of strawflower are produced on stout stems, making them perfect for fresh or dried arrangements. Strawlike bracts (modified leaves) give strawflower its color—usually rich yellow, gold, orange, bronze, and fiery red. White, pink, and salmon colors are in most mixes, too. Flowers may be semidouble or double, and grow up to 2½ inches across.

Set transplants after danger of frost passes, using seedlings started indoors five to six weeks earlier. Where the growing season is long, you can sow directly in the garden after the last frost. Locate in full sun, in well-drained soil. Once established, plants tolerate heat and some

drought, making them a good choice for dry spots and sunny hillsides.

Most strawflowers are sold as color mixes and grow 2 to 3 feet tall. A widely available dwarf form is the 'Bright Bikinis' mix, growing to only 14 inches tall. Those sold as the variety 'Monstrosum' produce flowers between 3 and 4 inches across, on plants up to 4 feet tall.

SUNFLOWER

Helianthus annuus

■ **Height:** To 12 feet
■ **Comments:** Often relegated to the back of the vegetable garden or along a fence row, sunflowers really deserve a place in nearly every summer flower garden. They're easy to grow, foolproof, and come in a range of heights, colors, and flower types.

Among the shortest sunflowers are 'Teddy Bear,' with golden yellow, double, chrysanthemumlike flowers up to 5 inches across; and 'Sunspot,' with 10-inch single, birdseed-producing flowers. Both grow to barely 2 feet tall and are perfect for a child's garden.

At about 4 feet is 'Italian White,' which produces creamy white flowers with dark centers.

One of the most colorful varieties in the 5- to 6-foot range is 'Color Fashion' with 6-inch single flowers of yellow, gold, mahogany, brownish red, and several bicolors. Similar varieties are 'Large Flowered Mixed' and 'Autumn Beauty.' For double, golden yellow flowers on plants 5 to 6 feet tall, use 'Sungold.'

The tallest, largest-flowered varieties have suitable names such as 'Mammoth,' 'Russian Mammoth,' and 'Giganteus.' These grow from 10 to 12 feet tall with flowers up to 1½ feet inches across, and are used for ornaments, snack food, and bird feed.

Sow directly in the garden after the last frost. Except in areas with a short growing season, little is gained by using transplants. Locate in full sun, in well-drained soil of average fertility. Sunflowers thrive on heat and grow best with regular watering; but, once established, they tolerate drought. Tall types may need support.

STRAWFLOWER

SUNFLOWER

ANNUALS PORTFOLIO *(continued)*

SWEET PEA

TITHONIA

VERBENA

SWEET PEA

Lathyrus odoratus

■ **Height:** To 6 feet

■ **Comments:** With its colorful, often fragrant flowers, sweet pea is a garden favorite. And it's easy to grow if timed for cool weather. Where summer's heat comes quickly, start seeds indoors in late winter. Use peat-moss pots, putting two to three seeds in each; do not thin seedlings. Set hardened seedlings in the garden four to six weeks later—a few weeks before the last frost. Or sow directly in the garden as soon as you can work the soil in spring. Where summers are cool, extend the flowering season with later plantings. In the Deep South and along the mildest parts of the Pacific Coast, sow in fall, too.

Locate in full sun or light shade out of drying winds. Soil must be well drained, rich, and moist. Support climbing types early. Apply a mulch in late spring to keep soil and roots cool and moist. Keep faded flowers picked.

Sweet pea flowers are solid or bicolored, and come in all colors but orange, yellow, and green. Dozens of climbing or bush varieties are available. Climbing types have tendrils and require support. They produce the largest flowers, on long stems suitable for cutting. Bush types have few or no tendrils, require no support, and generally grow less than 2 feet tall.

TITHONIA

Also called Mexican sunflower
Tithonia rotundifolia

■ **Height:** 3 to 6 feet

■ **Comments:** For heat resistance, drought tolerance, and lots of showy flowers, few annuals beat tithonia. The stiff-stemmed, daisylike flowers grow 2 to 3 inches across and come in warm tones of yellow, orange, and red. Plants become somewhat shrubby by season's end. Flowers, good for cutting, attract butterflies. Use in the back of the garden and as a temporary hedge.

Sow directly in the garden after the last frost, or use transplants started indoors six to seven weeks earlier. Locate in full sun, in nearly any soil. Avoid overfertilizing.

'Goldfinger' and 'Sundance' have orange-scarlet flowers and grow to only about 3 feet tall. 'Torch,' with orange-red flowers, and 'Yellow Torch' grow to nearly 6 feet tall.

VERBENA

Verbena x hybrida

■ **Height:** To 12 inches

■ **Comments:** Verbena, one of the best low-growing annuals, thrives in heat, requires little maintenance, and comes in a wide range of colors. Flowers are borne in clusters 1 to 2 inches across and include white, creamy yellow, pink, red, purple, and shades in between. Many have contrasting white eyes. Most types grow no more than 1 foot tall and are perfect in edgings, beds, rock gardens, window boxes, hanging baskets, and other containers. One type, sold as 'Grandiflora' or 'Mammoth' verbena, grows 1½ to 2 feet tall and is used for cut flowers.

Locate in full sun or light afternoon shade, in well-drained soil. Plants do best in rich, moist soil, but nearly any soil is suitable; established plants tolerate drought and heat well. Because verbena seeds are difficult to germinate, many gardeners buy transplants and set them out after the last frost. To produce seedlings, sow indoors 10 to 12 weeks before the last frost. Refrigerate seeds at least one week before sowing. Germinate in the dark at 70 degrees. When the first seed sprouts (about four weeks), move into light and cooler temperatures.

VINCA

Also called Madagascar periwinkle
Catharanthus roseus

■ **Height:** To 1½ feet

■ **Comments:** The bushy, tidy plants of vinca feature attractive, glossy leaves and colorful flowers of white, pink, or rose; many varieties have a rose eye. The single, star-shaped blooms are 1 inch or slightly more across. Use in mass plantings, beds, edgings, and containers.

Plant in full sun or partial shade, in moist, rich, well-drained soil. Vinca thrives on heat and, when established, tolerates drought. Sowing directly in the garden usually is unsuccessful because young seedlings grow very slowly. Buy transplants or sow seeds indoors 10 to 12 weeks before the last frost. The temperature of the seed flat should be near 70 degrees, and germination requires two to three weeks. Transplant only after all frost danger passes and the weather has warmed.

'Magic Carpet' mix has a creeping habit, growing only 6 inches tall and 2 feet wide. Use for low edgings, as an annual ground cover, in rock gardens, and in hanging baskets. Plants in the 'Little' series come in a full range of colors, some with contrasting eyes, and grow 10 inches tall. Several mixes in the 15- to 18-inch range are available.

VIOLA

Also called horned violet
Viola cornuta

■ **Height:** 6 to 8 inches
■ **Comments:** Traditionally, viola flowers were distinguished from pansy flowers by their small size and lack of face markings. Violas also bloomed more reliably the first year from seed and tended to stay in flower better than pansies under rugged conditions. However, with recent breeding introductions, the distinctions between the two plants are diminishing.

Low and compact, viola plants are perfect in edgings, rock gardens, window boxes, and other containers. They also blend well with spring bulbs. Violas do best in moderate temperatures and should receive full sun only where weather is cool; otherwise, partial shade. Soil must be rich, moist, and well drained; a mulch during summer helps. Keep faded flowers picked.

Time planting for cool spring weather by sowing seeds indoors in late winter and shifting hardened transplants to the garden in mid-spring. Violas tolerate moderate frosts and can be planted in early fall in mild-winter areas.

Johnny-jump-up, *V. tricolor,* requires similar culture. Plants grow 12 to 15 inches tall with dainty flowers marked with faces of white, yellow, and purple.

ZINNIA

Zinnia elegans

■ **Height:** 6 inches to 3 feet
■ **Comments:** Few annuals top zinnias for durability in rugged garden conditions, speed of growth, and range of heights, uses, flower colors, and sizes. Flowers come in all colors except blue. Some are striped, blotched, or otherwise bicolored. Blooms range from small, tight pompons to large doubles. Some blossoms have ruffled edges; some grow to 7 inches across.

Plant habits fall into three main categories: Dwarfs, which form low, compact mounds only 6 to 12 inches tall, are ideal in edgings, beds, pots, window boxes, and other containers. Intermediates produce plants knee-high or slightly taller, and work well in mass plantings, beds, and larger containers. Tall types reach 3 feet or slightly higher, producing flowers ideal for cuttings. They also are perfect for mass plantings and for use in the mid- to back portions of mixed flower beds.

Z. angustifolia, usually sold as 'Classic' zinnia, grows only about 10 inches tall and spreads to about 2 feet. Use in rock gardens, edgings, and hanging baskets and other containers. Plants are smothered with single, golden orange flowers. The distinctive foliage is narrow and linear.

Zinnias thrive on heat and do best in arid climates. Locate in areas with full sun and good air circulation; avoid overhead watering late in the day to prevent disease. Zinnias tolerate nearly any well-drained soil, but grow best in rich, moist soil. Sow directly in the garden after the last frost, or use transplants, not yet in flower, started indoors four to five weeks earlier. Pinch tips of transplants to encourage bushiness. Remove faded flowers.

VINCA

VIOLA

ZINNIA

BULBS

When you
plant a bulb, you plant a self-contained
package of foliage and flowers that
will reward you with color year after year.
Triggered from dormancy by time or
temperature, bulbs are one of the most
permanent and reliable of all flowering
plants. They help us welcome spring with
a brilliant burst of color or fill our summer
gardens with unusual beauty.

HARDY BULBS

In early spring, the orange-red tones of 'Love Song,' a kaufmanniana tulip, provide   *complementary color harmony to the purple hybrid crocus 'Remembrance.'*

Long before other plants, tiny bulbs such as winter aconite and snowdrop poke through the ground in spring. Their colorful show of life—along with that of other hardy bulbs—is certain to rekindle your gardening interests, if by remotest chance during winter you slipped into a horticultural hibernation,

Later, when spring-flowering trees, shrubs, and perennials come into bloom, hyacinths, daffodils, and tulips complete the palette with complementary colors. And as spring wanes, bulbs bridge the gap between the colors of the closing season and the flowers of summer.

BULB TYPES

For simplicity's sake, all of the plants in this chapter are referred to as bulbs, although a few of them are not true bulbs. They all have unique food-storing capabilities and are similar in their growth habits. All are planted while dormant and then grow, bloom, and store food before going dormant again. Their planting and care requirements are essentially the same.

True bulbs, such as daffodil and hyacinth, are actually complete plants within a tiny package. A bulb contains future roots, stems, leaves, and flowers. Fleshy scales surround the future growth and contain all the necessary food for the bulb to grow. After a bulb has bloomed, leaves manufacture food for the next year and transfer it underground to start the chain again the following year. As a bulb grows, tiny bulblets—which you can remove to grow as new plants—form around the base.

Corms, such as crocus, are modified stems filled with food-storage tissue. They usually are short and squat, and covered with a meshy material. Growth eyes appear at their tops. Corms disappear after they bloom, and new ones form for next year's growth. Some corms also produce cormels, which are similar to bulblets.

Rhizomes are thick food-storage stems that grow along the soil surface. Growth buds form on a rhizome for the next season's leaves and flowers; the original rhizome will not reflower.

Tubers, such as Grecian windflower, are

In early spring, the orange-red tones of 'Love Song,' a kaufmanniana tulip, provide complementary color harmony to the purple hybrid crocus 'Remembrance.'

underground, noncreeping food-storing stems. Tuberous roots are thick, fleshy, food-storing roots that look like tubers.

LANDSCAPING WITH BULBS

For a spring garden abloom all season, plant a number of bulb types with succeeding flowering times. Also, select varieties whose colors blend together and with surrounding trees, shrubs, and perennials that may be in bloom, too. Interplant bulbs into ground covers, or use them under trees and shrubs, along a walkway, in a rock garden, or as an accent planting. Plant them in geometric patterns or informal drifts. Also, select a site for bulbs where you can enjoy their flowers whether you're indoors or outside.

(Opposite) Clumps of tulips, hyacinths, and daffodils combine in mid-spring to brighten up a hillside, long before the leaves unfurl on the trees overhead.

TULIPS

Spring and tulips are practically synonymous. Tulips have such a vast array of sizes, colors, and bloom times that you could plant nothing but tulips and still have a garden with three months of color.

The earliest of all tulips to bloom are *Tulipa kaufmanniana* and its hybrids, often called water-lily tulips. Following their bloom, the fosteranas appear, with their large, cup-shaped blooms on stems up to 20 inches tall.

Single early tulips have the classic shape of traditional tulips on 10- to 16-inch stems. They are more weather resistant than other tulips, and are fragrant, too. Double early tulips are 6 to 12 inches high and have full flowers that last longer than single blooms.

Hybridizers crossed single early tulips with late-flowering varieties and created the triumph tulip, which blooms in mid-spring. Blooming with the triumphs are the greigi hybrids, which have striped or mottled foliage and slender buds on 7- to 14-inch stems.

Also blooming at the same time are the darwin hybrids, crosses between late-blooming darwins and early-blooming fosteranas. They are similar to the darwins but with red, yellow, or orange flowers. The darwins are the most popular of all tulips, for they come in all colors from pure white to inky black. Rembrandt tulips, a part of this group, have vivid stripes or blotches caused by a virus (a natural occurrence that doesn't harm the plants).

Blooming in late spring with the darwins are the similar cottage tulips with their large flowers and 3-foot stems. They come in all colors except blue and purple. The viridiflora, with green streaks on the outside of the petals, is a variation of the cottage tulip.

Also in bloom in late spring are parrot tulips, with large petals that are fringed, feathered, or twisted, and graceful lily-flowered tulips, with petals that are long, pointed, and curved outward. Double late tulips look like double early tulips, but with longer stems and more informal flowers. This is the best tulip for a massed bed in mixed colors.

(Far left) Species tulips are wild tulips or their hybrids. They are hardy, colorful, and especially useful in rock gardens.

(Near left) Mid- to late-blooming multiflowered tulips produce as many as six flowers per stem.

(Far left) Darwin hybrid tulips, like darwin tulips, grow 2 to 2½ feet high.

(Near left) Fringed tulips include fringed single early, darwin hybrid, darwin, and cottage tulips.

(Left) Tulips look best when planted in masses of the same color. Here, the red and golden tones of the cottage tulips form a background to the shorter parrot tulips of the same color combination.

(Opposite) Tulips take over a hillside garden as the daffodils and hyacinths start to fade. Mixing bulbs that have different blooming times ensures continuous color in spring.

DAFFODILS

(Right) 'Touché,' a trumpet daffodil, has a yellow trumpet and white segments, or petals. Other varieties may be all white ('Mount Hood') or all yellow ('King Alfred').

(Right) The hoop-petticoat daffodil gets its name from its unique flower form. The bright yellow blooms flower in early spring on 6-inch stems and are happy under trees or naturalized in the lawn.

(Opposite) One of the first daffodils to flower is 'Peeping Tom,' a cyclamineus variety. Growing 6 to 8 inches tall, it does well in rock gardens and with other early-flowering bulbs.

Daffodils and jonquils, all members of the narcissus genus, are among the most graceful of spring bulbs. With the proper selection of species and varieties, daffodil gardens can bloom over a three-month period from mid- to late winter until mid-spring, in white, yellow, gold, orange, and pink tones. Daffodils are perfect for the informal garden and excellent for naturalizing.

The flowers of daffodils and jonquils have two parts. The central part is called a trumpet or a cup, depending on its shape. The second part—six petals or segments—surrounds the central part. The two parts may be the same or different colors.

Daffodils and jonquils are classified into several groups based on their species derivation or shape, and grow from 4 to 20 inches tall.

Those that have a central part as long or longer than their petals are called trumpet daffodils; these are the largest and among the first of the larger hybrids to bloom. Next smaller in size are large-cupped and small-cupped daffodils. All of these have one flower per stem.

When the cup is split, or frilled, the flowers are known as split-corona daffodils. These daffodils bloom in mid- to late spring with double daffodils, which have many petals and do not form distinct cups or trumpets.

Snow may still be on the ground when *Narcissus bulbocodium*—the hoop-petticoat daffodil—and *N. cyclamineus* and its hybrids bloom. These hybrids have slender, often drooping flowers with petals that curve distinctly backward.

N. jonquilla and its hybrids, the jonquils, have small cups, a heavy fragrance, and slender, reed-like foliage. Flowers bloom in clusters of two to six. Hybrid daffodils bloom from early to late spring, depending on the variety.

One of the last daffodils to bloom is the tazetta, which has small, fragrant flowers with small cups. Tazettas bloom in clusters of four to eight flowers and are used as forced or cut flowers, as well as in the garden. They are joined by the triandrus daffodils, which have graceful, hanging flowers and petals that curve back behind the cups.

HYACINTHS AND GRAPE HYACINTHS

(Left) White, pink, and blue varieties of hyacinths will fill any garden—modern or old-fashioned—with foot-high flowers of vibrant color and rich fragrance.

The hyacinth genus has only one species, *Hyacinth orientalis,* but it's a species that's especially rewarding to the gardener. It and its many named varieties have a delicious scent so powerful it easily fills garden corners. To enjoy the aroma of hyacinths, plant them where you will walk by them often or put them outside windows you can open on warm days.

Hyacinths are more formal than other bulbs, and do well in massed beds or lining shrub and bulb beds and borders. Because its flower colors include white, pink, red, salmon, yellow, and blue, hyacinth harmonizes well with daffodils, tulips, and other bulbs that appear at the same time. Try pink or blue hyacinths under yellow forsythia to create a pleasing color harmony.

Hyacinths, like most bulbs, look best when at least three bulbs of the same variety are planted together in a clump, instead of being planted in a straight line across the front of the house or in mixed colors. Unfortunately, hyacinths, like tulips, become smaller and weaker over time, and need replacing every three to five years.

GRAPE HYACINTHS

The grape hyacinth is not a hyacinth at all, but rather belongs to the muscari genus. From a distance, however, the grape hyacinth looks like a 4- to 8-inch version of its larger cousin.

Grape hyacinths have a fragrance, but it's not as encompassing as the aroma of hyacinths. These little bulbs find a happy home under flowering trees, in rock gardens, and as a ground cover to taller daffodils and tulips. They naturalize easily and quickly, and soon can cover large areas of a lawn or woodland garden. Don't cut off faded flowers if you want the plants to drop their seeds and spread.

Most grape hyacinths are deep blue to purple, although a white variety exists. Grape hyacinths produce foliage in the fall, which can become unsightly. If it does, trim away the brown edges of the leaves (this will not hurt the plant).

(Opposite) The deep blue of grape hyacinth (shown here with taller tulips) is a great asset when designing flower beds. Use grape hyacinths in massed plantings or as dividers with other colors (especially yellow and red).

SEASON OPENERS

Glory-of-the-snow lights up the garden with 4- to 5-inch spikes of star-shaped, blue flowers with white centers. Pink and white varieties are available, too.

(Right) The blue, bell-shaped blooms of Siberian squill—or scilla—tuck neatly between the red and white flowers and red-striped foliage of the early-blooming 'Heart's Desire' tulip.

(Opposite) Flat-petaled white Grecian windflowers—or anemones—combine with larger and curvier 'Jeanne d'Arc' Dutch crocuses. Windflowers also may be pink or blue; crocuses, also yellow, purple, or lavender.

Long before other plants contribute color to the garden, early spring bulbs such as winter aconite (eranthis), snowdrop (galanthus), bulbous iris (*Iris reticulata* and *I. danfordiae*), and species crocus poke their heads through the ground or the snow. They are followed by large hybrid Dutch crocuses, which herald spring for about a month.

Next, a trio of blue bulbs comes into bloom in dormant lawns, or under the still-leafless trees. These are Siberian squill (*Scilla siberica*), glory-of-the-snow (*Chionodoxa luciliae*), and puschkinia. The Grecian windflower (*Anemone blanda*) soon carpets beds and borders with its daisylike flowers. All naturalize readily.

Set these early charmers where you will notice them most. Plant them in clumps by the front door or along a pathway. Tuck them into the rock garden or in front of shrubs. Big on color, most of these tough little bulbs will survive winters as cold as 25 degrees below zero.

SEASON STRETCHERS

To extend the colorful spring season, rely on late-flowering bulbs. They are as reliable as their early-blooming relatives and look beautiful on their own or teamed with flowering trees and shrubs, early perennials, and tulips, daffodils, and hyacinths.

Combine Dutch iris or wood hyacinth with late-blooming azaleas, dogwood, or Scotch broom. Dutch iris, hybrids of *Iris xiphium,* are 2 feet tall, with purple, blue, yellow, or white flowers. An airy configuration gives these flowers a stately look. Wood hyacinths (*Endymion hispanicus,* but sometimes listed in catalogs as *Hyacinthoides hispanicus* or *Scilla campanulata*) have dainty, bell-like flowers that generally are blue.

Summer snowflake (*Leucojum aestivum*) has clusters of white, bell-shaped blooms atop 1-foot stems. Summer snowflake resembles lily-of-the-valley, and because they bloom at the same time, the two make a good garden duo. Also white, but lower growing and with star-shaped flowers, is star-of-Bethlehem (*Ornithogalum umbellatum*), which thrives under poor conditions and minimum attention.

Delicate in appearance, guinea-hen tulip (*Fritillaria meleagris*) has purple and white checkered flowers resembling a lampshade. It contrasts sharply with its larger and more stately cousin, crown-imperial (*F. imperialis*), which works best as an accent in formal, late-blooming tulip beds.

For a wildflower look in a moist, shady corner, plant dog-tooth violet (erythronium species), which has nodding, lilylike flowers of white, rose, violet, or yellow; hardy cyclamen (*Cyclamen repandum*), whose lilac-pink flowers are small but demand attention; and violet wood sorrel (*Oxalis violacea*).

Alliums, which are related to onions, are striking additions to a flower bed. The tallest, *Allium giganteum,* reaches 5 feet in height and has purple flowers; *A. moly* grows a foot tall and has golden yellow blooms. One of the last to bloom in spring, alliums are joined by camassia, with its loose spikes of pale blue flowers, and foxtail lily (*Eremurus robustus*), which has tall, thick, dramatic spikes of peach, pink, orange, yellow, or white blooms.

Wood hyacinth—also known as Spanish bluebell—covers the ground under shrubs *with 10-inch spikes of delicate flowers. It also is available in pink and white varieties.*

Dutch irises display decorative blotched flower falls. Their ornamental markings and regal air make them a favorite often found in florists' cut-flower selections. For showiest display, set Dutch iris bulbs 4 inches deep.

The flowers of giant onion (from the allium family) can reach 5 inches across. Plant this tall bulb at the back of the border where lower-growing plants will hide its often unattractive, brown foliage. Set bulbs 10 inches deep.

HARDY BULB KNOW-HOW

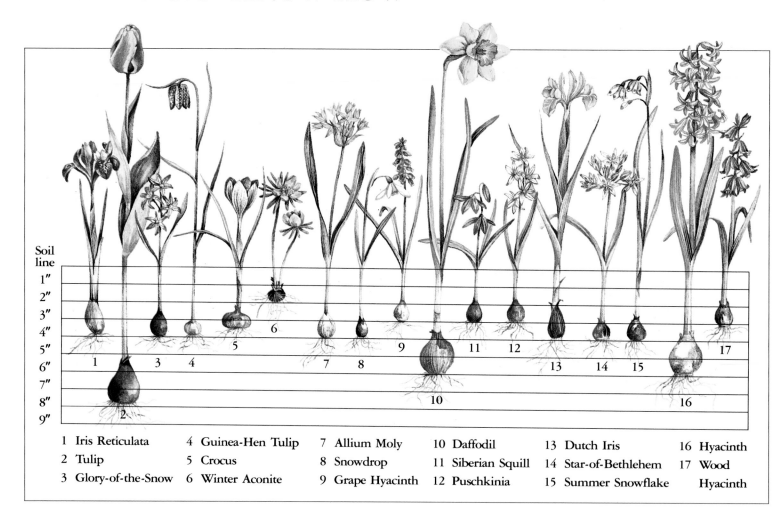

Soil line
1"
2"
3"
4"
5"
6"
7"
8"
9"

1 Iris Reticulata	4 Guinea-Hen Tulip	7 Allium Moly	10 Daffodil	13 Dutch Iris	16 Hyacinth
2 Tulip	5 Crocus	8 Snowdrop	11 Siberian Squill	14 Star-of-Bethlehem	17 Wood
3 Glory-of-the-Snow	6 Winter Aconite	9 Grape Hyacinth	12 Puschkinia	15 Summer Snowflake	Hyacinth

Planning for bulbs means planting many months before you'll see the results, but the effort is worth it. Plant at the correct depth as indicated on this chart or a depth about three times the width of the bulb.

First decide whether to make your bulb garden formal or informal. Formal gardens are symmetrical and have regular borders. Tulips and hyacinths stand stately in formal gardens. Informal gardens have bulbs planted in natural drifts. Whichever you choose, bulb gardens look best when bulbs of the same color are planted in clumps of three to 12 (depending on their size). Sketch your plan on paper, then follow the advice on these two pages to help ensure success. (For information about hardy lily care, see page 222.)

PLANTING

Always buy large, top-quality bulbs so you won't be disappointed with weak growth or

small flowers. Discard any soft or spongy bulbs. Until you plant your bulbs, store them in a dark, cool, dry area to keep them from growing or drying out (a covered box in an unheated garage is a good place).

Plant your hardy bulbs in soil with good drainage and aeration in an area that will receive light shade during the warmest part of the day. Before planting, add enough organic matter such as peat moss, compost, or leaf mold to equal one-fourth of the soil volume. Although bulbs contain their own food supply for the first season, add phosphorus-enriched bonemeal to the bottom of each planting hole to encourage root growth.

Plant bulbs any time in the fall before the soil freezes. Start with the smaller, earlier-flowering bulbs and finish with tulips, daffodils, and hyacinths. When planting bulbs in individual holes, use a narrow trowel or a tool specially made for planting bulbs. Consult the chart opposite to determine the planting depth, or plant bulbs at a depth three times their width. Plant small bulbs 3 to 6 inches apart; leave 6 to 12 inches between large bulbs.

If squirrels, chipmunks, or other small animals are a problem in your area and threaten to devour your bulbs, plant the bulbs in a buried wire basket or cage, or lay chicken wire on top of the bed you've finished planting.

Water well, mulch the beds, and label them.

SPRING CARE

Spring-flowering bulbs are about the easiest plants to care for, but a few chores in spring will keep bulbs at their blooming best.

Because the growth and flowering of bulbs depends on moisture reaching deep into the root zone, apply 1 inch of water per week if spring rains are inadequate.

To keep bulbs healthy and flowering at their peak, add fertilizer every year when the flowers start to fade. Sprinkle prepared bulb food or a 5–10–5 fertilizer over the ground according to label directions; water in.

When tulips, daffodils, hyacinths, and other large bulbs have finished blooming, cut off the dead flowers to direct energy into the bulbs. Let smaller bulbs go to seed to scatter and increase the colony.

Never remove the foliage from a bulb until it has completely browned and you can pull it away without force. Where neatness counts, braid the foliage or twirl it into a circle and tuck it under nearby plants. If you've planted bulbs in your lawn, do not mow the bulbs until their foliage has fully matured.

Because you may have trouble finding your bulbs when they are dormant, divide or transplant them in the spring when the foliage is still on the plants.

PLANTING BULBS

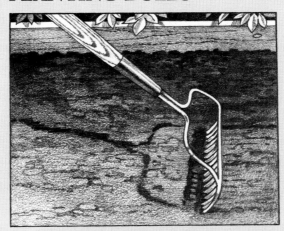

1 Because bulb roots grow deep, spade and prepare the bed to a depth of 1 foot. Rake to even the surface before planting the bulbs. Good soil preparation is key to the success of a bulb garden.

2 To make a bulb planting look natural, toss the bulbs on the ground in a random pattern and plant them where they fall. (You may have to adjust the positions slightly to maintain spacing.)

3 When planting a mass of bulbs, dig one large hole instead of lots of individual holes. Dig the hole 9 to 12 inches deep, then add improved soil until the hole's depth is correct for the bulbs you're planting.

HARDY LILIES

(Far left) Aurelian hybrid lilies grow 3 to 6 feet tall and have blooms of orange, pink, yellow, or white.

(Near left) Oriental hybrid lilies reach heights of 2½ to 7 feet. 'Uchida' shows the group's typical spotted, fragrant petals; its petals also are backswept. Other varieties have bowl-shaped or flat flowers.

W hen you add lilies to the summer flower garden, you add a long season of color and dazzling blooms. Depending on the type and the variety, lilies will bloom from late spring until early fall, providing a strong backdrop in mixed borders. Growing 2 to 9 feet tall, lilies have funnel- or bowl-shaped flowers that may be erect, outward facing, or nodding.

One of the first lilies to bloom is the 4- to 6-foot Turk's-cap lily (*Lilium martagon*), with drooping, reflexed flowers. This lily is followed by the 4-foot candidum hybrids, also known as Madonna lilies, with fragrant, pure-white flowers. Native to North America, the American hybrids bloom in early to midsummer. Their 4- to 8-foot plants have nodding, spotted flowers of red, pink, orange, and yellow, with highly recurved petals.

The Asiatic hybrids, which include the well-known mid-century hybrids, have midsummer flowers in many colors, both in solids and combinations. Flowering on the heels of the American and the Asiatic hybrids, the Aurelian hybrids also bloom in many colors, some with yellow throats or maroon stripes. The last lilies to bloom are *L. auratum,* the gold-banded lily—which has fragrant, slightly drooping white flowers with crimson spots and a central gold stripe on each petal—and the white, yellow, pink, or crimson Oriental hybrids.

LILY CARE

Plant lilies in a rich soil that drains well and in a place that receives at least six hours of sun daily. You can plant them in spring or fall, but fall is typical. Plant all lily bulbs—except those for Madonna and Turk's-cap lilies—8 inches deep, measuring from the base of the bulb. Place Madonna lily bulbs 1 inch below the surface; Turk's-cap bulbs, 2 inches deep. Lily bulbs are never dormant, so don't delay in planting them. Madonna lilies must be planted early enough to start top growth in fall if they are to bloom the next season. For all lily bulbs, sprinkle a handful of bonemeal in the bottom of each planting hole.

Lilies look best when planted in clumps of at least three bulbs of the same type and color. After planting, pack the soil gently to eliminate air pockets. In northern climates, mulch the planting areas with straw or leaves for winter protection.

Set lilies in a mixed border or in mass plantings, or use as accent plants. Shorter-growing varieties flourish in pots. Whether you grow lilies in the ground or in pots, feed them bonemeal once or twice a year. Remove flowers as they fade, and cut stems back after the foliage has turned yellow. Tall lilies need staking.

(Opposite) 'Enchantment' is an Asiatic hybrid lily. This group includes hybrids that grow 2 to 5 feet tall and have white, yellow, red, orange, pink, or lavender flowers.

TENDER BULBS

Tender bulbs, which sometimes are called summer bulbs, are less hardy than their spring-blooming cousins. Like their spring counterparts, however, they may be bulbs, corms, tubers, rhizomes, or tuberous roots. They fall under the heading of "tender bulbs" because they cannot withstand freezing temperatures. Except in the warmest parts of the country, they are planted in spring, then dug up in the fall and stored indoors.

DAHLIAS

Dahlias are the most versatile of tender bulbs. Actually tuberous roots, dahlias bring an almost unlimited selection of heights, colors, and flower types to the sunny garden. And in rich, moist soil, they'll bloom with minimum care from early summer until frost.

Dwarf dahlias grow a foot tall and are ideal as bedding plants. Though many bedding plants look best when massed in one color, dahlias are quite effective in beds of mixed colors. They also can intermingle with annuals and perennials. Their bright blooms range from 1 to 3 inches across and cover the plants all season.

Tall—or standard—dahlias grow 4 to 6 feet high and may produce blooms as large as dinner plates. They put on their best show in late summer and early fall, when most flower borders need fresh color. Tall dahlias need staking; set stakes at planting time so you won't damage the roots while driving in the stakes later on.

Dahlia flowers provide almost a rainbow's spectrum of color, blooming in every color except green and blue. Blossom styles include single, peony, anemone, cactus, ball, and pompon.

Dahlias are most often grown from tuberous roots, especially when named varieties are desired. Plant the roots 4 inches deep after all danger of frost has passed. To get a head start on the season, particularly where the season is short, start tuberous roots indoors. You also can start dahlias from seed; the plants will produce tuberous roots you can lift and transplant. However, dahlias grown from seed have an unpredictable flower form and color.

For bushy dahlias, pinch off the growing tips when the plants are several inches high. For extra-large flowers on standard dahlias, pinch off all but the central bud in the flower cluster.

After frost has blackened the tops of dahlias, carefully dig them from the ground, wash soil away, dry slightly in the sun, then store in dry peat moss or vermiculite in a dark area at 35 to 40 degrees. Check often to make sure they are not shriveling or growing; add water or let them dry out as needed.

CALADIUMS

Fancy-leaved caladiums are grown for their heart-shaped, tropical-looking foliage that is splashed with green, white, silver, pink, and red. At home in the ground or in pots, they brighten up any area in partial to full shade. They do especially well where summers are hot and humid.

In the fall, dig up the caladium tubers and store them in either dry vermiculite or peat moss at 60 degrees.

Colorful caladiums (combined here with ferns) brighten a shady garden spot. Plant tubers 1 inch deep and 1 foot apart in rich, moist soil after frost danger has passed. Or give tubers a head start indoors.

224

(Far left) The simplest of dahlias is the single type, such as this 'Mini-Top Mix.' Less showy than their more elegant cousins, single dahlias still make great additions to flower borders.

(Near left) Fanciful incurved dahlias look equally stunning in the flower garden or when cut and brought indoors. Here, 'Poetic' strikes an impressive pose.

Giant dahlias form a backdrop to dwarf dahlias, helping to extend a lively welcome to guests strolling into this garden through its grapevine-covered arbor.

TENDER BULBS *(continued)*

Two more summer bulbs sure to delight are tuberous begonias, whose iridescent blooms bring color to shady spots, and canna lilies, with spikes soaring to 6 feet.

TUBEROUS BEGONIAS

With their clusters of white, red, yellow, orange, salmon, or pink flowers, tuberous begonias can only be described as spectacular. Some blooms are solid colors; others are two-toned. Many have fringed petals. Resembling roses, camellias, or carnations, the single or double blooms of the tuberous begonia will appear all summer in a partially shaded garden.

Tuberous begonias can brighten up a drab corner when planted in containers, or light up a flower border under trees. Trailing types are tailor-made for hanging baskets. They prefer cool climates but will grow where it is hot if you mist their foliage and keep their roots cool and moist with a mulch.

For best results, start tuberous begonias indoors four to six weeks before planting outside. After the last frost, plant the tubers 1 inch deep and 8 inches apart in rich, fertile soil. Though most tender bulbs should remain in the ground in the fall until frost blackens their foliage, you should remove tuberous begonia tubers before the first frost. Store them in any dry packing material at 45 to 60 degrees.

CANNA LILIES

When you need a striking accent plant for your garden, choose the exotic canna lily. Its spikes support 4-inch flowers of white, cream, yellow, pink, orange, salmon, or red—some with solid colors, others spotted. The attractive, broad-leaved foliage may be bronze or green.

Canna rhizomes should have at least two growing eyes. Lay them flat in the planting hole, with their growing tips 1 inch below the soil line. Plant dwarf types 1 foot apart; standard types 2 feet apart. Give canna lilies full sun and moist, rich, fertile soil. Store at 45 to 50 degrees during winter.

Standard varieties of canna grow 5 to 6 feet tall. When garden space is at a premium, plant dwarf cannas, which reach a height of only about 3 feet.

Use tender bulbs alone or mix them with annuals and perennials. Dwarf dahlias like these often are used as edgings for larger plants. Pick flowers as they fade to ensure summer-long color.

Brightly colored tuberous begonias fill a shady garden with frilled blooms 2 to 8 inches wide. Protect tuberous begonias from strong winds, which could break their brittle stems.

TENDER BULBS *(continued)*

(Far left) Agapanthus—lily-of-the-Nile—has loose globes of fragrant flowers on 1½- to 3-foot stems. Though most are blue, 'Albus' is white. Plant rhizomes 1 inch deep and 1½ feet apart in sunny beds, borders, or containers.

(Near left) Funnel-shaped calla lilies (zantedeschia species) may be white, pink, or yellow; flower stalks grow 1 to 5 feet high. The arrow-shaped leaves often are spotted. Plant rhizomes 3 inches deep, 1 to 2 feet apart, in sun or part shade.

The summer stock of tender bulbs isn't limited to those discussed on pages 224–227. Here are more that deserve notice.

GLADIOLUS

Although their spiked blooms make striking garden displays, gladiolus are best known as cutting flowers. Their dramatic blooms may be solid or two-toned in all colors but blue, and are accented by sword-shaped foliage.

Gladiolus bloom two to three months after planting. To have a continuous supply of flowers for cutting, plant clumps of four or more corms every two weeks. Set stakes around the clumps at planting time to support the stems.

Plant gladiolus corms 4 to 6 inches deep and 4 to 6 inches apart. After the plants flower, dig the corms and store them in mesh bags or old panty hose hung from the ceiling of a 35- to 40-degree room. You do not need to wait until frost to dig gladiolus.

(Left) The petals of ranunculus are dry and appear made of paper. Double and semidouble flowers of yellow, white, red, orange, pink, or gold bloom on 1- to 1½-foot stems. Soak tubers, then plant them 2 inches deep and 8 inches apart in full sun.

OTHER FAVORITES

Easy to care for, summer bulbs are versatile and fit any garden plan. For a fragrant garden in full sun, choose the 20-inch-high sweet-scented gladiolus (acidanthera). (Plant its bulbs 2 inches deep and 5 inches apart.) Combine it with Peruvian lily (alstroemeria), which has large clusters of lily-shaped flowers of orange, gold, yellow, apricot, pink, red, or lavender on 1- to 4-foot stems. Some blooms are streaked or spotted in brown or green. Plant roots 6 inches deep and 15 inches apart. For fragrance and cut flowers, add freesia, whose wiry 1- to 1½-foot stems are covered with tubular flowers of pink, orange,

yellow, red, lavender, white, or blue. Plant the corms 2 inches deep and 2 inches apart.

For a touch of the unusual, grow pineapple lily (eucomis), whose greenish white, star-shaped flowers grow in a stiff cluster and resemble a pineapple. Set bulbs 6 inches deep, 10 inches apart. Tiger flower (tigridia) has two-toned, triangular flowers of red, white, rose, or yellow, with three blotched petals. Plant bulbs 3 inches deep, 6 inches apart. To cover a trellis, choose gloriosa lily, whose flowers are exotic and lilylike. Flowers have yellow centers, red tips, and wavy petals. Plant tubers 4 inches deep and 6 inches apart.

New gladiolus hybrids have a wide color range and interesting color combinations. And as cutting flowers, they are long lasting. Their flower petals can be plain or fancy, ruffled, wavy, crimped, pointed, or frilled.

ROSES

Gardeners
have been enjoying the beauty,
fragrance, and wonder of roses for
centuries. Since the dawn of civilization,
this queen of flowers has fascinated
and challenged many. No other flower has
so magnificently passed the tests of time
and preference. Today, roses remain
as much in people's hearts and gardens
as they did thousands of years ago.

PLANTING ROSES

Roses you purchase for your garden will be either bare root or in containers. Whichever you choose, you should plant your roses in light, rich, well-drained soil that has a pH between 6.0 and 6.5.

BARE-ROOT ROSES

Plant bare-root roses when they are dormant and the ground is not frozen. Depending on your climate, the best time is late winter or early spring. Where winter temperatures do not dip below zero, you can plant roses in the fall, too. If you do plant in the fall, add extra protection. Plant bare-root roses as soon as possible after you receive them. If you can't plant them for several days, keep them in a cool, dark spot. Be sure to keep the roots moist either with the packing material or with damp newspaper or peat moss. For instructions on planting bare-root roses, see the illustrations opposite.

CONTAINER ROSES

Buying container-grown roses allows you to extend the planting season into summer.

Plant container roses the same way as other containerized shrubs (see pages 102–103). If the roses come in metal or plastic containers, always remove the containers before planting.

To ensure fast, strong root growth of roses in compressed-fiber or cardboard containers, plant them without their containers, too. However, if the roses in these types of containers are in full leaf or flower, remove only the bottom of the container and cut slits into its sides so the roots will be unrestricted.

SPACING

In most climates, plant hybrid teas, grandifloras, and floribundas 2 feet apart. Where winters are mild, increase the planting distance; for dense hedging or edging, space a little closer together. Shrub and old garden roses grow large and need a planting distance of 4 to 6 feet. Set climbers you will train horizontally on a fence 8 to 10 feet apart. Plant miniature roses 8 to 18 inches apart, depending on their mature size.

LOCATION

Place roses where they can remain indefinitely, away from competing trees and shrubs.

Roses need at least 6 hours of sun daily; morning sun is best because it dries the plant foliage quickly, reducing the chance of disease. Where summer heat is intense, roses benefit from light afternoon shade. Miniature and climbing roses will grow with slightly less sun than their cousins. Protect roses from wind with a fence, hedge, or other barrier.

Growing magnificent roses starts with good planting techniques. Be sure your planting holes are at least 2 feet wide and 2 feet deep so the roots have ample room to grow. At planting time, add superphosphate to improved soil to ensure strong root growth.

PLANTING BARE-ROOT ROSES

1 Before planting, soak the roots of bare-root roses in water overnight. Prune roots that are too long, broken, or injured.

2 Dig a hole and mound improved soil in its bottom. Set the plant on the mound and spread the roots evenly around it.

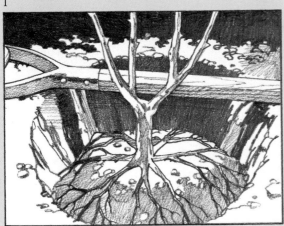

3 Use your shovel handle to make sure the bud union is level with the ground.

4 Backfill the planting hole two-thirds full, add water, then allow it to drain. Fill the hole with more soil, water again, then mound soil around the canes.

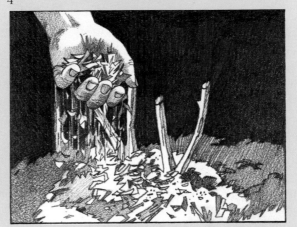

5 Prune roses back by one-third, and remove any dead or broken wood. This fosters new, strong canes.

6 Apply an organic mulch around and over the canes. After new growth begins, gently spray water on the canes to uncover them.

CARING FOR ROSES

Caring for your roses throughout the growing season will reward you with months of beautiful blooms from the onset of warm weather until long after the first frost.

WATERING

When roses receive the right amount of water, the plants grow better and the blooms are larger, have more substance and brighter colors, and last longer.

You can water roses several different ways. Overhead sprinkling is effective when done in the morning. That allows the foliage to dry out before nightfall and lessens the chance of disease. Overhead watering, however, will wash off any preventive sprays applied to the foliage.

You also can water roses with soaker hoses or other drip-irrigation systems permanently installed in the garden. Soaker hoses use less water than other types of irrigation. If you have only a few plants, water them by hand with a hose or watering can or use a soaker hose.

Apply enough water so the roses receive 1 inch of water per week. Use a rain gauge as a guide. For best results, water deep once a week instead of watering lightly more frequently; heavy waterings encourage deeper roots. If your soil is sandy or the weather is very hot or windy, water more often.

FERTILIZING

Use a prepared rose food or a balanced fertilizer such as 5–10–5. Feed roses at least three times a year: immediately after pruning, after the first bloom cycle, and two months before the first fall frost. To grow larger flowers, fertilize roses once a month during the growing season.

Spread the fertilizer evenly over premoistened soil according to label directions. Lightly work it into the top of the soil or mulch, and water well.

If you use liquid fertilizers only, apply them every two weeks because they leach from the soil quickly. Apply them to the foliage only if the temperature is below 90 degrees.

GENERAL CARE

When cutting fresh flowers or removing spent blooms, make the cuts at 45-degree angles above strong, five-leaflet leaves. Be sure to leave at least two sets of leaves on each cane to maintain plant vigor. On new plants, leave as much of the cane as possible.

For large, one-bloom-per-stem flowers on hybrid teas, remove all side flower buds as soon as they appear. You can rub them off with your fingers. Don't wait too long; you'll leave black scars. For more-even-blooming floribunda sprays, remove the central buds as they form.

To prevent diseases such as black spot or mildew, spray or dust rose foliage regularly. To control aphids, Japanese beetles, and other pests, treat as they appear.

MULCHING

Roses grow better if they are mulched. Leave the mulch in place all year long except in areas with short growing seasons. There, do not apply mulch until the soil has warmed up in spring; this will lengthen the blooming season.

In summer, mulch helps keep the soil cool, conserve moisture, and control weeds. Organic mulches, such as wood chips, shredded leaves, pine needles, or buckwheat hulls, will enrich the soil as they decompose. Don't use peat moss, however, because it's hard to rewet once dried.

OTHER GROWING-SEASON TIPS

Always keep your rose garden free of weeds. Weeds compete with rose plants for water and food, are breeding grounds for insects and diseases, and are unattractive. Remove weeds as soon as they appear. You can apply preemergence herbicides to rose beds in spring to prevent annual weeds from germinating (these weed controls won't harm the roses).

Remove flowers, too, as soon as they fade. This encourages new growth and faster reblooming. When working in the garden, keep an eye out for suckers, which are canes with distinct foliage that grow from the understock beneath the bud unions. Remove the suckers to prevent them from diverting the plants' growth.

WINTER PROTECTION

Different roses need different amounts of protection where winter temperatures drop below freezing. China, tea, and most pastel hybrid tea, grandiflora, and floribunda roses are tender. Most climbers and miniatures will survive unprotected to zero degrees. Shrub and old garden roses need protection only in areas where temperatures dip below minus 10 degrees.

Apply winter protection in fall immediately after the ground freezes. Remove it gradually in spring just before pruning. Materials good for winter protection include additional soil, oak leaves, or evergreen boughs.

WINTER CARE

In the coldest parts of the country, protect roses with plastic-foam cones. Wait until the ground freezes before covering the plants. Most roses will need heavy pruning to fit under the cones. Remove the covers on warm winter days to keep excess heat from stimulating plant growth too early.

Because tree roses are very tender, bury them, wrap them, or bring them indoors. To wrap, set four stakes around the plant. Place burlap around the stakes and secure it. Fill the area inside the burlap with leaves (oak, if possible, but never maple) or shredded newspaper.

Where temperatures drop below zero, take climber canes off their supports and secure them to the ground. Cover the canes with soil or leaves. Or, leave the canes in place and wrap them in burlap and leaves.

PRUNING ROSES

Large, healthy roses result from proper pruning. Many disease spores, especially black spot, overwinter on rose canes. Conscientious pruning means you'll cut away and discard many of your problems before they develop.

Pruning roses—including cutting healthy wood—produces vigorous, well-shaped plants full of blooms. Pruning also encourages new canes called basal breaks. Growing from the plants' bottoms, these canes enable plants to renew themselves year after year.

TOOLS COUNT

To do the job properly, buy the right tools. Use pruning shears with curved-edge blades, not the straight-edged anvil variety that can crush stems as they cut. You also will need long-handled lopping shears to cut out thick branches and prune large shrubs. Keep shears clean and oil them after use.

Keep your pruning shears sharp, too. Canes with jagged cuts do not heal properly, which allows insects and disease to get into the plants.

PRUNING POINTERS

Prune roses in late winter or in early spring, as soon as the buds begin to swell, but before they start to open.

Prune hybrid teas, grandifloras, and floribundas as illustrated opposite. Ideal pruning height is 1 to 1½ feet for hybrid teas and floribundas, and 1½ to 2 feet for grandifloras. When winter-kill is severe, prune until the pith—the core of the cane—is white.

If you use floribundas as a hedge, you can prune them higher and leave on more canes.

For shrub and old garden roses, prune lightly to remove old, weak, or dead wood, or to achieve the desired shape. These roses are best left growing as naturally as possible.

Polyanthas rarely suffer winter damage. In spring, cut their canes back to half of their length and remove the oldest canes.

Prune miniatures as you would prune a hybrid tea or floribunda, but on a smaller scale. Cut plants down to 4 to 8 inches, depending on their mature height.

Prune tree roses as you would bush roses, but remember, they are most attractive when symmetrical. Prune all canes to the same length for even growth.

Check the plants several weeks after pruning. A late frost or an unseen canker may have caused one or two canes to die back. Also, make sure you've left no short stubs.

Prune rose plants lightly during their first few years until they become well established and have developed a strong group of canes.

To ward off insects that could bore into cut canes, seal cane tips that are over ½ inch thick with pruning compound or orange shellac.

GENERAL PRUNING

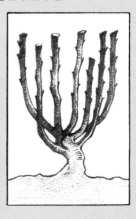
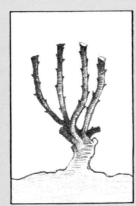

When pruning roses, first cut all dead or diseased canes flush with the bud union. Prune any broken or wounded canes or canes with cankers below the injuries. Next, cut out weak canes that are thinner than a pencil. Also remove canes growing into the center of the plant and canes that crisscross. This increases air circulation and discourages diseases. Finally, trim all but three or four of the newest and strongest canes flush with the bud union.

PRUNING CLIMBING ROSES

Because climbers bloom on old wood—the canes that grew the previous year—prune in the spring just to shape and to cut out canes that suffered winterkill.

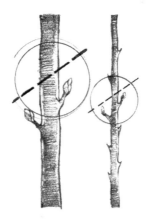

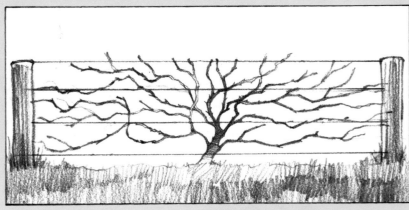

After a climber blooms, cut one or two old canes to their bases to make room for new canes. Thin dense growth and shorten canes that are too long. For maximum bloom, train a climber horizontally, tying the canes to a support.

Make all cuts at a 45-degree angle, about ¼ inch above a bud. The cut should slope downward, away from the bud, so water will run off. A cut too close to a bud may kill the bud; a cut too high above a bud may cause the cane to die back. Prune to an outward-facing bud to keep the plant open and nicely shaped.

USES FOR ROSES

(Right) Training climbers—even some shrub roses—along a split-rail fence colors the wood and softens straight lines. Here, 'Belinda'—a musk rose—flowers repeatedly, almost hiding the fence.

A formal rose garden is breathtaking. Laid out in a personal pattern, edged with boxwood or miniature roses, and accented with a statue or tree rose, it can be dramatic.

Even if you have limited space or desire an informal garden, you still can use this queen of flowers in your landscape. Any garden, as long as it is bathed in at least six hours of sunshine a day, can use roses, if only a few.

MIX AND MATCH

Mix roses with other plants. Intermingling roses with spring-flowering shrubs in a border, for example, results in color from early spring well into fall—much longer than either plant would provide alone. Or, use tall roses as backdrops to low-growing shrubs, and low-growing roses as edgings to tall evergreen shrubs.

Plant roses in the flower garden. They bring a continuity of color all summer as perennials go in and out of bloom. Mix annuals with roses to change the color scheme each year. Add spring-flowering bulbs to bring early color.

Roses are synonymous with fragrance. Fill the air with their sweet scent by planting them outside windows you'll open during warm weather. Or plant them along the patio where you spend your relaxing summer moments. Cut

(Opposite) Hybrid tea and floribunda roses create an unmatchable front-yard welcome mat. Plant roses where you can enjoy their beauty indoors as well, through your windows.

blooms to bring their fragrance and beauty indoors in arrangements or potpourris.

Roses are perfect for edging a walkway. Choose free-flowering floribundas or miniatures for never-ending color. Between sections of your property or on the property line itself, use roses as a hedge. Plant the bushes two or three deep in a staggered arrangement, setting the plants a little closer together than normal for fuller color effect. For a hedge to double as a screen, choose a tall rose such as 'Simplicity.'

Planting roses at the driveway entrance welcomes visitors. And if the roses are white or pale pink varieties, they will stand out at night to help mark your entrance. Finish the planting with a small spotlight and a low brick fence.

Choose sprawling roses such as 'Max Graf' or 'Red Cascade' to cover bare slopes or other areas that need a ground cover. Place them alongside steps to mark the change of grade.

Every garden has an eyesore; roses are perfect camouflage for the garden shed or the trash cans. Brighten a wall or fence, too, by planting roses in front of it. White climbers or floribundas are striking in front of a red brick wall.

SMALL SPACES

Small spaces are perfect for a rose garden. Use miniatures and low-growing floribundas in tiny pockets at the base of a flagpole, to grace a mailbox, to accent an outdoor light, or to brighten a rock garden.

When space is premium, plant roses in containers. They beautify any city balcony or rooftop as much as they enhance a suburban patio or deck. Move the containers around for a change of scene.

Intertwine climbing canes through an arbor for an attractive garden accent that provides shade as well as a focal point. To soften hard corners, use climbers to outline windows, eaves, and the front door.

Tree roses bring height and accent to the garden. Use them as a central focus in a formal planting, or underplant them with annuals and floribundas for an informal look.

239

OLD GARDEN ROSES

An old garden rose is any rose whose class predates the introduction of the hybrid tea in 1867. To the gardener, more than nostalgia or historical significance makes them popular. They stand on their own for their beauty, fragrance, easy care, charm, long life, and differing flower forms and colors. Most are quite hardy in winter, too.

OLD GARDEN ROSES SUBCLASSES

Albas are tall, dense, disease resistant, and covered with clusters of fragrant white or pink blooms. They bloom once a year. Bourbons, on the other hand, bloom throughout the season with clusters of fragrant, double flowers.

Centifolias are called cabbage roses because they have 100 or more overlapping petals; they also are called Provence roses for the section of France where they were once widely grown. They have globular, fragrant flowers of white to deep rose that bloom once a year on slender, arching branches.

Chinas have delicate, repeating flowers of pink or red and, like pastel tea roses, played an important role in the development of modern roses because of their repeat bloom. Unfortunately, both China and tea roses are tender.

Damasks are known for their fragrance. Except for autumn damasks, they bloom just once. The Gallacia, a French rose and the oldest one known, blooms once in spring with single or double flowers of pink, red, or purple.

Hybrid perpetuals are the link between old and modern roses, blooming repeatedly. Hybrid rugosas are shrubs derived from *Rosa rugosa;* they are rugged plants perfect for a seashore setting. Hybrid spinosissimas are mostly modern additions to the shrub border.

Noisettes are good climbers for mild areas, producing clusters of bloom in white, pink, red, purple, or yellow. They can grow with Portlands, which are sturdy, erect bushes with double, fragrant flowers. Both bloom all summer.

Species roses are robust native roses with single flowers. Some bloom once; others will flower all summer.

(Left) The eglantine or sweetbrier rose is a species rose with apple-scented foliage. This wild rose of lyric and lore has many hybrids that are 8- to 12-foot shrubs glistening with small, single or semidouble blooms and colorful seedpods known as hips.

(Left) Early American settlers planted 'Harison's Yellow' widely. It is a hybrid foetida, the class of rose that contributed the color yellow to modern hybrids. Unfortunately, it also contributed black spot.

(Opposite) Moss roses, such as this 'Crested Moss,' have hairy glands covering the sepals that look like moss and produce a marvelous fragrance. Most moss roses have globular, double flowers that bloom once in early summer.

MODERN ROSES

(Above) For unusual color, plant the hybrid tea 'Mikado,' an All-America Rose Selections winner for 1988. From afar, it looks bright red; up close, it is a blend of red with pink and gold.

(Opposite) No other apricot blend is as winter hardy or as disease resistant as 'Amber Queen.' A floribunda, its golden-toned petals are acclaimed for their fragrance and beauty.

A chance crossing of a hybrid perpetual with a tea rose in 1867 produced the first modern rose, 'La France.' This new rose—a hybrid tea—had neat growing habits and bloomed often, characteristics it inherited from the tea rose. And like the hybrid perpetual, it was hardy in winter. A wave of hybridizing followed and continues today.

HYBRID TEAS

The hybrid tea roses define the classic beauty of today's roses. As long, pointed buds open, they reveal swirls of petals and high-centered, elegant blooms in every color but blue. On plants 2 to 5 feet tall, many emit the fine and famous rose fragrance. Alone or in arrangements, hybrid teas are perfect for bringing indoors as cut flowers on long stems.

The list of outstanding hybrid teas for the garden is lengthy. Among the whites, select from 'Garden Party,' 'Pascali,' or 'Pristine.' If red is your favorite, plant 'Chrysler Imperial,' 'Mister Lincoln,' or 'Precious Platinum.' 'Tropicana' was the first orange-red, and remains among the best. 'Lady X' and 'Paradise' are good mauves. Pink or pink-blend roses are more plentiful than any other color; tops among these are 'Century Two,' 'Chicago Peace,' 'Color Magic,' 'Dainty Bess,' 'Duet,' 'Electron,' 'Royal Highness,' 'Swarthmore,' 'Tiffany,' and 'Touch of Class.' 'Peace,' a yellow blend, remains high on the list of favorites. Other good blends are 'Granada' and 'Folklore.'

FLORIBUNDAS

As its name implies, the floribunda produces an abundance of flowers. From one of its parents—a hybrid tea—it inherited its height and long cutting stems.

The floribunda is the perfect landscape rose, with sprays of flowers in bloom nearly all season. Plants are hardy, bushy, and compact, characteristics that enhance their use in hedges, borders, and mass plantings. Floribundas in general also are quite disease resistant.

Selecting a favorite floribunda is challenging because so many colors, flower sizes, and flower forms exist. Some have flat, decorative flowers; others, blooms that resemble small hybrid teas.

For a large, red-flowered hedge, choose 'Europeana.' A smaller red floribunda, excellent for edging, is 'Showbiz.' For a mass planting of white, select 'Iceberg' or 'Ivory Fashion.' Bright, eye-catching orange is found with 'Sunfire,' 'Impatient,' or 'Orangeade.' Create tall pink barriers with 'Simplicity' or 'Betty Prior,' and low-growing ones with 'Cherish,' 'Gene Boerner,' 'Regensberg,' or 'Sea Pearl.'

Few roses are as disease resistant as yellow 'Sunsprite,' or as floriferous as orange-blend 'First Edition.' 'Summer Fashion,' a yellow blend, has classic hybrid tea blooms; other blends are 'Apricot Nectar' and the mauve beauty 'Angel Face.'

243

MODERN ROSES *(continued)*

Though hybrid teas and floribundas (see pages 242–243) are the favorite modern roses of many gardeners, other rose growers have a fondness for polyanthas, grandifloras, and modern shrub roses—all of which have special allure of their own.

POLYANTHAS

Almost simultaneous with the hybrid tea came another class of modern roses, the polyantha. A cross between *Rosa multiflora* and *R. chinensis,* the roses in this class have low-growing plants smothered with clusters of 1-inch decorative flowers. Polyanthas widely grown today include 'The Fairy,' 'China Doll,' and 'Cecile Brunner,' all with pink flowers. Other popular polyanthas include a series of roses—in shades of orange and red—named for the famous Koster family of rose hybridizers.

GRANDIFLORAS

The grandiflora class was created in 1954 for the rose 'Queen Elizabeth,' a cross between a hybrid tea and a floribunda. A grandiflora exhibits the best traits of its parents: the flower form and long, cutting stem of the hybrid tea, and the hardiness, continuous flowering, and clustering of the floribunda. Usually tall, they often are planted behind other roses or used as a screen or in cutting gardens.

'Aquarius,' 'Pink Parfait,' and 'Sonia' produce pinkish flowers. 'Gold Medal' is an outstanding golden yellow.

SHRUB ROSES

Modern shrub roses fit into any landscape setting or border, providing color for longer periods than most shrubs. They vary in size from low-growing ground covers such as 'Max Graf' and 'Sea Foam' to tall plants like 'Dortmund,' 'Golden Wings,' 'Sparrieshoop,' and 'Bonica.' Most shrubs possess good disease resistance and require little maintenance.

(Left) Like many roses in its class, the polyantha 'Margo Koster' has small, cupped flowers that bloom throughout the summer.

(Below) The official rose of the 1984 summer Olympics, 'Olympiad' won an All-America Rose Selections medal the same year. This hybrid tea has brilliant red blooms that retain their color even as they age.

HELP IN SELECTING ROSES

Two national groups have programs to help home gardeners select roses.

■ All-America Rose Selections

One national rose organization is the All-America Rose Selections (AARS), a group of professional growers who test new varieties for two years in gardens across the country. Criteria for testing include habit, vigor, hardiness, disease resistance, bloom frequency, foliage, flower form, substance, color, fragrance, and novelty. Those with the highest scores are given the acclaimed AARS award. Look for these awards when choosing roses for your garden.

■ The American Rose Society

Amateur and professional rose growers nationwide belong to the American Rose Society. The organization categorizes all roses, old and modern, into 17 color classifications. Use these when making selections.

Color classifications are white, medium yellow, deep yellow, yellow blend, apricot blend, orange and orange blend, orange-red, light pink, medium pink, deep pink, pink blend, medium red, deep red, red blend, mauve, mauve blend, and russet.

Members of the American Rose Society are surveyed every three years to establish ratings for commercially available rose varieties. The rating system is based on a 10-point scale, with 10.0 indicating a perfect rose; anything under 6.0 is of questionable value. For results of this survey, contact the American Rose Society, Box 30000, Shreveport, LA 71130.

The American Rose Society has two national rose shows each year, and local and regional rose societies have shows, too. Visit one of these to help you decide which varieties you like most. Also, visit local rose gardens, private and public, and the garden at the American Rose Center in Shreveport, which demonstrates how to grow roses in small gardens.

Known for their hardiness, shrub roses such as the bushy 'Dortmund' shown here have few rivals for tolerating poor growing conditions and neglect.

Named to honor the 100th anniversary of the Rose Bowl parade, 'Tournament of Roses' is an All-America Rose Selections winner for 1989. A vigorous, 5-foot grandiflora, it has dark, glossy foliage and large blossoms of pink to coral.

CLIMBING, MINIATURE, AND TREE ROSES

Special structures and situations call for special plants. Take a look at what roses—with their myriad of forms and flowers—can do to fill your most special garden needs.

CLIMBING ROSES

Arbors, fences, walls, and trellises are made to display the beauty of climbing roses. Climbers are long-caned roses that can grow to great heights when supported. When trained horizontally, they can spill over fences and slopes and usually will produce more flowers. The class includes climbers that produce loose clusters of large flowers on fairly hardy plants, and climbing sports, or mutations, of bush roses. Climbing sports, though not as hardy, produce the same or better flowers than their parents.

For a vast cloud of red, decorative flowers, choose 'Blaze.' For a smaller area, 'Don Juan' offers velvety, fragrant, red flowers that resemble hybrid teas on long, cutting stems. 'America' has glowing coral-pink flowers and grows well accenting the base post of an outside light. In a large area, 'New Dawn' sprawls and is covered all season with pale pink blooms. For a touch of sunshine, plant 'Golden Showers.'

MINIATURE ROSES

Nearly every garden has enough space for several miniature roses. Use minis as low hedges, borders, accent plantings, or in containers.

Minis are small in all respects—plants, flowers, and leaves. They can grow to only a few inches tall, or be bushy, 1½-foot plants. Like their larger cousins, they come in many types. Some have a tiny reproduction of a hybrid tea flower; others look like petite floribundas.

Hundreds of excellent minis exist. Two, 'Debut' and 'New Beginning,' received the All-America Rose Selections award in 1989, the first time the award had gone to a miniature. Others have received the Award of Excellence from the American Rose Society; look for special symbols in rose catalogs designating the award winners.

The tiniest minis, with flowers no larger than your little fingernail, include white 'Cinderella' and 'Popcorn,' pink 'Baby Betsy McCall' and 'Bo-Peep,' and yellow 'Littlest Angel.'

Among larger plants, orange 'Starina' has for many years been the American Rose Society's highest-ranking rose. Closely related in color are the orange blends 'Mary Marshall' and 'Holy Toledo.' Among reds, 'Beauty Secret' rates well, as does the darkest red, 'Black Jade.'

Light colors stand out best in gardens viewed at night. Here, the white minis 'Pacesetter,' 'Simplex,' and 'Starglo,' and the apricot 'Jean Kenneally,' are good choices. Among the darker pastels, pink 'Judy Fischer' and mauve 'Lavender Lace' have large, attractive flowers.

Many varieties of minis have striking color combinations. 'Magic Carrousel' and 'Toy Clown' are white with red edges; 'Rainbow's End' is yellow edged in red; 'Over the Rainbow' is red on the inside of the petals and orange-yellow on the reverse. 'Avandel' is peach, yellow, and pink.

TREE ROSES

(Right) A potted miniature tree rose brings a touch of elegance to a garden. This 2-foot plant is an attention grabber and would look terrific near a low wall or front entry. For extra color around a tree rose, plant low-growing annuals around its base.

Tree roses are the crowning glories of the rose garden, accenting a flower bed, dressing up an entrance, or decorating a patio. They can function as the focal point of a formal garden, or stand informally in containers with other plants.

Any type of rose can be grafted on top of a stem to create a tree rose. Floriferous, spreading varieties will reward you with full, round heads. Some will even weep. To encourage straight stems, place a stake next to the trunk and secure it with soft ties.

When planting a tree rose, remember that it is a specimen of beauty and will attract the eye. So be sure it has an attractive, contrasting background. Plant a white tree rose against a red brick wall, for example, or a red variety against a white fence.

Tree roses are vulnerable to winter's cold, so where winter temperatures drop below freezing, move them indoors, wrap them in burlap (see page 235), or bury the canes in the ground.

(Opposite) What more inviting entrance to a garden could there be than an arbor of climbing roses? Use this landscape feature to say welcome and to hint at the beauty and color that lie beyond.

ROSE DISEASES

Disease	Description and Trouble Signs	Control
Black spot	Black spot is a fungus that causes round, black, ¼-inch spots to appear on the foliage. Eventually a yellow halo forms around each black spot, after which the entire leaf turns yellow and falls off.	If you had black spot the previous year, prune plants low in spring. This will remove many spores. Do not water overhead at night. Use a fungicide to prevent the disease.
Botrytis	Botrytis is a fungus that often keeps buds from opening, covering them with grayish brown, fuzzy growth. If buds do open, flowers are flecked with yellow or brown, and the petals become soft and brown.	Cut out and destroy all infected plant parts. Preventive sprays often are ineffective. The problem is most severe under cool, humid conditions and usually will disappear when weather improves.
Canker	Canker is a fungus that causes canes to die. Cankers usually appear in the early spring at pruning time. A part of the cane is healthy, but above the healthy part is a black, brown, or purple discoloration. Canker usually enters through a wound.	Chemicals can't control canker. Be careful to prevent wounds. In spring, prune canes below any sign of canker.
Crown gall	Crown gall is a bacterium that stunts growth and reduces flowering. Rough, round growths are found around the roots at or below the soil surface.	Prune small galls, disinfecting pruning shears between cuts. In severe cases, discard the plant and the surrounding soil.
Mildew, downy	Downy mildew causes foliage to develop purplish red to dark brown irregular spots. Leaves turn yellow and eventually fall from the plant. This fungus also causes gray, fuzzy growth on the undersides of the leaves.	Spray with a fungicide every seven to 10 days to prevent downy mildew. Remove and discard any infected leaves.
Mildew, powdery	Powdery mildew is a fungus that forms a white powder on rosebuds and leaves. It is most prevalent when nights are cool and days are warm, or where air circulation is poor. Mildew often causes serious disfiguration of the rose foliage.	Improve air circulation around plants to discourage powdery mildew. Do not water at night. Use a fungicide as a preventive, or spray with lime-sulfur to eradicate (apply only if the temperature remains below 80 degrees).
Mosaic	Mosaic is a virus that causes foliage to become mottled in yellow or develop a yellow netting or streaking. Growth becomes less vigorous, and the plants are more prone to winterkill.	Mosaic symptoms often disappear by themselves. In severe cases, remove the plant. There are no chemical controls.
Rust	Rust is a fungus that forms an orange-red powder on rosebuds, new growth, and leaves. The problem is primarily confined to the West Coast and is caused by mild, wet weather.	Inspect all new bushes for any sign of rust before planting, and don't plant any that show signs of the disease. Control with a commercial fungicide. Remove infected leaves.
Spot anthracnose	Spot anthracnose starts with the development of red, brown, or purple spots on the upper leaves. The centers of these spots eventually turn white, dry, and fall out. Affected leaves turn yellow and fall.	Spray with a fungicide every seven days as long as the symptoms of spot anthracnose persist. Avoid overhead watering.

ROSE INSECTS

Insect	Description and Trouble Signs	Control
Aphids	Aphids, or plant lice, are small but visible green, black, red, or brown insects that form colonies along flower buds and new shoot growth, starting in mid- to late spring. They harm roses by sucking their vital juices. A sticky substance called honeydew may appear on the leaves.	Knock aphids off the plant with your fingers or with a strong stream of water from the garden hose, or apply soapy water or a commercial insecticide.
Borers	Borers tunnel into canes and under the bark, hollowing out the pith and killing the shoot. Wilting of the top of the plant often indicates the presence of the borer. The cane usually will swell where the borer is hiding.	Prune just below each swelling, which indicate where a borer is hiding, then apply a sealing compound. Be careful not to injure canes when working in the garden.
Japanese beetles	Japanese beetles are shiny, copper and green, ¼-inch insects that can devour an entire garden in a short time. They eat holes in the flowers, particularly white and pastel ones; if hungry enough, they also eat the leaves.	If the infestation isn't too heavy, use your hands to remove Japanese beetles. Traps are sometimes effective, but often attract more beetles to the garden. Control the grubs in the soil for best results.
Leaf-cutting bees	Leaf-cutting bees cut neat circles into the edges of the leaves. The bees do not eat these leaf pieces, but rather use them to build their nests.	Prune severely damaged canes. Since leaf-cutting bees do not eat the foliage they cut away, chemicals are ineffective.
Leaf rollers	Leaf rollers are green or yellow caterpillars that grow to 1 inch long. They roll themselves up in the rose leaves and eat through them from the inside out. Another sign of these pests is tiny holes in the base of the flower buds.	Use commercial insecticides or organic controls for maximum effectiveness.
Midges	A midge is a tiny insect maggot that bores into a rose plant, causing the buds and the new shoots to suddenly blacken and die.	When you see signs of midge, prune the damage immediately and discard it. Spray a commercial insecticide on the tops of the plants and apply a systemic insecticide to the ground around the plants.
Nematodes	Nematodes are microscopic worms that cause disease symptoms in roses. Small knotty growths develop on the roots. Plants lose their vigor. Leaves turn yellow, wilt, and fall. Flowers become smaller.	Discard any plants infested with nematodes, and do not plant roses in the same spot for three to four years. Professional treatment of the soil may be necessary.
Rose scales	Rose scales are gray, brown, or white hard-shelled insects that encrust the stems and suck sap from the branches. Growth is stunted and flowers don't form. Plants eventually wilt and die.	Prune, discard canes with heavy infestations. Spray with dormant oil in early spring and with commercial systemic insecticide as insects appear in summer.
Rose slugs	Rose slugs are small, soft, yellow-green caterpillarlike pests. Starting with leaf undersides, they then eat the entire foliage, leaving skeletons. They can bore into the pith of pruned canes.	Spray rose slugs with a recommended commercial insecticide as soon as signs of damage appear.
Spider mites	The spider mite is too small to see, but its effects are quite obvious. Technically, it's not an insect, but it does the damage of one. Foliage turns dry and bronze or dull red. In advanced stages, webs will be seen.	Since spider mites do not like water, keep plants well watered, and hose down foliage undersides. When needed, apply a miticide three times at three-day intervals.
Thrips	Thrips are microscopic insects that bore into the bottoms of the flowers and suck juices from the petals. Buds become distorted and brown, and may not open. Thrips prefer white and pastel roses.	Since thrips hide in buds and flowers, cut the buds and flowers off at the first sign of infestation and destroy them. Apply insecticides to the tops of the plants.

SPECIAL GARDENS

The wonderful world of gardening is really too big for any one of us to enjoy all of its aspects, even in a lifetime. Instead, we often must focus our attentions in a singular gardening direction—such as one of those suggested in this chapter—to help create our own horticultural niche.

WILDFLOWER GARDENS

(Opposite) This garden of wildflowers gone rampant is the result of seeds sown from packets. Commercial seed mixes are tailored to a variety of climates and usually contain seeds for many regional flowers, plus other species that can adapt to the area.

Consider the lilies and other flowers of the field. They have been with us for ages but only recently have been claimed by home gardeners. Many of today's gardeners find that wildflowers are both beautiful and useful, particularly because they can cover broad, less-than-ideal spaces, such as shaded areas and low-lying wet spots. And as a plus, they need little care.

WILDFLOWERS IN HOME GARDENS

To prepare an area for wildflowers, till and amend the soil. Try to remove all weeds, spraying with an herbicide, if necessary.

Use seeds or seedlings. If you sow seed, buy good seed stock from local suppliers or collect seeds from nearby prairies, keeping in mind that some plants may be on conservation lists. In any case, consider colors and heights when making your wildflower choices. Blended colors can add visual spice to the garden. And height differences will create charming undulations.

Whether you use seeds or seedlings, select plants that will prosper in your region and that have enough bloom-time variety to span the growing seasons. Many will flower for several weeks, but none all summer long.

Arrange the seeds or plants to provide wall-to-wall wildflowers, or spread them in meandering beds separated by narrow paths. Avoid rows. Set out spring-blooming wildflowers in the fall, and summer- and fall-blooming plants in the spring or summer.

Resist the temptation to add petunias or other more-civilized plants in or around wildflowers. If you need to give the garden a bit of a finished look, consider enclosing the wildflowers with a casual stand of native sunflower, rudbeckia, or wild hollyhock.

Though you want to strive for a naturalized look throughout, when early bloomers go dormant, feel free to tidy up the garden. Untangle the red flax, coming in late, or the golden yarrow, in peak bloom, from dried-out companions or other encumbrances.

(Right) A tree-shaded patch of wildflowers can be rewarding in full bloom and soft light, especially when combined with small bulbs. In dappled sunlight, individual blooms take turns in the solar spotlight. The shifting light dramatizes each plant's unusual features.

WILDFLOWERS

Name	Description	Light and Soil	Propagation	Comments
ALUMROOT *Heuchera* sp.	Tiny red, white, or purple blossoms on stems 16 inches to 3 feet tall. Blooms May to August.	Shade; dry, well-drained soil	Seeds or divisions	Leaves mottled when young.
ANEMONE, RUE *Anemonella thalictroides*	Delicate pink and white blossoms on 5- to 9-inch stems. Blooms from March to June.	Shade; dry, well-drained soil	Seeds, stem cuttings, or layerings	Divide in fall after plant has died back.
BEE BALM **Oswego tea** *Monarda didyma*	Large pink or red blossoms on 2-foot stems from June to September.	Sun or shade; moist, acid soil	Seeds, cuttings, or divisions	Prefers light shade or partial sun.
BLACK-EYED SUSAN *Rudbeckia hirta*	Golden, daisylike flowers on 2-foot stems. Blooms in July and August.	Sun; well-drained soil	Seeds; also self-sows.	Often grows as a biennial.
BLUEBELLS *Mertensia* sp.	2-foot-tall stems with blue flowers in April and May.	Sun or partial shade; moist soil	Seeds or divisions	Plants disappear during the summer.
BUTTERCUP *Ranunculus* sp.	Yellow flowers April to August on stems 6 inches to 2 feet tall.	Shade; tolerates most soils.	Seeds or divisions	Can become weedy.
BUTTERFLY WEED *Asclepias tuberosa*	Clusters of small, red-orange blooms on 2-foot stems in July and August.	Sun; well-drained soil	Seeds or root cuttings	Brilliant colors.
CARDINAL FLOWER *Lobelia cardinalis*	Clusters of tubular, red flowers from July to September on plants 2 to 3 feet tall.	Partial shade; moist, acid soil	Offsets, divisions, and stem cuttings; also self-sows.	Keep well mulched.
CINQUEFOIL *Potentilla* sp.	Tiny yellow flowers, June to August, on 3- to 6-inch plants that turn red in fall.	Shade; well-drained, dry, acid soil	Seeds, divisions, or stem cuttings	Good ground cover.
COLUMBINE, WILD *Aquilegia* sp.	Finely cut red and yellow flowers from April through July on 1- to 2-foot plants.	Shade; well-drained, dry, slightly acid soil	Seeds; also self-sows.	Showy plant.
COMMON PUSSY-TOES *Antennaria rosea*	Charming ground cover with whitish flowers in May and June.	Sun; acid soil	Root cuttings	White, wooly herb found in mountain wilds.
CONEFLOWER, PRAIRIE *Ratibida columnifera*	Large yellow flowers, June to August, on plants up to 6 feet tall.	Sun; well-drained, dry soil	Seeds or divisions	Graceful and showy.
CONEFLOWER, PURPLE *Echinacea* sp.	Large, single, purple flowers from mid- to late summer on plants 2 to 5 feet tall.	Sun; well-drained, dry soil	Seeds or divisions	Tall and impressive.
DUTCHMAN'S-BREECHES *Dicentra cucullaria*	Unusually shaped white flowers in April and May; clustered on stems 6 to 12 inches tall.	Shade; well-drained, dry soil	Divisions or seeds	Spreads into clumps. Disappears after flowering.

Name	Description	Light and Soil	Propagation	Comments
EVENING PRIMROSE *Oenothera* sp.	Yellow, fragrant flowers July to August on plants 2 to 4 feet tall.	Sun; well-drained, dry soil	Seeds	Flowers open at night only. Treat as a biennial.
FLAG, BLUE *Iris* sp.	Large, purple blooms in May on plants 2 to 3 feet tall.	Sun; moist to wet, somewhat acid soil	Divisions; also self-sows.	Forms a dense colony.
FORGET-ME-NOT *Myosotis* sp.	Pale blue flowers with yellow centers. Blooms all summer if conditions are right.	Sun; moist to wet, well-drained soil	Divisions or seeds	Keep moist.
GENTIAN, CLOSED **Blue gentian** *Gentiana andrewsi*	Tubular, violet flowers August to September on plants to 2 feet tall.	Sun or partial shade; moist but well-drained, acid soil	Divisions or seeds	Flowers remain closed.
GERANIUM, WILD *Geranium maculatum*	Large, red-violet flowers in clusters on plants 2 feet tall.	Shade; well-drained, moist soil	Divisions or seeds	Effective in mass.
HEPATICA *Hepatica* sp.	Rose, white, or blue flowers from April to May on 6-inch plants.	Shade; well-drained, dry, slightly acid soil	Divisions or seeds; also self-sows.	Showy. Valued for early color.
JACK-IN-THE-PULPIT *Arisaema triphyllum*	Unusual vase-shaped, greenish brown flowers from April to June on plants 2 feet tall. Red berries later in the season.	Shade; well-drained, moist soil	Seeds; also self-sows.	Showy and attractive.
LADY'S-SLIPPER, YELLOW *Cypripedium calceolus*	Yellow flowers, often veined with blue, in May on plants 2½ feet tall.	Shade; well-drained, moist soil	Divisions	Showy. Give an annual topdressing of compost.
LOBELIA, BLUE *Lobelia siphilitica*	Tiny blue flowers from August to October on terminal clusters of plants 2 to 3 feet tall.	Sun or partial shade; well-drained, moist soil	Divisions, offsets, cuttings, or seeds	Valuable for late-summer color.
MARIGOLD, MARSH *Caltha* sp.	Small clusters of brilliant yellow flowers in April and May on plants 2 feet tall.	Sun; moist to wet soil	Divisions	Plants disappear in summer.
MEADOW RUE, TALL *Thalictrum polygamum*	Large clusters of white flowers from August to September on plants 10 feet tall.	Sun; well-drained, moist to wet soil	Divisions, stem cuttings, or seeds	Use as background plant.
PASQUEFLOWER *Anemone* sp.	White to lavender flowers March to April on 16-inch-tall plants.	Sun; well-drained, dry soil	Seeds or root cuttings	Early and attractive.

255

WILDFLOWERS *(continued)*

Name	Description	Light and Soil	Propagation	Comments
PHLOX, BLUE *Phlox divaricata*	Clusters of pale blue flowers in April and May on stems 6 to 15 inches tall. Small leaves opposite each other on stem.	Partial shade; well-drained, dry soil	Divisions or stem cuttings	Often forms large clumps.
POPPY, CALIFORNIA *Eschscholzia* sp.	Brilliant orange, cuplike flowers from April to June on plants 10 to 20 inches tall.	Sun; well-drained, dry soil	Seeds	Vigorous and hardy.
PRAIRIE ROSE *Rosa setigera*	Pink flowers from May to July in small clusters. Branches grow to 15 feet long.	Sun; well-drained, dry soil	Seeds or stem layering	Branches are thornless.
PRIMULA *Primula veris*	Bright yellow and fragrant flowers in early spring on 4- to 8-inch stems.	Shade; moist soil (even bog conditions)	Seeds	Blooms second year. Charming but not as sturdy as polyanthus primroses.
SAND VERBENA *Abronia* sp.	Small pink, yellow, and lilac flowers from May to September on low plants.	Sun; well-drained, dry soil	Seeds	Trailing stems creep along the ground.
SHOOTING-STAR *Dodecatheon* sp.	Clusters of small, attractive, red-violet flowers in May and June on 1-foot-long stalks.	Light shade; well-drained, moist soil	Divisions, root cuttings, or seeds	Plants disappear in summer.
SNAKEROOT, BLACK *Cimicifuga racemosa*	Tiny, white flowers in spike clusters from July to September on plants up to 8 feet tall.	Shade; well-drained, moist soil	Divisions or seeds	Dried plants work well in fall arrangements.
SPRING-BEAUTY *Claytonia* sp.	Delicate, pinkish white blooms from March to May on plants 4 to 6 inches tall.	Shade; well-drained, dry soil	Divisions or seeds; often self-sows.	Good ground cover in shady areas.
TRILLIUM *Trillium* sp.	White and purple flowers from April to June. Erect stems are about 1 foot long.	Shade; well-drained, moist soil	Divisions or seeds	Effective in mass. Showy.
VIOLET *Viola* sp.	Flowers from April to June on 6- to 8-inch plants.	Shade; well-drained, moist soil	Divisions or seeds; also self-sows.	Can become a weed.
WOOD ASTER, BLUE *Aster cordifolius*	Open clusters of small, light purple flowers in August and September on plants up to 4 feet tall.	Partial to full shade; well-drained, moist soil	Divisions	Good background plant.
YUCCA Spanish-bayonet *Yucca aloifolia*	Southern native; slow grower; white flowers tinged with purple in late summer.	Sun; well-drained soil	Cuttings or seeds	Evergreen, sword-shaped leaves. Most suffer drought easily.

FERNS

For those deeply shaded, moist spots in your wildflower garden (or yard), consider using ferns. Though they are non-flowering, their handsome foliage and exciting leaf patterns make alluring additions to their surroundings. They can clothe and decorate a rising piece of ground or a neglected glen. Or they can bring excitement to any tree-filled area. On a smaller scale, one large tree can become the inspiration for a collection of ferns.

■ Ferns make good neighbors

In a mixed planting, ferns will contribute indirectly to the well-being of adjacent plants. They provide protection against winds and act as a ground cover to conserve moisture. Ferns also help retard the growth of weeds, which would compete for soil nutrients. And, if you are starting a new wildflower garden, ferns will supply enough shade for delicate wildflowers to grow.

THE RIGHT ENVIRONMENT

Ferns prefer somewhat moist ground, and, if watered regularly, will enhance a cool setting.

Well-defined planting areas will command more respect than random beds, which have the look of haphazard attention. Clustered plantings demonstrate that a gardener has studied the merits of ferns and carefully interspersed them with flowering plant varieties.

■ Planting ferns

Ferns do best when transplanted in the early spring or in the fall, though you can transplant them in the summer, too, if you avoid moving them on a very hot day.

Underlay your planting area with coarse gravel, then fill it with leaf mold mixed with good soil. Do not bury the fern crowns, which could cause them to rot. Wet down your plantings with a fine spray of water, and surround the new plantings with mulch.

In cold-winter areas, plant ferns in a sheltered ravine, if possible, to provide extra protection.

To allow ferns and their neighboring plants to grow without crowding each other out, be sure to learn each plant's space requirements. If the setting still looks bare, fill in with violets and small, colorful spring bulbs.

CHOICE OF FERNS

There are so many fern choices that citing particular species and families is almost a disservice. Each section of the country has at least a few native ferns that gardeners can put to good use. Start by buying suitable specimens from local suppliers, or purchase plants or ask for diggings from woodland owners.

For beginning recommendations, try any of these: ostrich, one of the tallest and stateliest ferns; maidenhair, with its lacy fronds on black, wiry stems; the finely toothed northern lady fern; holly, toothed and dark green; royal, which grows in tall, dramatic clumps; and cinnamon, whose wide fronds turn cinnamon brown.

Too often used alone, ferns can team with other plants for exciting results. These ferns provide a rich, dark backdrop that helps focus attention on colorful azalea blooms.

HERB GARDENS

The appeal of herbs is in their differences, from basil to garlic to thyme. There are so many—crimson-flowered monarda, tall-branched angelica, or downy, gray-leaved lamb's-ear, for example—that choosing from among them is difficult. Your garden's climate and soil condition will help eliminate some possibilities, however.

For beginning herb gardeners, start with familiar plants, then branch out, seeking new uses and beauty. In making choices for your herb garden, remember to consider colors and textures. Plant neighboring herbs that have contrasting colors or textures so both plants can stand out.

Also consider heights. The ultimate size of your plants could range all the way from peck size to bushel-basket size. Feathery dill and fennel can grow to people sizes, for instance. Once you have established your preferences and have tracked down the seedlings you require, spend the first summer concentrating on cultivation and propagation to develop sturdy plants for successive seasons.

THE GARDEN DESIGN

The scope of herb gardens can stretch from tiny window boxes to giant formal designs that echo the patterns of medieval times. Formal herb gardens traditionally are planted in geometric shapes, one of the simplest being four beds intersected by crisscrossing paths. (According to the ancients, this cross pattern helped ward off evil spirits.)

Whatever design you decide upon, herbs require full sun and well-drained soil. So pick an open, sunny site. Before planting, work in plenty of compost and manure.

Some gardeners sculpt a large bowl-shaped cavity for their herb gardens. This form creates well-drained soil along the rim, and moist bottomland in the middle for herbs such as balm and mint. The south-facing slope allows you to plant herbs that love as much sun as they can get, and the north-facing slope is ideal for those that like it less sunny.

(Above) Purple basil, wild senna, lemon balm, love-in-a-mist, dill, and bee balm surround an ornamental beehive, creating an herb garden that pleases the eye as well as the nose.

(Left) If space is limited, plant herbs in small pots. Or push flue tiles into the ground and fill with herbs for a tasteful, scentful display.

Arrange herbs around a large, central display. Here the feathery foliage of artemisia and fuzzy leaves of lamb's-ear create a pleasant frame for the taller wormwood in the center of the bed.

HERBS PORTFOLIO

SWEET BASIL

CHIVE

DILL

BASIL, SWEET

Ocimum basilicum

■ **Type:** Perennial in milder climates; annual in northern states

■ **Care:** Start seeds six to eight weeks before transplanting outdoors, or sow seeds after danger of frost passes. Plant in average soil, and in sun or partial shade. Garden-ready plants are available by mail. In cool locations, sow every year. (To forgo the annual seeding, try cutting back the plant in fall, covering it lightly for winter, then watching for new shoots in spring.) Encourage bushiness by pinching and clipping through summer.

■ **Comments:** Basil leaves are good in salads and add zest to any tomato dish. Routinely, fresh leaves are used through summer; in autumn, whole, dead plants are pulled up and the leaves stored in jars for winter use. Because of the fleshy quality of its leaves, basil needs a few weeks more drying time than do some other herbs. Purple-leafed strains add a new color scheme to pesto or spaghetti.

CATNIP

Also called catmint
Nepeta cataria

■ **Type:** Perennial

■ **Care:** Set out seeds or divisions in sun or partial shade in light, well-drained soil in fall or early spring.

■ **Comments:** Catnip spreads rapidly and will grow to 3 feet tall. This is a popular herb, particularly with cats. To show their appreciation, cats tend to roll over these plants, damaging them. (This plant's pungent fragrance pleases many people, too.) For gardeners who are also bird-watchers, catnip isn't recommended. However, planted in containers, away from predators, catnip graces a terrace nicely.

The heart-shaped, grayish green leaves are tasty, fresh or dried. Brew in water for a delicious tea.

CHIVE

Allium schoenoprasum

■ **Type:** Perennial

■ **Care:** In early spring, plant seeds or divisions in a sunny spot with moist soil. Pinch back to encourage vigorous growth. Because their leaves are the main product, chives need not be dug up and replanted each year. For best results, divide the clumps every second or third year in spring.

■ **Comments:** Chives have a more delicate flavor than onions. On their own, they form clumps 10 to 12 inches tall. Their rose-purple blossoms are dainty. Expect to begin clipping the slender hollow leaves within a month or two after planting the seeds. Chives do not suffer from frequent clippings. Still, you're probably best off planting enough of a crop so you needn't go back to the same plant too often. Chives are decorative enough for use as a border planting.

DILL

Anethum graveolens

■ **Type:** Annual

■ **Care:** In early spring, after the danger of frost passes, gently press seeds into good, moist soil in a sunny location. Thin the plants later so they have 10 to 12 inches of space in each direction. The more you water them, the faster the plants will grow. Too much dryness can rush the flowering before the plants are fully grown. Gather plants for seed harvesting just before the golden flowers fade. Cut the ripening heads and spread them thinly on sheets. (If temperatures get above 98 degrees, move the drying operation into shade.) When the heads are dry, thresh with a light rod, and clean and store the seeds in cotton sacks in a dry place.

■ **Comments:** An old-world herb, dill is claimed to be soporific in seed form, a bit milder sedative in dried-leaf form. If you love dill as a flavor for fish, chicken, and pickles, sow seeds in intervals spring into summer for a continuous harvest. Because of its strong flavor, a little dill goes a long way.

FENNEL

Foeniculum vulgare

■ **Type:** Annual or biennial
■ **Care:** Fennel needs bright sun with good, somewhat alkaline soil that is not allowed to remain wet. Sow seeds in the fall for dynamic growth the following year. Or dig up fennel roots in the fall, overwinter them in sand in a frost-free area, then replant them outside in spring. Divide the roots then, if needed.
■ **Comments:** Fennel looks much like dill, but has a stronger, aniselike flavor. It can serve as an ornamental plant along a back wall or be the focal point in a garden. Use fresh leaves on salads. The seeds, when well dried, are favored for chewing. The herb also is praised as a flavor for herring, mackerel, or pike.

GARLIC

Allium sativum

■ **Type:** Best grown and harvested as an annual
■ **Care:** Grow from bulbs bought in nurseries or at the supermarket. One garlic bulb, broken into individual cloves, is enough to launch an extensive home planting. In spring, set the cloves in a sunny location, pointy side up, in rich soil with compost mingled in. Top with a little manure later. Plant cloves in clusters or rows with enough room for easy harvest. In fall, lift the garlic bulbs carefully with a garden fork. Wait until the stalks are dry before storing in a net bag. Or braid tops to form a rope. Hang in a cool, dark, well-ventilated area.
■ **Comments:** Garlic comes from southern Europe at altitudes that assure cool temperatures. If you want the taste of garlic before harvesting the bulbs, clip a few leaves.

MARJORAM, SWEET

Origanum majorana

■ **Type:** Usually grown as an annual for its fragrant flowers. Can become a perennial shrub in mild climates.
■ **Care:** Sow seeds indoors, eight to 10 weeks before moving the seedlings to the garden after all danger of frost passes. (Because the seeds are so small, plant them first in a seed pan, then transplant into a seedling flat.) Shield seedlings from hot sun while they grow indoors, and later when moved out into the garden rich in manure or compost. Harvest the fragrant leaves just before the flowers bloom.
■ **Comments:** Sweet marjoram's flavor comes from its tiny gray-green leaves and its small white flowers. To prevent plants grown as perennials from becoming woody, keep the flowers and leaves trimmed.

In northern climates, buy small plants in the fall to grow indoors and use during cold months. Too much sun can scorch the leaves, so keep a close watch. Use the leaves fresh or, if they accumulate too fast, dry them for use in the future.

Leaves, fresh or dried, are good in salads and oil dressings, and particularly with lamb. They also add zest to cooked peas or beans, and can serve as the mystery flavor in sausage.

MINT

Mentha species

■ **Type:** Perennial
■ **Care:** Plant seeds or divisions in early spring in good soil in sun. Divide every few years.
■ **Comments:** Popular mints are peppermint, spearmint, water mint, bergamot, apple mint, and pennyroyal.

Most valuable for medicinal purposes, these plants produce essential oils for mentholated cold remedies.

Fun-loving gardeners, however, focus on possible pleasures, and brew the fresh leaves in concoctions that taste good on a hot summer day. Mint juleps are traditional for the Kentucky Derby. Grow mint indoors in winter for other social events, or use stored, dried leaves.

The plant produces no seeds but propagates itself easily from stolons—so much so that it can become invasive. Some gardeners suggest planting mint in a bucket buried in the ground to restrict root growth.

GARLIC

MARJORAM

MINT

261

HERBS PORTFOLIO *(continued)*

NASTURTIUM

OREGANO

PARSLEY

MUSTARD

Brassica juncea

■ **Type:** Annual

■ **Care:** Sow seeds in good, rich soil early and frequently until hot summer weather sets in; if the weather cools in August, reseed to extend the harvest. Keep well watered.

Just before the seedpods ripen—they will be golden brown—pull up the plants and hang them in bundles to dry. When the pods are crisp, thresh out the seeds, grind them with mortar and pestle, then store in powdered form. Later, add enough vinegar or water to make a mustard paste.

■ **Comments:** Mustard offers healthful benefits. It is a good source of vitamins A and C, and has ample amounts of calcium, iron, potassium, and dietary fibers.

Though mustard has a sharp, pungent flavor, you can eat its young leaves raw in lieu of lettuce. In a broth, its greens make a good vegetable dish. Mustard greens are a traditional southern dish. Curly-leaved varieties resemble and cook down like kale.

NASTURTIUM

Tropaeolum species

■ **Type:** Annual

■ **Care:** Plant seeds after danger of frost passes in full sun where summers are moderate; otherwise, in partial shade. Nasturtium will thrive in ordinary—even poor or sandy—soil.

■ **Comments:** Nasturtium often is included in organic gardens because its unusual scent may discourage the presence of damaging insects. Its leaves spice up a serving of cottage cheese; its flowers brighten a salad; and, strangest of all, its pickled seed can spark a meat dish. Known as Indian-cress, this product was popularized by the British.

Nasturtium grows quickly, with flowers in ranges of golden orange. Favored by hybridizers, varieties now span from dwarf to trailing or high climbers. New colors are jewellike, and new strains have double blooms.

OREGANO

Also called wild marjoram
Origanum vulgare

■ **Type:** Perennial or annual

■ **Care:** Even though most varieties of oregano are perennials, it still is wise to replace them every three years. After danger of frost passes, sow seeds in partial shade and in a dry location (oregano does particularly well on a well-drained hillside). Space plants 18 to 20 inches apart. Pinch back plants to encourage bushiness. Debud to keep the plants from flowering so new leaves will continue to appear. In cold climates, cover plants in the fall with 2 to 3 inches of straw or leaf mulch to prevent winterkill.

■ **Comments:** Oregano leaves make a fine flavoring for spicy foods. In some areas of the country, oregano is known as the pizza herb. It grows widely and spreads on underground stems. It has oval leaves and flowers in shades of pink to purple.

PARSLEY

Petroselinum crispum

■ **Type:** Biennial, but best grown as annual

■ **Care:** Buy new seed each year; homegrown seed, which is smaller than commercial seed, is difficult to propagate and hard to see. In late fall or early spring, sow seeds outdoors in sun in average soil. If grown as a biennial, harvest leaves before flowers bloom.

■ **Comments:** Parsley often is taken for granted, yet its sprigs are indispensable to spark a bland meal, add color to a special dish, or dress a glass of tomato juice. Parsley also is an essential ingredient in bouquet garni and in fines herbes.

Parsley is considered difficult to grow from seed, but often the problem is just slow germination. Speed up germination by sowing seeds in trays of warmed compost. Or, hasten germination by starting seeds between layers of wet blotting paper.

ROSEMARY

Rosmarinus officinalis

■ **Type:** Perennial
■ **Care:** Prefers light, sandy soil laced with lime, and a south-facing planting area. Start new plants by sowing seeds indoors in spring or in a row outdoors after the danger of frost passes. Move seedlings to permanent locations in the fall. To protect plants from winterkill, trim back. This should encourage new branching the second spring. If the seedling process doesn't work, take cuttings from a sturdy bush both before and after flowering. Remove excess leaves and bury the cuttings two-thirds of their length in sandy soil. In the second year of growth, harvest leaves if plants look sturdy.
■ **Comments:** A woody shrub, rosemary, once made happy in the right location, can live for generations. It grows gnarled, producing pale blue flowers in the spring.

The piney taste of rosemary leaves complements meat dishes, particularly lamb or pork.

SAGE

Salvia officinalis

■ **Type:** Perennial
■ **Care:** Sow seeds outdoors in early spring, plant stem cuttings (which yields faster results), or plant root divisions. Set in well-drained soil in a sunny spot. Mulch in winter. To develop more plants, take cuttings in spring from the heels of growing stems.
■ **Comments:** Use sage's narrow leaves in cooked dishes. Sage has such a strong scent and taste, use it alone as a poultry dressing or with pork in sausage. Though its flavor is considered masterful, its looks aren't: the shrubs have uninspiring forms. It has gray-green foliage and is related to western sagebrush.

Some varieties have purple or variegated leaves that carry many blooms. The fuzzy leaf textures protect sage from excessive evaporation, a convenience for a desert plant.

TARRAGON

Artemisia dracunculus

■ **Type:** Perennial
■ **Care:** Plant stem cuttings or transplants in early spring in a sunny, well-drained location. Tarragon will tolerate poor soil. Clip leaves frequently to keep new leaves coming. To propagate, buy small plants or divide larger ones; replace plants every few years to maintain full flavor. For best flavor, cut plants to ground level just before they flower, then store the leaves in a cool, dark place. If the season is long, repeat the process on other tarragon plants.
■ **Comments:** Tarragon is good in soups and flavored vinegars. The French strain is strong in taste, the Russian a bit rougher. Both need pruning to be kept in check.

THYME

Thymus species

■ **Type:** Perennial
■ **Care:** Sow seeds indoors four to six weeks before the last frost, outdoors after danger of frost passes. Or plant stem cuttings or root divisions. Plant in sunny location in average, well-drained soil. Reap leaves sparingly the first year and twice a year thereafter.
■ **Comments:** Thyme has a sharp, bittersweet flavor that adds zest to stews, soups, salads, and meat. There also is a lemon-scented variety, which, because of the strength of its flavor, you should use with care.

If you have a beehive, thyme makes good company for it. Planted nearby, the herb will attract bees, giving the honey a new taste, particularly during the hot, summer months.

Thyme colonizes well and produces pale rose flowers in May.

If you lack sufficient growing space, group thyme with sweet basil, rosemary, and tarragon in a reed basket filled with good soil. Set the basket beside a sunny terrace or on a wall.

ROSEMARY

SAGE

THYME

ROCK GARDENS

Teaming stones with native plants to form a rock garden often is the best—and most visually pleasing—solution to landscape problems such as eroding slopes, inclines too upright to mow, and steep grade changes. To avoid a helter-skelter look, start with a rough sketch of where you'll place the rocks and set the plants.

THE RIGHT ROCKS

Depending on their composition, rocks can add sparkle to a ground-cover grouping, or help stabilize a steep, barren slope. Fortunately, there are enough kinds of boulders, rocks, and pebbles to meet each requirement.

The best rocks are those that look at home in your setting—those natural to your area or rocks that harmonize well with the rocks used in other parts of your landscaping (in your house foundation or patio, for example). Shun novelty rocks that call attention to themselves.

To avoid the look of a geological collection, try to use rocks of the same general kind. Weathered rocks evoke a feeling of permanence. Lightweight porous rocks, such as limestone, are not only easier to position initially, but also absorb moisture to act as a buffer during dry spells. Nonporous rocks, such as granite, can cause surrounding soil to dry out faster. Also, steer clear of soft and scaly rocks, shale, and unweathered sandstone.

For best effect, keep the design informal. The rocks themselves should seem as if they have been embedded in the setting for centuries.

■ Hard labor

Whatever kinds of rock you select, be prepared to apply some muscle. Before moving a single stone, however, plan carefully where you'll place the rocks. You don't want to have to move them any farther than necessary.

Just two or three huge boulders (about 3 feet in diameter) usually are enough for any rock garden. Have the boulders positioned by machine as close as possible to their final resting place to help reduce backbreaking labor.

PLANT CHOICES

Plant choices for rock gardens are many but vary region by region, based upon temperature differences and soil quality.

Coastal California sites might be planted with armeria (also called sea pink or thrift), golden poppy, yarrow, and marguerite. In the drier and hotter regions of the same state, try penstemon, nigella, pulsatilla, and dwarf rudbeckia.

In areas with freezing winters, rely on bulbous plantings of iris and daylily, plus such billowing plants as Queen-Anne's-lace, bachelor's-button, and taller black-eyed susan.

A tribe of native plants—California poppy, ceanothus, isotoma, armeria, yarrow, marguerite, juniper, oleander, and eucalyptus—tame a windswept hill in northern California, bringing color and life to what was once a rocky wasteland.

Yards leveled for easier lawn mowing often leave a homeowner faced with abrupt grade changes— and a gardening challenge. A well-designed rock garden will hold a slope beautifully.

In the Rocky Mountain states, native plants such as antennaria (pussy-toes) and arctostaphylos (kinnikinick), together with *Anemone pulsatilla* and aquilegia—the blue columbine—are considered fine ornament.

Southwestern desert plants are quite different from those in all other areas, and it's a good idea to capitalize on these differences. Agave, yucca, and euphorbia, along with plants of the genus crassula, adjust well to the desert climate.

In the Southeast, high temperatures combine with greater rainfall, resulting in high humidity. Try heat-resistant annuals, such as marigolds, zinnias, and salvia, and petunias. Perennials and small deciduous shrubs make good choices for the Southeast, too. Regardless of your area, where the grade change is steep, help keep the soil in check by adding creeping evergreens and small ornamental shrubs. And don't neglect spicing up your rock garden with annuals. Their addition could be just the splash of color a rock garden needs.

The basic aim in all regions is to make native plants thrive in your garden. To do so, be patient. Give plants a chance to mature among the warm and companionable rocks. The result will be a rock garden with low maintenance and high eye appeal.

265

SHADE GARDENS

Don't give up when the only place you have to garden is shady, whether it be in the shadow of your house or the shade of giant trees too valuable to cut down. You may need to make some mental adjustments, but a shade garden can be as attractive and rewarding as its sunny counterpart.

In addition, shade plants require less water, and their flowers almost always last longer. And, more than likely, you'll find that doing garden chores in cool shade instead of hot sun is more refreshing.

MAKE THE MOST OF IT

With the many sun-loving gardening possibilities already eliminated (unless you're willing to rotate container-grown plants from your shade garden into the sun for a few hours each day), you need focus only on the remaining plant alternatives and the amount of usable space. The preparation steps are simple: Trim trees upward slightly to admit more early-morning and late-afternoon sunlight, and enrich the soil.

■ Plants for shade

For a thriving, colorful shade garden, try hostas (see the next page), shade-loving woodland plants and wildflowers (see chart, opposite), bleeding-heart, bishop's weed (or goutweed), bee balm, bugleweed (*Ajuga reptans*), Christmas rose (*Helleborus niger*), lenten rose (*Helleborus orientalis*), coralbells, hardy ageratum, anchusa, globeflower, leadwort, lobelia, lungwort, meadowsweet, and astilbe. Annuals that will add color to your shade garden include coleus, impatiens, begonia, cynoglossum, mignonette, and nicotiana.

Other shade plants to consider are lily-of-the-valley, meadow rue, primrose, snakeroot, foxglove, ferns, violets, and trillium.

Add small bulbs—scilla, muscari, and snowdrops—where they can catch early-morning sun in spring.

A crowded, shady place needn't be neglected. Fibrous begonia, cyclamen, Japanese maple, ferns, and colorful potted azaleas create an inviting side-yard nook.

Consider adding *Aquilegia caerulea* (blue columbine) or *A. canadensis,* which is yellow with red spurs, to your shady setting. Also consider dogwood, hawthorn, or magnolia—whichever grows best in your area—in shrub sizes. Add a bench where you can sit in the cool shade and enjoy your accomplishments.

Plan an informal arrangement because it will look best. As you tend your shade garden, save any good volunteer plants.

Shade-loving hostas in bloom form a ring of charm around the base of a stately tree. Attractive and varied foliage is the hallmark of hostas, whose leaves can be wide or narrow, smooth or quilted, solid or variegated.

THE HOSTA FAMILY

Shady areas are ideal for an informal grouping of different hosta types. You might plant the various types in separate locations so their sculptural beauty stands out, or interlace them for pleasure en masse. Most varieties have flowering spires that reach well above their plant mounds. Hostas have thick, durable roots that last a generation, and leaves in every shade of green and many blues, with lighter edgings and quilted surfaces.

The variations are so numerous, you might enjoy this funkia plant family as a specialty in and of itself. Primping is about the only chore that demands your attention: Tattered leaves need to be removed to make room for new leaves.

Dubbed the shade lily, the hosta is one of our most popular and versatile perennials, and the fact that it does well in shade adds to its worth. Many other perennials prefer or need sunlight in large doses. With their great variety, hostas often steal the spotlight in shade gardens.

WILDFLOWERS AND WOODLAND PLANTS FOR SHADE

- Arbutus, trailing
- Bloodroot
- Cardinal flower
- Columbine, golden
- Dog-tooth violet
- Dutchman's-breeches
- Ferns (cinnamon, lady, maidenhair, ostrich)
- Foamflower
- Forget-me-not, true
- Gentian, fringed
- Goatsbeard
- Hepatica
- Jack-in-the-pulpit
- Jacob's-ladder
- Lady's-slipper (pink, yellow)
- Lily-of-the-valley
- Loosestrife
- Mallow, swamp rose
- Marsh marigold
- Mayapple
- Milkweed
- Moccasin flower
- Partridgeberry
- Phlox, creeping
- Pitcher plant
- Shooting-star
- Snakeroot
- Solomon's-seal
- Spiderwort
- Spring-beauty
- Swamp milkweed
- Sweet william
- Trillium
- Violet
- Wild ginger

DESERT GARDENS

Lots of heat and little water may mean certain disaster for most gardens, but careful selection of plants that love desertlike conditions can change a barren wasteland into an exotic oasis.

THE SECRET TO SUCCESS

The key to a flourishing desert garden is to work with the environment, not against it. Trying to provide the right conditions in a desert setting for plants that like lots of humidity and rain will only doom your efforts. Instead, go native with your plant selections.

■ Desert-garden strategies

Gather the seeds of those plants that grow naturally in desert areas. Attempt to imitate nature, establishing gardens that provide similar conditions to what the desert offers.

Starting a seedling bedding is a good idea, too. Plant more than enough for your own use so you can remove the less-vigorous plants. Save seeds from one year to the next. Be patient, too, with dry-area plants. They tend to grow slowly because of their meager supply of nutrients and water.

Also, remember that technically the United States has no true desert. In fact, if your area receives more than 15 inches of rain a year, you should not attempt to grow true desert species.

■ A bonus from desert gardens

One big plus of desert gardens is that they generally require little care—once you've accomplished the initial work. The very nature of plants suited for desert gardens makes them less demanding than other plants. Combine this with little or no lawn maintenance, and with the low-care materials that work well in a desert garden (such as flagstone and pebbles), and the result is a truly unique garden that gives you plenty of time to sit back and admire its beauty.

These glorious, familiar-looking succulents are large versions of popular houseplants: aloe, jade or ice plant, cactus, and echeveria. Deserts grow them on a scale grander than the home.

(Above, top) Cacti come in many forms, from rabbit-ears (shown) to cob, barrel, and snowball. Where the climate can be extreme, determined gardeners protect their desert gardens within the confines of a courtyard.

(Above) The adobe-and-wood architecture of this southwestern house serves as the backdrop for the unrefined habits of daylily and native sage. Fairy roses in the foreground lend a more civilized air.

269

WATER GARDENS

A water garden can add a striking new dimension to your home's setting. Any container made watertight can house a water garden, but for a spectacular display, try a pond or concrete pool.

HOW DEEP?

You will need a pool or tub deep enough to accommodate potted aquatics set on the bottom, plus 6 to 12 inches of water above the rims of those pots. The final depth should be at least 18 inches for plants and most fish to cohabit.

When planning a pond or pool, keep size and shape in mind. A small pond takes less care than a big one. Use a pond shape that will blend with your yard. And be sure to include a system to recirculate water to keep it from stagnating.

Most water plants are grown in soil-filled containers submerged in water. If you use a single large plant in a big tub, plant it directly in the bottom of the container and fill the tub with water. At planting time, fill an appropriate container with garden loam, then incorporate slow-release fertilizer at the rate suggested on the package. Ground covers near the water's edge can soften the lines of a water garden.

To better enjoy a water garden, build a small pier so you can look down on the expanding flower blooms and pond wildlife. Or arrange a series of stepping-stones to guide visitors past prime features of your waterscape.

Even with a concrete pool, the main goal is a natural look. Here, potted water lilies flourish in a sunken, concrete-lined pool.

WATER-GARDEN PLANTS

Name	Plant Needs	Plant Height	Description	Comments
ARROW ARUM *Peltandra virginica*	Moist soil	2'–3'	Cultivated for bold foliage, mass effect.	Best at edge of pool large enough to cope with a fast-spreading mass.
ARROWHEAD *Sagittaria latifolia*	Shallow water	1'–2'	Hardy. White flowers in summer.	Also will grow in boggy soil at edge of pool.
BULRUSH *Scirpus* sp.	Shallow water	3'–9'	Grasslike leaves; chocolate-colored flowers in summer.	Invasive. Plant where it is easy to control.
CARDINAL FLOWER *Lobelia cardinalis*	Marsh or shallow water	2'	Hardy. Fire-red spikes July to September.	For border or shallow running water.
CATTAIL *Typha latifolia*	Shallow water	1½'–4'	Swordlike blades; dark brown spikes.	Effective bordering pool. To restrain, plant in tubs and sink 2 to 4 inches in water.
CINNAMON FERN *Osmunda cinnamomea*	Moist soil	3'–5'	Tall fronds in circular masses. Hardy; tropical look.	Use in partial shade at pool edge as a background for plants in water.
FLOWERING RUSH *Butomus umbellatus*	Shallow water	3'–4'	Pink flowers July to September. Hardy.	Grow in submerged pot. Divide and repot each year or plant won't flower.
FORGET-ME-NOT *Myosotis scorpioides*	Marsh or shallow water	2'	Clear, blue flowers bloom May to October.	Needs only an inch of water. Also grows in any ground that stays wet or swampy.
GOATSBEARD *Aruncus dioicus*	Moist soil	4'–6'	Delicate foliage; showy white flowers in June. Hardy.	For pool border as background. Delicacy contrasts well with heaviness of other plants. Needs a shady location.
GOLDEN-CLUB *Orontium aquaticum*	Shallow water	1'–1½'	Tiny, yellow flowers in spring; floating or aerial leaves.	Thrives planted to depth of 8 inches.
GRASS PINK ORCHID *Calopogon tuberosus*	Moist soil	1'–1½'	Hardy. Rare, native. Fragrant, pink blooms.	On conservation list in many states. Needs acid soil and shade.
HORSETAIL *Equisetum hyemale*	Moist soil or shallow water	1'–4'	Rushlike, ridged, leafless stems.	Grow at pool's edge (or in pots submerged nearly to rim). Needs partial shade.
LEOPARD PLANT *Ligularia tussilaginea 'aureo-maculata'*	Moist soil	1'–1½'	Green leaves spotted yellow. Showy.	Ideal for lighting up a shady area.
LOTUS *Nelumbo* sp.	Shallow water	2'–3'	Pink flowers; shieldlike leaves rise 2 to 3 feet above water.	Hardy if roots don't freeze. Plant in containers of soil, then submerge in water.
MARSH MARIGOLD *Caltha palustris*	Marsh or shallow water	15"	Buttercuplike flowers appear April through June. Hardy.	Lovely at edge of pool to reflect in water. Succeeds in moist soil.

Name	Plant Needs	Plant Height	Description	Comments
MEADOW BEAUTY *Rhexia virginica*	Moist soil	1'–2'	Rosy purple flowers in summer.	Provides good color among moist rocks, such as near a waterfall or rock border.
OSTRICH FERN *Matteuccia pensylvanica*	Moist soil	6'–9'	Bold leaves give massive effect. Hardy.	Can grow in full shade.
PAPER PLANT *Cyperus papyrus*	Marsh or shallow water	4'–6'	Threadlike leaves; triangular stems.	For large ponds. For smaller ponds, try *C. alternifolius.*
PICKEREL WEED *Pontederia cordata*	Shallow water	2'	Dark green foliage; violet-blue spikes bloom spring to fall.	Depth of water shouldn't exceed a foot. Best at pool edge in about 3 inches of water.
RABBITEAR IRIS *Iris laevigata*	Shallow water	2'	Blue or white flowers in June and July. Looks somewhat like Japanese iris.	Tolerates water year-round, so is preferred over Japanese iris in continuously wet spots.
SWAMP PINK *Helonias bullata*	Moist soil	1'–2'	Leaves in basal rosette; pink, fragrant flowers in spring.	Does best in boggy, acid soil.
SWEET FLAG *Acorus calamus*	Shallow water	6"–3'	Yellow-green blades; clublike green spikes.	Use in water at edge of pool or in moist soil around outside.
TARTARIAN DOGWOOD *Cornus alba*	Moist soil	6'	Lovely red stems; dingy, white flowers.	Prune random stems of this shrub before new growth begins in spring.
WATER ARUM *Calla palustris*	Moist soil	1'	Flowers white inside, green outside in late spring.	Does best in mud at pool's edge. Provides good transition to dry-land plantings.
WATER CHESTNUT *Trapa natans*	Floating	2"–4"	Feathery leaves below water and solid rosette above; small, white flowers; edible seeds.	Propagate by dropping seeds to the bottom of the pool and overwintering them there.
WATERCRESS *Nasturtium officinale*	Shallow water	4"–6"	Hardy. Edible, bright green foliage.	Thrives in sun or shade, and in cold running water.
WATER HYACINTH *Eichhornia crassipes*	Floating	9"	Glossy, green leaves; violet flowers.	Tender. Spreads like a weed in the South. Available only in states where supplies already exist.
WATER LILY *Nymphaea odorata*	Deep water	3"–5"	Many species, many colors. Spring through summer bloom.	Plant in container of rich soil. Submerge, with 6 to 12 inches of water above the container. Divide every few years.
WATER PLANTAIN *Alisma plantago-aquatica*	Deep or shallow water	1'–3'	Heart-shaped, plantainlike leaves; white flowers through the summer.	Blooms best in shallow water. Leaves narrower in deep water. Invasive.
YELLOW FLAG *Iris pseudacorus*	Moist soil	2½'	Yellow flowers in spring.	For double pleasure, plant at border so plants reflect in the water. This can be a very showy flower.

ORNAMENTAL GRASSES

(Right) Tall cordgrass and tasseled fountain grass, center, grow near bluish sheep fescue, teaming to make a pleasing grassy trio. These quite-unlike strains suggest the possibilities available to a fancy-grass gardener.

(Opposite) The differences in colors, arching stems, and sturdiness make each of these ornamental mounds stand out from its neighbors. The green and white ribbon grass in the center has sharp blades that tend to keep youngsters from running in and around it. In short, this variety gets respect.

More than 150 kinds of grasses grow in the United States. Many have agricultural value as food for us or forage for animals. For gardens, however, there are ornamental strains that provide showy displays.

Most fancy grasses have long, slender leaves and minute, if any, flowers; all are useful in landscaping for their delicacy, soft colors, or plumelike flower clusters.

Grow annual grasses from seeds sown in an open, sunny place in spring. Start perennial grasses from transplants or root divisions. Allow enough room between plants to avoid overcrowding. Because grasses grow worldwide, varieties exist for every kind of soil. Start a sampling of varieties in a back corner of your yard until you find the decorative grasses that work for your yard.

ORNATE OPTIONS

For striking effect, plant giant reeds that reach up to 20 feet in rich soil. Bamboos do well in the South beside a tranquil stream, or in clusters in a moist hollow. Pampas grass is not hardy in winter frosts, but some northern gardeners grow it like dahlias, lifting and storing the roots in a cellar space through winter.

Blue fescue is a small beauty with needle-thin, blue-gray clusters. Planted in bouquet-size mounds in geometric patterns, it is excellent in a formal garden. Ribbon grass, with its green and white stripes, grows quickly; green and yellow zebra grass is equally prolific.

If you lack big spaces for tall grasses, consider modest terrace displays of smaller grasses. Fescue, Japanese sedge, and quaking grasses do well in close confines.

CONTAINER GARDENS

Container gardeners devote themselves to their craft for many good reasons: Some have no land to cultivate; others just prefer their gardening adventures in containers such as ceramic bowls, clay strawberry pots, and hanging baskets. Still others like the ease of container gardening (less weeding and bending over, for example). And gardeners who move often like taking their gardens with them to their new residences.

THE MOBILE NATURE OF POTS

One advantage of container gardens—with the exception of most window boxes—is their mobility. If your container tomatoes do poorly in a back corner of the lot, you can move them into brighter sunlight. And if your morning-glories wither in strong afternoon sunlight, you are free to reposition them so they get the sunlight they prefer.

You also can take advantage of that mobility to rotate containers frequently so every side of a potted plant receives equal sunshine for equal growth. You can even mix and match container plants to provide new arrangements as often as you're so inclined. Try, for example, a pot of dwarf sunflowers, some brilliant geraniums, or one dramatic hibiscus plant as a porch display.

■ **The nitty-gritty of container gardening**
Consider all container choices, from stone urns to half barrels, troughs, and ceramic bowls. The choices are limited only by imagination.

With each container, cut one or more holes to provide good drainage. Cover the holes with shards (be sure not to plug the holes to allow proper drainage), or add a layer of pebbles. Then fill with a mix of good soil and compost.

Because full to overflowing containers require more nutrients than a pot can supply, you'll need to feed sufficiently.

Check often, too, for proper moisture. Sun and heat can quickly turn a bright spot into a microdesert. Water if the soil surface feels dry to the touch. You may need to water container plants twice daily in extremely hot weather.

(Opposite) This group of containers—brimming with bold bedding plants—bunches together to bring a show of color to a shady spot.

(Left) Containers can go beyond clay pots. Here, watering cans overflow with blooms, extending a whimsical welcome to all who climb the stairs.

(Below) For variety of view, change window-box displays with the seasons. Plant spring bulbs in fall (cover with pines and holly boughs through winter); later, set in annuals for summer flowering.

CUTTING GARDENS

A garden designed solely for cutting can supply endless fresh-cut or slow-dried specimens. So you can reach individual flowers easily, be sure to define a main path or web of paths.

Many flower lovers agree that a garden set aside solely for cutting is essential. It can multiply your total flower bloom two times over and give you an opportunity to field-test new varieties before they make their way into a fully designed formal bed. Immediately, it can provide an abundance of new choices in flower form, color, and fragrance. A cutting garden also helps preserve the good looks of a main border whose beauty would be marred if too many blooms were snipped for floral arrangements.

Such a garden can make you feel bounteous, too, as you give away huge bouquets to friends (and smaller nosegays to chance acquaintances).

If well planned, a cutting garden will supply flowers from early spring through late fall.

CUTTING-GARDEN CUES

Grow a cutting garden in a sunny—but out of the way—spot. Such a specialty is not grown for beauty outdoors, but for the beauty of floral arrangements. If neatness counts, screen out the garden with small shrubs so it does not intrude on your grand plan. Or cultivate it behind a border, where the coming and going of blooms will go unnoticed.

■ Rows or random planting?

A popular way to grow flowers for a cutting garden is in rows, though random plantings work just as well. For either, make sure you have easy access to the blooms. Define a packed-earth path (top with mulch, if you want, to keep the muddy times to a minimum), or lay concrete slabs that you can rearrange each growing season. Still easier is to make the garden small enough so you can reach all of its flowers without walking a path.

■ Little work

One of the pluses of cutting gardens is that they require little work. Prepare the soil by spading in a compost mixture in the fall, plant your garden, and keep weeds in check.

Since the garden is grown for cut flowers, remove yellowing foliage only if you feel like it. You may want to clip off spent flower heads, though, to prolong the flowering period.

■ The choicest of flowers

Include perennials, biennials, and annuals in your cutting garden, but set the perennials apart from the others. That way, the perennials' roots will go undisturbed as you plant and replant the annuals and biennials.

When choosing cutting plants, begin with old-fashioned flowers such as foxglove, pansy, hollyhock, narcissus, zinnia, and marigold, trying several sizes of each. Also grow a few perennials for handing out year after year: lilac,

peony, forsythia, and mock orange. Add a few feathery flowers such as cleome, lythrum, and liatris to add softness to a stiff-looking bouquet.

Or, if you like, grow only new hybrids. The choices are amazing and inexhaustible. The red-cap primula with scarlet flower heads and a fringed lilac-pink skirt has flowers like those of a poker plant. Some new blooms are iridescent and as brilliant as colors resulting from light shone through a prism.

■ Making a bouquet

In flower arranging, there are no rules. Instinct and availability often determine combinations and arrangements. You are free to mix 200-year-old-type chrysanthemum with its new hybrid counterparts, or go colonial by combining yellow tulip with clove pink and larkspur. Phlox with black-eyed susan, coreopsis, and gaillardia is another grand combination.

When arranging flowers, an easy style to imitate is country charm. Pack a crock with zinnia, marigold, and blue salvia. Then, for an outdoor bouquet fine for any celebration, add teddy-bear sunflower.

DRIED FLOWERS

Dried flowers allow you to extend your garden pleasures. They beautifully preserve remembrances of things past—a rose you grew with pride, choice dahlias you couldn't bear to let go, bright blue delphiniums you longed to enjoy just a bit more. The aim, always, is to preserve the original colors without damaging the flower form.

PICKING FLOWERS

First you need to learn which flowers dry well (see chart, right), although there is no reason you can't attempt to save blooms not tried before.

The timing of harvests also is crucial—at or just before peak bloom is best. Try, too, to collect your flowers when the muggy days of summer have passed. This assures that the picked flowers won't be full of excess moisture, which might misshape them as they dry.

Immediately place the picked flowers in a drying medium, before they have time to wilt. In the drying space, keep the surrounding air dry, using a dehumidifier if needed.

■ Drying compounds

Flowers that dry easily on their own are called everlastings, and have rich colors and rugged forms. Field-grown grasses—such as cloud grass, quaking grass, and animated oats—fall in this category.

Everlastings dry just by hanging upside down, but many other flowers need to be buried in a drying compound (see chart, right). Initially, this compound was sand, applied gently. Later borax, a crystalline salt, became popular. Today, the most-used material is silica gel, which is sugarlike in appearance. (For drying foliage, glycerin often is used.) Between uses, free the drying material of any accumulated moisture by setting it out in the sun or under a heat lamp, then store it in a sealed can.

■ Dried arrangements

Whether in informal or formal arrangements, dried flowers excel. But the care you take in arranging the flowers can enhance their appearance considerably.

When making your arrangement, first insert foliage into a container filled with florist's foam. Use the foliage as a guide for floral heights. (If flower and leaf stems are short, lengthen them with florist's tape and wire.) Place larger and darker flowers in the lower center. Fill in with more flowers, making sure some extend below the rim of the container. Finally, keep your creation out of direct sunlight.

DRIED-FLOWER BASICS

Drying Method	Time*		Plants
Silica gel	2 to 3 days		Coralbells, lantana, miniature rose, viola
	3 to 5 days		Dwarf dahlia, dwarf marigold, feverfew, larkspur, pansy, small zinnia, tea rose
	4 to 5 days		Buttercup, delphinium, hydrangea, large zinnia, peony, shasta daisy
	5 to 6 days		Aster, calendula, large dahlia, lilac, marigold, snapdragon
Borax	Double the drying times for silica gel.		Same plants recommended for silica gel
Pressing in books	3 to 4 weeks		Buttercup, daisy, delphinium, dusty-miller, fern, florets, hydrangea, lobelia, pansy, sweet alyssum, verbena, viola
Air drying	2 to 3 weeks		*Garden flowers:* Annual statice, artemisia, bells-of-Ireland, blue salvia, celosia, delphinium, globe amaranth, heather, honesty, hydrangea, larkspur, physalis, strawflower, yarrow *Field flowers:* dock, goldenrod, pampas grass, tansy, teasel
Glycerin	1 to 2 weeks		Aspidistra, beech, crab apple, eucalyptus, holly, laurel, oak, peony, pyracantha, sycamore, yew

***Drying times vary according to local climate. Be sure to monitor each plant's progress during the drying process.**

After lifting your blooms from the drying medium, hang them in small bunches from the rafters, or lay individual blooms on wood-framed wire trays. A dark, dry attic such as this one is perfect for drying—and storing—flowers.

WILDLIFE GARDENS

A wildlife garden brings one more living dimension to your yard. Providing basic needs—food, water, and shelter—assures that birds and friendly furry critters will flock to your wildlife garden.

FOOD

To give wildlife a big choice of foods, offer them a variety of seed-, nectar-, and fruit-producing plants. Supplementing plants with bird feeders will attract an even larger crowd of visitors to your wildlife garden.

■ Trees

Trees top the list as sources of food. Favorite wildlife tree species include beech, red and white oak, red maple, white pine, hemlock, red cedar, serviceberry, flowering dogwood, flowering crab, spruce, mulberry, Russian olive, box elder, wild cherry, hawthorn, mountain ash, and hackberry.

■ Shrubs and vines

Fruit-bearing shrubs and vines that are especially inviting to wildlife include blackberry, raspberry, elderberry, wild grape, honeysuckle, viburnum, nannyberry, gooseberry, highbrush cranberry, pyracantha, currant, bittersweet, and red osier dogwood.

■ Flowers and herbs

Annual and perennial flowers, such as bee balm, sunflower, poppy, aster, daisy, marigold, cosmos, verbena, and tithonia, will entice both birds and butterflies into your yard. Allow seedpods to form on perennials and clip most faded blooms on annuals to promote new flowers.

Herbs that attract wildlife include yarrow, mint, chamomile, borage, chive, sweet basil, and lavender.

■ Native species

If you have space, it's a good idea to let a corner of your yard go native. Many common meadow plants, such as milkweed, clover, Queen-Anne's-lace, goldenrod, black-eyed susan, wild sunflower, and mullein, are as beautiful as cultivated flowers when tucked into an out-of-the-way corner of your garden.

WATER

A birdbath, shallow saucer, or 3-inch-deep tray filled with water will give birds, squirrels, and other small animals a spot for a refreshing drink. Set the containers near enough to trees and shrubs for hasty retreats when predators come prowling. And keep them clean and filled—even during winter, if possible.

Eventually, consider adding a pool. You can fill it with fish, and the pool will make a good home for frogs and turtles. Add rocks in and around the pool so amphibians and reptiles can sun themselves.

SHELTER

The trees and shrubs you plant, plus those already on your property, will shelter wildlife from their predators and extreme weather. For best results, leave densely wooded areas undisturbed in your backyard.

To encourage thick growth—and more natural cover—keep pruning to a minimum and allow fallen branches to remain on the ground.

■ Nesting sites

Trees and shrubs provide potential nesting sites for birds and squirrels. Some bird species prefer birdhouses, however, and installing a few nesting structures will increase your chances of attracting resident birds.

■ Open spaces

Though woodland areas are a necessary ingredient in any wildlife refuge, leave some open spaces in your plan, too. A grassy area will tempt worm-hunting robins. An open air space will give baby birds plenty of room to try their wings for the first time. And perhaps best of all, an open patch of land will let you enjoy a clear view of your backyard oasis and its visitors.

Place bird feeders near your house for selfish reasons: They allow closer acquaintance with feathered guests, such as this hummingbird zipping in to feast on sugar water for a quick burst of energy.

Butterflies add flittering color to wildlife gardens. This brightly hued monarch has found a summer stopover until time to make its winter migration.

(Opposite) Entice wildlife visitors by offering three essentials: water, food, and shelter. This garden provides all three in a pleasing, natural setting.

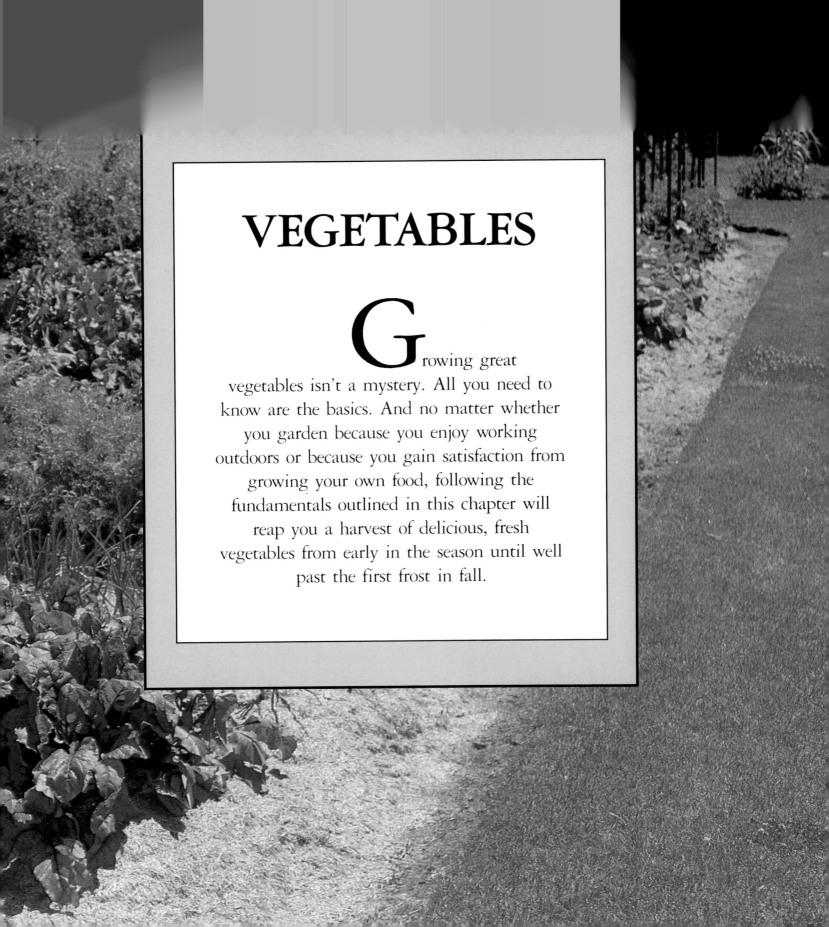

VEGETABLES

G
rowing great vegetables isn't a mystery. All you need to know are the basics. And no matter whether you garden because you enjoy working outdoors or because you gain satisfaction from growing your own food, following the fundamentals outlined in this chapter will reap you a harvest of delicious, fresh vegetables from early in the season until well past the first frost in fall.

PLANNING YOUR VEGETABLE GARDEN

(Opposite) Because they need little space and grow quickly, gardens devoted to salad greens are easy to plan and care for. Plant your garden close to the kitchen so you can harvest greens easily whenever you need them.

The first steps to good garden planning are finding an acceptable site and choosing the right vegetables. Then, before you begin, consider your gardening style and your plans for pests.

CHOOSING A GARDEN SITE

Most important of all to successful vegetable gardening is finding a sunny spot. Select a site that receives at least six to eight hours of sunlight a day. The more light, the better.

Low-lying areas are a bad choice because they drain poorly. Their soggy soil can cause root rot, which kills plants. In addition, low areas collect cold air in spring and fall and are the first to frost over, killing many plants that would have survived on higher ground.

Also, keep your garden away from trees and large shrubs. Both will compete with your plants for the moisture and nutrients in the soil. Large trees will shade the garden, too, and reduce the yield of fruiting vegetables.

Gentle slopes are excellent for home gardens. If you have a steep slope, terrace it to make it manageable. Otherwise, you'll have problems with soil erosion. If your site has extremely rocky or hard soil, consider a raised-bed garden.

(Right) Raised beds are best in cool, wet areas or in gardens with compacted rocky soil. The mounded soil provides excellent drainage, which allows you to start your gardening earlier in the season.

Try to place your garden close to the house. Vegetables need lots of water, and hauling heavy hoses over long distances to water garden areas can become tiresome. The ideal spot is right next to the kitchen, where you can pick fresh vegetables and herbs for every meal.

Also, consider having several gardens in different locations. Why not grow lettuce, radishes, green onions, and herbs by the kitchen and other vegetables in another spot?

Good soil is another feature to look for when selecting a garden spot. Good soil is loose, crumbles in your hands, and is rich in nutrients. But don't despair if the soil in your backyard doesn't measure up. You can improve any soil by adding lots of organic matter, such as leaves, grass clippings, rotted manure, or compost (see page 16).

WHAT VEGETABLES?

After you select your garden site, make a list of the vegetables you want to grow, studying their food, water, and space requirements. When you're done, you'll know approximately how much garden space you'll need. You might want to sketch the entire garden on paper, with the vegetables spaced according to seed-packet instructions. Grow only what you need, and only what your family really likes to eat.

Plant any perennial vegetables to one side of the garden where you won't disturb them. These crops include artichoke (in warm areas), asparagus, many herbs, raspberry, rhubarb, and strawberry. Certain perennial plants—such as horseradish, Jerusalem artichoke, and mint—can become pests. Experienced gardeners plant these in confined areas or in spots where their rambling habits won't cause problems.

Study seed catalogs to choose vegetable varieties suited to your area. Agricultural extension services often have lists of recommended plants based on local field trials. Temperature, rainfall, season length, and disease resistance are taken into consideration for these recommendations. By choosing the right variety, you'll greatly increase your chance for success.

PLANNING YOUR VEGETABLE GARDEN *(continued)*

If you don't have enough room for a big vegetable garden, don't worry. Plant breeders have developed many vegetable varieties that produce well in small areas, even containers. The key words to look for are mini, baby, bush, and patio. Vegetables with any of those words in their names will do well in tight spots.

WHAT'S YOUR GARDEN STYLE?

Once you've decided where to put the garden and what to plant in it, you need to choose a garden style that best fits your personality. Every gardener is different. No one can tell you what's right or wrong. But good garden planning takes personal style into consideration.

■ Raised-bed gardens
One popular method of growing vegetables is raised-bed gardening. This is similar to the Chinese mound system that dates back thousands of years. The beds are made by mounding soil 6 to 8 inches high and about 4 feet across. This width makes it easy to weed, thin, and pick vegetables from any side of the bed.

Raised beds are most appropriate in cool, wet climates because they heat up quickly in spring and dry out rapidly in summer. They also are excellent on ground you can't work properly—compacted clay or rock, for example. In such situations, buy black loam and mix it with peat and organic material to make the beds.

Leave 1- to 2-foot-wide pathways between your beds. Cover the pathways with black plastic and a layer of bark, wood chips, or, for more permanence, pebbles. Some gardeners use cedar, redwood, or green-treated boards to contain their raised gardens.

■ Traditional gardens
The traditional method of power tilling or spading an area on a flat surface works well in most instances, and is preferred in areas with sandy

soil and hot, dry conditions. Mulch this flat surface with plastic in cool areas to add heat for crops that like warm weather, or cover it with organic materials in warm areas to protect crops that prefer cooler surroundings. Organic materials also help retain the moisture in the soil, which is especially important in areas prone to drought or high summer heat. Good organic mulches include compost (see page 16), rotted manure, grass clippings, seaweed, and shredded leaves. One or more of these are available in most areas, and all are free or inexpensive.

Gardens do not have to be big to produce a lot. This garden measures only 4 feet by 16 feet, yet has enough space to grow more than 20 varieties of fresh vegetables (see the garden key, below right).

preferring instead to rely solely on organic controls. For example, they use diatomaceous earth to kill flea beetles, set out shallow pans of beer to drown slugs at night, and use predator insects such as ladybugs and lacewings to control crop-devastating insects. If you choose not to use insecticides, study specialized literature to learn more about gardening without poisons.

In many instances, damage to your vegetables from insects can be severe—up to 50 percent—but still not result in a loss of your crop. One of the simplest methods of dealing with this problem in the home garden is to grow twice as much as you intend to use. Though not foolproof, this method works more often than not.

GARDEN KEY

A. Basil, 'Spicy Globe'
B. Marigold, 'Janie'
C. Lettuce, 'Summer Baby Bibb'
D. Lettuce, 'Little Gem' romaine
E. Lettuce, 'Tetue de Nimes' romaine
F. Lettuce, 'Lollo Rossa' loose-leaf
G. Tah Tsai greens
H. Pak-choi, 'Mei Qung Choi'
I. 'Santoh Round Leaf' greens
J. Beet, 'Little Ball'

K. Carrot, 'Planet'
L. Pearl onion, 'Barletta'
M. Pea, 'Precovil'
N. Eggplant, 'Easter'
O. Basil, 'Green Ruffles'
P. Basil, 'Purple Ruffles'
Q. Alpine strawberry, 'Baron Solemacher'
R. Pepper, 'Super Chili'
S. Tomato, 'Sweet 100'

UNINVITED GUESTS

Whether you grow your garden in the country, suburbs, or city, plan on uninvited guests. The only real solution for keeping animals out of a large garden is a 6-foot fence with chicken wire around the bottom firmly planted 6 inches into the ground. In small gardens, you can surround plants with circular wire cages.

Treat insects with both organic controls and a limited use of insecticides. Some gardeners, however, don't like to use insecticides at all,

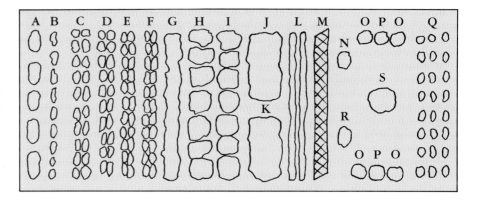

PLANTING AND CARING FOR VEGETABLES

Although every crop is a bit different, you can increase your garden's yield by heeding the following basic steps.

■ Prepare a good bed

Make sure your soil is easy to work and fertile. A soil analysis will tell you what to do to achieve just the right pH, texture, and fertility. Many county extension offices will do the analysis for you. Add as much organic matter, which decays into humus, as possible into the soil to enrich it.

■ Buy good seed

Buy seed only from reputable companies. Good seed is certified disease free and produces vegetables with good taste, texture, aroma, and size.

If you grow your own plants indoors, harden them off before setting them in the garden. Young plants need to be acclimated to the bright light and cooler temperatures outside. Do this by moving them slowly from shade to bright light for seven to 10 days. If a frost threatens, bring the seedlings indoors at night.

If you plant a number of crops, label them all. It's easy to forget what you've planted where.

■ Plant healthy transplants

Buy small, stocky plants (about 4 inches tall) for transplanting. These will do better than larger plants. The plants should have a deep, healthy green color. Don't buy diseased, wilted, or tall, spindly plants.

■ Space properly

Don't crowd plants. If you do set your plants more closely together than recommended on the seed packages (when using the space-saving technique called interplanting outlined on page 292, for example), plan on paying closer attention to how the plants are doing.

■ Protect plants

Protect your plants from insect damage, frost, and wind, particularly when they are young.

Simple paper collars wrapped around plant stems will thwart cutworms. Make cloches from plastic milk bottles and place them over plants at night to protect the plants from sudden dips in temperature. Set window screens and wood shingles by plants to prevent the wind from damaging them.

■ Apply mulch

Apply a thick layer of organic mulch to stop many weeds from growing and keep the soil around plants moist. Excellent organic mulches are straw, grass clippings, shredded leaves, pine needles, and compost (see pages 16–17).

In cool climates, use black plastic as a mulch around plants that like warmer weather. Be sure to water the soil before laying the plastic.

Caring for the plants in your vegetable garden—as is this gardener, who is covering heat-loving plants to protect them from a cold snap—can yield bountiful harvests later on.

■ Provide water

Don't use the old 1-inch-per-week watering formula. All seedlings need constantly moist soil around them. Older plants need water whenever the soil is dry several inches down. Feel the soil with your fingers to see how dry it is. Water by hand, use a soaker hose, or install a drip-irrigation system.

■ Feed your plants

Use organic or inorganic fertilizers to stimulate healthy growth. Good organic fertilizers include rotted manure, compost, blood meal, bonemeal, and seaweed.

A 10–10–10 inorganic fertilizer supplies all three of the elements essential to plant growth: nitrogen, phosphorus, and potash. Brush or wash off any inorganic fertilizer that lands directly on a plant. Never fertilize seedlings because the nitrogen can burn their foliage. When fertilizing, follow package directions exactly.

■ Thin crowded plants

Thin your plants regularly because vegetables that must compete for moisture and nutrients do not do well. Since the roots of plants often intermingle, snip tiny seedlings with scissors to avoid pulling out bunches at a time.

■ Weed

Dig or pull up any weeds that appear. If you use a hoe, don't dig deeply. Otherwise, you may hurt the shallow roots of many vegetables.

■ Kill pests

Kill as many insects as you can using organic controls. If you use insecticides, follow the directions carefully.

■ Watch for disease

Keep an eye out for plant disease. Remove and destroy infected plants or parts of plants.

■ Harvest constantly

Even if you don't use the vegetables, keep picking to stimulate further production. Most vegetables stop producing if allowed to go to seed.

CARE TIPS

To control cutworms, which kill seedlings by eating around their base, wrap the bottom inch or two of the plants' stems with foil or newspaper collars. Set the plants so the collars extend an inch below the soil. Remove the collars after the plants become established.

Cut the bottoms off plastic gallon milk containers and place the containers over individual plants to protect them from low temperatures. At night, keep the openings of these homemade cloches capped to prevent heat loss. Open them during the day if temperatures get too hot.

If needed, protect plants from wind and sun with two window screens fastened together to resemble an A-frame. Anchor the screens with small wooden stakes to keep high winds from knocking them over.

SPACE-SAVING TECHNIQUES

Whether your garden is small or you want to make more efficient use of a large garden, your goal is to produce as high a yield from as little space as possible. Here are a few techniques that work as well today as they have for thousands of years.

INTERPLANTING

Interplanting means using one area of the garden for more than one crop at the same time. It is sometimes referred to as intensive gardening. Successful interplanting requires combining companion plants in a logical pattern.

Good interplanting combinations mix quick- and slow-maturing crops, or they shelter cool-loving plants in the shade of larger plants that like hotter temperatures.

For instance, plant radishes in a row of carrots. The radishes germinate quickly and mark the row. The carrots pop through the soil much later, after the radishes have already started to leaf. Harvesting mature radishes will leave spaces between the young carrot plants—a natural thinning process that promotes good root growth in the carrots. Other vegetables that do well together are beets, lettuce, spinach, and Swiss chard interplanted with broccoli or cauliflower. The larger plants shade the leafy vegetables, which thrive in the cool and moist soil under their companion plants.

SUCCESSION PLANTING

Succession planting, often called double cropping, is commonsense gardening. You plant a crop immediately in any space left empty by the harvest of an earlier crop. Some vegetables—such as peas, radishes, green onions, and lettuce—mature quickly. By planting a second crop in the space left by the earlier crop, you double or even triple the number of harvests in a single season. This method also lets you plant small plantings frequently, so your crop of a certain vegetable doesn't come in all at once. Better a few heads of lettuce every week than dozens of heads all at once.

(Above) Interplant several crops in the same area to get the most from a small space. Harvest quick-maturing crops before they compete with their companion plants. Here, onions happily rub elbows with cabbages.

(Left) As soon as you pick one crop, plant another. This will provide you a succession of small crops, doubling, perhaps even tripling, your harvest.

VERTICAL GARDENING

If you're short on space, try vertical gardening. Growing vegetables up fences, trellises, poles, sticks, and wire takes up only a fraction of the ground space of regular gardening. Some plants even prefer growing vertically. Cucumbers and pole beans are two that thrive when grown this way. Prepare solid supports before planting the vegetables so you won't have to disturb the roots after the plants have begun to grow.

Some vining plants need a little help to get started. Wrap them gently around the support to guide them initially. Once they start, though, there's no stopping them. If plants climb a little too high, snip off their growing tips to make them branch out and become bushier.

Melons grown vertically may require some support because of their weight. Provide homemade slings made from old nylons, sheets, or towels for any fruit that starts to break off. Try not to disturb the vines, however.

Crops grown vertically often have better shape and less disease than fruit produced on the ground. But they do require more waterings. Mulch them to keep the ground moist.

CONTAINER GARDENING

Growing your own vegetables in containers on balconies, patios, or porches is a simple way to make the most of your space. Since you can move containers easily from one spot to another, you can take advantage of the different conditions offered in your yard. For example, put potted plants that like hot temperatures in areas of bright sun, and potted leafy vegetables that like cool, moist surroundings in shady spots.

Anything that will hold soil can become a container for growing vegetables. You can use household odds and ends or construct elaborate containers from scratch. Good ready-made containers are gallon cans, plastic milk jugs, clay pots, plastic pots, barrels, strawberry jars, baskets, wheelbarrows, buckets, or garbage cans.

If the containers do not have drain holes, cut some. Put broken clay shards or an inch of pebbles in the bottom of each container.

The size of the container should match the size of the grown plant. If you grow an eggplant or tomato plant in a small pot, for example, you're asking for trouble. As the plants grow, they create an extensive root system that demands space. And when the tops of big plants get heavy, they sometimes tip small pots over.

Use a sterilized potting soil, not garden soil, for container-grown plants. Garden soil usually compacts too much in containers. If you must use garden soil, mix it with equal parts peat and either vermiculite or perlite.

Water container plants often. Test the soil by pushing your finger several inches down. If your finger comes up dry, water the plant. Vegetables require lots of water to grow rapidly

Fresh vegetables grow well in space-saving containers as long as you start them in a good soil mixture and water them frequently—as often as twice a day—in hot weather. Choose bush or baby varieties suited to patio gardening.

EXTENDING THE SEASON

In areas where the growing season is short, you can use a number of techniques and products to get an early harvest in the spring and a late harvest in the fall.

Start plants in a cold frame as early in the season as possible. Your cold frame need not be complex or expensive: an old window slanted over a support will do. Face the frame to the south or southeast to collect the most daytime heat. Or, heat your cold frames with cables.

Unheated cold frames require insulation on cold nights (a blanket over the glass or plastic). During the day, you may need to open your cold frame to prevent overheating young plants.

Once spring arrives, make sure your started plants are set into the garden as early as possible.

Even though cool-loving plants thrive in cold temperatures, their seedlings need protection from unexpected frost in the first few days after planting. Cover them at night with commercial protectors or homemade cloches, such as the bottom halves of gallon milk containers (see page 291). Once cool-loving plants are growing well, they can withstand some frost.

Plants that prefer warmth do not tolerate frost, yet you still can set them in the garden early. Use black or clear plastic as a mulch. Plant your seedlings through holes cut in the plastic. Cover the rows with a tent made of clear plastic. Cut small holes along both sides of the tunnel to ventilate it. If daytime temperatures get hot, open one end. Close the end again at night to trap heat inside. You can start melons and cucumbers three to four weeks ahead of the normal planting time this way.

In the fall, when the temperature drops to freezing, one simple way to protect plants is to turn a sprinkler on in the garden. Leave the sprinkler on until the temperature rises above freezing the next day. Usually, weeks of mild weather follow the first heavy frost.

Extend the season, too, by covering plants late in the afternoon with old blankets, tarps, paper bags—anything at all. These do not keep out the cold; instead, they trap heat absorbed by the soil during the day. This heat, rising during the night, protects the plants from freezing.

Many synthetic materials are now available in rolls or sheets to protect plants, especially young ones, from cold and insects. Vent the sheet during the day if temperatures get too hot.

Some hot caps capture heat in the day in a covering filled with water. As temperatures drop during the night, the water gives off heat to keep plants warm.

Use plastic tunnels to get a jump on the season. Make small holes along the sides to keep plants from overheating during the day. Open the ends during the day for circulation; close them at night to keep the heat in. For additional heat, put clear or black plastic on the ground around the seedlings.

Get a jump on the growing season by hardening off your seedlings in a cold frame.

Or, grow leaf crops in cold frames in late fall or very early spring to extend the season.

VEGETABLES PORTFOLIO

GLOBE ARTICHOKE

ASPARAGUS

ARTICHOKE, GLOBE

Globe artichokes, a gourmet's delight, are perennials. Grow them year after year in your backyard garden. In the North, protect plants from killing frosts.

■ **Varieties:** 'Green Globe' is the standard variety, but is especially suited for warmer areas.

■ **Planting:** In warmer areas, plant globe artichokes in a permanent bed where you won't disturb them. Spade the ground deeply. Enrich the soil with well-rotted manure or compost. Use 10–10–10 fertilizer according to package directions. Plants need full sun to develop properly, so try to plant them with a southern exposure. Planting them near a wall or wooden fence helps protect them from cold snaps in spring.

Start your own plants from seeds indoors (eight weeks before the frost-free date), buy nursery transplants, or order dormant roots. After all danger of frost passes, set globe artichokes into the garden, allowing 4 feet between rows and plants.

■ **Care:** Water the plants frequently. Surround them with a thick layer of mulch to keep the soil moist during summer hot spells. Hand-pull any weeds close to the plants.

Older plants produce numerous suckers at the base of the stem. Cut these off, along with 3 inches of root, to make new plants. Frost will kill artichokes so, in cold areas, cut the plants back to 1 foot at the end of the season. Dig up the roots and plant them in large clay pots. Bring them inside. Water the plants occasionally, just enough to keep them alive. In spring, three weeks before setting the plants outdoors, start watering regularly and fertilize.

■ **Harvest:** Pick artichokes while the scales on the buds are still tight and flat. Homegrown artichokes are tenderest when no larger than 3 inches wide. Keep picking to stimulate further production. Some gardeners, however, will let artichokes go to bloom so they can dry the thistlelike flowers for arrangements.

ASPARAGUS

An asparagus bed is a lifetime investment. Once this vegetable establishes itself, it produces for decades. But it does require patience to get it established, so pick asparagus only after two to three years of growth.

■ **Varieties:** No variety is universally recommended. Asparagus will grow well in all regions except along the Gulf Coast, but each area has different growing requirements. Varieties have been bred with these variations in mind, so look for plants that will grow in your area.

■ **Planting:** To have a healthy asparagus bed, dig a trench about 16 inches deep, then fill it with 10 inches of soil mixed with manure or compost. Choose a sunny spot that will remain undisturbed all season long and for years to come. The site also should be near a source of water.

After preparing the bed, set out crowns in the trenches. You can find crowns in local stores or order them through the mail. Crowns are sold by age, and either one- or two-year-old crowns are fine. You also can grow asparagus from seed, but that delays harvest by an additional year. Plant the crowns 8 inches deep and 2 feet or more apart. Cover them with several inches of rich soil. Gradually fill in the trench as the spears grow.

■ **Care:** Because asparagus grows so quickly, give it heavy applications of nutrient-packed manure or compost or fertilizer. Keep the beds mulched at all times to hinder weeds and to increase soil moisture. Remove any weeds that grow through the mulch. Water frequently to encourage as much fern growth as possible. Healthy ferns create large root systems and new buds for next year's crop. After plants die back in the fall, remove all dead ferns to prevent insect infestations and disease the following year. In cold areas, apply a fall mulch to protect the crowns from winter damage.

■ **Harvest:** Never pick asparagus when it is an immature plant. When spears are thicker than a little finger, start to pick lightly. Pick spears before they start to form little branches. To snap off the tender and delicious portion of each spear, bend it to one side just above the tough lower section. Stop picking by early July. For healthy root growth and long-term production, always leave some spears to create new ferns.

BEANS

Beans, one of the most popular vegetables, take very little space, have few problems, and produce bountiful crops.

■ **Varieties:** Grow both bush and vining varieties. The bush varieties mature rapidly and are easy to grow in successive plantings. The vining varieties take longer to mature but are prolific. Beans are eaten in three ways: pod and all (snap beans), as immature seeds (limas), and as mature dry beans (shelled and stored for later use). You can use some varieties in all three ways.

■ **Planting:** Plant beans in a sunny, well-drained location after the soil has thoroughly warmed. Bean seeds rot in cool, damp soil. Make successive sowings of bush beans every two weeks for an extended harvest. Plant pole, lima, and dry beans only once. Space rows of bush beans 2 to 2½ feet apart, with seeds placed 2 to 3 inches apart. Plant pole beans in hills 2 to 3 feet apart, with four or five seeds per pole. After the beans have sprouted, thin to three plants per pole. Lima beans need a little more space, with seeds spaced every 8 inches in rows 2 to 2½ feet apart.

■ **Care:** Side-dress beans with fertilizer when plants are 4 to 6 inches high. Use mulch to keep soil constantly moist. Weed regularly, but to avoid spreading viruses, work in the bean patch only when it's dry.

■ **Harvest:** Because bean plants will stop producing if the pods develop seeds, pick all snap and lima beans before they mature. The beans should be tender, and the seeds should not have swelled enough to cause visible bulges in the shells. Pinch limas when small and tender. Allow dry beans to mature on the bush. Dry them

well, then harvest by beating them against a hard object, such as the side of a garbage can. Store in an airtight glass jar.

BEET

You can eat both the tops and the tender roots of the succulent beet. The red-veined, deep green leaves are decorative, making beets a natural for patio, container, or border planting.

■ **Varieties:** Beets come in a fascinating number of colors, shapes, and varieties. Some varieties yield crops quickly. Some are grown for their tender tops (not their roots). Still others thrive in the late season, get very large, and store well. Choose the variety that matches your needs.

■ **Planting:** Plant beets in the early spring as soon as you can work the ground. The soil should be loose to encourage root growth. If you have compact soil, try a raised bed. Beets prefer soil with a pH of 6.5 to 7.5.

Each seed is really a pod containing a number of seeds. Beet seeds occasionally do not germinate well. Sow them more thickly than recommended on the package. To stretch the season, make successive plantings.

Thin the seedlings when they are 5 inches tall, leaving them 4 to 6 inches apart. The thinnings make a delicious meal even though their roots haven't fully formed.

■ **Care:** Rapidly grown beets will taste far better than those allowed to linger, so encourage quick growth by watering heavily. Mulch to keep the soil moist around the roots. Pick weeds when small to avoid injuring beet roots and to eliminate competition for food and water.

■ **Harvest:** Harvest fast-maturing beets when their roots swell to 2 or 3 inches in diameter. If they get any larger, they can become tough and woody. Slow-maturing beets get much larger and you don't have to pick them so young. Harvest the tops throughout the season for tasty steamed greens. Store harvested beets in sand, peat, or leaves in a cool, dark place.

BEAN

BEET—cylindrical

BEET—'Golden'

VEGETABLES PORTFOLIO *(continued)*

BROCCOLI

BRUSSELS SPROUTS

BROCCOLI

Broccoli grows beautifully in most home gardens as long as you protect it from rabbits and insects. After you pick the large central buds—the heads—the plants will produce delicious, though smaller, buds.

■ **Varieties:** Many varieties do well in the home garden. Try two each year. Choose the one you like better and grow it again the following year with yet another variety. Keep doing this each year. This is a simple (and fun) way to find out which variety does best in your garden.

The purple-headed variety turns green when cooked. Some catalogs list it as a cauliflower.

■ **Planting:** Get broccoli into the garden as early as possible. Start your own seeds 4 to 6 weeks ahead of the frost-free date in your area. Or buy started transplants from a reliable garden center. Buy compact, stocky plants.

Set seedlings outdoors as soon as you can work the soil. If frost threatens, protect the seedlings with cloches. To prevent cutworm damage, wrap stiff paper around the stem of each plant before planting. At least 1 inch of the collar should extend below the soil line, with 2 inches above. Space rows about 2 feet apart, with at least 20 inches of space between the plants. Grow spinach, lettuce, or Swiss chard in the shade of broccoli.

■ **Care:** Give broccoli lots of water. Use a thick mulch around each plant to keep soil moist. Weed regularly. Broccoli has two mortal enemies: rabbits and cabbageworms. Protect the plants with a fence or small, individual wire cages. Because rabbits stop feeding on broccoli when it gets big, remove the cages when the plants get large. To combat worms, spray broccoli plants at weekly intervals with *Bacillus thuringiensis,* a biological control that kills worms but is totally safe to animals and humans. Organic gardeners accept its use.

■ **Harvest:** Pick the green flower buds before they start to spread into little yellow flowers. The buds should be firm and tight, just as they are in the grocery store. Cut the bud with a sharp knife an inch or two down the stalk.

Heads that start to flower are past their prime, although the flowers are decorative and edible. A number of smaller buds will form below the central bud after you pick it. Harvest these in the same way as the original, larger bud. Keep harvesting to force continued production.

BRUSSELS SPROUTS

Brussels sprouts are a close relative of cabbage. The plant produces a tall stalk covered with miniature cabbages about the size of walnuts. Brussels sprouts like to mature in cool weather. Flavor improves after light frosts.

■ **Varieties:** Try two varieties the first year, then choose the one you like better and grow it again the following year with yet another variety. Order seed from a catalog or pick up plants grown locally. Buy short, stocky plants (no more than 4 inches tall). Locally grown seedlings often are not identified by variety—a good reason to start your own plants from seed.

■ **Planting:** Work organic matter and commercial fertilizer into the soil before planting. Get brussels sprouts into the garden as early as you can. Experiment with a second crop later in the season to see which time period produces a better crop. Space seedlings 1½ to 2 feet apart in rows about 2½ feet apart. Attach cutworm collars if this insect is a problem in your area. Plant leafy crops underneath the brussels sprouts if space is at a premium. The taller brussels sprouts will provide cool, moist conditions for quick-maturing lettuce or spinach.

■ **Care:** For healthier and more productive plants, side-dress brussels sprouts with manure or commercial fertilizer every two weeks. Water plants frequently and use a thick mulch to prevent water loss from the soil. Remove only those leaves that turn yellow and die.

Cabbageworms and insects such as grasshoppers will attack brussels sprouts. To kill worms, spray at weekly intervals with *Bacillus thuringiensis*. Use carbaryl to kill other insect pests.

■ **Harvest:** For best taste, harvest brussels sprouts when they are compact and only about

1 inch in diameter. Pick the larger sprouts first, from the bottom up along the tall stem. If frost threatens, don't worry—it won't harm the plant.

CABBAGE

Cabbage, a popular vegetable because it stores well, thrives in cool-weather areas. In southern gardens, it often is replaced by other leafy greens such as collards.

■ **Varieties:** Early-, mid-, and late-season varieties of cabbage exist. The ones that mature late in the season store the best. Study the catalogs carefully to see which varieties are recommended for your area and to find varieties that match your needs. Plant more than one variety to extend the harvest.

■ **Planting:** Start seeds indoors about six to eight weeks before the frost-free date in your area. If you buy seedlings at a garden center, choose healthy, stocky plants no larger than 4 inches tall. Get seedlings into the garden two to four weeks before the frost-free date, just as soon as you can work the soil. If there is an unexpected frost, use cloches to protect the young plants. Plant late-maturing varieties later in the season. If cutworms are common in your area, use cutworm collars around the stems of the young plants. Protect seedlings with wire cages or a fence if rodents are a nuisance. Remove these when heads begin to form.

■ **Care:** Provide cabbage with cool, moist soil enriched with lots of organic matter and 10–10–10 fertilizer. Apply a thick mulch around the bases of the plants to keep them moist. Encourage quick and uniform growth for the best heads. Watch for damage by cabbageworms. If you see small holes in the leaves, immediately spray with *Bacillus thuringiensis* at weekly intervals. Handpick worms whenever you see them.

■ **Harvest:** Begin harvesting before the heads mature. Twist the heads off or cut them with a knife. Cabbage plants often produce several smaller heads to replace the one picked early in the season.

CARROT

Carrots grow easily in a small area, resist cold, and, if stored under moist, cool conditions, stay fresh up to four months. They also yield more fruit per square inch of garden soil than most other vegetables and are tasty cooked or raw.

■ **Varieties:** If you have deep, loose soil, grow some of the longer-rooted varieties. If you have clayey soil, stick to the stubbier crops such as 'Planet.' Try new varieties to find the ones that do well in your garden and appeal to your taste.

■ **Planting:** Prepare your bed well. The looser the soil, the better. If you have compacted soil, grow carrots in a raised bed. Get carrots into the ground as soon as you can work the soil in the spring. Carrot seeds are extremely fine and are difficult to sow evenly or in an uncrowded manner. Some gardeners mix the seed with sand or vermiculite to make sowing easier. Others use a saltshaker. Still others mix in radish seeds, which germinate faster and work as a good row marker. Carrot seeds can take up to three weeks to germinate. Keep them moist because uniform moisture at this stage is critical. If you can't watch your carrots closely, apply a ½-inch layer of mulch over the row.

■ **Care:** Thin carrots early by snipping off the ferns with a scissors. Or wait and pull up the larger carrots just as they reach edible stage. The smaller carrots then will have space to mature as the season progesses. Keep after weeds. Mulch works well around carrots to keep them free of weeds, but some weeds still will grow. Don't let the weeds get big. Otherwise, when you pull large weeds, you may pull up young carrots. Water frequently during dry spells. Carrots will be sweeter if grown rapidly.

■ **Harvest:** Start picking carrots as soon as they are large enough to eat. These young carrots are delicious, and picking them helps the other carrots thrive. Also, when carrots get large, they can be difficult to pull. Dig off to the side with a spade to harvest large bunches of carrots all at once. Store harvested carrots in sand, peat, or leaves for later use.

CABBAGE

CARROT—baby

CARROT—'Planet'

299

VEGETABLES PORTFOLIO *(continued)*

CAULIFLOWER

SWISS CHARD

CAULIFLOWER

Cauliflower suffers from a reputation of being hard to grow, probably because some of the varieties have to be blanched (protected from the sun). But the truth is that blanching isn't difficult, and some varieties are self-blanching or don't need blanching at all.

■ **Varieties:** You can buy cauliflower that produces white or purple heads. The purple heads turn deep green when cooked and taste like broccoli. Purple-headed varieties do not require blanching. Some of the white varieties are self-blanching because their leaves curl up and over the curd.

■ **Planting:** Start cauliflower seeds indoors six to eight weeks before the frost-free date in your area. Get the young seedlings into the ground two to four weeks before the frost-free date. If you expect a frost, protect the plants with cloches. You also can buy seedlings from local nurseries. Avoid tall, spindly plants.

If cutworms are a problem in your area, put a cutworm collar around the stem of each seedling before planting. Start a second planting later in the season for a fall crop.

■ **Care:** For a good harvest, provide your cauliflower with cool temperatures, ample moisture, and organic-rich soil. The only way to control the temperature is to get the plants in at the right time. As for moisture, water frequently and keep a thick layer of mulch around the plants. For rich soil, side-dress with 10–10–10 fertilizer every two weeks. Spray plants with *Bacillus thuringiensis* at weekly intervals to kill cabbageworms.

Once the curds begin to form, gather and tie the leaves together to form protective canopies. This blanching step is necessary because sunlight striking the buds causes discoloration and grainy texture. Do this on a dry day. Wet curds may rot. Purple and self-blanching varieties don't need blanching.

■ **Harvest:** After tying the leaves, check the curds daily (untie the leaves and peek in). When the curds are large, cut them off at the base with a sharp knife.

CELERIAC

Celeriac is a tasty, easily—but rarely—grown celery-flavored plant great in soups and salads.
■ **Varieties:** The most readily available varieties include: 'Alabaster,' 'Giant Prague,' 'Large Smooth Prague,' 'Marble Hall,' and 'Zwindra.'
■ **Planting:** Start seeds indoors eight to 10 weeks before the frost-free date in your area. Set the seedlings in the garden when night temperatures are higher than 45 degrees.
■ **Care:** Keep the plants growing rapidly with frequent waterings and a thick organic mulch. Weed regularly. When the base of the plant begins to expand into a turniplike root, cover it with soil. This will blanch it, keeping it white, tender, and sweet.
■ **Harvest:** Wait until the stem is 3 to 4 inches wide before harvesting. Cut the root below the bulge with a sharp knife. Frost will sweeten its taste. To store the plant in the garden in cold areas, cover it with a thick mulch.

CELERY

Celery can be tricky to grow from seed, but if you use transplants purchased at a garden center, it is not difficult at all. You'll get large plants with crunchy, delicious stalks.
■ **Varieties:** Celery can be green or gold. When choosing seeds or seedlings, look for varieties that don't need blanching. A number of varieties also resist fusarium yellows and blight.
■ **Planting:** Start celery from seed indoors eight to 12 weeks before the frost-free date in your area. Press the seeds into a moist growing medium and keep them exposed to light. Plant seedlings after night temperatures stay above 45 degrees.
■ **Care:** Water celery frequently. Flood the area around the base of the stem whenever the soil starts to dry out. Use a mulch to keep the ground moist and cool. Mulch to help control weeds. Pull weeds immediately, before they can compete with the young celery plants.

If you blanch your celery to improve its taste, you will lose many of its vitamins. If you do blanch the plants, wait until they're almost mature. Put boards along their sides, mound soil on the stalks, or cover the bottoms of the plants with milk carton halves. Keep the leafy tops of the stalks exposed to light, however.

■ **Harvest:** As soon as the celery plants produce medium-sized stalks, harvest some of them. Pick off one or two of the outer stalks from each plant, leaving the central core to grow. At the end of the season, pull up the entire plants, cut off their roots, and enjoy.

CHARD, SWISS

Swiss chard is a member of the beet family, but the taste of its cooked tops resembles that of spinach. Unlike spinach, though, Swiss chard leaves are not very tasty eaten raw in salads. Swiss chard resists heat and drought, and grows without bolting to seed, right up until frost. It also is packed with vitamins.

■ **Varieties:** Swiss chard comes in both red and green forms. Good green varieties are 'Fordhook Giant' and 'Lucullus.' 'Rhubarb Chard' is a popular red variety. Both color forms are attractive enough to mingle with flowers in beds and borders.

■ **Planting:** Avoid setting Swiss chard into acid soil. Although it can adapt to a wide variety of soil types and exposures, Swiss chard, like beets, prefers soil with a pH of 6.5 to 7.5. Lime or wood ash will raise the pH if a soil test shows that's needed. Sow seeds in the garden as soon as you can work the ground. Because each seed actually is a cluster of three to four seeds, space seeds an inch or so apart in the row. Rows should be 1½ to 2 feet apart.

■ **Care:** As seedlings emerge, thin the plants to stand about 8 to 10 inches apart. Don't worry if you don't have the time to thin, though, because even crowded plants produce well. Mulch around the plants to retain moisture in the soil. Keep the soil moist with frequent waterings if needed. To stimulate new growth, fertilize lightly each time you pick leaves off a plant.

■ **Harvest:** Pick the outer leaves when they are small (less than 8 inches) and cook like spinach.

Let the inner growing buds continue to produce new leaves. Do not pick all the leaves from one plant. If leaves get big, strip out the midrib and serve it like asparagus (don't expect it to taste like asparagus, though). In the fall, Swiss chard lends itself to cold-frame or greenhouse culture for an extended harvest into the winter. Or simply place protective caps over garden plants for pickings well past the first hard frost.

CHINESE CABBAGE

Because of its mild flavor, Chinese cabbage is excellent raw in salads and coleslaw, but it is even better cooked in stir-fried dishes.

■ **Varieties:** The three kinds of Chinese cabbage are: Chinese chard cabbage or bok choy, which is loose-leaved, easy to grow, and quick maturing; Chinese mustard greens, which are good for succession cropping; and true Chinese cabbage, which forms long, narrow heads over an extended season. True Chinese cabbage is the toughest of the three to grow.

■ **Planting:** Prepare a bed rich in organic matter for good drainage, aeration, and water retention. Mix peat, compost, or well-rotted manure into the soil with a sprinkling of commercial fertilizer. Plant Chinese chard cabbage and Chinese mustard greens in spring and fall. Plant several plantings for an extended harvest. Plant true Chinese cabbage for fall harvest in the North and for winter harvest in the South.

■ **Care:** As plants emerge, thin to stand every 8 to 12 inches. Surround the plants with a thick mulch to keep soil moist and cool. Keep plants moist for best growth (the faster the growth, the better the taste). Feed young plants with supplemental applications of a high-nitrogen fertilizer every 10 to 14 days until just before harvest. If you like, blanch Chinese cabbage by placing milk cartons over the plants' lower portions, but leave the tops exposed. Blanching improves the taste, but destroys vitamins.

■ **Harvest:** Pick leaves as soon as needed on leafy, nonheading varieties. For heading varieties, pull plants when heads are large and firm. Strip off damaged leaves and cut off the roots.

CHINESE CABBAGE—bok choy

CHINESE CABBAGE—true

VEGETABLES PORTFOLIO *(continued)*

COLLARDS

CORN—'Illini Gold'

COLLARDS

Collards are leafy members of the cabbage family that yield heavily over a long harvest season. Because collards tolerate hot weather, they are widely grown in the South, where cabbages do poorly. In northern gardens, collards grow well as a mid-season crop when planted after earlier crops mature.

■ **Varieties:** The best varieties are 'Georgia' and 'Vates' (a compact, dwarflike variety).

■ **Planting:** Prepare a bed of loose soil enriched with organic matter and a sprinkling of fertilizer. Sow seeds any time during the spring, spacing rows about 2 feet apart. Replace an early crop of peas with collards to take advantage of the nitrogen left behind by peas.

■ **Care:** As plants mature, thin to at least 6 inches apart. Thinnings are both delicious and nutritious. Keep plants moist at all times. Because collards have shallow roots that damage easily when hoed, retard weed growth with a 2- to 4-inch mulch applied when the plants are several inches high. Side-dress with nitrogen-rich fertilizer every three to four weeks to stimulate leafier growth. If cabbageworms attack, spray weekly with *Bacillus thuringiensis.*

■ **Harvest:** Pick the outer leaves of collards as they develop, leaving the inner leaf buds to grow for later pickings. Don't remove all the leaves from one plant.

CORN

Fresh corn tastes so much better than store-bought or market corn that it's almost a different vegetable. Although corn takes up a lot of space in the home garden, it's well worth it.

■ **Varieties:** For a harvest throughout the summer and into the fall, plant some early, mid-season, and late varieties. Both popcorn and supersweet corn hybrids (labeled supersweet, extra sweet, shrunken 2, or Sh2 in catalogs) grow well in home gardens, but you must isolate them to prevent cross-pollination with other varieties. Sugary enhanced (SE) or everlasting heritage (EH) varieties need no isolation.

■ **Planting:** Wait until the soil is completely warm before sowing corn seeds, which will rot in cool, damp soil. For rapid growth, warm days and nights are critical. Corn is wind-pollinated, so plant corn in a block of three or four short rows, rather than in one long row. To provide an initial food supply for the seeds, dig a furrow 3 inches deep and sprinkle any complete fertilizer along the bottom. Cover the fertilizer with a thin layer of soil, then plant the seeds 1 inch below the original soil level. Space seeds about 4 inches apart in rows 2 feet apart. If you plant corn in hills, space the hills about 3 feet apart and sow five seeds to a hill.

Isolate varieties to avoid cross-pollination. For instance, if allowed to cross-pollinate, popcorn can ruin sweet corn and sweet corn can ruin supersweet hybrids. Isolate either by time (plant so crops tassel 10 days apart) or by space (have 1,000 feet between different varieties). Obviously, the easiest and most practical method for home gardeners is to isolate by time.

■ **Care:** After the seedlings emerge, surround them with mulch (except in cool, wet areas). Keep plants well watered. When the stalks are a foot high, side-dress with fertilizer. Do this one more time when the plants begin to tassel.

Keep an eye out for smut, which forms a big gray to black ball on infected ears. Remove and destroy the smut ball immediately.

Protect the crop from deer and raccoons by building a high fence around the patch. Run a wire around the top and connect it to a battery. Other simple tricks some gardeners use to keep out marauders—such as growing pumpkins and squash beside the corn—do not work.

■ **Harvest:** Pick ears when the kernels fill out and exude a milky substance when punctured with a fingernail. Because the pointed tips of the ears mature last, you'll need to husk one or two ears to judge whether a crop is mature. Other signs of ripeness include brown silk, a deep green color, and a firm, full feel (squeeze the ear). Pick corn just before you cook it because corn sugar starts turning into starch immediately after it's picked. The supersweet and sugary enhanced (SE or EH) corns stay fresher longest.

CUCUMBER

Cucumbers have little nutritional value, but the taste of fresh or pickled cucumbers makes up for this shortcoming.

■ **Varieties:** Cucumbers generally are classified as slicing varieties or pickling varieties. Slicing varieties are delicious in salads and, when still young, can be picked for pickles, although this isn't recommended. Pickling varieties produce many small fruits. Both types come in vining and bush varieties. Bush varieties still vine but take up a lot less space, making them ideal for containers or compact gardens. Breeders also have produced unique varieties: some produce mostly or all female flowers (gynoecious) and some do not need pollinating (parthenocarpic). Some of these varieties are seedless or have only a few seeds.

■ **Planting:** Plant cucumbers in a bright, sunny location only after the soil has warmed. The bed should be loose and contain lots of organic matter and added fertilizer. Use a black or clear plastic mulch in cold areas to increase heat. To increase production and save space, plant cucumbers to climb a trellis of wire or wooden lath. The fruits of cucumbers grown this way often are straighter.

■ **Care:** As soon as the plants begin to vine, start training them up the support. Most varieties will take to vertical growth if you train them to climb at the outset. If necessary, loosely tie the young plants to the support with soft twine. Keep vines moist at all times. Use a thick mulch (if you're not using plastic) to lessen competition from weeds. If a vine outgrows its support, pinch off the growing tip. This will cause the plant to branch. As the season ends, encourage the growth of the larger fruits by pinching off all flowers and any immature fruit.

■ **Harvest:** Always pick fruits as soon as they are ready. Fruits allowed to mature on the vine give off a hormone that causes the vine to stop producing and eventually kills it.

With a sharp knife, cut cucumbers that are tender and tasty. Pick them much smaller than those found in grocery stores. Overripe cucumbers will begin to turn yellow. They can become bitter and thick skinned, and often have hard, indigestible seeds.

EGGPLANT

Eggplant—a native of India and the Mideast and somewhat of a newcomer to U.S. gardens—comes in an interesting variety of shapes and colors, and needs a long period of warm weather to mature. Each plant, if properly grown, produces many fruits throughout the season.

■ **Varieties:** More than 30 varieties are available; most adapt readily to container growing. One of the best is 'Black Beauty.' Also good is 'Dusky,' which matures more rapidly. 'Easter' bears fruit the size of chicken eggs, but tastes just like traditional eggplant.

■ **Planting:** Start plants from seeds eight to 10 weeks before the frost-free date in your area. Or purchase healthy transplants at a garden center. If you start seedlings on your own, harden the plants in a cold frame or on a porch for one week before planting. Plant seedlings 2 or more feet apart after all danger of frost passes. Place cutworm collars around the stems if cutworms have ever been a problem in your garden. If an unexpected cold snap hits, protect eggplants with cloches.

■ **Care:** To get a good crop of eggplant, mulch around the plants. Water frequently in dry or hot weather. Because hoeing will damage the plant's shallow roots, handpick weeds near the plants. Side-dress with fertilizer several times during the growing season. Some eggplants need support as they grow. Use bamboo stakes and a soft cloth to tie the stems to the support.

■ **Harvest:** Harvest eggplant when much smaller than the size sold in stores. Smaller eggplants have a glossy skin and a tasty, firm, seedless flesh. Cut the stem just above the eggplant with a sharp knife. The plant is prickly, so wear gloves while harvesting. As the season ends, encourage the growth of the few remaining fruits by pinching off all blossoms and immature fruit. Or, if you prefer, pot up the plants and bring them inside for an extended harvest.

CUCUMBER—pickling

CUCUMBER—slicing

EGGPLANT—'Easter'

303

VEGETABLES PORTFOLIO *(continued)*

ENDIVE

HORSERADISH

ENDIVE

Endive, a succulent green crop, has outer green leaves that have a distinct, somewhat bitter taste; its inner, creamy white leaves have a buttery texture and more delicate flavor. Endive is easy to grow and matures in two to three months depending on the variety.

■ **Varieties:** Endive comes in broad-leaved varieties (often called escarole or Batavian endive) and curly varieties. Three favorites are 'Florida Deep Heart,' 'Full-Heart Batavian,' and 'Green Curled.' The first two prefer warmer areas.

■ **Planting:** For best taste, plant endive for cool-weather maturity (in the North, plant it in midsummer for a fall harvest). Prepare a loose, rich bed with lots of organic matter. For an early crop, start plants indoors or in a cold frame. Set seeds in the garden as soon as you can work the ground. Sow seeds in rows 1½ to 2 feet apart. Sow several times to extend the harvest.

■ **Care:** As seedlings emerge, thin them to stand 6 inches apart. Plant thinned plants as transplants. To encourage leafiness, side-dress with high-nitrogen fertilizer every few weeks. Mulch plants to preserve soil moisture. Water frequently in dry weather to force quick growth. Blanching helps produce creamy white centers and prevents leaves from becoming tough and bitter, but causes the plants to lose vitamins. To blanch, pull dry leaves up into a loose head and secure. Or shade the plants with a board supported by bricks. After a rain, untie or expose the leaves just long enough to dry.

■ **Harvest:** Slide a sharp knife under the blanched head and cut to harvest. Wash well and keep chilled in a crisper until needed.

HORSERADISH

Horseradish is a prolific perennial that takes little care. Grated, its root is a super condiment.

■ **Varieties:** The best-known variety is 'Maliner Kren.' Roots available in grocery stores will grow as well as those from catalogs or local garden centers.

■ **Planting:** Prepare a separate bed for horseradish, which can become a weed if left uncontrolled. The bed must be loose and rich. Add compost, rotted manure, or peat, along with fertilizer, to stimulate healthy root growth. For best results, plant the roots as soon as possible in spring. Space plants 12 inches apart in a block.

■ **Care:** When tiny shoots appear, apply grass clippings, shredded leaves, or straw around the plants. Water often to encourage vigorous growth. Remove weeds by hand. Side-dress with fertilizer twice during growing season.

■ **Harvest:** Dig roots as needed after the first fall frost, but only if the bed is thriving. Sometimes it is best to wait until the second season to begin harvesting. Always leave some roots in the bed to keep it alive for the next season.

JERUSALEM ARTICHOKE

Jerusalem artichokes—members of the sunflower family—form edible tubers low in starch and calories. They make an excellent potato substitute. The plants grow up to 8 feet tall, producing long leaves on a fuzzy stalk that form either yellow or light purple flowers.

■ **Varieties:** Buy tubers from grocery stores, garden centers, or mail-order houses.

■ **Planting:** Prepare a separate bed in full sun for Jerusalem artichokes because they can be invasive in the home garden. The soil should be loose and slightly acid (mix in acidic peat moss). Also mix in fertilizer to stimulate root growth. Plant as early as possible in the spring. Cut each tuber into several sections. Plant sections 6 inches deep and 2 feet apart in all directions to form blocks. A heavy feeder, Jerusalem artichoke will respond favorably to applications of organic or chemical fertilizers.

■ **Care:** As the tubers begin to sprout, surround them with a thick layer of mulch, such as grass clippings, shredded leaves, or straw. Handpick any weeds before they get large. Water frequently. Side-dress with extra fertilizer every few weeks during the season.

Although the flowers are attractive, pinch off flower buds to force better tuber development.

Wear gloves and a long shirt since some gardeners are allergic to these plants. In the fall, cut stalks to the ground to keep the patch clean. This will prevent disease and eliminate winter homes for insects.

■ **Harvest:** Do not harvest the first season. The following fall, dig tubers carefully to prevent damaging the skins. Or leave the tubers in the ground under a heavy mulch for wintertime harvesting. Leave some tubers in the ground for the following year's crop. Store harvested tubers in peat, sand, or leaves.

KALE

Kale, like other members of the cabbage family, likes it cool. Once growing, kale is a tough plant and can put up with a lot of abuse, including hard frosts and heavy freezes. Its deeply crinkled blue-green leaves make it a natural for striking ornamental plantings.

■ **Varieties:** The two main types of kale are Scotch and Siberian. These come in both smooth and curly-leaved varieties. Three of the best varieties for the home garden are 'Vates,' 'Dwarf Blue Curled,' and 'Dwarf Siberian.'

■ **Planting:** Because it is hardy and its flavor improves with a mild frost, grow kale so it matures in cool to cold weather. Sow seeds ½ inch deep in rows 1½ feet apart. Or scatter seeds over a wide band for wide-row gardening.

■ **Care:** Early in the season, watch for flea beetles. Dust the plants with diatomaceous earth or spray with carbaryl. Mulch around plants to keep roots cool and damp throughout the season. Water frequently if soil dries. Handpick any weeds that pop up through the mulch. Do not cultivate close to the plants; you may damage their shallow root system. To increase yield, side-dress with fertilizer every few weeks.

■ **Harvest:** Pick leaves before they reach 8 inches in length. The central buds of the kale plants will supply a continuous harvest if you pick only the outer leaves as they mature. If you want to harvest the crop in the North during winter, cover the plants with a thick layer of mulch (up to 12 inches of straw).

KOHLRABI

Similar in cultural requirements to cabbage, kohlrabi produces an edible, swollen stem. It's an odd-looking plant, good either raw or cooked. Although the plant isn't popular, most people like its turniplike taste after trying it.

■ **Varieties:** Three popular varieties are 'Grand Duke,' 'Early Purple Vienna,' and 'Early White Vienna.' 'Grand Duke' produces larger and milder knobs. It also resists black rot.

■ **Planting:** Because kohlrabi does best when it matures in cool weather, sow its seeds as soon as you can work the ground in the spring. Mix in lots of organic matter and some commercial fertilizer. Space rows about 2 feet apart. For an even earlier crop, start seeds indoors six to eight weeks before the frost-free date, then transplant to the garden three to four weeks before that date. Protect if necessary with cloches. Planting seedlings instead of seeds is highly recommended—but not essential—in northern gardens. Because kohlrabi matures early, it's a good candidate for interplanting with later-maturing onions. Or plant kohlrabi later in the season to mature in the cool weeks of fall.

■ **Care:** Provide kohlrabi with plenty of sun and a cool, moist soil. Add a thick mulch as soon as the plants emerge to preserve soil moisture. Water whenever the soil dries out. Avoid cultivating around the plant since it has a shallow root system. Spray weekly with *Bacillus thuringiensis* to prevent cabbageworm attack. If a plant wilts unexpectedly, check its roots for maggots. Kill root maggots with diazinon, or prevent them by surrounding plants with root maggot mats (5x5-inch pieces of carpet underlayment).

■ **Harvest:** Pick before the knobs grow wider than 2 inches. Kohlrabi will become tough and stringy if it ripens beyond that point. Trim leaves, which are edible but rarely eaten, and roots. Parboil the knob. Remove outer peeling before eating. Protect late plantings with mulch to extend the harvest into late fall.

KALE

KOHLRABI

VEGETABLES PORTFOLIO *(continued)*

LEEK

LETTUCE—butterhead

LETTUCE—cos (romaine)

LEEK

Coveted for their subtle onion flavor, leeks require from 75 to 150 days to mature, depending on the variety. They're easy to grow and store well when left in the garden. This is a prized vegetable among gourmets and is expensive in most stores. Leeks look like elongated onions and, when cut, unfold like a newspaper.

■ **Varieties:** Common varieties include 'Broad London' ('Large American Flag'), 'Giant Musselburgh,' and 'King Richard.'

■ **Planting:** Start seeds indoors eight weeks before outdoor planting (usually four weeks before the frost-free date). Give seedlings a crew cut whenever they grow taller than 3 inches. When planting seeds directly in the garden, sow ½ inch deep and cover with sifted soil. When plants are 8 inches tall, thin to 5 inches apart. Plant the thinned seedlings the same distance apart in another row. Space rows 1½ feet apart. When planting transplants, set them into a 6- to 8-inch-deep trench. As plants mature, fill in the trench to just below the leaves. This blanching procedure will produce tender, white stalks. The longer the white portion, the better the vegetable. Or, blanch the stems by piling soil up around them as the season progresses. Either method works well. Watch for onion thrips and root maggots, which you can kill with carbaryl and diazinon.

■ **Care:** Nip weeds as soon as they begin to invade the rows. A good mulch will make the job easier. If rain is insufficient, soak with a garden hose to maintain soil moisture. Side-dress with fertilizer throughout the growing season.

■ **Harvest:** Pull leeks when the stems are between 1 and 2 inches in diameter. Cut off the top leaves and the roots. Rinse the stems if you notice sand or soil in the folds. Leeks are extremely tough and can withstand severe frost.

To harvest all winter, apply a thick mulch before the ground hardens, then dig up stalks as you need them.

LETTUCE

Lettuce is one of the most popular and diverse vegetables available to the home gardener. It grows quickly, is easy to care for, and comes in a variety of forms and flavors.

■ **Varieties:** The four types of lettuce are: butterhead, cos or romaine (upright), crisp-head, and loose-leaf. Every gardener has a favorite type, but loose-leaf varieties are slightly more popular because they're easiest to grow and they provide a continuous supply of leaves. Good loose-leaf varieties are 'Black-Seeded Simpson,' 'Salad Bowl,' and 'Oak Leaf.' The most popular crisp-head types are 'Great Lakes,' 'Iceberg,' and 'Ithaca.' The all-time favorite butterhead variety is 'Buttercrunch.' The favorite upright varieties are 'Little Gem' and 'Paris Island Cos.'

■ **Planting:** Because lettuce is a short-season crop that resists cold, sow seeds as soon as you can get into the garden. Pour a small amount of seed into one hand, then grip the seed between the forefinger and thumb of the other hand. Plant the seed as if sprinkling salt. Cover with no more than ¼ inch of fine soil, then sprinkle with water. Make small, successive plantings at two-week intervals to extend the season. Or start seeds indoors to get a jump on the outdoor growing season. Start seeds of crisp-head varieties eight weeks before the frost-free date, setting the seedlings into the garden three to four weeks before that date. Other types also can be started indoors or in cold frames to yield early crops. Most lettuce varieties grow well mingled with flowers (the light green is refreshing) or in the shade of slow-growing vegetables, such as cabbage, cauliflower, or broccoli. Lettuce also does well in containers, including strawberry jars and hanging baskets.

■ **Care:** Begin thinning your lettuce plants as soon as they are up and established. When seedlings are about 4 inches high, thin to 3 inches between plants; later, 6 inches; then 12 to 18 inches between mature plants. Use thinnings in early salads, or transplant them to another section of the garden. To encourage abundant leaf growth, work a high-nitrogen fertilizer into the soil at planting time, then sidedress with the same mixture during the growing season. Never let fertilizer granules come in contact with the leaves. Use mulch to avoid having to cultivate around the plants. Most lettuce varieties become bitter and unusable during hot midsummer weather, but don't let that stop you from sowing seeds again in early August for a good-tasting fall harvest.

■ **Harvest:** Harvest loose-leaf varieties through the season by picking the outer leaves as they mature. To do this, pinch the leaves off at the base of the plant. Or cut the entire plant to 1 inch with a sharp knife. It will grow back.

Harvest crisp-head, butterhead, and cos varieties only after the entire plant has matured. Remove the head by cutting off the entire plant at soil level with a knife.

MUSKMELON (CANTALOUPE)

Muskmelon has a wonderful aroma and taste. It requires a long season of warm, bright days to mature properly. Improved varieties and growing techniques have made it a realistic crop for northern gardeners.

■ **Varieties:** Choose varieties to suit your growing season and space. Bush varieties are best for compact and container gardens; vining varieties, though, are more prolific. Buy varieties that resist the diseases common in your area. Many catalogs now feature gourmet melons from other countries; these more exotic varieties are well worth trying.

■ **Planting:** Prepare the planting area by adding lots of compost or rotted manure. Plant muskmelons after all danger of frost passes. If you like, get a jump on the season by starting some seeds indoors three weeks before planting outdoors. Use individual peat pots to avoid disturbing the roots during transplanting. If you plant before the frost-free date, protect the plants with cloches.

In northern areas, use a black or clear plastic mulch to retain heat and moisture in the soil. Always water the soil well before laying a plastic mulch. Never use black plastic in hot or dry areas. For direct planting, sow seeds five to a hill or cluster, about 1 inch deep. Place hills 4 to 6 feet apart. Muskmelon thrives when planted in a corn patch. It also does well grown vertically on wires or trellises.

■ **Care:** After seedlings develop their third set of true leaves, thin them to stand only three plants per hill.

If not using plastic, surround the plants with an organic mulch such as grass clippings or shredded leaves. This mulch will make weeding almost unnecessary and keep you out of the patch (the vines are easily damaged). Water frequently, never allowing the soil to dry out. Drip-irrigation systems work well for muskmelons since they water the plant without getting the foliage wet, which often can cause disease. Fertilize every few weeks since muskmelons are heavy feeders.

When a vine has several fruits, snip off its growing tip to encourage branching. When fruits are several inches in diameter, place boards, shingles, or roofing paper under them to hasten ripening and to prevent rot. Watch for cucumber beetles. Kill them with carbaryl.

■ **Harvest:** Pick the melons when they have an irresistible odor and tannish yellow color, and when they slip easily from the vine. Even though a melon may become large, it isn't necessarily ripe. Any melons that do not pull away easily aren't ripe. As the season nears its end, pinch off small fruits to force the ripening of the larger fruits.

LETTUCE—crisp-head

LETTUCE—loose-leaf

MUSKMELON

VEGETABLES PORTFOLIO *(continued)*

MUSTARD

OKRA

OKRA—'Burgundy'

MUSTARD

Mustard greens have long been a favorite dish in the South, but their popularity is catching on elsewhere. The greens mature in about 40 days, making them a good spring and fall crop.

■ **Varieties:** Both curly- and broad-leaved varieties exist. A favorite curly type is 'Southern Giant Curled.' Broad-leaved varieties include 'Florida Broad Leaf' and the flavorful 'Tendergreen' (mustard spinach).

■ **Planting:** Plan on early spring, fall, or even winter yields because, in warm weather, mustard runs to seed. Sow seeds ½ inch deep in rows 1½ to 2 feet apart. Some northern gardeners like to sow seeds in the fall and overwinter young plants under insulating mulch. In spring, they pull back the mulch so the young seedlings can resume growth for an extra-early harvest.

■ **Care:** Weed and thin plants as soon as they emerge. Mature plants should be 6 to 8 inches apart in the row. Eat all thinnings for an early crop. Side-dress seedlings with a nitrogen-rich fertilizer to stimulate lush leaf growth. Mulch to keep soil moist; water whenever necessary. Constant moisture is the key to success with mustard, which will turn hot and spicy during drought. Should mustard ever go to seed, cut off the flowers, unless you want the plant to spread in the garden. The bright yellow flowers are quite lovely and form small pods filled with seeds you can grind into a powder as a base for homemade mustard.

■ **Harvest:** Pick outer leaves as the mustard greens mature. Start picking early since the young leaves are the most delicious. Older leaves can turn tough and bitter, but taste better if cooked. Young leaves are excellent in salads.

OKRA

Traditionally grown in the South, where it's sometimes called gumbo, okra requires temperatures well above 60 degrees and a well-drained, fertile soil. Its elongated seedpods are excellent additions to soups and stews, or they can be cooked and served on their own.

■ **Varieties:** Tall varieties, such as 'Clemson Spineless,' may grow to 4 feet. They make attractive garden hedges, with handsome foliage and showy, yellow, hibiscuslike flowers. Shorter varieties, such as 'Dwarf Green Long Pod,' grow 2 feet tall.

■ **Planting:** Mix compost, manure, or peat into soil. A slow-growing crop, okra does fine in any fertile, well-drained soil.

Sprinkle commercial fertilizer into the planting area a day or two before planting. In regions with short growing seasons, start seeds indoors eight weeks before the frost-free date. Use individual peat pots to avoid disturbing plants at time of transplanting. Plant in the garden after all danger of frost passes and the ground is thoroughly warm.

■ **Care:** If you sow seeds in the garden, thin plants to 6 inches apart. Mulch with grass clippings or shredded leaves. Keep after weeds, never allowing them to interfere with seedling growth. Water whenever soil dries out. Fertilize every two weeks. If your area is prone to windstorms, stake the plants. Some growers pinch off the growing tips when they pick the first pods to encourage lateral branching. Carbaryl will kill any insects, including corn earworms, that might attack the plants.

■ **Harvest:** Pick pods when they are immature (small and soft). The size varies with the variety. Some growers let the pods mature, then eat the seeds inside, but this is rare. If pods mature on the plants, the plants will die. Pick all pods if frost is possible. Some people are allergic to okra and must wear gloves when working with it. Okra has a natural gumminess when cooked.

ONION

Onions belong in every garden because they take up little space, are easy to grow, and produce a crop you can store for a long time—well into winter. They also come in many shapes, colors, and flavors suitable for lots of recipes.

■ **Varieties:** Not all onions do well in all areas, so choose varieties that match the day length in your area and suit your needs: scallions (often called bunching onions) for fresh use and for salads, sweet onions for delicious hamburgers or onion rings, and storage onions for use during winter.

■ **Planting:** Start onions from seeds, seedlings, or sets. Sets are dormant onion bulbs saved from the year before. You can grow your own sets from seeds or buy them from local garden centers. Small sets are better than large ones, which sometimes go to seed. Sets produce large onions the first year. Start with seedlings when growing the varieties that produce scallions early in growth, sweet onions for summer use, and sizable onions for storage late in the season. Seeds produce scallions, sweet onions, and sets for the following year.

The secret to successful onion growing is to get the plants into the ground as early in the season as possible. Onions form bulbs according to day length, and once the days get long, no bulbs will form. Start onions indoors up to eight weeks before the frost-free date. Set young transplants in the garden three to four weeks before the frost-free date; protect with cloches if necessary. When planting sets, make sure the pointed ends are up. Plant sets shallow so the tips just peek out of the soil.

■ **Care:** Keep onions weed free. Do all weeding by hand to avoid harming the shallow roots. Use a mulch to control weeds and keep the soil moist. Water whenever the soil starts to dry out, but stop watering toward the end of the season. If root maggots have been a problem in the past, apply diazinon when preparing the bed for the onions. If plants start to turn yellow early in the season, spray with a chemical to control thrips. Grow onions in a new place each year to avoid disease and insect problems.

■ **Harvest:** Pick scallions at any stage. Pull summer onions whenever needed. Let onions you plan to store mature completely. At the end of the season, when most of the stalks have weakened and fallen, push any remaining ones over with a rake or walk on them. Let the stalks dry out. When all stalks are dry, pull the onions. Spread them on the ground to dry for several days. To store, braid the onions and hang them, or cut off the stems about an inch from the onions and lay the onions out on wire supports. Store in a cool, dry place (air circulation prevents rotting). Or, keep the onions refrigerated. If any onions have thick necks, use them immediately. To inhibit onions' tear-producing substance, peel them under cold running water.

PARSNIP

Parsnips are an often-overlooked, but nutritious and good-tasting, vegetable. They have a sweet, nutty flavor that adds zest to any soup or stew. Try them cooked like carrots or mashed like potatoes, too.

■ **Varieties:** Three recommended varieties are 'All American,' 'Harris Model,' and 'Hollow Crown.'

■ **Planting:** Since parsnips can reach a depth of 15 inches, prepare a deep bed by loosening the soil with a spade or tiller. Remove all debris such as rocks, sticks, or large clumps of earth. Add lots of peat, compost, or rotted manure to the bed and mix in commercial fertilizer. Because parsnips take a long time to germinate, sow seeds as early in spring as possible. Interplant radishes to mark the rows. To prevent crusting, mix peat moss or dried grass clippings with the soil used to cover the seeds.

■ **Care:** Keep the soil moist at all times to prevent seedlings from drying out. Thin young plants to stand several inches apart, then mulch around them. Thin again later in the season to about 6 inches apart. Remove all weeds immediately to prevent competition for water and nutrients.

■ **Harvest:** Because the flavor of parsnips improves after several frosts, keep them in the ground until late fall. If you want to overwinter any plants, cover them with a thick layer of mulch. Dig all remaining parsnips in early spring. Dig parsnips with a spade or garden fork. Pulled parsnips sometimes break off underground. Harvested parsnips store well in cool temperatures in moist peat moss or sand.

ONION

ONION—'Barletta Pearl'

VEGETABLES PORTFOLIO *(continued)*

PEPPER—'Mexi Bell'

PEPPER—'Super Chili'

PEPPER—'Yolo Wonder'

PEANUT

Peanuts are a main crop in many southern areas, where they do well in loose soil with a light clay content. They are still a novelty item in the North, although they can thrive there, too.

■ **Varieties:** Peanuts produce either erect or creeping (vining or runner) plants. The three main types are: Spanish (erect), Valencia (erect), and Virginia (erect or creeping). Creeping varieties will spread over a large area; production of erect varieties is more concentrated.

Choose a variety with a maturity date appropriate to your climate. The Spanish varieties mature the fastest; the creeping Virginia varieties take much longer. Read catalogs carefully.

■ **Planting:** Choose a warm, sunny spot with excellent drainage for a peanut bed. Young seeds will rot in cool or overly damp soil. Spade or till the soil. (Use a raised bed if you have compact or rocky soil.) Add compost or rotted manure to the bed. Or sprinkle in commercial fertilizer high in potassium and phosphorus.

In the North, start peanuts indoors in peat pots four weeks before the frost-free date. For seeding directly in the garden, plant peanuts 4 inches deep in hot areas, no more than 2 inches deep in the North.

■ **Care:** Thin young plants to stand 8 to 12 inches apart (3 feet for runner types). Hoe all weeds while the plants are young. Work the soil thoroughly to form a loose mound around each plant, then apply a thick mulch.

Water when the soil dries out. Dust the plants with gypsum (provides needed calcium) from early to late bloom. The plants form pegs or little shoots that grow down from the plants into the ground. Peanuts develop on the peg ends about 60 days after flowering.

■ **Harvest:** When plants start to yellow, dig a few peanuts. Not all peanuts mature at the same time, so be patient and dig up the peanut patch only when you think most peanuts have ripened. Delay harvest as long as possible, but do not allow the soil to freeze. Cut off the top portions of the vines before harvesting. Dig peanuts with a spading fork. Hang the plants to dry for several weeks—or longer—in a warm, well-ventilated spot. Store unshelled peanuts in a mesh bag, or shell and store in an airtight jar.

PEAS

Fresh peas are what gardening is all about—they're so much better than anything you can buy. Picked at just the right moment, peas match sweet corn as a garden delicacy.

■ **Varieties:** The main categories of peas are shell or English peas (peas eaten without the pods), snow or edible-pod peas (immature peas eaten with the pod), snap peas (more-mature peas eaten with the pod), petits pois (tiny shell peas), and dry peas (shell peas dried on the vine). Choose early-, mid-, and late-season varieties for an extended season. Also, choose varieties by height to match your growing method.

■ **Planting:** Mix compost, peat, manure, and commercial fertilizer into your garden bed. For support, lay chicken wire down the center of each double row. Or use brush. Fences along the outside of the garden also make good vertical supports. Bush varieties need no support.

Sow peas in spring as soon as you can work the soil. Peas will burn out quickly if hot weather strikes while the plants are still small. Plant the seeds every 3 inches on both sides of the wire or brush. Space double rows 2 feet apart.

■ **Care:** Keep plants moist at all times. Mulch helps to keep soil moist and cool. Water only the bases of plants if a white powdery material (downy or powdery mildew) begins to appear on foliage. Pull all weeds as they sprout.

■ **Harvest:** Pick one or two pods daily to check pea size. The peas should be small and tender. If you let them grow big, the peas will become tasteless and mealy. When picking pods, hold onto the vine with one hand and pinch off the pod with the other. Avoid damaging the vines, which are brittle and easily broken.

PEPPER

Peppers are warm-weather vegetables that require about 2½ months to fully develop. Somewhat finicky, peppers need even temperatures and uniform moisture to develop fully.

■ **Varieties:** Pepper varieties, of which there are hundreds, are divided into two main classes: sweet and hot. Eat sweet peppers raw in salads, cooked, or dried. Dry hot peppers and serve in a variety of spicy recipes. Good varieties of sweet peppers include: 'Bell Boy,' 'California Wonder,' 'New Ace,' 'Tokyo Bell,' and 'Yolo Wonder.' Favorite varieties of hot peppers are 'Hot Portugal,' 'Hungarian Wax,' 'Mexi Bell,' and 'Long Red Cayenne.' 'Super Chili' is as good looking as it is edible.

■ **Planting:** Start pepper plants from seeds indoors six to eight weeks before the last expected frost. Or purchase transplants from a local garden center. Plant only after the soil is thoroughly warm. Set in a sunny spot. Prepare a loose bed with lots of organic matter to retain moisture. Put cutworm collars on the plants if these insects have been a problem before. Space plants roughly 2 feet apart. To protect young plants from cold and sun until they are growing well, use cloches or shades (such as a shingle placed next to each plant).

■ **Care:** Provide uniform moisture to help the plants grow and produce abundantly. Water whenever the soil starts to dry out. Improper watering can result in sunken brown spots on the fruit. Mulch around each plant with an organic material such as grass clippings or shredded leaves. Pull all weeds as soon as they appear. Avoid cultivating around the bases of the plants because their root systems are shallow. Fertilize regularly to stimulate production.

■ **Harvest:** Pick sweet peppers when either green (immature) or red (mature). Let hot peppers dry as much as possible on the plants themselves. Then pick the hot peppers and continue the drying process in a hot, airy spot. Grind or shred hot peppers for use. Always wear rubber gloves when handling hot peppers.

POTATO

Potatoes are inexpensive to buy at the grocery store and do take up a lot of space in the garden, but because they're easy to grow and because new potatoes are so sweet and delicious, many home gardeners make sacrifices to have them.

■ **Varieties:** For summer use, try 'Irish Cobbler,' 'Norland,' or 'Russet.' Good storing varieties are 'Katahdin' and 'Kennebec.'

■ **Planting:** To start your crop, obtain certified seed potatoes, which are guaranteed to be disease free, from your garden center. You can use potatoes from local grocery stores, but they often take longer to sprout because they have been sprayed with a growth inhibitor. They also may carry disease. Experts disagree about whether to plant the potatoes whole or sliced ("eyes"). Some think whole potatoes produce larger individual potatoes and healthier crops. Experiment with both whole potatoes and slices. Slices or portions of potato must have at least one eye, or growing point, per piece. Cut them two days before planting to let the wounds dry out. Dust the wet portions with fungicide to prevent rot. Place whole potatoes or the pieces (cut side down) in a trench 4 inches deep. Potatoes are a cool-season crop, so get them into the garden as soon as you can. To prevent rot, do not plant in wet soil.

■ **Care:** Water potatoes frequently. Use mulch to keep soil moist. Cover any exposed portions of potatoes to keep them from turning green. Pull all weeds. Fertilize several times at two-week intervals. Use carbaryl sprays—only if necessary—to kill chewing insects that damage leaves and stems. To avoid killing bees, apply carbaryl only when the plants are not in flower.

■ **Harvest:** When the plants begin to flower, look for new potatoes just under the soil surface. Carefully pull some soil away, then break the tiny potatoes off. Try not to damage the main root system. Cover the area with soil and let the plants continue to produce other potatoes. At the end of the season, the foliage turns brown and dies. Remove and compost all the dead foliage. With a spade, dig into the soil to the side of the plants. Lift and break up the soil to expose all tubers. Let the tubers dry in the sun. Use any with broken skin right away since they will not store well.

POTATO—'Finnish'

POTATO—'Russet'

311

VEGETABLES PORTFOLIO *(continued)*

PUMPKIN

RADISH—'Black Spanish'

PUMPKIN

Because they grow into large, spreading vines that quickly cover a wide area, most varieties of pumpkins require more space than many gardeners can afford. Pumpkins can, however, tolerate more shade than other squash, so you might find an unused garden corner for them. Or plant them between corn rows or along a fence.

■ **Varieties:** Pumpkins come in all sizes. Giant-size varieties include 'Big Max,' 'Big Tom,' and 'Howden's Field.' Intermediate-size varieties, often used for cooking, include 'Jackpot' and 'Spirit Hybrid.' Smaller varieties, such as 'Small Sugar' and 'Spookie,' are just right for gardens short on space. Several naked-seed varieties, such as 'Lady Godiva' and 'Triple Treat,' are grown just for their delicious seeds. A recent introduction, 'Cinderella,' is a bush variety requiring less space than the rambling varieties. 'Autumn Gold,' unlike other pumpkins, has colored fruit right from the start.

■ **Planting:** Provide pumpkins with a bed of rich soil and lots of moisture. Mix in commercial fertilizer and rotted manure, compost, or peat. Plant seeds in hills after all danger of frost passes. Pumpkins thrive in open fields or mixed with corn. Sow five seeds per hill.

■ **Care:** When seedlings are several inches tall, thin them to the three healthiest seedlings per hill. Mulch around the plants to retain moisture in the soil. Weed around the plants by hand to prevent competition. To provide steady moisture and stimulate rapid growth, some gardeners place a gallon jug, punched with small holes in the bottom and filled with water, on each hill.

■ **Harvest:** After the fruit turns bright orange, use a sharp knife to cut it from the vine. Leave at least an inch or two of stem on each pumpkin. Never carry the pumpkins by these stems. Leave pumpkins in the sun for several days to cure. Bring them inside and store for two weeks in high temperatures to finish the curing process.

Store in cooler temperatures for long-term holding. Never allow pumpkins to freeze. This causes rot, making pumpkins soft and mushy.

RADISH

The foolproof summer radish reaches maturity within 20 to 30 days after planting, changing so fast you can almost watch it grow. It's nearly indestructible and can grow anywhere, from raised beds to flowerpots. Winter radishes take longer to mature, store well, and can be eaten raw or cooked.

■ **Varieties:** Favorite summer varieties include 'Cherry Belle,' 'Sparkler,' and 'White Icicle.' Good winter varieties are 'Black Spanish,' 'China Rose,' and 'White Chinese.' 'Easter Egg' produces different colors in every crop.

■ **Planting:** Sow seeds of summer varieties in early spring as soon as you can work the ground. Radishes like loose soil amended with organic matter and sprinkled with commercial fertilizer high in potassium and phosphorus. Radishes are such a quick growing crop that small, successive plantings make the most sense. Interplant radish seeds with slower maturing crops, such as carrots. The radishes will mark the location of the carrots, and, as you harvest the radishes, you will be thinning the young carrots automatically. Plant winter radishes so they will mature in the fall and be ready for storage before frost. In the North, plant in early to late July.

■ **Care:** For juicy, tender roots, force rapid growth in cool weather. Water the plants generously. Thin the larger radishes to give younger ones space. Mulch around plants to hinder weeds and keep the soil constantly moist.

If root maggots have been a problem, treat your soil with diazinon early in spring before planting. Flea beetles often riddle young leaves with holes, but do little damage to the edible roots. If you want, sprinkle the leaves with diatomaceous earth to discourage these pests.

■ **Harvest:** Because small radishes are tender and juicy and large radishes get woody and hot, pull radishes when they are no larger than a marble. Harvest winter radishes when they mature at the end of the season. Use a spading fork for monster varieties. Store radishes in moist peat, sawdust, or sand.

RHUBARB

An easy-to-grow perennial, rhubarb demands little, if any, attention from the home gardener. Prized for their flavorful stalks, these attractive plants appear unfailingly in the early spring each year. Rhubarb grows best where the ground freezes in winter.

■ **Varieties:** Three commonly grown varieties are 'MacDonald,' 'Valentine,' and 'Victoria.'

■ **Planting:** Because rhubarb is a perennial, plant it in an unused corner of the garden where the plants will be undisturbed by annual cultivation. Rhubarb prefers full sun but will tolerate some shade. Prepare the bed by digging deep holes and filling them with compost, rotted manure, or peat. Mix in some soil and commercial fertilizer. Buy roots from a reliable nursery or divide an established clump in two with a sharp spade. Place the roots or divisions, nodes up, in the holes. The buds or nodes should be 1 to 2 inches below the soil surface. Space plants 4 feet apart. You also can start rhubarb from seed. The light, flat seeds do well in humus-rich soil kept continually moist. Seeds are less reliable starters than roots since they may produce plants somewhat different from their parents.

■ **Care:** Keep the soil around the plants moist at all times. Use a thick layer of mulch to help you do this. The mulch also will hinder weeds. If any weeds do appear, pull them immediately so the young plants can establish themselves without competition. Side-dress with fertilizer. Remove any flower stalks that appear. Do not let the plants go to seed. Divide the plants with a spade if their stems start to get smaller, usually after five or six years. Do this in the spring, making sure each division has several eyes or buds. Replant the divisions as you did the original mother plant.

■ **Harvest:** Because early harvest damages young plants, do not harvest during the first year. During the second year, harvest lightly for several weeks. In subsequent years, harvest heavily for six or so weeks at the start of each season. To pick, grasp stalks at the base of each plant and pull up with a twisting motion. The stalks will pop out. Remove larger stalks first, never taking more than half of the leaves from a single plant at one time. Cut leaves from pulled stalks and compost them. Eat only the stems of the plants since the leafy areas contain poisonous oxalic acid.

RUTABAGA

Rutabagas grow much the same way turnips do, but are really a turnip-cabbage cross, so they do better in northern areas than their cousin. A solid, tasty root crop, rutabagas store even better than turnips, but take longer to mature.

■ **Varieties:** Two popular varieties are 'American Purple Top' and 'Macomber.'

■ **Planting:** Plant in loose soil. If your soil is compact or rocky, make a raised bed for this crop. Add compost, peat, or well-rotted manure to the bed. Sprinkle this mixture with fertilizer for rapid root growth. Sow seeds in both spring and summer for two crops. The later seeding will provide roots for winter storage and is preferred by northern gardeners.

■ **Care:** When the seedlings are about 4 inches high, thin them to stand about 6 inches apart. Weed carefully to stop all competition for water and nutrients. Apply a thick mulch to keep soil moist, cool, and weed free. Water whenever necessary. If root maggots have been a problem, mix diazinon into the soil before planting. Flea beetles sometimes attack young plants, fraying the leaves, but rarely do serious damage. The roots still taste fine.

■ **Harvest:** Dig roots as needed. Smaller roots often are the best. During winter, leave roots in the garden covered with a heavy mulch. Or, for convenience, pull roots and store indoors in moist peat, sawdust, or sand. Rutabagas often taste best after heavy frost or freeze.

RADISH—'Easter Egg'

RHUBARB

313

VEGETABLES PORTFOLIO *(continued)*

SPINACH

SQUASH—scallop

SQUASH—winter

SALSIFY

Salsify, or oyster plant, is the most unusual root crop vegetable you can grow because, when cooked, the long white roots taste somewhat like fresh oysters. Salsify is a slow grower that requires about four months to mature fully, but it takes up little room in the garden. Plant it among other crops, such as lettuce or cabbage, if space is at a premium.

■ **Varieties:** The most common salsify variety is 'Sandwich Island Mammoth.'

■ **Planting:** Provide a well-prepared bed free of clumps, sticks, and stones. Work in lots of organic matter such as peat, compost, or well-rotted manure to make it easy for the long roots to penetrate the soil. Sprinkle this mixture with some commercial fertilizer to stimulate vigorous root growth. Plant seeds as soon as you can work the soil in spring.

■ **Care:** Because salsify cannot compete with invading weeds, keep the area weed free. When the seedlings reach 3 inches tall, thin them to stand 6 inches apart. Apply a thick layer of mulch to the bed to keep soil cool, moist, and weed free. Water as needed.

■ **Harvest:** Pick roots when crowns are 1 inch in diameter. Mulch heavily if you want to store roots in the ground for a spring harvest. Because the carbohydrates in the roots turn to sugar after frosts, many gardeners prefer the taste of roots harvested after winter.

SPINACH

Spinach is a dual-purpose vegetable you can cook or serve raw. With a high vitamin A content, it also is one of the most nutritious vegetables you can grow.

■ **Varieties:** Some commonly planted varieties include 'Melody Hybrid,' 'Viking,' and 'Winter Bloomsdale.'

■ **Planting:** Prepare a loose bed for spinach. To retain water, which is essential for good leaf growth, work in lots of peat, manure, or compost. Add commercial fertilizer to supply the young plants with nitrogen. Spinach grows best during the cooler temperatures of spring and fall. During hot weather, it bolts.

Plant spinach as soon as you can work the soil in spring. Sow seeds at 10-day intervals until warm weather arrives.

■ **Care:** Keep the plants well supplied with water. Use a mulch to keep the soil moist and cool. Handpick all weeds before they get large and compete with the seedlings for nutrients and water. When the seedlings are several inches tall, thin them to stand about 4 inches apart. Eat the thinnings for an early crop.

■ **Harvest:** Harvest outer leaves as needed, leaving the central bud to produce more. Or harvest the whole plant, either by pulling it or cutting it back to 1 inch. Plants that have been cut often will sprout again. Because heat makes the plants bitter and unusable, pull the entire crop when hot weather arrives.

SQUASH

Squash is a warm-weather crop that takes more room in the home garden than most vegetables, but, given the right conditions, it outproduces other choices. Many new bush forms of squash are now available that you can use in place of the old-fashioned, space-taking vining varieties.

■ **Varieties:** Of the summer soft-skinned varieties, the most commonly planted are: 'Early Prolific Straightneck' (yellow), 'Zucchini Elite,' 'Fordhook Zucchini,' 'Cocozelle Bush' (green), 'White Bush Patty Pan,' and 'Scallopini Hybrid.' Fall and winter hard-skinned varieties include: 'Royal Acorn,' 'Bush Buttercup,' 'Bush Acorn,' 'Table King,' and 'Bush Gold Nugget.' 'Spaghetti' is a novelty variety that produces tasty pulp that looks like spaghetti when cooked and removed from the squash shell. When choosing a variety, consider space needed, days to maturity, yield, and disease resistance.

■ **Planting:** If space is limited, choose bush varieties only, or grow squash vertically on a trellis or wire. Prepare the bed with compost, peat, or well-rotted manure, then add commercial fertilizer. Plant squash in hills or clusters when the soil warms, spacing six seeds about 2 inches apart. A common misconception is that the soil must be mounded, but this is a matter of choice. The advantage of raised hills is that, like raised beds, they drain well and dry out quickly. Space the hills about 6 feet apart. In cool, wet areas, mulch with clear or black plastic.

■ **Care:** When the seedlings emerge, thin them to three healthy plants per hill. Apply a thick organic mulch around the plants if you are not using black or clear plastic. Water plants regularly. Use drip irrigation if possible; otherwise, flood the bases of plants with water to avoid mildew. Side-dress with fertilizer every 10 days for healthy growth. If vines get out of hand, snip the growing tips to encourage lateral branching.

Watch for borers, cucumber beetles, and squash bugs. Kill them with carbaryl. (Avoid using carbaryl during blooming since it kills bees.) Destroying cucumber beetles will help prevent bacterial wilt, one of the worst diseases in the squash patch.

■ **Harvest:** Summer squash develops quickly, so check fruits daily as they begin to form. Though certainly edible when large, summer squash tastes better and is tenderer when harvested while still small. Cut off zucchini and straightnecks when they are only a few inches long, and pattypans when no larger than a quarter. Harvest all fruits whether you can eat them or not. Give away or compost what you can't use. If you allow fruits to ripen on the plants, they give off a hormone that causes the plants to shrivel and die. Constant picking also stimulates increased production. Flowers of summer squash are edible. Choose the male flowers (those without small squashes developing at their bases; plants produce male flowers first).

Allow winter squash, on the other hand, to mature completely before picking it. Wait until the stems begin to dry and wither. Cut the fruits from the vines, leaving an inch or two attached to each squash. Do not carry squash by these stems. Place the squash (except acorn squash) in a sunny, dry location for several days, then move it inside to a warm, dry area for several weeks. This curing process allows the shells of the fruits to harden. Store them in a dark room at temperatures between 55 and 60 degrees. Store acorn squash, which can be eaten young or mature, according to taste, in cool temperatures from the start.

SUNFLOWER

Grown for their bright yellow flowers and tasty, nutritious seeds, sunflowers are everyone's favorite. Fun to grow, they're great for the kids' garden. Their seeds also make feed for poultry and wild birds, including cardinals and finches.

■ **Varieties:** Several large-flowered varieties are now available, including 'Black Striped Russian,' 'Gray Striped Russian,' and 'Mammoth.'

■ **Planting:** Plant sunflowers, a warm-weather crop, after all danger of frost passes. Pick a site with full sun and a rich, well-drained soil. Prepare the bed by loosening it with a spade and adding peat, compost, or manure. Sow seeds about 1 inch deep and about 1 foot apart. Plant sunflowers on the north side of the garden since they will grow tall and shade other plants. Plant shade-tolerant vegetables such as lettuce, spinach, and Swiss chard nearby.

■ **Care:** Once the plants are up and growing, mulch to keep weed competition to a minimum. Keep the plants well watered and fertilized. Thin the plants if their growth is retarded.

■ **Harvest:** Allow the seeds to mature on the plant before harvesting. Keep birds from getting to the seed-bearing flowers by covering them with nylon netting or cheesecloth. When seeds have turned color and pop easily off the heads, cut the heads off with a sharp knife. On particularly large stalks, you may have to use a hatchet. Hang the heads in a warm, dry area with good ventilation to let the seeds cure. When the seeds are fully dry, rub your thumb across them to pop them off the heads. Store dried seeds in airtight glass jars, keeping the humidity low to prevent mold. Storing in the refrigerator works well.

SQUASH—zucchini

SUNFLOWER

VEGETABLES PORTFOLIO *(continued)*

TOMATO—'Better Boy'

TOMATO—'Early Girl'

SWEET POTATO

Sweet potatoes are a warm-weather crop grown primarily in the South. Northern gardeners have success starting with slips distributed by mail-order houses.

■ **Varieties:** Good varieties are 'Centennial,' 'Goldrush,' 'Jersey Orange,' and 'Nemagold.'

■ **Planting:** Pay close attention to soil preparation, which is vital for growing sweet potatoes. Loosen compact soil by digging thoroughly and adding compost, peat moss, or well-rotted manure. A moderately fertile, sandy loam is ideal. Make a 1-foot ridge of soil. Do this in the fall for spring planting. Start sweet potato slips indoors by sprouting whole potatoes. Break off slips and pot up in peat pots. Harden plants off by moving them outdoors over a period of 10 days. Transplant them after all danger of frost passes. Or buy started, hardened slips at garden centers or through the mail at the correct planting time.

Plant seedlings about 1 foot from each other in rows 3½ to 4 feet apart. Make a hole and slide the slip into it with only the top leaves exposed. Water immediately.

■ **Care:** Cultivate the plants regularly during the early stages of growth to hinder weeds. Draw up loose soil around each plant. Mulch to reduce the need for late-season cultivation, which can damage the vines. Water as needed.

■ **Harvest:** Before the first heavy fall frost, dig the tubers, taking care not to injure them. Eat damaged tubers right away since they'll rot in storage. Sun-dry undamaged tubers for several hours. Cure them by placing them in a warm room (75 to 85 degrees) for about 10 days.

TOMATO

Almost a universal vegetable, the tomato provides rewarding yields in practically any soil and with little care. The tomato, a warm-season crop, grows in nearly any sunny spot.

■ **Varieties:** Tomatoes come in several hundred varieties, some of which are best suited to your area, depending on length of season and overall climate. Study catalogs carefully.

Most tomatoes grow vigorous vines (indeterminate). Others grow more compact bushes (determinate). The bush varieties come in earlier and take up less space. They are good for small gardens and container gardening.

Tomatoes come in a fascinating array of colors and shapes. They range in color from pink to white to yellow. Their size differences can be just as remarkable, ranging from small ones the size of marbles to giants that weigh in at several pounds. Breeders offer many varieties resistant to common diseases. Each variety is labeled to indicate this resistance. The letters V, F, N, S, and C behind a variety name indicate that a plant will resist verticillium wilt, fusarium wilt, nematodes, stemphylium, and cladosporium.

■ **Planting:** Because tomatoes require a long growing season, start seeds eight weeks before transplanting. Or buy seedlings from a garden center. Plant seedlings after all danger of frost passes. (Or gamble by setting plants outside early, protecting them from the cold at night.) Set plants 2 feet apart in rows 3 feet apart. Plant caged or staked seedlings closer. Strip the lower leaves from each seedling and bury the entire stem. If cutworms are a problem, place a collar around the stem of each plant.

■ **Care:** Keep the soil moist. In the far North, use clear or black plastic as a heat-retaining mulch, watering the ground before laying it. In other areas, mulch around the plants with a thick layer of organic mulch. Pull weeds by hand; a hoe could damage plant roots. Fertilize lightly to encourage healthy growth. Control the vining habit of indeterminate varieties by pinching off the suckers that sprout from the joints where the leaf stems join the main stems.

■ **Harvest:** For juiciest fruit and sweetest taste, ripen tomatoes on the vine. Ripe tomatoes will pop off the vine with just a slight tug. Refrigerate ripe tomatoes. For canning, pick tomatoes before they completely ripen because of their higher acidity at this stage. When frost threatens, pick green tomatoes, wrap in newspapers, and store in a cool, dark place until fully ripe. Compost tomato vines at the season's end to prevent diseases and pests from overwintering.

TURNIP

Turnips were at one time the most popular garden vegetable, but since have fallen out of favor. Still, they are delicious, easy to grow in the South, and nutritious, offering both greens and roots as hearty meals. Turnips also store well.

■ **Varieties:** Common varieties include 'Just Right,' 'Purple Top White Globe,' 'Seven Top' (grown for its leaves), 'Shogoin,' 'Tokyo Cross,' and 'Tokyo Market.'

■ **Planting:** Prepare a loose bed. Clean out all roots, debris, and rocks, and work peat, manure, or compost into the soil to give it a light, airy feel. Add some commercial fertilizer to the soil just before planting. Plant as early in the spring and as late in the fall as possible, giving turnips just enough time to mature before warm weather arrives in the summer and cold weather arrives in the winter. Turnips like to mature in cool weather.

■ **Care:** Thin plants to 4 inches apart. Eat the thinnings as greens. Use a thick mulch to keep soil moist and cool. Because roots taste best if they mature rapidly, water frequently. Never allow weeds to compete with the plants for nutrients and water. Do not feed again unless you're growing the plants only for their leaves.

■ **Harvest:** Harvest greens at 4 inches. Pick turnips when they are no more than 2 to 3 inches in diameter. Older turnips get woody.

WATERMELON

Homegrown watermelons have a sweet taste and delightful texture. To produce a good crop, most varieties need a long, warm summer and plenty of soil nutrients. With proper planning, every gardener can savor a harvest of melons.

■ **Varieties:** Most watermelons grow well in the South, but northern gardeners should take special care when selecting a variety to ensure a good crop. If you live in the North, always use early varieties.

■ **Planting:** Provide loose, rich soil and a warm location. Before planting, work as much well-rotted manure and compost into the soil as you can. In the North, start seeds indoors four weeks before normal planting time, usually two to three weeks after the frost-free date. Use individual peat pots to avoid disturbing roots during transplanting. If you like, gamble by setting plants out early, protecting them with cloches during cold snaps. Or wait until the ground is warm and sow the seeds outdoors. Plant hills of watermelons 6 feet apart, six seeds per hill. Later, when the plants are up and growing, thin them to the three healthiest plants per hill.

■ **Care:** Use black or clear plastic in northern areas as a heat-giving mulch, watering the ground before laying the plastic. Do not use plastic in the South. Water the young vines frequently. Keep the bed free of weeds, taking care not to damage the vines. If not using plastic, lay an organic mulch. Because watermelons are heavy feeders, side-dress with fertilizer at regular intervals. Some gardeners set a can or jug of water with diluted fertilizer into or on top of each hill to drip nutrients to young plants. Watch for striped cucumber beetles, which carry disease. Kill them with carbaryl.

■ **Harvest:** Picking watermelons at just the right moment can be tricky since they won't ripen if picked too early. Note the day the female flowers blossom. (The female will have a little fruit on it.) On this day, bees pollinate the plant. Small varieties, such as 'Petite Sweet,' mature 28 days later. Larger ones, like 'Charleston Gray,' take 35 to 40 days. By knowing the day of flowering and the length of time your variety takes to mature, you can pick the fruit at just the right stage of ripeness. Catalogs, however, don't always supply this information so try some of these tricks: Check the round spot on the bottom of the fruit; it turns from white or cream-colored to yellow as the fruit ripens. Practice thumping the melon with your knuckles; the sound changes with advancing ripeness. Some growers squeeze the melon; if it cracks slightly, the melon is ripe. As the season draws to a close, encourage the ripening of the few remaining large fruits by picking all the immature fruits.

TURNIP

WATERMELON

VEGETABLE DISEASES

Disease	Description and Trouble Signs	Control
Anthracnose	Appears as brownish sunken spots. Infected fruit often oozes pinkish material. Infects many vegetables including beans, peppers, tomatoes, and especially vine crops.	Prevent by buying chemically treated seed, or by treating seed yourself with a fungicide. Spray plants with a fungicide to prevent further spread.
Aster yellows	Leafhoppers infect plants with this disease, which results in stunted, yellow plants. Common in celery, lettuce, and spinach.	Prevent by using chemical sprays to kill leafhoppers.
Blights	Several blights cause watery spots to appear on foliage. Beans, peas, potatoes, and tomatoes are susceptible.	Avoid working in the garden when foliage is wet. Prevent with applications of fungicide.
Clubroot	Shows up as distorted, thickened roots in cole crops (such as cabbage and broccoli), causing plants to wilt and die. Most often a problem with cabbage.	Prevent by adding lime to the soil. Use gypsum if you do not want to change the soil pH.
Damping-off	Affects seedlings as they germinate. The bottom of the stem turns mushy, causing the plant to topple. Damping-off is extremely common and one of the main concerns of serious growers starting plants from seed.	Prevent by using a sterile growing medium such as sphagnum moss, vermiculite, or perlite. Or buy a sterile mixture. Treat seeds with a fungicide.
Mildews	Two of the most common mildews are powdery and downy. Both cause a white material to form on foliage. Mildews are a common problem in damp, cool, or overly hot and dry weather, infecting many plants.	Prevent by watering around plant stems; avoid sprinkling foliage. Destroy infected plants. Thin remaining plants for better air circulation. Apply fungicide in severe cases.
Mosaics	A number of mosaic viruses can create severe problems in the home garden. They cause mottled leaves, misshapen plants, wilting, and death.	Prevent by planting resistant varieties. Use chemicals to kill insects carrying the virus. Destroy infected plants immediately to stop spread of the disease. Keep tobacco out of the garden. If you smoke, wash hands thoroughly before gardening to prevent tobacco mosaic virus.
Rot	Rot infects plants at many stages of growth from seed to storage.	Prevent rot by planting seeds at the right time. Use treated seed. In cool, moist areas, build raised beds. Avoid setting plants in low areas with poor drainage. Avoid storing damaged vegetables. Cure them properly before storage.
Smut	Black to whitish gray growths bulge out from ears of corn during the growing season. Usually infects only a small number of plants.	Pick the growths off before they mature. Burn or throw them into the garbage.
Wilts	Bacterial, fusarium, and verticillium wilts are three of the worst diseases in the garden. Plants turn yellow, wilt, and die. The diseases infect many different crops.	Prevent by buying resistant varieties. Rotate crops each year. Kill insects such as cucumber beetles with sprays.

VEGETABLE INSECTS

Insect	Description and Trouble Signs	Control
Aphids	Aphids, or plant lice, are small sucking insects that damage numerous vegetables. They come in a wide variety of colors, and cluster along stems and on leaves. Plants may become stunted or deformed. Aphids also carry disease.	Cut off and destroy heavily infected plant parts. Spray with a hose or rinse off with soapy water. Use chemical controls in severe cases. Prevent by killing ants that support aphid colonies.
Beetles	Beetles feed on foliage and fruit. Beetle types include the asparagus, bean, striped or spotted cucumber, flea, and Colorado potato. In many cases the larvae are equally destructive. Some beetles carry disease.	Handpick larger beetles. Dust plants with diatomaceous earth to kill flea beetles. Use chemical controls if necessary. Prevent by cleaning debris out of the garden in the fall.
Borers	Borers work their way into the stems and fruits of several vegetables. Squash vine borers get into the lower stems of cucumber, muskmelon, squash, and watermelon, causing the vines to wilt or die.	Cut borers out of the stem with a knife. Mound soil over the stem. Use chemical controls around the base of the plant before it flowers.
Caterpillars	These butterfly and moth larvae come in many forms, including cabbage looper, cabbageworm, corn earworm, and tomato hornworm. They damage leaves and fruit.	Handpick. Look carefully because they blend in with the background. Use *Bacillus thuringiensis* (a biological control sold as B.t., Dipel, or Thuricide) or chemical sprays.
Cutworms	Cutworms curl around the bases of many vegetables, killing them by eating rings around their stems.	Protect seedlings with collars made of newspaper, cardboard, or aluminum foil (see page 291); or enclose with old cans or the bottoms of plastic milk containers.
Grasshoppers	A few grasshoppers do little damage, but when concentrated—especially during a drought—they destroy entire patches of vegetables. They particularly like cole crops, such as cabbage and broccoli.	Prevent by tilling gardens thoroughly in the fall to expose clusters of ricelike grasshopper eggs that birds will eat. Use chemicals during the season for severe infestations.
Leafhoppers	Leafhoppers are small insects, typically wedge shaped and green. They suck juices from many vegetables, causing plants to lose vigor and turn yellow. They also carry disease.	Use a chemical spray.
Maggots	Maggots are fly larvae that generally attack roots or plant parts below ground level. These pests include seed-corn, cabbage-root, and onion maggots, as well as leaf miners, which tunnel through leaves rather than roots.	Prevent by placing root maggot mats (5×5-inch carpet underlayments) around bases of plants. Or treat the soil with chemicals before planting.
Red spider mites	Minuscule red spider mites cause leaves to turn yellow, then drop off. Look for webbing. Mites like dry conditions.	Wash plants with a gentle spray. Kill with a miticide.
Slugs and snails	Slugs are snails without shells. These insects work at night, leaving behind slimy trails that sparkle in the morning sun. They eat jagged holes in leaves and prefer moist conditions.	Handpick. Set out shallow dishes of beer for these pests to crawl in and drown. Use commercial poison bait (protect pets).
Weevils	More than a dozen varieties of weevil threaten plants. Both the larvae and adults cause damage by eating U-shaped holes in leaves and burrowing into fruit and roots.	Use chemicals if weevils become a major problem in your garden.

FRUITS AND NUTS

H omegrown
fruits and nuts offer flavor, freshness,
and convenience no market can match.
From blueberry bushes to walnut trees,
your yard can look lovely—and help
feed the family—when you grow
beautiful, edible foods among your
purely ornamental plants.

FRUIT TREE BASICS

Growing your own fruits allows you to select from among the best-tasting varieties, many of which are unavailable at groceries because they don't ship well. Your own fruit may never make it to your kitchen, too, but for a different reason: It's so delicious eaten fresh from the bush.

DECIDING FACTORS

Whatever the garden spot, a fruit is available to fill it. Taller apple or pear trees provide shade and framing. Semidwarf trees are excellent as accents. Dwarfs grow in containers on balconies. Bush fruits blend in with other shrubbery. Grape or kiwi covers an arbor for instant shade, and strawberry is good as a ground cover, in hanging baskets, or to form living walls.

Hardiness is the first item to consider when choosing fruit varieties. Where there is much heat or cold, plant only specially adapted varieties. Check with your garden center or catalog, or buy the kinds you see thriving around you.

Select the best microclimate your yard has to offer. You want early bloomers like apple and peach to stay cold until spring is certain. Avoid planting early bloomers in warm areas that seldom frost, or near south-facing walls; both entice blossoms to open too early.

Space may limit you to a semidwarf tree that grows 12 to 15 feet tall, a dwarf of 8 to 10 feet, or a miniature of only 6 feet. But don't despair. Smaller trees bear large fruit sooner and are easier to prune, spray, and pick. They can give you more varieties in the same space. A single dwarf tree can yield up to six bushels of fruit.

Pollination takes two trees for apple, pear, most plums, sweet or bush cherry, and some peaches. But even self-fruiting varieties will bear better if another variety is within 100 feet, allowing bees to travel easily between. If the pollinator dies or blooms at the wrong time, set a bucket of blooming branches of a different variety beneath the tree. Or shake the blossoms of a different variety over your miniature tree.

Taste is most important in selecting varieties, though you can always use most fruits in some way that's delicious. It is not always possible to taste your choice before you plant, but try to make note of desirable varieties when you sample them. Learn to graft or bud these on the trees you already have.

Sun is vital to fruit production. Some trees will live, grow, even bear in semishade. But all do best in full sun.

Soil for most fruits and nuts should be slightly acid, with pH between 5.5 and 6.5. Only blueberries like soil as acid as 4.0. Have your soil tested, and add lime to raise the soil's pH or sulfur to lower it.

Poor drainage can kill the best fruit stock. Dig a hole and fill it with water to check. The water should drain away overnight. If not, select another site or improve drainage by breaking up deep hardpan, installing drainage tile, digging a small ditch for runoff, or planting on a mound. (See pages 86–87.)

PLANTING

Early spring before buds swell is the best time to plant most fruit trees, especially where winters are harsh. In milder areas, you also can plant fruit trees after their leaves drop in the fall. You can plant container-grown stock anytime during the growing season.

Space standard trees 20 feet or more apart; dwarfs as far apart as their mature height. For best results, prepare your planting hole before you buy or receive your tree. Dig it 2 feet wider than you expect the root ball to be. Place dark topsoil in one pile, and the lighter-colored subsoil in another. (See pages 86–87.)

When you get bare-root stock in the mail, open the package and sink the roots in water in a cool, dark place. If you cannot plant within 24 hours, heel-in the roots by leaning them against the side of a shallow trench and covering them with soil.

To permanently plant all fruit trees, fill the hole halfway with good, loamy topsoil, soak, and let drain. Place the tree at the level it grew in the nursery unless otherwise noted (see pages 330–341). If in doubt, set it shallower, not deeper.

These cherry trees burst into delicate blossoms with the coming of spring. After a fanciful shower of petals, fruits begin to grow, then ripen in early summer.

With balled trees, remove any cords. Then loosen the burlap from around the trunk and use it to lower the root ball into the hole, leaving the burlap to rot. If potted trees have tangled roots, cut or pull some of them apart.

Then fill the hole. Use subsoil, if necessary, on the top. Make a saucerlike depression around the trunk to catch water for the roots, but keep the trunk and center high and dry to prevent rot.

CARE AFTER PLANTING

Most trees of any size need at least one stake on the windward side. Use one or more soft, loose ties to stop excessive, but not all, swaying. Three equally spaced stakes should offer sufficient support. Remove these as soon as the tree gains enough strength. Wrapping the trunk will prevent sunscald and other damage.

Prune out all but three to five well-placed branches; shorten these by a third. Remove any encircling wires or labels before they get tight. Water as you plant, then deeply once a week the first summer. A layer of mulch will save water, decrease stress, and eliminate competition from grass, as well as prevent lawn-mower nicks. Keep the mulch about 6 inches from the trunk so rodents won't hide there and gnaw on the tree bark. New trees need little or no fertilizer.

PRUNING FRUITS

Pruning fruit trees and bushes in the early years forms a strong scaffold of productive wood. If you've not pruned much before, don't let your inexperience frighten you from the job. Bad pruning is better for fruit than none at all. Plus, you will gain a feel for it as you work.

PRUNING FRUIT TREES

For a foolproof start, follow these basic steps.

Work in late winter or early spring while trees are dormant and sap is still. Wounds heal best then, and flower buds are easy to see.

Use sharp pruning shears or, for bigger cuts, lopping shears. Scissor-type shears with two sharp sides are better than the anvil types with one sharp and one blunt side. For mature trees, a pruning saw will make correctly angled cuts more easily than a regular saw.

Look the tree over and decide which branches you want to keep. The more horizontal and less vertical, the better. In some cases, you can bend and secure branches at a 45-degree angle for better shaping. Keep the brace in place for a year.

When pruning, first cut away all dead, broken, or diseased branches. Then remove suckers from around the base and water sprouts along the limbs unless you need to train one as a main branch. Because you want no stubs, make cuts nearly flush with the branch, but try not to cut away the branch collar. Leaving the collar promotes faster healing. Often, lines of growth will indicate the branch collar.

To remove a large, heavy branch without tearing, use the three-cut method shown on page 91.

Open up the middle of the tree so the sun can get to all the fruit. Cut above an outward-facing bud so new growth spreads rather than crowds.

Remove spindly, crowding, or crossing branches. Cut back to desired height.

Cut off all noticeable egg cases and as many branch tips as you can (that's where insects often lay their eggs). Finally, dispose of the debris.

TRAINING TECHNIQUES

The central-leader or pyramid system has a single, dominant central trunk and lateral branches at regular intervals. Thin annually so the center gets good light. Use this method to train apple, pear, sweet cherry, and quince.

The open-center system or vase shape has three or four main limbs at wide angles with five or so secondary branches on each. This works well for plum, peach, nectarine, apricot, and sour cherry.

The modified-leader system gives the central leader and the lateral branches equal importance. Select three or four widely spaced branches and remove the rest. This is best for nut trees, but also is used for apple and pear.

GRAPES

Grapes are most productive if trained using a four-cane technique known as the Kniffin system. Begin by planting single canes, cutting them back to two or three buds. While the canes grow the first year, build a trellis with 7-foot posts sunk 2½ feet into the ground and set 15 to 18 feet apart. Attach two lengthwise wires, one 30 inches high, the other at the post tops.

The second spring choose the strongest cane for your trunk. Cut it off at the level of the top wire, tie it loosely to the top wire, and cut away all other canes.

The third spring and thereafter, select two pencil-sized canes near each wire, one on each side of the main stem. Cut these four canes back to 12 to 15 buds each, and attach them to the wires. Select four more canes near the base of the first ones. Cut this set back to two buds each for the next year's production. Remove everything else, which is usually quite a lot.

■ Training grapes on an arbor

To train grapes on an arbor, prune to develop a main trunk. Cut back the side growth, even in summer, to throw all of the energy into getting that one stem to the arbor top. Then let growth spread as you wish, but remove all but about 60 buds every spring.

BUSH FRUITS

Bush fruits need pruning to keep them from turning into a thicket where only birds can reach the best berries. If you combine pruning with a system of support that keeps the canes off the ground, the plants will be neater, less susceptible to disease, and more productive.

A single stake with a circle of canes tied to it tepee-style helps control raspberries. T posts and double wires work well for bramble fruits.

Whatever system you use, spring pruning is necessary to shorten and thin out canes. Better air circulation will reduce the chance of disease, increase yields and quality, and make maintenance and berry picking easier.

TAMING CANES

Contain bramble fruits with T-shaped posts and double wires. Tie blackberries to the wires. Let raspberries grow between and bend over the wires. Prune to a height or length of no more than 5 feet.

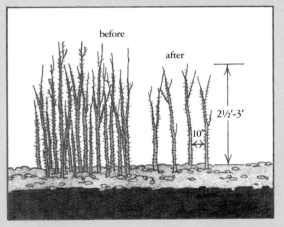

Pruning raspberries is simple as long as you remember that biennial fruiting canes sprout from perennial crowns. Once you pick the berries, remove the old canes. In spring, cut to the height and thin to the spacing indicated, keeping the strongest canes. After picking, remove old canes.

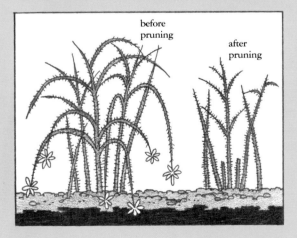

Blackberries have central canes that produce much longer side shoots. Fruit grows on these laterals, which you should shorten to 12 inches every spring. Also trim back the tips of the main plants. Remove old, spent canes after harvest.

ESPALIERING

This pear tree follows an adapted fan pattern. Such severe pruning throws extra vigor into the fruit, making it of the finest quality as well as easy to pick. The tree takes very little space but is unique in both interest and accomplishment.

Europeans fruit growers developed espaliering years ago to get more fruit from less space. Basically, this technique involves pruning to a specific pattern of height and width, but with so little depth that the tree is almost flat. Usually, espaliered trees are placed against walls or trellises, or on freestanding structures.

Today, most espaliers are dwarf fruit trees, especially apple, pear, peach, and nectarine. These trees have the advantages of a workable height and abundant, early fruiting.

An espaliered fruit tree needs the same basic care as any other, including at least six hours of unobstructed sun each day. A south-facing wall, however, can become sizzling hot when summer temperatures go above 90 degrees. A southeast or southwest wall is better.

■ Offer support

Support is the primary need of espaliers, at least in the beginning. You must tie the branches until they harden into definite patterns. Sink

ESPALIER PATTERNS

(Left) Triple horizontal cordon: Three pairs of equally spaced horizontal shoots grow from the central leader. Prune side shoots on laterals to about 6 inches.

(Right) Six grid: Select a single horizontal cordon. Then train six equally spaced shoots upward, three on each trunk side.

(Left) Palmette verrier: Begin as above, left, but with closer spacing. Then direct laterals up and into the form of U's.

(Right) Belgian fence: Prune as for a single horizontal tier. Then train neighboring lateral branches to cross and form a diamond shape. Tie the branches to each other temporarily.

two stout posts into the ground at least 8 feet apart. (Be sure the support is far enough from the house or wall to allow plenty of working room in back of the tree.) Steady the posts by connecting them to the house, if necessary. Stretch 14-gauge wire at intervals of 1 to 2 feet between the posts.

■ Pruning

The pattern you choose dictates your pruning. The key to shaping a tree is identifying the leaf buds and choosing the ones that will contribute the most to the design. Usually, fat, bulging buds are the fruiting buds; narrow buds are leaf buds. In general, to shape a tree, prune heavily in late winter or early spring. Train the new growth in midsummer, and prune any secondary growth in the late summer or early fall. Prune just above a bud and remove all growth that doesn't fit the pattern.

During the first year, remove flower buds to send all the tree's energy into developing roots and branches. By the third year, the tree should begin producing some fruit, and soon it will be a bountiful horticultural work of art.

SPECIAL TIPS

Fruit and nut plants can delight you for many years with their fresh produce. Here are tips to help those plants produce their yield as far into the future as possible.

WATER AND FOOD

Fruit and nut trees need ample water, especially between bloom and harvest. If you don't have enough groundwater, or get less than an inch of rain each week, it's time to get out the hose.

First, dig a 4-inch trench 6 to 12 inches wide around the plant at the drip line (the farthest tip of the branches). Run water slowly into the trench until it soaks into the ground. To check, see if a thin, stiff wire (such as a straightened coat hanger) slips easily deep into the soil. Newly set plants will need water two or three times a week for the first month. After that, water deeply but only as needed. Avoid overwatering, as well as frequent, light waterings.

Feed fruit trees with an all-purpose fertilizer two to four times between early spring and midsummer. If growth is too leafy, feed less. If leaf color or growth is poor, add trace elements.

MULCH

When mulched, nut trees and most fruit trees thrive. (Citrus trees, an exception, do better without mulch.) Mulch reduces moisture evaporation, so less water is needed. Roots, worms, and beneficial organisms grow better because mulched soil remains cooler in summer. Mulch also prevents weeds or grass from sharing nutrients or moisture with tree roots; and it means less freezing, thawing, and heaving in winter, and less erosion. Organic mulches enrich the soil as they decompose. And mulch helps prevent damage to trees from lawn equipment.

ANIMAL DAMAGE

In hard winters, hungry rodents may gnaw on the tree bark. To discourage this, keep the mulch 6 inches from the tree trunk to leave an open area, which rodents dislike.

Wrapping the trunk with heavy paper in the winter will prevent sunscald, as well as some rodent damage. But, to keep animals at bay, it's best to wrap a cylinder of wire mesh several inches away from and around the trunk, and at least 2 feet up the tree. Where snowfall is deep, wrap the lower branches in aluminum foil or remove the snow from beneath the tree to prevent critters from nibbling on the branches.

Deer are less likely to damage young fruit trees if you hang a few bars of soap in each tree. The deer don't like the smell of soap. Any kind of soap will do, and you don't even have to unwrap the soap.

If raccoons or squirrels are a problem, keep a dog nearby to discourage them. If that fails, catch the invaders in a box trap and release them in the wild.

Birds will want your fruit, too (and they deserve some for their help in insect control). To preserve your share, provide water for birds—they often peck at fruit just to get a drink—or plant a mulberry or other trap fruit nearby for the birds to eat. Or dangle reflecting pie pans or strings of beads and small mirrors from the branches. Many growers find that a single swath

Miniatures like this 'Nectar Babe' nectarine bear fruit soon, often during their second year. Rotate or relocate container plants to catch more sun or show their best sides. In northern areas, move container trees into an unheated shed or garage during winter.

of cheesecloth will save enough cherries. As a last resort, encase whole trees in netting from the time fruit begins to develop until harvest.

FRUIT DROP

Dropped fruit is nature's way of thinning your crop. Dry spells could make all of the fruit fall, but some drop is necessary, even in optimum conditions. To increase quality and size of fruit, you may need to thin more.

About six weeks after bloom and after the normal May or June drop, remove all diseased, shriveled, or wormy fruits. Later, thin again so fruits will be 6 to 8 inches apart for apple, pear, and peach, and 4 inches apart for plum. After thinning, you still may need to buttress a fruit-laden limb. If a branch sags, use a pole stuck into the ground for support.

INSECTS AND DISEASE

You can grow good fruit with few or no poison sprays. A single dormant oil spray applied in late winter—either before or after pruning—will suffocate insect eggs and scale without hurting beneficial insects.

After that, carefully watch your plants so you can stop problems while they still are small. You soon will learn to spot egg cases as you prune bare branches, when it's easy to remove and destroy them. During the growing season, check the undersides of leaves often or take a flashlight out and see who's coming to dine after dark. Quick handpicking will rid a lot of pests. Get a bug book so you can tell friends from foes.

Other biological controls, such as *Bacillus thuringiensis,* kill a particular pest without harming the environment and increasingly are available.

For perfect fruit, get a spray schedule from your county extension agent and follow it, usually with a combination fungicide and insecticide about every eight days from petal fall until one week before harvest. Don't use insecticides during bloom because they will kill bees, which are vital to pollination. When you must spray, do so in late afternoon when fewer bees and

Peach trees, such as this beauty in blossom, and nectarine trees bear the second or third season after planting. Where peach trees grow (in at least 30 states), most nut trees thrive, too.

beneficial insects are around. Mow clover and dandelions first to avoid attracting additional bees, then use the least-toxic chemical or spray.

Apply all fungicides, miticides, and insecticides with care, on windless days, and always according to label instructions.

329

TREE FRUITS PORTFOLIO

APPLE—'Dorsett Golden'

APPLE—'Golden Delicious'

APPLE—'Granny Smith'

APPLE

Crunchy apples are probably the most widely grown fruit in the world. At one time, almost every backyard had an apple tree that gave shade and held swings, plus stocked the pantry shelves. But such a standard apple tree could take up as much as 1,600 square feet of yard and overwhelm a homeowner with bushels of fruit ripening at once.

Modern growers, even commercial ones, are choosing smaller trees. Genetic dwarfs grow only 4 to 6 feet tall, can be grown in containers on porch or patio, and can satisfy a family without requiring canning. Dwarfs and semidwarfs still will fill the larder, but with more varieties, over a longer time, and with more freshness and less work. Dwarf trees are man-made by joining two or more trees. This makes dwarfs more expensive initially, but the advantages far outweigh the price. Some dwarfs require support.

Fruit trees are budded or grafted for their desirable features, so trees from seeds may not be as sturdy or productive.

■ **Varieties:** Old-fashioned varieties still are available from growers and mail-order nurseries. New discoveries offer advantages that would amaze Johnny Appleseed.

'Lodi,' 'Transparent,' 'Anoka,' and 'Stark's Earliest'—summer apples that ripen starting in early July—are best for cooking, and need to be used rather quickly. Fall apples, like 'Delicious,' 'Jonathan,' and most well-known varieties, on the other hand, ripen from September to frost and keep for months.

'Liberty,' 'Priscilla,' 'Prima,' 'Redfree,' and 'Sir Prize' resist pests and diseases. Spur-type trees, such as 'Starkrimson Delicious,' produce fewer branches and limbs, and need less pruning than standard trees; still, they produce larger and more fruit than dwarf trees, which are smaller.

Tip-bearing types like 'Tydeman's Red,' 'Rome Beauty,' and 'Granny Smith' bear fruit on the ends of shoots from the previous season's growth as well as on spurs.

Some varieties are especially adapted to certain areas. 'Anna,' 'Dorsett,' and 'Tropical Beauty' bear in warm climates.

You can buy trees that have had several varieties grafted on them. Or you can bud or graft more varieties to the trees you have. This aids pollination and, more importantly, yields a greater variety of fruit at different times.

■ **Planting and care:** Plant apple trees in early spring in the North, late fall in the South. Keep the swelling or bud union above the soil line. Be sure to remove any shoots that develop from the rootstock.

Apple trees tend to be alternate bearers: heavy crop one year, small one the next. You can even out the harvest somewhat by carefully thinning the fruit when it is about the size of a thumbnail. Be sure, however, not to remove spurs. In a fruitful year, when a tree produces more apples than it can ripen with any size or quality, you will need to remove more apples than you leave on the tree.

■ **Pruning:** Most apple trees are best trained to the central-leader or pyramid system. With this, they become established and bear sooner. 'Golden Delicious' and its offspring are vigorous growers that tend toward too much height, so using the open-center or vase system helps keep them down to workable size.

Spur-type apples will keep renewing their spurs if you remove one out of every 10 spurs each spring. For tip-bearing varieties, head-back long shoots to force branching and production of more bearing wood.

When pruning old, neglected trees, or when shortening tall trees, do not prune severely all in one year. Instead, spread the job over three springs to maintain the tree's natural balance and avoid shock.

■ **Pollination:** Apple trees produce best when two or more varieties bloom at the same time within 100 feet of each other. If your growing space is limited, depend on your neighbor's tree, graft more than one variety on the same tree, or plant two trees in the same hole. But the ideal is to have three different kinds of reliable pollinators. Your nursery can best advise you on these choices.

■ **Harvesting and storage:** A waxy coat on the skin, as well as brown seeds and true fruit color, all indicate ripeness. But taste is the best sign. Take a bite. If the fruit tastes sour and is hard or brittle, wait. But if the apple tastes juicy and sweet, and is medium soft, pick the rest. To pick, pull upward with a twisting motion. Ripe fruit parts easily from the stem.

Pick apples you'll store before they're completely ripe. Store them in a cool, but not freezing, cellar, shed, or garage. To keep the apples from taking on foreign tastes and odors, store them away from other fruits and vegetables. Check periodically and remove bad apples. Fall apples will keep until late winter in a cellar, and as long as the following May in plastic bags in the refrigerator.

■ **Insects and diseases:** Apples are prone to plenty of pests and diseases, but if you spray with dormant oil and follow the suggestions on pages 329 and 342–343, problems should be minimal. Resistant varieties will do even better. All-purpose spraying is most effective right after petal drop and again at the fruitlet stage.

Keep apple trees clean and avoid overfeeding to maintain control over fire blight disease. Cut out and bag for trash pickup diseased limbs, fruit, and leaves. Avoid heavy pruning or over-application of nitrogen fertilizer because this stimulates rapid, weak growth.

APRICOT

Ripe apricots, golden and juicy, are one of the most delicious and delightful products of the home fruit garden. The trees are easy to grow, attractive with glossy-green foliage, and vigorous. Their delicate white blossoms often are the first to open in spring, scenting the air with a gardenialike sweetness.

■ **Varieties:** 'Moongold,' 'Sungold,' 'Scout,' and 'Hardy Iowa' are good for the northern states. 'Manchurian,' often a bush apricot, is the hardiest and is an excellent rootstock. But most

are seedlings and vary greatly in fruit quality. 'Blenheim,' 'Hungarian,' 'Moorpack,' 'Royal,' 'Tilton,' and 'Wilson Delicious' are popular apricots.

Dwarf and miniature varieties do well in containers. For winter, move them indoors to a cool cellar so dormancy continues; or move them to an unheated garage or porch, making sure to bundle them up when night temperatures drop below 25 degrees.

■ **Planting and care:** Plant in early spring. Because apricot flowers open so early, plant on a northern slope or behind a protective evergreen hedge. These trees grow fast, so don't overfeed. They also tend to set more fruit than their branches can support, so thin after fruit drop and again later if needed. Leave fruit to develop at 4- to 6-inch intervals.

■ **Pruning:** Apricot trees do best with an open-leader or vase shape. On a new tree, choose three branches spaced around the trunk at nearly the same height. Cut them back to one or two buds each. Prune the top back to 1 or 2 inches above the highest branch and remove all else. Apricots bear on spurs that produce for about three years. As the tree grows, keep the center open.

■ **Pollination:** Most apricots are self-fruiting, having both male and female flowers on each tree. 'Moongold' and 'Sungold' need a second variety nearby. In cold climates, it's best to plant two varieties to encourage a heavier fruit set and a better chance for a crop in the face of late-spring frosts.

■ **Harvesting and storage:** Pick when golden yellow and fairly soft to the touch by twisting lightly. If ripe enough, the fruit will come off easily. Apricots will keep for about three weeks if stored in a cool place, or you can freeze, can, or dry them.

■ **Insects and diseases:** Apricots are remarkably resistant. To avoid verticillium wilt, plant in soil where you haven't grown raspberry, strawberry, tomato, potato, pepper, or melon in the last few years.

APPLE—'Red Delicious'

APRICOT

TREE FRUITS PORTFOLIO *(continued)*

CHERRY

CITRUS—grapefruit

CITRUS—kumquat

CHERRY

Cherry trees bloom with clouds of pink and white flowers in early spring. Harvest comes conveniently at the beginning of summer before you get too busy with other crops.

■ **Varieties:** There are two kinds of cherry trees: sweet and sour. Tart or pie cherries are easiest to grow because they tolerate hot summers, fog, and cold weather better than sweet cherries. 'Montmorency' is a longtime favorite sour variety. 'Early Richmond' and 'Suda' also are good. The dwarf 'North Star,' 'Meteor,' and 'Early Montmore' bear great quantities of fruit. Among the sweet varieties, 'Bing,' 'Lambert,' 'Black Tartarian,' 'Royal Ann,' and 'Stella' are favorites. 'Garden Bing' is a good miniature.

■ **Planting and care:** Plant sour cherry in late fall in mild climates; elsewhere, in early spring. Space the trees 20 to 25 feet apart. Plant sweet cherry in spring, also 20 to 25 feet apart. Because cherries ripen earlier than other fruits, don't plant cherries among other fruits that will need spraying while the cherries are ripening.

No fertilizer is needed until the trees are well settled. Then, a yearly feeding of an all-purpose fertilizer keeps growth vigorous and yields delicious.

Cherries, especially the sweet ones, are very fussy about proper watering. Water deeply and regularly during dry spells.

■ **Pruning:** Sweet cherry trees grow naturally in a pyramidal form, so they do best trained using the central-leader method. So do dwarf sour cherry trees. For standard sour cherry trees, use the modified-leader system to get more sunlight to the center.

Sweet cherry trees tend to grow too vertical. Prune them in late winter while still dormant to lateral growing twigs or buds; repeat yearly. In three years, you should have good form. Also, use boards to brace branches to wider angles, or weight them down with sand-filled milk jugs.

As trees mature, they need little pruning. Sweet cherry spurs bear for 10 years or more. Sour cherry trees bear on two- to five-year-old spurs. Keep the center open and shorten long branches as needed.

■ **Pollination:** Sour cherry trees are self-fruiting. Among the sweet cherries, so is 'Stella,' which also is a good pollinator for other varieties. Other sweet cherries, however, not only need two trees, but a particular two. 'Bing,' 'Lambert,' and 'Napoleon,' for instance, will not pollinate each other. 'Black Tartarian' will pollinate all three, plus also pollinate 'Yellow Glass' or 'Royal Ann.'

■ **Harvesting and storage:** Sweet cherries become firm when ripe. Sour cherries part easily from the stem. Fruit will keep longer if you pick it with the stem attached. You can pile the cherries in containers without fear of bruising. Soft varieties will keep in the refrigerator for about a week; firm-fleshed ones, two to three weeks.

■ **Insects and diseases:** Although there are many possible pests, you can control most using few, if any, sprays. Birds are more of a problem. Dangling reflectors or swaths of netting may help keep birds away. Complete cover is the only sure solution, though this seldom is necessary since cherries generally bear enough fruit to share. Because plenty of other food is available when the later varieties ripen, birds bother them much less.

CITRUS

Oranges and their relatives hang like golden orbs on small trees with thick, glossy green leaves. For weeks at a time, they perfume the neighborhood with their fragrant blossoms. All demand warm, sunny weather year-round; as a result, most are successful only in zones 9 and 10, though citrus will survive in the southern parts of Zone 8. In borderline areas, develop a more-protected microclimate by planting citrus near a south or west wall, painting nearby walls a light color to reflect heat, or tucking citrus close to protecting evergreens. See page 368 for instructions on growing citrus indoors.

■ **Varieties:** Several important varieties of the common or sweet orange exist, with 'Navel' among the favorites. Because the varieties vary widely in their bearing season, you can plant several to extend the harvest. 'Washington,'

'Hamlin,' 'Pineapple,' and 'Valencia' bear in that order. 'Satsuma,' 'Parson Brown,' and 'Gim Gong' also are good for home growers.

With an exotic red pulp, the blood oranges are no more difficult to grow. 'Ruby,' 'Torocco,' 'Temple,' 'Moro Blood,' and 'French Perfume' are outstanding. 'Meyer' is a good lemon for dooryard planting, and the 'Ponderosa' lemon bears huge fruits. Calamondins and kumquats are easy to grow and produce baby fruits, which you can use in many ways.

Grapefruits, most successful in desert regions, are available in pink and white. 'Marsh' is an excellent seedless white; 'Foster' and 'Ruby' are pink and bear early.

Tangerines are small and easy to peel. Both 'Fremont,' which ripens in November, and 'Dancy,' which ripens in December, are hardy.

Among the limes, 'Mexican' is the hardiest. 'Lakeland Lime' produces all year.

Juicy tangelos are a cross between a tangerine and a grapefruit, and have a delicious tart taste.

■ **Planting and care:** Citrus trees need good drainage. In California, plant them from March to May. In the Gulf states, plant in late spring and early summer. Plant no deeper than the trees grew at the nursery. The bud union should be about 4 inches above ground.

Wrap the trunk with tree tape or heavy paper to prevent sunscald. Water well every two weeks, but let the soil dry out in between.

Citrus does better without mulch; however, keep the ground around the trunk bare and free of weeds and grass.

Keep the soil slightly acid. Citrus prefers a pH of 6.0 to 6.5. Test every few years and add dolomitic limestone to raise the pH, sulfur to lower. In Florida, feed three times a year with citrus fertilizer. In California, add only nitrogen.

■ **Pruning:** If the nursery didn't head-back your tree, prune it after planting. Further pruning is unneeded as long as the tree develops to a central-leader system. Rub off any young sprouts that appear beneath the bud union.

■ **Pollination:** Most citrus are self-fruiting.

■ **Harvesting and storage:** Ripe citrus can stay on the tree more than three months before overripening. But for peak flavor, pick fruits as soon as possible after they mature. Cut them from the branches; don't pull them.

■ **Insects and diseases:** An all-purpose spray usually will protect citrus against invaders. Spray in early spring, just after petal fall, and again four to six weeks later. If aphids or thrips infest the citrus, spray with 1½ tablespoons of malathion per gallon of water.

FIG

Although reliably hardy only in zones 7 to 9, the fig is grown in ethnic neighborhoods as far north as Chicago and Boston, either in containers or with special winter care.

■ **Varieties:** 'Capri' and 'Smyrna' are grown commercially in California and the Southwest. 'Celeste,' 'Black Mission,' 'Kadota,' and the everbearing 'Brown Turkey' produce fruit in much of the rest of the country.

■ **Planting and care:** Set extra deep in the ground, especially where danger of freezing exists. Mulch well to discourage nematodes. For container plants, either bring them inside before frost, wrap entire plants in heavy insulation like old rugs, or, where winter temperatures go below 10 degrees, cut the roots on one side and bury the whole plant in a horizontal trench.

■ **Pruning:** Keep plants trimmed to the size you can protect. Grow as open-centered shrubs.

■ **Pollination:** 'Capri' is used to pollinate 'Smyrna,' but these require the special fig-wasp, which is even more sensitive to climate than are the plants. Fortunately, 'Celeste,' 'Black Mission,' 'Kadota,' 'Brown Turkey,' and 'Texas Everbearing' all are self-fruiting and don't need the wasp.

■ **Harvesting and storage:** Fig flowers develop inside the fruit, which is ripe when the neck bends over on the stem. If the fruit is milky, it is not ready, but will ripen at room temperature. Figs are good fresh, canned, frozen, or dried.

■ **Insects and diseases:** Fig resists insects and diseases well. Use clean culture and refer to pages 342–343.

CITRUS—tangelo

CITRUS—tangerine

FIG

333

TREE FRUITS PORTFOLIO *(continued)*

NECTARINE

PEACH

PEAR

PEACH AND NECTARINE

Although touchy about weather, peaches will grow in at least 30 states. Check with your county extension office or nursery to learn if your area and your favorite variety are compatible.

■ **Varieties:** Peaches and nectarines are either clingstone (a fruit whose flesh sticks to the seed) or freestone (a fruit whose flesh doesn't cling to the seed).

'Mercicrest' nectarine and 'Reliance' peach are among the hardiest varieties, and can take temperatures far below zero. 'Elberta' and 'Hale' peaches are old favorites. 'Pocahontas,' 'Cherokee,' 'Lexington,' 'Redbud,' and 'Suredrop' are good nectarines.

Many varieties also come in dwarf sizes. 'Bonanza,' 'Compact Redhaven,' and 'Nectar Babe'—genetic dwarfs or miniatures that grow as short as 4 feet—are good in containers.

■ **Planting and care:** Keep these out of the direct path of winter winds, perhaps in a pocket protected by buildings or evergreens. However, avoid southern-facing slopes and south walls, which may lure them into early bloom.

Plant in early spring with 25 feet between standard trees, 10 to 15 feet between dwarfs. Mulch well, but do not feed young trees. Expect fruit the second or third season.

You will need to thin the fruit unless a late frost does it for you. Thin when fruit is about the size of a thumbnail and the tree goes into a rest period. Leave one fruit to each 4 to 8 inches of stem—more for early-ripening varieties. If branches bend too much, thin again.

■ **Pruning:** Cut back the main stem of a new tree to about 3 feet and stake until it's well established. Train to a vase or open-center shape. Prune annually in late winter. Every few years, remove some old branches. The part where the peaches grew last year won't fruit again, so encourage strong new growth by thinning one-third to one-half of the old growth. Keep the center open. Prune long, vertical shoots to an outward-pointing bud.

Genetic dwarfs are not as vigorous but need little pruning.

■ **Pollination:** Most peaches and nectarines are self-fruiting, except for 'J.H. Hale,' its relatives, and 'Mikado.' Check before buying.

■ **Harvesting and storage:** Allow peaches to ripen fully on the tree. Yellow-fleshed varieties turn orange; white-fleshed ones turn from green to yellow-white. Some develop a red blush. Nectarines take on an orange to red cast. When ripe, all come loose from the stem easily. Taste to check. Eat at once or refrigerate.

■ **Insects and diseases:** Be prepared to treat peach-leaf curl and bacterial cankers; also, do your best to prevent borers. Regular applications of an all-purpose spray work best for peaches and nectarines. (See pages 342–343.)

PEAR

Pears thrive wherever apples do and have been favorites for as long. With their white blossoms, handsome foliage and fruit, and, in winter, interesting bare branches shaped like a ballerina's skirt, they make beautiful, edible landscaping additions.

■ **Varieties:** Many old, gritty pears are 'Kieffers.' These don't taste great, but are productive and reliable. Much-improved varieties and dwarfs now are available. 'Bartlett' is the most famous, 'Surecrop' the most resistant to fire blight, and 'Lincoln' one of the hardiest. 'Clapp Favorite' and 'Moonglow' bear fruit early.

■ **Planting and care:** Plant in early spring much like apples. Drainage is vital. Mulch and water during drought, but be careful not to overfeed since this stimulates disease.

Pears seldom need much thinning unless the crop is unusually heavy.

■ **Pruning:** Pears are determined to grow vertically, but vertical branches seldom bear much fruit. Train either to a modified-leader or an open-center system, continually cutting back upward-growing branches to encourage horizontal growth. Once trees reach the fruiting stage, prune lightly, if at all.

■ **Pollination:** A single 'Kieffer' may bear because of other trees in the neighborhood, but for sure pollination, plant two varieties. Any combination, except 'Bartlett' with 'Seckel,' works.

■ **Harvesting and storage:** Pears are one of the few fruits that should not fully ripen on the tree. Harvest when the small spots on the skin turn brown. Most, except 'Bartlett' and 'Kieffer,' will separate from the stem when ready to pick. 'Bartlett' and 'Kieffer' need a twist to loosen. Because pears bear on the same spurs every year, be careful not to break them off when removing fruit.

To store, wrap each pear in paper and stow in shallow boxes in a cool, dark place. To hasten ripening, place several in a plastic bag and seal. Check the fruit often.

■ **Insects and diseases:** Fire blight is the principal disease. Whenever terminal shoots or flowers look like they have been scorched by fire, remove and destroy them. Insects can spread the disease, so you may need a spray program similar to the one outlined for apples (see pages 330–331). Plant resistant varieties.

PLUM

There are plums for every state in the country, but no one kind grows everywhere. The small size of plum trees, even the standard varieties, simplifies pruning, spraying, and harvesting.

■ **Varieties:** Plums include two European types—'European' and 'Damson'—which are the sweetest and often are used for prunes. 'Damson' plums usually are blue or purple, but some are yellow. They are best used for cooking and preserves. 'Damson' trees are fairly small, so they're highly suitable for small yards.

Japanese plums actually originated in China and are primarily red or reddish orange. They are softer and juicier, but less sweet, than the European-type plums, and are most suited to warmer areas and the far western region of the United States. There also are wild native plums, a fourth group.

Double-check to be sure the varieties you want to plant are hardy in your area.

■ **Planting and care:** Plant in early spring. European varieties can be set out in late fall, too. Space standard trees 20 feet apart with the graft union above the soil line. A north-facing slope is ideal, especially for early-blooming Japanese varieties. Standards will last up to 20 years; dwarfs bear for 15 years.

Mulch well and water when needed, especially when trees are young and from blossom time until harvest. Once trees are settled, feed each spring with 1 to 3 pounds of ammonium sulfate, adjusting the amount to the size of the trees. Cut this rate in half for dwarf varieties.

Thinning is seldom necessary for 'European,' never for 'Damson.' For Japanese, thin to 4 to 6 inches apart and divide all clusters.

■ **Pruning:** Train 'European' and 'Damson' plums to a central-leader or cone shape, Japanese varieties to the open-center system. Established European-type trees require little pruning. Japanese are more vigorous and need somewhat severe pruning all their lives.

■ **Pollination:** This varies, so double-check pollination requirements for any tree you buy. 'Stanley' and 'Damson' are self-fertile. Others, such as 'South Dakota,' 'Superior,' 'Mt. Royal,' 'Shiro,' or 'Santa Rosa,' need two or more trees planted in the same area.

■ **Harvesting and storage:** Color varies too much to help in judging ripeness. Ripe fruit separates easily with a little twist, is slightly soft, and has a whitish bloom or powdery coating. Shaking the tree and then gathering the fallen plums is OK. If you pick and store early varieties before they are fully ripe, they will keep for several weeks in a cool place. Late varieties will last one to three months, depending on kind.

■ **Insects and diseases:** Many problems can occur, but few are serious. All are easy to control with a regular spray program, as outlined by your county extension agent. Wood with large, dark swellings is probably suffering from black knot. Remove and destroy.

PLUM—Japanese

PLUM—'Santa Rosa'

BUSH FRUITS PORTFOLIO

BLACKBERRY

BLACKBERRY—'Black Satin'

BLACKBERRY

True blackberries are larger and more elongated than black raspberries. As wild thickets disappear, the convenience of having them in your own yard in neat rows more than ever is worth their care.

■ **Varieties:** Blackberries are either cane or vine. The cane varieties thrive everywhere except in extremely cold or warm regions. Vine types grow only in warmer climates, and include the redder boysenberries and loganberries, and the large, near-black dewberries. 'Thornfree' requires little pruning. Cane types like 'Black Satin,' 'Early Ebony King,' and 'Darrow' support themselves but are easier to pick and prune with added support, even if just a single wire. Vines should have double wires (see page 325).

■ **Planting and care:** Soak the roots in water an hour or two before planting in early spring. Then set out in rows spaced 8 to 10 feet apart, with plants 3 to 5 feet apart in each row. If you use the spaces between for vegetables or flowers the first year, the extra cultivation will result in a bonus production of vegetables and flowers, and the cleaner berry patch will yield more berries on stronger canes.

To keep the berry planting vigorous, side-dress with 5–10–10 fertilizer along the row at bloom time, then give a lighter application shortly after harvest. Mulch to control weeds.

As root suckers appear during the growing season, remove them to keep your ordered rows from growing into a thicket.

Thin canes to four or five per plant for uprights and 12 to 16 for vines.

■ **Pruning:** Cut canes back to about 6 inches after planting. Build a support within a few months.

Keep in mind that each cane emerges and puts out lateral branches one year, blooms and bears the next, then dies. To improve fruiting, cut back lateral branches to about 12 inches in the spring. Throughout the summer, cut back tips so canes do not exceed 2½ to 3 feet. At the end of the season, cut out all spent canes at soil level and destroy them.

■ **Pollination:** Blackberries are self-fruiting.
■ **Harvesting and storage:** To harvest at peak ripeness, pick when colors begin to turn. Otherwise, bugs will move in to do it for you. Berries should be sweet but still firm. Pick daily in the morning.
■ **Insects and diseases:** Pests and diseases seldom present serious problems for blackberries. Plant resistant varieties, remove and destroy weak and diseased canes immediately, and keep the patch free of weeds to discourage insects.

BLUEBERRY

Blueberry bushes with pinkish white flowers in spring, luscious blue fruits in summer, and brilliant red foliage in fall are fine additions to shrub borders. They grow 6 to 8 feet tall and make good hedges, too.

■ **Varieties:** Of the many different types only the high-bush and the rabbit-eye kinds are recommended for the home garden. 'Earliblue' and 'Collins' are good early producers; 'Stanley' and 'Bluecrop' are top-producing midseason kinds. For late harvest, try 'Jersey' or 'Coville.'

■ **Planting and care:** Blueberries require an acid soil, down to a pH of 4.0. Apply four pints of powdered sulfur per 100 square feet for every full point you need to lower the pH.

Plant blueberries in spring or fall, 4 to 7 feet apart, in rows 8 feet apart. Buy only 2- to 4-year-old plants. Mix plenty of peat moss in the holes and do not plant too deep. Mulch with an acid material like oak leaves or pine needles.

As spring buds begin to swell on established plants, give each bush 4 ounces of ammonium sulfate. Increase by 1 ounce each year to 8 ounces for mature bushes.

■ **Pruning:** Little trimming is needed except to remove old and weak stems in late winter or early spring every year. Remove some of the side shoots to give bearing branches better air circulation and sunlight. On mature bushes, cut off one or two of the oldest branches each year.

■ **Pollination:** 'Northblue' and 'Tophat' are new, self-fruiting dwarf varieties. Others need two or more varieties for cross-pollination.

■ **Harvesting and storage:** Bushes take 6 to 10 years to reach full production. Berry production lasts long enough for you to pick each bush for six to seven weeks. After the berries turn blue, leave them on several days longer until they are sweet and come off easily. Handle them carefully; they bruise easily. The berries will keep in the refrigerator about a week; they freeze well, too.

■ **Insects and diseases:** Blueberries are rarely bothered by insects and diseases. Shriveled, dried up, mummified berries result from a fungus. Use a fungicide according to label instructions. Birds are the most serious pest, and the only complete solution to that problem is to cover the entire bush with netting.

BUSH CHERRY

Bush cherries are ideal for small yards, as windbreaks and screens, or in the far northern states where it is too cold for cherry trees. They grow 5 to 10 feet tall and produce up to two bushels of tart and tangy fruit a year. The fragrant white flowers are quite spectacular in early spring.

■ **Varieties:** 'Hansen' is a small bush developed in South Dakota. It has larger, purple fruit. 'Nanking' hedge cherry grows taller and has scarlet, super-juicy fruits ½ inch across.

■ **Planting and care:** Plant as early in spring as possible. Set shrubs 8 to 10 feet apart. Mulch to control weeds. Shrubs require little maintenance. Keep fertilizer applications small.

■ **Pruning:** Cut plants back halfway when planting. Thereafter, plants need little pruning. Clip them to any height, but they will produce more if left untrimmed.

■ **Pollination:** Bush cherries are self-fruiting, but two or more shrubs will give better pollination and top crops.

■ **Harvesting and storage:** When cherries begin to ripen in midsummer, check shrubs daily to catch fruit at peak flavor. Remove cherry and stem from the bush, but take care not to in-

jure the tiny fruit spurs. Plants bear quickly, sometimes even the first year.

■ **Insects and diseases:** Bush cherries seldom need sprays, and birds don't bother them much.

CURRANT AND GOOSEBERRY

Both members of the ribes genus, currants and gooseberries require little care, except for picking. They are the alternate host of the white pine blister rust, but even in the few areas where these fruits are regulated, danger of the disease exists only if a white pine tree is within 900 feet. New varieties are totally resistant.

■ **Varieties:** 'Wilder,' 'Red Lake,' 'Cascade,' and 'Perfection' are the best red currants. 'White Grape' is a productive white (or yellow) currant. Black currant is suspected of carrying disease. Among the gooseberries, 'Welcome' and 'Pixwell' are the most common. 'Oregon Green' and 'Downing' are good green berries. 'Poorman' and 'Fredonia' are the best red.

■ **Planting and care:** Both fruits do best in cooler regions and will thrive in full sun to semi-shade. Because they leaf out so early in the spring, set plants out in the fall where possible. Space 5 feet apart. Mulch well. The plants will bear in two years.

■ **Pruning:** After planting, trim tops back to 6 to 12 inches. As plants develop, prune annually by removing old canes at the soil line. Aim for three each of one-, two-, and three-year-old canes per plant. Remove growth that roots between plants or you will have a thicket of weak, unproductive canes.

■ **Pollination:** All are self-fruiting.

■ **Harvesting and storage:** Berries ripen early in summer around the Fourth of July. Pick currant stems just short of ripe for the best jelly. Separate them with a fork. Gooseberries can remain ripe on the bush for two weeks. Wear gloves and strip berries from one stem at a time.

■ **Insects and diseases:** Pests and diseases present few problems for either fruit. Birds will want their share—and yours, too. (See pages 328–329 for help in controlling birds.)

BLUEBERRY

CURRANT—'Red Lake'

BUSH FRUITS PORTFOLIO *(continued)*

GRAPE—'Concord'

GRAPE—'Thompson Seedless'

GRAPE

The days of a grape arbor in every yard need not pass, for grapes take little room or care and produce reliably for as long as 75 years.

■ **Varieties:** Check with your county agent to learn the best varieties for your area. 'Beta,' 'Blue Jay,' 'Edelweiss,' and 'Red Amber' are hardy to temperatures as low as 30 degrees below zero. The purple 'Concord' and green 'Niagara' are standard for much of the country. Good seedless varieties include 'Concord Seedless,' 'Himrod,' 'Thompson Seedless,' 'Reliance Pink,' and 'Romulus.' In the South, muscadines are larger and resist disease better.

■ **Planting and care:** Choose a site protected from winds and late frosts. If possible, plant on an east-west line for maximum sun. Plant as early in spring as possible, or in fall. If you plant in fall, mound soil over the crown of the plant for the first winter. Set plants at the same depth as at the nursery in large holes 7 to 8 feet apart.

Mulch the soil beneath grapes and feed them every spring with all-purpose food, up to 1 pound per mature vine. Do not overfeed. You probably will have to water only during drought, but be sure vines get enough moisture when fruit begins to mature.

■ **Pruning:** See page 325.

■ **Pollination:** Except the muscadine types, all are self-fruiting but will produce bigger crops with two or more varieties.

■ **Harvesting and storage:** Let taste, not change of fruit color, be your guide. When the grapes are sweet and bursting with juice, cut off—do not pull—the entire cluster. Vines begin to bear two to three years after planting.

■ **Insects and diseases:** Good air circulation usually will prevent most potential insect and disease problems. If necessary, apply an all-purpose spray according to label directions.

KIWI

Like grape, kiwi is a vigorous-growing arbor fruit. It has fragrant, creamy white flowers in May. The leaves have reddish petioles. Its superb-tasting fruit has green flesh and a circle of black, edible seeds. Kiwi stores up to 16 weeks in the refrigerator. Kiwis are very high in vitamin C, up to 20 times that of some citrus.

■ **Varieties:** The common kiwi (*Actinidia chinensis*) is hardy only to 10 degrees, but the hardy kiwi (*A. arguta*) can withstand northern winters as low as 25 degrees below zero. Hardy kiwis bear grape- to plum-size fruit with smooth skins that need no peeling. Each female vine produces five to 10 gallons of this ready-to-eat fruit.

■ **Planting and care:** Plant kiwis in spring or fall 10 to 15 feet apart with 1 pound of organic fertilizer or 2 to 4 ounces of slow-release formula for each plant. At the end of the first growing season, apply a half pound of complete fertilizer per plant. Increase the amount each year until you are giving each vine 3 pounds a year, with two-thirds applied before new growth appears and the rest after fruit set.

■ **Pruning:** These vines are so vigorous they'll need a strong trellis soon after planting.

Prune both sexes heavily in late winter to prevent bleeding. (Female vines have flowers with pistils; flowers on male vines have stamens with pollen.) Don't remove older, spurred branches, which bear the fruit; instead, shorten them to within two to four buds of last year's fruit. Remove old branches after their second year of fruiting; also remove any damaged or crowding wood from current growth and all branches that would let fruit touch the ground.

Remove basal suckers whenever they appear. Prune males more severely after flowering to conserve space.

■ **Pollination:** Most kiwis require a male and a female vine. Only one male is needed for five to eight females, but since males seem less vigorous, give yours extra care. 'Issai,' a new self-fruiting kind, also serves as a good pollinator.

■ **Harvesting and storage:** Though the fruit may look mature in midsummer, leave it until late September or early October. The riper it is, the sweeter. After picking, refrigerate the fruit at once. For best softness and flavor, let it stand at room temperature 48 hours before eating it.

■ **Insects and diseases:** Seldom a problem.

RASPBERRY

Raspberries are easy to grow. Many, like 'Fall Gold,' are so delicious they never get to the kitchen because they make superb on-the-spot garden snacks.

■ **Varieties:** Raspberries are either summer-fruiting or everbearing. The first group produces berries on the previous season's canes in early to midsummer. Everbearers do the same, but bear on the current season's growth, too. They often fruit the first autumn after planting.

Popular red raspberries include 'Fallred,' 'Hilton,' 'Latham,' and 'Thornless Canby.' For black raspberries, try 'Bristol,' 'Allen,' 'Black Hawk,' or 'Morrison.' Purple varieties include 'Clyde,' 'Amethyst,' and 'Purple Autumn.' Among the yellows, choose 'Amber,' 'Golden West,' or 'Fall Gold.' Check with your county extension agent or nursery to see which grows best in your area.

■ **Planting and care:** Plant in early spring or late summer 3 feet apart in rows 5 to 8 feet apart. Provide humus-rich soil. Plant red raspberries 2 to 3 inches deeper than their depth at the nursery. Set others at the same depth.

■ **Pruning:** Head-back every spring and remove canes after bearing, just as you would for blackberries (see page 325). Cut black raspberries at 1½ to 2 feet; purple, red, and yellow raspberries at 2½ to 3 feet.

■ **Pollination:** All are self-fruiting.

■ **Harvesting and storage:** Check every morning for proper color. Ripe berries will come off easily. Because they keep only a few days in the refrigerator, eat or process them right away.

■ **Insects and diseases:** Problems with insects and diseases are few if you purchase only healthy, disease-resistant plants. Remove and destroy all spent or diseased canes.

STRAWBERRY

Because they are perennial and can grow as a ground cover, strawberries are among the easiest of garden plants. Alpine varieties, such as the one shown on pages 320–321, grow from seed and bear the first summer. With no runners, they are ideal for edging flower beds. For easier care, plant in strawberry jars or vertical planters.

■ **Varieties:** 'Fairfax,' 'Surecrop,' 'Cyclone,' and 'Dunlap' are good June bearers. Favorite everbearers are 'Ozark Beauty,' 'Ogallala,' and 'Sequoia.' 'Sweetheart' is an everbearer you can start from seed. Newer day-neutral varieties, such as 'Tristar,' 'Selva,' and 'Brighton,' produce flowers and fruit all summer long regardless of the length of daylight hours (unlike most conventional strawberry varieties, which form flowers and fruit only during the short days of autumn, with the spring crop formed the preceding fall). Alpines include 'Alexandria,' 'Yellow Wonder,' and 'Ruegen Improved.' Check for local stars. You need only one kind, but several will stretch the season.

■ **Planting and care:** Plant strawberries as soon as you can after buying them to help prevent transplant shock. Keep plants in the refrigerator if there is any delay. Plant in well-prepared soil with extra compost worked in. Most important is to get the crown or growing point right at the soil line. Set plants 1 to 2 feet apart. Allow runners to fill wide rows, direct them specifically, or remove them as they develop for largest berries. Pinching off blooms the first year will result in bigger crops later. A bed will last up to five years, but starting alternating beds every year works best. (Do this by plowing under an old bed and starting a new bed annually. Coupled with another, established bed, this procedure results in a new bed coming on and an established bed in production each year.)

Mulch with clean straw or leaves after the soil has frozen. Rake the mulch into the space between rows once growth begins in the spring.

■ **Pollination:** Strawberries are self-fruiting.

■ **Harvesting and storage:** Check color and taste for ripeness. Most varieties produce for 10 to 15 days. Remove all rotted and stunted fruit. Refrigerated fruit will keep about a week.

■ **Insects and diseases:** Birds are more of a problem than insects and diseases. Use netting.

RASPBERRY

STRAWBERRY

NUTS PORTFOLIO

ALMOND

HICKORY

ALMOND

The almond is closely related to the peach and is hardy wherever peaches grow. But because almond trees bloom up to a month sooner, frost or chill often kills their blossoms. Reliable crops can be grown only on the Pacific Coast.

Almond trees, which stand 15 to 30 feet tall at maturity, take three to four years to bear nuts.
■ **Planting and care:** Plant 20 to 30 feet apart in early spring in light, sandy soil. A heavy soil can kill almond trees. Most nut trees have a long taproot that makes them more difficult to transplant than other trees, so start with a small tree.

At planting time, head-back the tree. The next spring, prune again leaving three or four healthy branches growing at wide angles. Once the tree is established, prune to remove old wood, or crowding or crossing branches. The almond needs only an occasional dose of well-rotted manure.
■ **Pollination:** Most almond trees need another variety for pollination. If space is limited, plant both in the same hole.
■ **Harvesting:** When most of the hulls in the center of the tree split, shake the nuts down. Remove kernels from the inner shells and allow them to dry before using them. Properly dried, almonds will keep for several weeks at room temperature, for several months in a cool and dry place, and for more than a year in a freezer.

CHESTNUT

Although only a few treasured specimens of the American chestnut remain since the blight in the early 1900s, the search continues for resistant species and hybrids. One of the most promising of these is the Chinese chestnut.

The chestnut reaches 30 to 40 feet tall, taking three to four years to bear nuts. It's hardy to Zone 6.
■ **Planting and care:** Plant 20 to 30 feet apart in early spring, on a northern slope, if possible, to delay early flowers.

Chestnuts prefer a deep, fertile, slightly acid soil with plenty of humus. They are subject to oak-root fungus in soggy soils. Additional fertilizer is seldom needed if soil is well prepared at planting time. Mulch for optimum growth.

Train to the central-leader system, pruning suckers so tree doesn't become bushlike.
■ **Pollination:** Chestnuts need a pollinator. For greater harvests, plant two varieties. If space is limited, plant both in the same hole.
■ **Harvesting:** As nuts mature in the fall, they drop to the ground. To prevent mold and insect injury, gather them daily. Soak nuts in water and defective husks will float; discard them. Dry the nuts or kernels in the sun for two days before storing. Properly dried, chestnuts will keep for several weeks at room temperature, for several months in a cool and dry place, and for more than a year in a freezer.

HAZELNUT

Also called filbert, the hazelnut is perhaps the easiest nut for home gardeners to grow because its tree is the smallest of the nut trees—reaching only 6 to 20 feet in height—and it is satisfied with almost any soil. Hazelnuts produce best when grown as tall shrubs, but also can be trained as trees, or planted in clumps or 6 feet apart in a hedge. Hazelnuts are hardy to Zone 3 and take three to six years to bear nuts.
■ **Planting and care:** Plant 15 to 40 feet apart in early winter in warm areas; in cold areas, very early spring. Choose a protected spot with northern exposure to delay blooming. Prepare the soil with plenty of rotted manure or compost, plus sphagnum peat.

Wrap the trunk to prevent sunscald. Mulch well. If foliage pales, feed with an all-purpose fertilizer. Head-back at planting time and train trees to a central leader. For shrub forms, prune excessive sucker growth every year, but avoid large cuts because wounds heal slowly.
■ **Pollination:** Another variety of the same type is required for pollination.
■ **Harvesting:** Gather nuts as they drop. As for chestnuts, soak, discarding any floaters. Spread

out to dry. Properly dried, hazelnuts will keep for several weeks at room temperature, for several months in a cool and dry place, and for more than a year in a freezer.

HICKORY NUT AND PECAN

Prized as shade trees with golden brown autumn color and often interesting shagbark, hickory and pecan trees are of the carya genus.

Varieties adapted to the climate bear delicious nuts to Zone 4. Pecans, however, require a growing environment that's not only frost-free but fairly warm 180 to 220 days.

Hickories reach a height of 120 feet and need five to 10 years before bearing nuts. Pecans can reach 100 feet tall, and will bear about 10 pounds of nuts when 10 years old and 100 pounds of nuts when mature.

■ **Planting and care:** Plant 30 to 50 feet apart. Planting holes must be deep enough to hold 3-foot-long taproots without bending them. It is safer to plant the nuts. If you buy a tree, set it 2 to 3 inches deeper than it grew at the nursery. Water as you fill to settle soil. At planting time, cut the tree back one-third to one-half to compensate for root loss. Mulch well.

Hickories will need little more care. Don't prune pecan trees again until the top can shade the trunk. Then remove lower limbs, one each year. Until then, keep these lower branches headed back and secondary to the main trunk.

■ **Pollination:** Needs more than one variety.

■ **Harvesting:** Gather nuts as they fall, or shake the tree. Pecans keep better unshelled. Refrigerate after shelling and use soon. Properly dried, hickory nuts and pecans will keep for several weeks at room temperature, for several months in a cool and dry place, and for more than a year in a freezer.

WALNUT

Walnut trees provide fairly good shade, with high branches that leaf out late and do not interfere with grass. They do need ample room. Black walnut grows in every state east of the Rockies. 'Thomas' varieties are improved. The roots and leaves are toxic to some plantings, such as dogwood and tomato.

English or Persian walnuts usually are grown on the West Coast, but 'Crath Carpathian' is hardy from Virginia into Canada. It produces thin-shelled, mild-flavored nuts.

Walnuts like rich, slightly acid soil. They are hardy to Zone 3; butternut, which also is called white walnut, is the hardiest. Fungus prevalent in some areas may shorten the butternut's life. Butternut likes soil on the alkaline side.

Heartnut is a Japanese walnut that is very good through the central, more moderate climates. It is shorter and more spreading, and lives about 30 years.

Walnuts reach heights of 30 to 90 feet and take five to eight years to bear nuts.

■ **Planting and care:** Nuts of grafted varieties are superior to seedlings. Plant 30 to 50 feet apart in early spring. If earlier bearing is desired, prune back the taproot a few inches. Make the hole deep enough to accommodate the rest. Prune walnut trees to a modified central-leader system. Once established, walnut trees need little pruning.

Mulch to keep grass and weeds from competing. Water as needed. Feed young trees yearly in early spring. Dispose of leaves and husks of black walnut in the fall. Because they're toxic, do not use them for compost or mulch.

■ **Pollination:** Walnuts are self-pollinating, but using two or more trees improves the yield.

■ **Harvesting.** Shake nuts from the tree and store in or out of the shell. They will keep for several months in their shells in a cool, dry place. To remove the extremely hard husks, drive over the nuts with a car. Then dry the nuts in the sun for a few days. Crack black walnuts and butternuts by standing them on end and hitting the end with a hammer. Wash kernels to remove stains. (Baking soda will remove the stains from your hands.) Dry the nuts.

Store in airtight containers. Properly dried, walnuts will keep for several weeks at room temperature, for several months in a cool and dry place, and for more than a year in a freezer.

BLACK WALNUT

ENGLISH WALNUT

FRUIT AND NUT DISEASES

Disease	Description and Trouble Signs	Control
Bacterial canker	Gummy cankers, lesions, or damp-looking patches form on branches and trunk of apple, apricot, nectarine, peach, pear, plum, and especially cherry. Since the canker curtails passage of water and nutrients, the part of the branch beyond the canker may die.	Remove and destroy infected wood after leaves fall. Use sharp tools and disinfect them by wiping with alcohol between cuts. Plant disease-resistant varieties like sweet cherry 'Sam'; avoid 'Bing,' 'Lambert,' and 'Royal Ann.' Sprays are not completely effective. Dormant copper spray may help.
Black knot	On apricot, cherry, and plum, conspicuous long black swellings appear on smaller twigs; on larger branches, galls—hard, round knots—appear. These may girdle and kill branches beyond, or even the whole tree.	Prune out diseased wood in early spring, cutting at least 4 inches below the swelling. Apply lime sulfur while dormant, or captan during growing season. Remove or treat nearby wild cherry or plum.
Brown rot	Brown rot is a fungus that causes spots on peaches, nectarines, plums, apricots, cherries, and sometimes apples and pears. Spots spread, shriveling or mummifying the fruit completely. Brown rot causes blight on blossoms and twigs, and hastens rotting of harvested fruit.	Compost or bury all dropped fruit after harvest. Remove and destroy any mummies left in the tree before spring. Prune tree for maximum air circulation and spray penetration. Wash peaches with hot water or a chlorine solution as you pick them. For serious infestations, spray with captan, sulfur, or benomyl.
Fire blight	Growth on pear, some apple, and crab apple wilts, turns brown or black as though charred by fire, then hangs down. Cankers may develop. The disease can appear suddenly and spread quickly.	Plant resistant varieties with proper drainage and pH. Follow good cultural practices. Do not overfeed or overwater. Prune out and destroy blighted twigs well below infection. Disinfect tools if cutting during the growing season. Destroy old, diseased trees nearby. Plant apple and pear as far apart as you can.
Leaf spots	Well-defined spots develop on leaves of plum, apricot, cherry, nectarine, peach, and cane fruit. Spots spread and change colors, and the centers drop out. If disease infects fruit spurs, fruit will drop. Leaves may fall early, making the tree more susceptible to winter injury and less productive the next year.	Plant resistant varieties. Remove and destroy diseased leaves. Avoid excessive humidity or wetting of the foliage, especially late in the day when it will not dry before nightfall. Spray at fruitlet and leaf fall with ferbam, captan, Bordeaux, fixed copper, or lime sulfur.
Peach-leaf curl	Leaves of peach and nectarine curl and twist as though infected with blisters. Very common, but need not be serious.	Remove diseased leaves to compost. Fertilize trees with compost. Spray with fungicide before buds break in spring and later just after leaves fall. Or spray leaves with onion water at first sign of curl.
Powdery mildew	A white, dusty growth appears on the undersides, or both the tops and bottoms of leaves, and on new growth of apple, cherry, and sometimes pear. Leaves turn yellow and drop, stunting growth. Fruit may be stunted, shriveled, or cracked.	Prune out distorted or badly mildewed twigs as they are noticed. Plant resistant varieties like 'McIntosh' and 'Delicious.' Regular spray programs should provide control. For severe infestation, spray with lime sulfur, benomyl, or other fungicide.
Scab	Brown, corky patches first appear on leaves, then on fruit of apple and pear. Scab is especially prevalent in damp areas or seasons.	Rake leaves and provide good sanitation to keep disease from overwintering. Prune for good air circulation. Spray as needed—as often as every three days in wet springs—with captan, lime sulfur, or benomyl. Soak soil under tree with spray.
Verticillium wilt	Branches of all kinds of fruit die suddenly from bottom to top. Tree fruits show black sapwood under the bark. Bush fruits turn grayish blue, wilt, and die.	Avoid planting near or after susceptible plants like tomato, melon, and pepper. Remove infected plant parts, disinfecting tools with bleach after each cut; the rest of the plant usually will recover.

FRUIT AND NUT INSECTS

Insect	Description and Trouble Signs	Control
Aphids	Aphids are tiny greenish or reddish bugs that fix themselves to the bottoms of apple, pear, and plum leaves and suck plant juices. Leaves may curl. Aphids may produce a sticky honeydew that attracts ants and sometimes forms a black mold. Woolly apple aphids leave white, cottony puffs along twigs.	Spray with dormant oil in late winter, then a regular program of all-purpose spray through the season. For severe infestations, spray with malathion, carbaryl, or diazinon according to label directions. Encourage or import lacewings, ladybugs, or trichogamma wasps.
Cherry fruit flies	Cherry fruit fly larvae are the little yellowish worms found when pitting cherries. The adult is black and smaller than a housefly with four black bands on its wings.	Use a spray program advised by your county extension agent from bloom until 14 days before harvest. Or spray with diazinon or malathion at seven-day intervals as soon as you notice flies or maggots.
Coddling moths	Worms are about ¾ inch long. Adults are gray moths with brown patches on the tips of their front wings; they are ½ to ¾ inch wide with their wings spread. Infested apples and pears have holes from the side or blossom end to the core.	Scrape off all loose bark before spraying with dormant oil. Then apply a 2- to 4-inch band of Tanglefoot or petroleum jelly around the trunk to trap many of the remaining larvae. Do this with or without applying an all-purpose spray.
Japanese beetles	Insects are ½ inch long with copper-colored bodies and metallic-green wing covers. They chew large holes in the leaves of grape and raspberry, especially in sunny locations.	For a small infestation, remove by hand. Or use one of several kinds of beetle traps available. For severe problems, apply spores of *Bacillus popilliae*—milky spore disease—to surrounding soil areas. Or spray with malathion or carbaryl.
Peach-tree borers	Worms with brown heads and cream-colored bodies, about 1 inch long when mature, tunnel into the trunks of peach, nectarine, apricot, cherry, and plum. They can girdle or kill a tree, or weaken it, making it susceptible to other enemies. A thick, gummy substance forms at the entrance to the bored hole. A fine, sawdustlike substance comes from the holes.	Let gum remain because it seals the holes. Plant garlic around the trunk to repel borers. Tie a bar of strong soap into the tree's lowest crotch so rains can wash it down the trunk. Or treat in mid-September with a 20-percent solution of lindane, soaking the infested area and surrounding soil with at least a gallon for each mature tree, a half gallon for smaller trees. Inspect for holes in spring, then push in a flexible wire to kill worms, or cut them out with a knife.
San Jose scales	Disklike scales, about $1/12$ inch in diameter, encrust twigs and branches. When mature, legs emerge and crusty shells begin to crawl. They feed on foliage and fruit of apple, apricot, currant, gooseberry, peach, nectarine, pear, plum, and sweet cherry, causing small reddish spots. Can kill limbs or entire trees.	Coat all parts of tree thoroughly with dormant oil spray in early spring. Ladybugs and their larvae provide good control. If scales persist, spray with diazinon or malathion after crawlers hatch.
Spider mites	Spider mites turn leaves brown and create silvery webs on the undersides and in the leaf axils of apple, plum, pear, and other deciduous fruit. The tiny mites suck plant juices from the leaves. Foliage may look tarnished.	Spray with dormant oil in early spring. Mites thrive on dusty conditions. Spray with water at high pressure to remove them. For severe infestation, use diazinon or malathion.
Tent caterpillars	Hairy caterpillars emerge from large webs in branches to eat. Usually 20 or more leave each tent, and can nearly defoliate their branch.	Remove webbing in the evening when most worms are inside. Use a long stick with a rag on the end. If you like, soak the rag in kerosene. Kill and burn all the worms you can. (Do not burn tents in the trees, however.) Use sticky band on trunk (see control for coddling moths, above) to trap many more as they try to climb back. Using Tanglefoot or petroleum jelly on a regular basis may prevent infestations.

343

HOUSEPLANTS

Living, growing indoor plants add beauty to our rooms, oxygen and moisture to the air, and good feelings to our lives. For some gardeners, houseplants are the only garden; for others, the most carefully observed. And though each grower and home is unique, many indoor plants adapt easily to new surroundings, making the selection of just the right plants a pleasant and seldom-difficult task.

CARING FOR HOUSEPLANTS

I t isn't hard to have blooming orchids in a bay window, green foliage climbing the poles of room dividers or billowing from hanging planters, herbs on the kitchen windowsill, or hyacinths filling the room with fragrance and the feeling of spring.

Unfortunately, it also isn't hard to have wilting, dying, sad-looking failures.

Much as today's homes need plants, a house can be a hostile environment: low light, desertlike dryness, heat, drafts, and gardeners whose busy schedules lead to infrequent waterings compensated by overwatering.

The conditions you offer your houseplants often mean the difference between their success and failure.

THE RIGHT CONDITIONS

All houseplants require light, humidity (or lack of it), water, and food. The problem: What's great for one plant could be a killer for another. The secret: Find the right plants, put them in the right place, and give them the right care.

■ Light

Determining the right light is the first requirement for thriving houseplants. If you have few or north windows, try plants like ferns, Chinese evergreen, split-leaf philodendron, grape ivy, cast-iron plant, sansevieria, pothos, and parlor palm. Or try growing plants under artificial light (see pages 354–355).

Medium-light conditions are ideal for spider plant, dieffenbachia, dracaena, false aralia, rubber plant, fiddle-leaf fig, prayer plant, peperomia, philodendron, pilea, wandering Jew, zebra plant, Norfolk Island pine, and asparagus fern.

A south bay window, though too bright for African violets and foliage plants, is ideal for cactus, citrus, orchids, and most blooming plants such as azalea, hibiscus, and geranium.

For light guidelines, check plant labels, the window exposure of successful plants, and the "Foliage Plants Portfolio" and the "Flowering Plants Portfolio" on pages 356–373. If a plant doesn't thrive in one spot, try it elsewhere.

■ Humidity

Most plants need more humidity than usually is found in a home, especially when the furnace or air conditioner is running. You can ease this problem in several ways short of buying a whole-house humidifier.

Frequent misting of the plants will help. So will setting them on trays of pebbles kept wet (but don't let the pots themselves sit in water). Just grouping plants together helps, too, because they emit moisture.

During weather extremes, when the furnace or air conditioner runs nonstop, you might run a cool vaporizer or put a problem plant in a plastic bag. And be sure to make use of the places in your home with the highest humidity: the laundry, bathroom, and over the kitchen sink.

■ Water

Although the need for water is obvious, the solution is all too subtle. You can kill your plants with either neglect or kindness.

Mini spathiphyllum, now available in compact varieties only 14 inches tall, has foliage that survives in low light. However, for best bloom, give the plants bright light. Wash foliage often with soapy water to fend off pests.

Always use tepid water. Cold water can slow growth or injure roots. Softened water also is hard on plants. If your water is high in chlorine, let it sit a day uncovered before using it.

If you are uncertain of your ability to tell when a plant needs water, or if you're busy, consider buying or making pots that hold water in reserve for plants to use as needed (see page 349). Otherwise, just take a look at your plants' condition often, and use your finger to test the soil surface for moisture. Small pots may need water every day or two. Large ones may go a week between waterings. A hanging basket of petunias in the summer sun on your patio may need water twice a day. Check often; experience soon will tell you what to do.

The amount of water, fortunately, is easier to figure than the frequency. Add water until it drains through the hole in the bottom of the pot and shows in the saucer. This ensures that the entire root area receives a thorough soaking. The roots need air, too, so be sure to empty the saucer 20 minutes after watering.

■ Food
Feeding instructions may seem more confusing than those for watering, but they also are less critical. Buy a good, balanced houseplant fertilizer for most indoor plants, a specialized one if you have many African violets, orchids, bromeliads, or such.

Read the label carefully. The three numbers, such as 10–20–10, refer to the levels of nitrogen, phosphorus, and potassium. Nitrogen gives the plant lush foliage. Phosphorus keeps roots and stems strong and healthy. Potassium or potash encourages blooms.

Water the day before feeding. Fertilizers—most for houseplants come in solution form—can burn if the soil is dry. Getting the solution on the leaves will give them a good foliar feeding; avoid fertilizing the flowers, however, or it could result in spotting. Follow directions or give *less*. Never give more.

Plants need little feeding in the winter when they are almost dormant, more in the spring and summer when they are growing more actively.

For plants that have grown large, such as the rubber plant taking over the bedroom or the philodendron covering the window, give the minimum amount of food to purposely keep growth slow.

Do not feed seedlings until they have their first true leaves, and then use a diluted dose. Hold feeding of new or repotted plants for several weeks until they've had time to adjust to their new home. And remember, feeding is seldom the cure for a sick plant.

■ Bringing home a new plant
When you get a new plant, expect a few leaves to drop while it adjusts to the new surroundings. Try to keep the humidity high. You also may want to keep new arrivals isolated for a few weeks to make sure they are hiding no bugs or diseases that might spread.

Streptocarpus is a showy gesneriad that blooms for months. Also called cape primrose or Bavarian bells, its flowers can be white, pink, rose, blue, or purple. Always snip off dead blooms, stems, and leaves for more blooming power.

CONTAINERS AND REPOTTING

If a plant is thriving, assume it is happy in its pot. Most flowering houseplants, such as African violet and geranium, prefer to be somewhat pot-bound. Gloxinia and Christmas cactus have been known to bloom in the same pot for 20 years. Some plants, though, may need repotting right after you bring them home, especially if they are young and actively growing.

WHEN TO REPOT

Young seedlings and cuttings need repotting frequently for growth to continue unchecked. With an older plant, if you notice that its growth slows, it wilts too soon after watering, its lower leaves turn yellow, or new leaves stay small, it's time to look at the root ball.

First, be sure the soil is moist enough so it won't crumble. Then knock the plant out of the pot. Healthy white roots should be numerous around the outside of the root ball, but not crowded into a solid mass or winding round and round in a tangle. Repot if the roots have nowhere left to grow.

If you receive a gift planter with several plants crowded together, repot them soon so they will have room to spread naturally.

SOILS

You can buy potting soil or mix your own. For an all-purpose formula, use one part sand, one part humus, and two parts loamy soil. Sterilize any of the ingredients that could contain weed seeds, insects, or diseases by baking them in a 200-degree oven for 45 minutes. Purchased potting soils already are sterilized.

For succulents or African violets, add more sand or humus or buy special mixes. Orchids need a special soilless mixture such as fern bark or osmunda fiber. You'll find such mixtures where orchids are sold.

Many of the commercial potting soils are light and therefore better than homemade mixtures for use in large pots you might have to move.

Whatever you use, be sure the soil is neither powdery dry nor soggy. Store it in a closed plastic bag or container to keep out insects.

HOW TO REPOT

Select your new pot, usually ½ to 1 inch larger in diameter than the old one. Seedlings should go in 2-inch pots and cuttings in up to 4-inch pots, depending on the plant size. Lay out all your supplies on newspapers or a garbage bag.

CONTAINERS

■ Clay pots have been used for ages and work well because they let air in and moisture out. They come in many sizes and heights, including lovely hand-molded shapes. Always soak new clay pots overnight before using. Scrub old pots between plantings, or, if disease has been a problem, boil them.

■ Glazed or plastic pots stay clean more easily than clay pots. They also are cheaper, lighter, and come in more colors. Plants in glazed or plastic pots need fewer waterings, but because these pots let in less air, watering and feeding must be more exact.

■ All containers should have a drainage hole in the bottom. If you want to use decorative items like old crocks, put pots with drainage holes inside the crocks.

■ You also can use plastic buckets, milk cartons, window boxes, and such. Use a drill, hot ice pick, or knife to cut a drain hole, if needed.

REPOTTING A HOUSEPLANT

1 Put a crockery shard over the bottom hole to keep the soil in the pot. Large pots should have a layer of shards on the bottom.

2 To loosen the plant, put one hand over the soil and around the stem. Turn the pot over and rap it firmly against a hard surface.

3 Usually the soil and roots come out in a compact unit. If not, run a knife between the soil and pot to loosen.

4 Place the plant in the center of the pot with the base of the stem about ½ to 1 inch below the pot rim. This leaves room for watering.

Provide drainage, then partially fill the pot with soil. For large plants, you may want to carefully measure the amount of soil needed. Then gently turn the plant out of the old pot, keeping the root ball intact as much as possible unless it has become a snarl. If that's happened, loosen some of the roots around the edges and bottom; trim broken or soft and smelly roots.

Center the plant and fill in soil around the roots or the root ball. Use a stick if you need it to press the soil firmly into narrow spaces.

Water well from the top to settle the soil, filling any air spaces. Set the pot in a saucer to collect the water that should drain from the hole. After 20 minutes, dump any water in the saucer. Keep the plant from direct sunlight for several days until it recovers from the operation.

To make a pot that will give the plant water as it needs it, place a strip of old nylon stocking along the side and down through the hole in the bottom of the pot. Plant as usual. Then set the pot on a container of water—a plastic margarine tub works fine—with two holes in the lid. Extend the stocking into the reservoir through one hole. Add water through the other hole. The plant will take up a steady supply of moisture.

PROBLEM SOLVING

Simple little tricks not only can perk up houseplants with troubles, but also can make a big difference in the appearance of even the healthiest plants. Follow these tips to avoid—or remedy—houseplant problems.

■ **Protect plants**
Avoid subjecting your plants to high temperatures and drafts, warm or cold. Keep plants away from heat ducts; on bitter-cold nights, slip a piece of cardboard or some newspapers between leaves and icy windows. (In general, though, the cooler your house, the better. Turning down your thermostat before you go to bed will save money and houseplants.)

Plants such as cyclamen won't bloom and grow for long in a typical home, so enjoy them while they last and don't feel bad when they go.

■ **Turn pots**
Give your plants a quarter to half turn each week. (Some experts even say to turn them counterclockwise.) This will give your plants nice rounded shapes. Turning also lets you see the other sides of your plants and the shades and shapes of leaves and flowers.

■ **Rejuvenate plants**
Take pot in hand and remove the dead leaves that sneak under the lushest foliage. Give the pot a firm tap on a hard surface to settle the roots. Soak the pot in the sink for a half hour to dissolve the salts in the soil (soaking also will moisten the pores of a clay pot).

■ **Shape up your plants**
To give shape to plants like philodendron and ivy, wind the long, trailing branches up over the pot in a pleasing pattern, then pin them to the soil at several points with hairpins, bent pipe cleaners, or unbent paper clips. Do this every few months. The branches probably will root at these points, giving you a lusher-looking, bushier plant.

Some plants need to be trimmed into shape. Remember that taking off end growth encourages side branches, usually just below the cut.

FIRST AID FOR HOUSEPLANTS

Take a close look at any under-the-weather houseplant, and its symptoms often will tell you what's wrong. Here's a list of common maladies and their solutions.

Symptom	Cause	Remedy
Leaves brown on tips; lower ones yellow, then fall. Stems mushy or soft. Buds drop. Soil soggy.	Too much water.	Let soil dry before watering again. Provide drainage. Don't let pot sit in water. Repot if necessary.
Leaves brown on tips; lower ones brown, then die. Buds drop. Soil hard.	Not enough water.	Immerse whole pot in water for a half hour. Let excess drain away. Water more often.
Leaves fade, have yellow or brown spots or edges. Cactus pales.	Too much light.	Move plant. Use curtains to filter the light. If using artificial light, move farther from source.
Long, spindly stems, weak or pale growth, new leaves undersized.	Too little light.	Move plant to brighter spot. Add some artificial light, if needed.
Quick, weak growth, spindly and streaked with yellow. Crust on pots.	Too much fertilizer.	Flush out soil by watering several times an hour with tepid water. Cut down on feeding.
Yellow leaves, green veins. New growth weak and droopy.	Too little fertilizer.	Feed. Set feeding schedule based on plant's needs and size, and the season.
Leaf edges curl under, turn crispy and brown.	Air too dry, too hot, or both.	Add humidity, mist, or move plant to cooler spot—often nearer the window.
Buds and flowers do not form.	Wrong day length. (Poinsettias and certain plants need short days.)	Move to room that is dark at night or cover each evening to keep out light.

HOUSEPLANT BEAUTY TIPS

(Left) To clean the dust from large, smooth-leaved plants, hold one hand under a leaf and wipe gently with a rag in the other.

(Right) Use a dry cotton swab, pipe cleaner, or watercolor brush to softly clean hairy-leaved plants, such as African violet and gloxinia.

(Left) Encourage thicker, bushier plants by pinching new growth at the tips. Energy then goes to the side branches.

(Right) Prune an indoor tree to give it a pleasing and sturdy shape. Always cut away any dead or broken branches.

■ Keep your plants clean

Help your plants breathe by cleaning their leaves. You can clean many plants quickly under the shower if you have unsoftened water. Wrap plastic bags around the bases to keep the soil in the pots, then wash with lukewarm water at medium force. Let the plants drip-dry. If chemical residue in the water leaves white spots, wipe the spots away with a clean, soft cloth.

If the weather is warm, set plants outdoors in the rain. Shower large plants with a spray bottle.

You can give your plants that florist shine with special sprays or liquids, or with a cloth dipped in milk. But try not to get any of these solutions on the leaf undersides. You might clog the stomata, which leaves breathe through.

■ Control insects

Watch closely for insects and wash them away with soapy water. Vigilance is the best cure for insect problems. If you use sprays, put the plants in plastic bags to concentrate the effect. Higher humidity also eases plant stress. Systemic insecticides go into the soil and up through the roots to the entire plant to kill insects.

PLANT PROPAGATION

Watching seeds sprout is fascinating. But taking a piece of a plant and causing new roots to grow seems almost magical. A stem cutting can root into a new, sizable plant in as little as two weeks.

PROPAGATION METHODS

Depending on the plant, choose from among the following propagation methods: seeds, root divisions, runners and offsets, cuttings (leaf, stem, or root), and air layering. All but seeding are asexual or vegetative forms of propagation that will give you a new plant exactly like the old one.

Use pots, flats, jars, or terrariums to start cuttings. Choose a container that's deep enough for roots to develop and one that makes it possible to enclose the plant to keep the humidity high. One way to do this is to turn over a clear plastic bag, brace it on sticks, then pull it down over the rim of the pot.

■ The right medium
Some plants will root right in plain soil or water, but the best medium is sterile. The medium you choose also must hold the plants upright and hold both air and moisture around the roots. Vermiculite or perlite works well. So does a mixture of half coarse sand and half peat moss. Or substitute perlite for the sand.

Fill your container, water well, and press the medium down firmly, leveling it off within an inch of the top.

■ Cuttings
The most common method of propagating houseplants is with stem or leaf cuttings.

Make stem cuttings of coleus, geranium, begonia, ivy, hoya, philodendron, pilea, Swedish ivy, and such.

With a clean, sharp knife, cut a shoot 4 to 6 inches long from a healthy tip of the original plant. For the good of the parent plant, cut just above a leaf joint. Then make another clean, slanting cut just below the next leaf joint up the shoot. Remove the bottom leaf or leaves so they won't rot beneath the medium. Also remove any flower buds or blossoms so the shoot will not waste its strength on flowering.

Now use a knife to make a row in the medium. Plant each cutting an inch deep or more, pressing the medium firmly around it with your fingers. Water gently. The stems will take two to four weeks to root. Give them light, but not direct sunlight, during this time. For maximum humidity, cover with a plastic bag. You also may want to mist the stems the first few days.

To check for new roots, pull gently on one cutting. If it does not pull out, carefully dig up the cuttings and plant in regular soil.

Leaf cuttings, like a single leaf of African violet or a leaf section of snake plant, should receive the same basic treatment, but may take several weeks or more to form new plantlets at the base.

You also can propagate plants like philodendron, pothos, wax plant, and dracaena from pieces of stem or cane that contain a leaf bud.

■ Air layering
To tame ceiling-touching indoor rubber plants and dracaenas, try air layering.

Pick a stem and make a cut about 6 to 12 inches long and ½ inch deep into the stem where you want the new plant's roots to form. Insert a matchstick to keep this wound open. Then split a water-swollen peat pellet in half and cup it over the wound (or use damp peat moss). Wrap with plastic, binding above and below the cut to hold moisture.

Roots will form in several months. Then cut off the new plant and pot it up gently.

■ Seeds
Coleus, Christmas cherry, gloxinia, cineraria, herbs, palms, and asparagus fern all start well from seed.

Sow seeds in a fine medium; cover the seeds to the same depth as their thickness. Then cover with plastic until the seeds germinate. This method is much slower than propagating from cuttings, and the seedlings can vary in flower or leaf color.

PROPAGATING HOUSEPLANTS

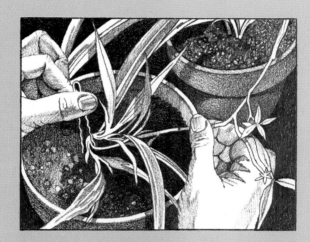

(Left) To split one plant into two or more, pull gently on the roots, pry them apart, or, if necessary, use a sharp knife to cut them. Then repot each root division.

(Right) To root plantlets, firm them into a small pot of planting medium, before or after cutting the connecting stem.

(Left) To restart an old, long-stemmed giant, air-layer the woody stem, then place in a peat moss ball. When roots form, cut the stem just below the root ball, then plant.

(Right) To propagate dieffenbachia, cut the stem and root in water. Or section the cane; place in a pot of medium.

(Left) Some leaves will root in water. Transplant the new plant to medium as soon as roots form, before they grow brittle.

(Right) To curtail rot and help roots form more quickly and surely, you can, if you like, dip the leaf ends into a root-inducing hormone.

GROWING UNDER LIGHTS

To assure that your plants get the right light, you could take two of the same plant, put one in a sunny spot, the other on a dark coffee table, and switch them weekly. Or you could move all your plants daily for a few sunny hours. But much easier and more successful is growing them under artificial light.

HOW TO BEGIN

Your first step may be snuggling your plants up to the lights you already have and watching how well they grow. Once you see how seedlings respond to even a little desk lamp, or how violets bloom on the shelf closest to your light over the sink, you will know better how much to invest in lighting.

When selecting lights, keep in mind that light is made up of wavelengths that we see as colors, and that some lights are stronger in some colors than in others. White light, for example, carries all the colors of the rainbow; reading light, on the other hand, is mostly green and yellow—two colors plants don't use.

For foliage, plants need cool blue and violet tones; to bloom, they need warm red and orange. Therefore, use only cool light on foliage plants, cool and warm on flowering ones.

The ideal setup includes both fluorescent and incandescent bulbs, but this can get complicated for the average indoor gardener. In addition, incandescent bulbs can do more harm than good because they produce a lot of heat.

Grow-light tubes combine the benefits of both bulb types. They emit very few of the unneeded light wavelengths, so they appear less bright. And they're available with either a pinkish or bluish glow.

ARTIFICIAL-LIGHT BASICS

Plant Type	These Do Well	Light Needed	Comments
Foliage plants	Pilea, peperomia, coleus, grape ivy, philodendron, Swedish ivy, aluminum plant, spider plant	14 to 16 hours of light per day; place 6 to 12 inches below fluorescent lights.	If using incandescent light, keep plants 1½ to 2 feet below lights.
Flowering plants	Cyclamen, mums, calceolaria, gloxinia, geranium, and begonia	12 to 16 hours per day. Place florists' plants 6 to 10 inches below lights; geraniums, 6 to 8; begonias, 6 to 12.	Experiment with height and place of geraniums and begonias to find what works.
Ferns	Asparagus, pteris species, and nephrolepis species	14 to 16 hours of light a day; place 8 to 12 inches below lights.	Be careful foliage doesn't burn under lights.
Cacti and other succulents	Echeveria, haworthia, agave, aloe, kalanchoe, sedum, euphorbia, and sansevieria	About 16 hours of light per day. Keep succulents within 6 inches of light; desert cactus, 4 inches.	In fall, slowly reduce to 12 hours a day to induce bloom on plants such as kalanchoe and holiday cactus.
Gesneriads such as African violet and achimenes	All respond beautifully under lights.	14 to 16 hours of light per day; place 4 to 10 inches from light depending on kind.	Gesneriads are probably the most popular plants for grow-light cultivation.
Orchids	Epidendrum, florist orchid, dancing-lady, moth orchid, lady-slipper, coelogyne	Start with 14 hours a day. First group should be 3 inches from lights, second up to 12 inches.	Orchids need higher light intensity, warm or grow-light bulbs. They take months to adjust, but then do well.

For peak efficiency, buy tubes at least 3 feet long. The fixtures are inexpensive and cost only pennies a day to run. Reflect light back on the plants by painting the area with white latex paint, setting pots on trays of perlite, or using aluminum foil.

■ How much light?
Provide too much light and your plants will grow stubby with yellow or very dark green leaves; offer too little and they will get leggy and flower poorly. To adjust light intensity, raise or lower the lights or individual pots.

As a rule, flowering plants need higher light intensity than foliage plants. Place the tops of foliage plants no more than 15 inches from the bulbs, flowering plants 10 inches or closer, seedlings within 3 inches. See what works best. Also, turn and rearrange your plants as needed.

■ How many hours in a day?
Darkness is important for plant growth, so give your plants at least six hours of total darkness a day. Try to operate the lights at the same time every day. An automatic timer will save you a lot of time turning lights on and off.

With lights, you can grow plants anywhere. And many plants gain a richer, darker color and more and brighter blooms. Keep tubes and reflectors clean, and replace tubes yearly. Watch plants on top; they will be warmer and might dry out faster.

FOLIAGE PLANTS PORTFOLIO

AIRPLANE PLANT

ASPIDISTRA

ALOE

Also called burn plant
Aloe species

Aloe is a succulent that thrives in hot, dry conditions. This attractive houseplant also is an ever-handy first-aid kit. Pluck a leaf, peel away the skin and spines, and use the fluid to treat burns, mosquito bites, diaper rash, and all sorts of minor skin irritations.

■ **Light:** Place in bright south windows for best results, although plant will tolerate moderate light. Outside in summer, plant in some shade or move into the sun gradually.

■ **Water:** Allow to dry between waterings. Offer even less water in winter.

■ **Comments:** Increase plants with offsets. Aloe makes a fine gift, especially to new mothers. It blooms if the light is bright enough long enough, but seldom indoors.

ARALIA

Dizygotheca or *polyscias* species

Lacy *Dizygotheca elegantissima,* or false aralia or thread leaf, is an indoor shrub that grows slowly to 5 feet and has delicate, dark green to almost reddish brown leaves arranged like fingers in a fan shape. The polyscias species, including balfour or Chinese aralia, are small outdoor trees with the erect growth habit of false aralia but wider leaves. These trees are dark green with three round leaflets 2 to 4 inches across. Some varieties are variegated and slightly cupped.

■ **Light:** Provide false aralia with bright indirect light. It will thrive for years with only artificial overhead light. A summer outdoors under a tree does it good. (Be sure to stake it to protect it from the wind.) For balfour aralia, provide bright light indoors, filtered shade outside. It does well, too, with artificial light.

■ **Water:** Water false aralia thoroughly and keep soil evenly moist. For balfour aralia, keep soil barely but evenly moist, with good drainage and extra humidity.

■ **Comments:** Use standard potting soil mix for both types. Feed false aralia lightly every

two weeks during active growth period. For a dramatic presentation, buy several small false aralias and grow for a year, then repot to a single large container. Propagate both types by stem cuttings or root divisions.

AIRPLANE PLANT

Also called spider plant
Chlorophytum comosum

Popular and dependable, airplane plant has long, thin, arching leaves of dark green, often with one or more white stripes down the middle. The stems grow out, produce little white flowers, then are soon weighted down with plantlets. A shelf or hanging basket shows airplane plant at its best.

■ **Light:** Place in bright light, although plant will grow slowly even in a north window. Outdoors, provide shade and wind protection.

■ **Water:** Let soil dry, then water generously.

■ **Comments:** Offer a feeding of diluted fish emulsion once a month to encourage longer leaves and more offspring. Runners root easily in soil or water before or after separation. Do not feed the runners until they become established. Use standard potting mix. Lack of humidity causes tips to brown. When this happens, just cut them off. Repot when the plant becomes root-bound.

ASPIDISTRA

Also called barroom plant or cast-iron plant
Aspidistra elatior

Aspidistra elatior has long, tapered, dark green or variegated leaves that arise on stems from a crown.

■ **Light:** Place near window out of direct sun for most luxuriant look, although plant will survive in dark corners. Barroom or cast-iron plant is ideal for dim apartments or offices.

■ **Water:** Let dry between soakings. Overwatering causes more problems than neglect.

■ **Comments:** Place in areas with temperatures from 45 to 85 degrees. The solid green varieties prefer rich soil. Variegated varieties will revert to all green in rich soil. Too much sun will yellow leaves. White spots with brown margins are caused by a fungus; remove and burn the affected leaves. If scale insects appear (white males; brown, oyster-shaped females), wash them off with soapy water. Trim off brown leaf tips. Propagate by cutting root ball apart with a sharp knife.

AVOCADO

Also called alligator pear
Persea americana

Avocado is an almost-cost-free houseplant because it is easy to grow from the pits of the fruit. When the plant gets six leaves, cut it back to two. Also pinch branch tips as they form to keep plants from getting too tall and skinny.

■ **Light:** Place in bright to indirect sun. Grows in full sun outdoors in subtropics.

■ **Water:** Let dry between waterings. Good drainage should prevent root rot.

■ **Comments:** To start, select the ripest fruit. Remove the pit, wash away any remaining fruit, then let the pit sit in a warm spot overnight to make it easier for you to peel the skin. After peeling the skin, insert three toothpicks around the fattest part of the pit. Then rest the picks on the edge of a jar so that water just covers the flat-bottom end where the roots will form. Pot up when rooted.

Or slice a dime-thin sliver from the top and bottom of the pit with a razor blade; throw away the slivers and plant the seed in a 6-inch pot of fairly rich soil. Leave a third of the seed, the pointy end, above the soil line.

The seed will split as a tiny stem arises—in four to eight weeks, soonest at 85 degrees. Keep the seed out of direct sunlight until growth starts.

BABY'S-TEARS

Also called Japanese moss or Irish moss
Helxine soleiroli or *Soleirolia soleiroli*

Baby's-tears is an ideal ground cover in terrariums. Its slender, horizontal stems, crowded with tiny round leaves, won't grow far over the edge of a pot because they must have contact with the soil.

■ **Light:** Place in bright indirect light.

■ **Water:** Provide even moisture and high humidity.

■ **Comments:** Combine baby's-tears only with plants that are fairly thirsty. The leaves resent wetting, and the plant is sensitive to cooking or heating gas. Prefers soil high in humus. Propagate by division.

English babytears or bead plant, *Nertera granadensis,* is much like true baby's-tears, but the leaves are a bit larger and a waxy green. Requirements are essentially the same, but English babytears may be a shade easier to grow than baby's-tears.

BANANA PLANT

Musa acuminata or *M. nana 'cavendishi'*

Growing to 6 feet indoors, banana plant is an interesting plant even without fruit. Production is possible but don't get your hopes up.

■ **Light:** Place in bright indirect light or sunny spots. Grows in full sun where hardy outdoors.

■ **Water:** Keep evenly moist. The leaves will fold down from the center rib and turn brown when plants are thirsty.

■ **Comments:** Protect the large, light green leaves from the wind. Banana plants are heavy feeders and lusty drinkers. Place them in rich, porous soil and feed a liquid fertilizer every other month from March to September. Summer the plants, which are pest free, outside if you can.

Use a knife or scissors to trim away damaged leaves. When the stem deteriorates—after several years or one bearing, whichever comes first—cut it away for your compost pile and let one of the many babies take over. To divide and repot the suckers that form underground at the base, dig down carefully, separate sprouts and roots, and pot up the new plant.

AVOCADO

BANANA PLANT

FOLIAGE PLANTS PORTFOLIO *(continued)*

CALADIUM

COLEUS

CROTON

CALADIUM

Caladium species

The plants in the caladium species offer a wide choice of spectacular color in intricately marked leaves of white, pink, red, green, silver, and combinations of each. Remove their insignificant blooms.

■ **Light:** Indoors, place in bright indirect light; outdoors, shade. Hot sun can scorch the leaves.

■ **Water:** Water when the soil surface is dry. With drainage, and when in full leaf, caladiums can drink a lot. They like heat and humidity.

■ **Comments:** Start the bulbs indoors in April in trays of vermiculite with bottom heat. Repot as they grow. Put outdoors only after the ground is warm and the danger of frost passes. Lift bulbs and bring in for winter or let pots go bone-dry for two months. Acid soil gives deepest colors. Propagate by bulb divisions.

CHINESE EVERGREEN

Also called Chinese waterplant
Aglaonema species

Chinese evergreen is very adaptable. Some varieties grow 15 to 24 inches tall and are suitable for terrariums. Others grow 3 feet tall. Lance-shaped leaves grow on long, thick stalks. Variegated kinds are just as easy to grow but may require more light for best dappling.

■ **Light:** Place in north windows or near the center of rooms.

■ **Water:** Keep evenly moist. Plant can grow in water alone. Add charcoal to keep water clear; add soluble fertilizer occasionally after changing the water completely.

■ **Comments:** Use any all-purpose soil mixture. Propagate by root division or by stem cuttings. Will tolerate heat and low humidity.

COLEUS

Also called painted nettle
Coleus species

Coleus grows easily. Its velvety leaves come in combinations of reds, greens, yellows, bronze, and chartreuse; its leaf edges may be scalloped or ruffled. New dwarf varieties are compact.

■ **Light:** Provide bright or indirect light indoors, sun or shade outside. Good on the north or east side of buildings. Lack of light dulls colors and causes leaves to drop.

■ **Water:** Keep evenly moist for lush growth. Leaves will wilt if thirsty, revive with water or evening dew.

■ **Comments:** Remove spikes of purple flowers and pinch as needed for bushy growth. Use a standard soil mix. Feed once a month during the growing season.

Replace old plants with new cuttings once a year or start from seeds for new colors. Plants will root in water.

If mealybugs appear, treat plant with soapy water or replace. Avoid insect bombs, which can harm the plant.

CORDYLINE

Also called ti, good-luck plant, or dracaena 'tricolor'
Cordyline terminalis hybrids

Cordyline is closely related and similar to dracaena in needs. Lancelike leaves are flushed with cream, red, or purple on green. *C. australis* 'purpurea' has purplish bronze, yuccalike foliage. For growth tips, see Dracaena, opposite.

CROTON

Codiaeum species

Crotons are fussy about drafts, dryness, full sun, and cold, and protest any of these conditions by dropping their leaves. But if conditions are right, their long, waxy leaves are spectacular, with bright colors, patterns, and blotches of yellow, pink, red, and bronze.

■ **Light:** Provide strong light at least four hours a day, or the leaves will revert to green. Colors return with a summer outdoors, but harden the plant carefully both going out in summer and coming back in the fall.

■ **Water:** Keep soil evenly moist but not soggy. Mist daily to provide lots of humidity.

■ **Comments:** Use a rich potting mixture with good drainage. Feed every other month from early spring through midsummer. Multiply by stem cuttings, or air-layer in spring or summer.

DIEFFENBACHIA

Also called dumb cane
Dieffenbachia species

Dumb cane gets its name from the fact that its sap can cause swelling of the tongue and vocal cords and a loss of voice. The sap is not really harmful, but avoid putting your fingers near your mouth or eyes after handling.

This evergreen grows vertically 6 feet or more with a thick trunk and large, patterned 1½-foot leaves that arch gracefully. Of the smaller varieties, 'Rudolph Roehrs' has oval leaves of chartreuse marked with ivory.
■ **Light:** Offer north, east, or west light with no more than two hours of daily sun. Plant tolerates a wide range of light, but full sun can yellow its foliage.
■ **Water:** Let the soil dry on the surface between waterings, but don't wait too long or the leaves will discolor and droop. Occasionally, immerse the whole pot or move the plant to a steamy bathroom. If the plant is large, place it on a platform with casters to make the move easier and less dangerous.
■ **Comments:** This tropical native likes heat. Use standard potting mix and feed monthly in spring and summer. Expect lower leaves to die. When the leggy stem becomes unsightly, air-layer or take a cutting of the top. Dieffenbachia will root in water. A new stem will sprout on the stub, so cut to the height you want.

DRACAENA

Dracaena species

The plants of the dracaena species vary in appearance but all are easy to grow and similar in habit. Corn plant has leaves that resemble corn leaves, only thicker and darker green with stripes. Stalks will grow very tall, often woody and bare, with a cluster of leaves at the end.

D. deremensis 'Warnecki' is rugged and adapts well to unfavorable conditions. Gold-dust dracaena, or 'Florida Beauty,' is compact and bushy, seldom exceeding 1½ feet. Its oval leaves are dusted with yellow and cream and it is more exacting than other dracaena types.

Dragon tree has stiffer, sword-shaped, gray-green leaves that sometimes turn red or white at the edges in sunlight. Its stems may veer in interesting directions.
■ **Light:** Place in east windows or out of direct sun in south or west exposures. Leaf edges will develop brown spot in too much sun. With only artificial light, plants grow more slowly.
■ **Water:** Keep soil just moist to the touch. Lower leaves may drop if plant gets too dry. Too much or too little water will cause browning of the tips. Trim them off with scissors. Syringe the foliage to keep it shiny clean.
■ **Comments:** Strip lower leaves for accent. Use a loose, humus-rich soil mix with good drainage. Feed every three months year-round. Usually pest free, but watch for mealybugs or scales; if present, treat plant with insecticidal soap.

Plant three in a tub with leaf tops at different heights for dramatic effect. Propagate from tip cuttings or pieces of stem with buds, or by air-layering. New growth will sprout from stub.

FATSIA

Fatsia japonica or *Aralia sieboldi*

Fatsia has shiny green leaves with an exaggerated maple shape. It grows 5 feet tall indoors; for summering outdoors, plant it alone in a tub.
■ **Light:** Place in bright sunny or indirect light indoors, full or filtered shade outside. Too much sun causes yellow leaves.
■ **Water:** Keep evenly moist.
■ **Comments:** Pinch back if you want a bushy plant. Otherwise, expect long, gracefully curving trunks. Fatsia has small white flowers followed by black fruit. Root from stem cuttings.

DIEFFENBACHIA

DRACAENA

FATSIA

FOLIAGE PLANTS PORTFOLIO *(continued)*

BOSTON FERN

MAIDENHAIR FERN

FERNS

"Ferns" applies to a class of plants with about 6,000 species in 150 different families. Most grow in the wild on the moist floor of the forest. Some are epiphytes growing like orchids in tall trees, some are vines that climb trees, and some stand in water. They are among the oldest-known plants on Earth and were probably dominant in the time of the dinosaurs.

In Victorian times, ferns were the most popular houseplants. They faded from the scene, however, because they couldn't stand the fumes from the gas and coal used to heat homes. Now that we have those problems pretty well licked, ferns are returning to our homes in hanging baskets, wall brackets, and green groupings. Their diverse forms make them fascinating.

■ **Light:** Place in bright light indoors but not direct sun. Ferns grow in nature where light intensity is low. Boston fern can take a little early morning sun, but it is unnecessary. Never expose variegated pteris ferns to the sun, just bright light.

■ **Water:** Provide an even moisture supply, with a little less water during dark winter days. On sunny days, mist foliage early in the morning. Skip dark days, and don't mist so late that the foliage remains wet overnight. This could lead to fungus, which is generally incurable.

Yellowing, other than that of natural aging or disease, indicates excess moisture or poor drainage. Use about an inch of clay chips in the bottoms of fern pots. For added humidity, which is the key to success with ferns, group the pots on trays of pebbles, use a humidifier, or turn down the thermostat. Never, though, let a pot stand in water.

■ **Comments:** Grow ferns in a peat-rich, porous soil mix or a soilless mix such as osmunda fiber or peat with some sand. Avoid touching new fronds. Also avoid drafts and overwatering. Feed ferns with care once every six months using a slow-release formula high in nitrogen. Always water before feeding. Summer ferns outside only if you harden them carefully; provide filtered light and shelter them from winds.

Watch for thrips or red spiders and for fern scales—small sucking plant mites with shell-like coverings. Male scales are white; females are brown. Pick off if only a few scales are present, then treat the plant with soap and rinse. For a large infestation, destroy the plant before the pests spread.

Propagate ferns any time of year by dividing roots, separating plantlets, or planting spores (the dusty seedlike particles from the undersides of the leaves). Sow the spores on a firm surface of moist peat. Cover with glass or plastic. Germination requires one to six months of good light at 65- to 70-degree temperatures.

Asparagus fern or *Asparagus sprengeri* often is used in spring planters, usually remaining as the sole survivor after the annuals bloom themselves to death. This fern—noted for its dainty, trailing fronds of short, light green, needlelike foliage—will bloom, sometimes after several seasons, with delicate pink flowers followed by red berries. It's easy to grow, but is a heavy feeder. Cut back ragged fronds to keep plants looking dainty.

Bird's-nest fern or *Asplenium nidus* is easy to grow. Its bold, broad chartreuse leaves uncurl from the center of the plant rosette and extend to 3 feet, though 1½ feet is more common.

Boston fern or *Nephrolepis exaltata 'bostoniensis'* is the most popular of ferns and comes in many forms. Its leaves vary from 8 inches to 5 feet. Whitman, curly, and crested ferns are mutations of the Boston, which itself comes from the sword fern. New strains are creating new interest.

Bear's-paw, hare's-foot and false hare's-foot, rabbit's-foot, and squirrel-foot ferns (several species) have creeping, brown, furlike rhizomes that grow over the soil surface and edge of the pot or hanging basket for added interest. Growth is easy. To start, break off a foot and pot it separately.

Brake fern (pteris species) has pale to dark green ribbonlike, forking fronds. Ribbon brake has a white line through each leaf segment. 'Riverton' is ruffled and lobed. Some have tasseled tips or are banded with a silver stripe. Brake ferns do well under artificial lights and are sometimes called table ferns. Too much moisture causes the fronds to turn black and rot off.

Hawaiian tree fern or *Cibotium chamissoi* needs plenty of room and is best placed on a high pedestal so you can see the fronds from underneath. Water the trunk twice daily to always keep it wet.

Holly fern or *Cyrtomium falcatum* has toothed, dark green leaflet fronds that look like holly. Holly fern will tolerate less humidity and more warmth and cold than most ferns.

Holly fern (tsusima) or *Polystichum tsusimense* also is called Christmas or hedge fern. Tsusima holly fern is quite different from holly fern, with much daintier and more finely divided leaflets. The tough fronds will grow to 2 feet long. This fern is excellent in hanging baskets, but can be kept small enough for some terrariums or dish gardens. Moisture control is critical because roots rot quickly if oversoaked. Plantlets develop on mature fronds.

Maidenhair fern or *Adiantum cuneatum* is more difficult to grow than many ferns. It has an intricate pattern of little hand-shaped leaflets. Its individual fronds start to yellow in six to nine months. It likes cool temperatures, less than 65 degrees, and plenty of humidity. Peat-rich or soilless mixes are best.

Staghorn fern (platycerium species) is perhaps the most amazing of ferns because of its large antler-shaped fronds that grow from a paperlike base. It usually is grown vertically on a ball of spaghnum on a board or bark support. Water by immersing the support and the base of the plant in water twice a week. Mist early on sunny days.

FICUS

Ficus species

Like ferns, the plants of the ficus family are variable, and all are interesting and useful houseplants.

■ **Light:** Place all figs in bright indirect sun. Full sun through glass can burn them.

■ **Water:** Water well when the soil surface dries. As plants grow, be sure water reaches the bottom of the pot but does not gather and sit.

■ **Comments:** Use a general all-purpose potting soil lightened with a little sand or perlite. Feed three or four times a year unless the plant is growing too fast. Keep the leaves dusted and add a little Volck (dormant oil spray) to soapy water to give gloss and ward off scales. Pinch if you want branching. Propagate with tip cuttings in water or media, or air-layer leggy plants.

Celeste and **brown turkey figs** are the edible forms. They drop their hand-shaped leaves in the winter but still have fascinating forms. In sight or stashed, they need a light watering on occasion. Add a bit of dolomitic lime once a year to sweeten the soil. The flowers are inside the fruit. Prune when dormant to maintain shape. Start with nursery-grown rootstock rather than seedlings.

Creeping or **climbing fig** is a small-leaved woody vine with aerial roots. It is good for terrariums or for peeking over the edges of pots or hanging baskets. It is especially lovely on stone or brick walls.

Fiddle-leaf fig is a near relative of the rubber plant but its leaves are shaped somewhat like violins with wavy margins. It can grow 6 to 15 feet tall and is both dramatic and durable.

Rubber plant is quite well known: large, shiny, oval leaves; red stems and underveining; and new leaves that are red as they unfurl. Rubber plant defies neglect and lack of light and bleeds a milky sap when wounded.

Weeping fig or *Ficus benjamina* is the most elegant of the family. It is the most common indoor tree and has small, waxy, pointed leaves along slightly drooping branches. Its shredding papery bark is almost like birch. New leaves are a delicate apple green.

Weeping fig is more expensive and less adaptable than other figs, but still well worth trying. Buy it in summer to minimize the shock of moving; if it sheds many leaves, find a better spot.

FIDDLE-LEAF FIG

RUBBER PLANT

FOLIAGE PLANTS PORTFOLIO *(continued)*

ENGLISH IVY

SWEDISH IVY

JADE PLANT

FITTONIA

Also called nerve plant
Fittonia verschaffelti

Fittonia is a low creeper with unique markings. Its dark shiny, oval leaves have veins of white, pink, or red. When flowers appear, they grow erect as white spikes.
■ **Light:** Grow in a north window or back from the sun in other exposures.
■ **Water:** Keep evenly moist, not soggy. Leaves droop quickly when dry. Fittonia likes humidity and is striking in terrariums.
■ **Comments:** Use standard soil mix with added organic matter. Feed lightly once or twice a year. Prune as needed and multiply by stem cuttings, preferably in spring.

IVY, ENGLISH

Hedera helix

English ivy is a hardy ground cover turned houseplant. You can train plants on supports for special shapes or to surround windows. Several named varieties offer a choice of leaf shapes, sizes, variegations, textures, and habit.
■ **Light:** Offer filtered light or a north window.
■ **Water:** Keep evenly moist but also well drained, and a bit drier in the winter.
■ **Comments:** Place in cool spots. The one major enemy of ivies is the spider mite. If a plant seems to sulk and its leaves look tarnished, hold a piece of white paper under the leaves and tap. If present, the mites—hardly more than tiny crawling specks but devastating to the plant—will show up on the paper. Shower or mist both sides of leaves weekly, or use insecticidal soap or a systemic insecticide on affected plants. Ivy roots easily in water.

IVY, GERMAN, GRAPE, SWEDISH

German, grape, and Swedish ivy belong to different genera but have the same growing habit as English ivy (see above). Swedish ivy has round crinkled leaves and German ivy has smooth, thin, bright green, ivy-shaped leaves.

Grape ivy has tendrils and three green leaflets with rust-colored undersides. Swedish prefers more light, and both it and the German are easier to grow in warm houses. Use a good all-purpose soil mix.

JADE PLANT

Crassula argentea

Jade plant is a popular succulent with jade-colored, round, fleshy leaves. It easily grows 3 feet or taller. Mature plants may have fragrant clusters of tiny pink or white flowers in the fall if you summer them outdoors, but ease them into the sun and back inside in steps.
■ **Light:** Place in direct sunlight.
■ **Water:** Watch overwatering. Let the soil dry between waterings. You may go even two weeks between waterings.
■ **Comments:** Repot using any soil. Plants usually live for years, even when root-bound. Don't feed plants except lightly in summer, or they may grow too fast. Prune if you wish for a more treelike shape. Leaves or tip cuttings root easily. Let them lie exposed for a week to form a callus before inserting in sand or perlite.

MARANTA

Also called prayer plant
Maranta leuconeura

Prayer plant gets its name from the fact that at night its leaves fold together. The oval leaves have intricate texture and color and the plant has a low spreading habit. As a rain-forest native, prayer plant likes water and humidity. Leaf edges brown otherwise.
■ **Light:** Place in medium to low light. Avoid all but cool morning sun. Lower light will intensify the plant's colors.
■ **Water:** Keep evenly moist and mist daily. Use tepid water. Leave slightly drier in winter.
■ **Comments:** Use a peat-rich soil mix and feed lightly only during the summer, not more than once a month. In January, trim back the older leaves or cut stems back to the soil. Calathea, a close cousin, is good in terrariums.

NEPHTHYTIS

Also called arrowhead plant, trileaf wonder, or African evergreen

Syngonium podophyllum

Nephthytis is a familiar and easy plant with thin, arrow-shaped, and richly mottled leaves, about 6 inches long. The plant doesn't hang but will climb as directed, even around odd shapes.

■ **Light:** Provide medium light, although plant is fairly tolerant.

■ **Water:** Keep evenly moist.

■ **Comments:** Protect from drafts, sudden temperature changes, direct sunlight, and over-watering. To maintain size, take cuttings with attached aerial roots often or divide.

NORFOLK ISLAND PINE

Also called star pine

Araucaria species

Norfolk Island pine, the ideal indoor ever-green, is adapted from a tropical giant. Its soft, short needles appear on horizontal branches from the trunk at yearly intervals in tiers of six.

■ **Light:** Place in medium light but not direct sunlight indoors or out. If the light is too low, too much space will develop between tiers.

■ **Water:** Allow to dry between waterings. Plants will tolerate generous watering if drainage is excellent.

■ **Comments:** Decorate these easy plants as Christmas trees, but avoid heavy or hot bulbs. Norfolk Island pine is ideal for the person who is away all day because it prefers cool rooms. Repot every two or three years and top-dress every March. Feed no more than once a month during spring and summer. If needles turn brown, cut off affected branches flush with the trunk. Side cuttings will give a one-sided plant. If the plant gets leggy, cut off the entire top and root it.

PALMS

Palms are dramatic plants that create a lush tropical atmosphere and are easy to grow if you give them what they need. Several varieties are well suited to containers indoors or out.

■ **Light:** Provide bright light indoors, even a bit of full sun in winter. Outside, filtered shade is best for most varieties (full sun is OK for European fan palm if offered gradually).

■ **Water:** Offer even moisture. Palms are *not* desert plants. Moisture is of prime importance to prevent leaf browning (other than natural dying from age). A plant in a 9-inch pot requires 1½ quarts of water each week, but avoid getting plants soggy.

■ **Comments:** Remove unwanted chemicals from the soil by washing water through the pot. Pots should be deep to give roots enough room. Top-dress yearly. Repot only if so root-bound that water won't soak through. Use a porous, lime-type soil with excellent drainage.

Mist often because palms like humidity. Sponge leaves to keep them clean and to prevent scales or mealybugs. Pests are not usually serious problems, however.

Feed a slow-release houseplant food every three or four months. Growth is slow. When your plants are near the size you want, feed them just once in the spring. Feed potential gi-ants (fishtail and fan palms) and wide spreaders (howea and areca) less frequently than the natu-rally short ones (parlor or neanthe bella and bamboo).

Palms benefit from summering outdoors. Pots may sit on top of or be sunk into the soil (for less-frequent watering), and should receive filtered light with wind protection. Brown tips can indicate a need for water, leaching, or mois-ter air, or indicate natural aging. Snip off brown areas with scissors. Propagation by seeds or off-sets is possible, but usually is done for fun be-cause the process is slow and impractical.

NEPHTHYTIS

NORFOLK ISLAND PINE

PALM—howea species

FOLIAGE PLANTS PORTFOLIO *(continued)*

SADDLE-LEAF PHILODENDRON

SPLIT-LEAF PHILODENDRON

PILEA—creeping charlie

PEPEROMIA

Peperomia species

Foliage patterns and textures make peperomia one of the most popular houseplant families. Thick, semisucculent leaves may be smooth, shiny green, two-toned, corrugated, or deeply ridged, with red, pink, or green trailing or upright stems. Emerald-ripple peperomia has deeply ridged and quilted, dark green and brown, almost heart-shaped leaves; ivy peperomia has a silver sheen on its round leaves; watermelon peperomia has green and white stripes; waxy-leaved *P. obtusifolia* climbs when young, trails at maturity.
■ **Light:** Place in medium to bright light, but not direct sun. A bright north window is fine, but diffuse the sun in other windows or put plants in the room's interior.
■ **Water:** Allow to dry between waterings during winter. Keep evenly moist during active growth. Plants rot easily if kept too wet. They like humidity and thrive in terrariums.
■ **Comments:** Keep in warm rooms. Use standard potting mix with added sand or perlite; repot infrequently. Feed no more than once a month during active growth, not at all in winter.

Watch for stem rot at the soil line or below. If the problem is advanced, take cuttings and discard the plant.

Stunted plants whose leaves are disfigured with concentric markings have ring spot, a virus. Destroy the affected plants and take no cuttings.

Root tip cuttings of branching varieties, leaves of others. Plant just the base of the leaf in the medium. Crowns also can be divided on some peperomias.

PHILODENDRONS

Philodendron species

Philodendrons compose the largest, most popular, and most adaptable family of indoor plants. The most common variety has smooth, 3- to 4-inch heart-shaped leaves, grows quickly, and vines or hangs gracefully with tips upturned. Among the self-heading types, the selloum or saddle-leaf philodendron sends up leaves as large as 2 feet long on lengthier stems from a central rosette.

Monstera deliciosa, often called the split-leaf philodendron or Swiss-cheese plant, is not a philodendron but takes the same care. Red emerald philodendron blooms on rare occasions with overwhelming fragrance. Others have velvety or fiddle-shaped leaves. Imbe has long, slightly twisted stems. All are rain-forest natives but tolerate our less-humid homes.
■ **Light:** Place in bright indirect light, although plants will live in low light.
■ **Water:** Provide ample water, keeping soil evenly moist. Many types appreciate a support wrapped with moist sphagnum moss. The support provides extra humidity, roots tend to grow into it, and it lets all the leaves show their best side. When watering the soil, water the sphagnum, too.
■ **Comments:** Wash leaves often to remove dust and grease. This also will discourage mealybugs and scales. Use an acid, peat-based soil with some sand and crushed charcoal added. Feed the plants every three or four months. Low humidity or soggy soil can cause leaves to dry and turn brown. Trim the dead parts with scissors. If new growth has smaller leaves, give plants brighter light.

Large types send out long, ropelike aerial roots. Stick these into the soil or clip them off. The large types also sometimes form offsets around their bases that you can separate. As the lower leaves drop on older plants, cut off or air-layer the top. Leave a short stub to start leafing again. Vines easily root from cuttings.

Pothos or devil's ivy has leaves similar to the common philodendron vine, but with white or yellow variegation. It is just a tad fussier and needs a little less water, but otherwise grows much the same, even in the same pot.

PILEA

Pilea species

The pilea genus includes such unlikely relatives as the tiny-leaved artillery plant, ivylike creep-

ing charlie, and aluminum plant. 'Moon Valley' has deeply veined, textured leaves of apple green and brown, and clusters of tiny pink flowers. 'Silver Tree' is dark maroon and silver.
■ **Light:** Provide bright or indirect sun.
■ **Water:** Keep evenly moist.
■ **Comments:** Add extra peat moss for a rich potting soil. Feed lightly every two months, and keep the humidity high. Pinch leggy growing tips. Propagate by stem cuttings or division.

SANSEVIERIA

Also called snake plant, hemp plant, or mother-in-law's tongue
Sansevieria species

The common names for sansevieria all degrade a noble plant of many uses. The tall leaves make prime vertical accents in arrangements. The plant also endures where others falter, surviving dim daylight, haphazard watering, heat, dust, and dry air.

A pot-bound, mature plant will sometimes send up tall spikes of dainty, white blooms with delightful fragrance only at night.
■ **Light:** Provide bright light, even an east window. Sansevierias, though, can exist for a long time in dim corners.
■ **Water:** Offer low humidity because sansevierias are succulent. Keep the soil on the dry side. Water only once every two weeks during fall and winter.
■ **Comments:** Feed no more than once a month and only in spring and summer. Increase by root division or from cuttings of leaf sections. Cuttings of variegated varieties may revert to all green. The dwarf rosette form, 'Hahni,' also is popular. It grows only 6 to 8 inches tall.

SCHEFFLERA

Also called Australian umbrella tree, Queensland umbrella tree, or octopus tree
Brassaia actinophylla

Schefflera's shiny horizontal leaves look like wheels, with six to eight leaflet spokes about 1½ inches wide and 5 to 9 inches long.

■ **Light:** Give strong light but not direct sun. Turn the plant to help it develop on all sides.
■ **Water:** Let the soil surface dry between waterings. Schefflera is more tolerant of low humidity than most houseplants.
■ **Comments:** Feed lightly once or twice a year. Multiply by potting any suckers from around the base or by air-layering.

UMBRELLA PLANT

Also called Nile grass
Cyperus alternifolius

Umbrella plant bears no resemblance to the Australian umbrella tree (see Schefflera, left). It is related instead to the ancient Egyptian papyrus. This plant has feathery top growth that complements the older, coarser foliage. Stiff stems grow from a clump, and palmlike leaves radiate from the top of the stem. Little flowers bloom from June to October and form additional umbrellas above the foliage. Varieties range from 6 inches to 4 feet tall. The small ones do well in terrariums. Also useful for water gardens.
■ **Light:** Keep away from sunny windows.
■ **Water:** Provide constant moisture. Umbrella plant is one of the very few houseplants whose pot can stand in a saucer constantly full of water.
■ **Comments:** Feed every two weeks during spring and summer. Likes cool rooms, 60 degrees. Divide plants or root leaf rosettes.

WANDERING JEW

Tradescantia or *zebrina* species

The two wandering Jew types are unrelated except in form, but both are no-kill plants with similar red, purple, green, and silver leaf markings, and trailing habit.
■ **Light:** Provide full sun to indirect light—the brighter the light, the deeper the colors.
■ **Water:** Offer humidity and keep soil evenly moist. Plant will grow in water alone.
■ **Comments:** Pinch constantly to keep plants from getting leggy. Or double the runners back to the soil and pin them down to root. Cuttings root easily at any time.

SCHEFFLERA

UMBRELLA PLANT

WANDERING JEW

FLOWERING PLANTS PORTFOLIO

AFRICAN VIOLET

AMARYLLIS

ACHIMENES

Also called magic flower
Achimenes species
With a little care, achimenes produces showers of many-colored blooms from spring until fall. The requirements: 60-degree night temperatures and constant moisture.
■ **Light:** Protect from midday sun (for example, place in an east window).
■ **Water:** Be sure to keep achimenes moist. If it dries out, it goes into instant dormancy.
■ **Comments:** Start rhizomes in moist sphagnum or vermiculite in spring, then transfer several to a pot or hanging basket of half peat and half sand and soil. Feed twice a month during bloom. When blossoming tapers off in late October, decrease water and let the plants die down naturally. Take rhizomes out of the pot and store in dry sand or vermiculite in a spot with 50-degree temperatures until spring.

AFRICAN VIOLET

Saintpaulia species
African violets are among the most treasured and most challenging of houseplants. They grow easily and can be almost everblooming if you fill their needs. Flowers come in shades of white and pink to purple, double or single, with rich form variations. Velvety leaves have different edgings and colors, deep purple to metallic.
■ **Light:** Place in bright indirect light. East windows are best; north windows in the summer or other directions with curtains to filter the direct sun also work. Plants like artificial light. Even 40-watt incandescent bulbs, 2 feet above the plants for 18 hours a day, will double the number of blooms and increase the size of the plants by a foot. Put plants 4 inches below fluorescent tubes. Move plants from under lights when in full bloom to enjoy them at their best.
■ **Water:** Plant in wick-watering pots (see page 349) for best results. Otherwise, water only when the soil surface dries. Tepid water in shade will not hurt leaves, but cold water or full sun will spot them terribly.

■ **Comments:** Keep plants in warm rooms, 60 to 75 degrees, day and night. Avoid sudden changes. For humidity, set plants on trays of pebbles; don't mist directly on hairy leaves. Potting soil should be rich and porous. Buy some made just for African violets, or add peat, perlite, sand, or leaf mold to regular mixes. Feed with an African violet food, usually a diluted addition to each watering. Or add the food to the water reservoir if using wick-watering pots.

If the foliage looks burned, check for too much sun or cold. Use plastic pots because leaves that touch the rim of a clay pot, where soluble salts accumulate, often rot and die. If using a clay pot, dip the rim in paraffin before planting or crimp a narrow strip of foil over the edge.

Watch carefully for mealybugs. Treat with soap or systemic insecticide.

Crowns sometimes need dividing. Leaf cuttings usually root easily but rather slowly. Stick cuttings in a medium with the leaves just above the surface; cover with a plastic bag to hold in humidity. Several baby plants will form at the base in eight weeks or so. Pot them separately.

AMARYLLIS

Hippeastrum species
Amaryllis bulbs produce dark green, straplike foliage with tall stems bearing several huge, lily-like flowers in one of many brilliant colors. They often are given as gifts and may rebloom for 50 years or more.

Choose pink, red, white, or striped flowers, and select bulbs from 4 to 6 inches in diameter with many live roots. Set the bulb on top of a jar of water for a week to wet the roots. Then plant in a pot with a diameter not more than 2 inches larger than the bulb itself, exposing the top half of the bulb.

Use a rich soil mix. Water well and set in a shady spot; leaves appear in about four weeks.
■ **Light:** Once leaves appear (see above), move plant to a bright spot—a southern window if possible, east or west as second choice. If you have only northern light, shine a 100-watt bulb on the plant for a few hours every evening.

■ **Water:** To prevent rot, water well after planting, then sparingly until growth starts. As soon as the flower stalk appears, increase water. Plants are thirsty when in bloom.

■ **Comments:** To hurry or hold back the bloom, choose a warmer or cooler room temperature. Flowers will last about three weeks at 75 degrees, up to 10 weeks at 65 degrees.

Feed every two or three weeks at half the recommended dose during the growing period. Cut off each flower as it fades, then the stalk at the base. After bloom, set the pot in indirect light until leaves turn brown. Or sink the pot to its rim in semishade outdoors after spring frost is past. Before fall frost, bring the pot in, cut off leaves to the neck of the bulb, and store at 70 degrees for four weeks. Then move to a cool place and store dry, on its side, until new growth begins in about six to eight weeks. Top-dress and start watering again. The bulb will produce offsets. Separate for new plants.

AZALEA

Rhododendron species

Azaleas are available almost year-round with bright, showy flowers in white or many shades of pink. They will bloom for several weeks indoors with bright light and cool night temperatures—below 65 degrees, if possible.

■ **Light:** Give up to four hours of direct sunlight daily.

■ **Water:** Water generously. After 15 minutes, water again. Or sink whole pots in water for a half hour (never longer). Plants are quite potbound when blooming and have many thirsty roots with little extra room for moisture.

■ **Comments:** Cut off the dead blooms. After bloom, feed with acid fertilizer every two weeks until fall, monthly after that. Never feed while the plant is in bloom. Summer the plants outdoors in filtered light. To pot outside or in a larger pot, use plenty of peat to make soil more acidic. Cut the root ball in several places around the outside and with an X on the bottom, then

pull the roots apart. If you don't repot, top-dress with acid peat in fall. Water as needed. Watch for red spiders.

BEGONIA

Begonia species

Begonias come in three forms: wax or fibrous, rex or rhizomes, and tuberous. The round red or green leaves and pink flowers of the first form are the most common; angel-wing also belongs to this class. The rex family is grown for its striking large leaves of many shapes and colors.

Tuberous begonias are mostly grown outdoors in the shade, and are excellently suited to hanging baskets and patio plantings. Their flowers are spectacular in their fullness, forms, and bright colors: yellow, orange, red, and pink.

■ **Light:** Place outdoors in open shade with some early eastern sunlight. Indoors in winter, give plants a bright window, but filter the glare with sheer curtains. Rex will take less light.

■ **Water:** Keep these shallow-rooted plants evenly but not overly moist, and increase humidity. Wax and beefsteak can dry between waterings; water tubers only as needed, especially right before and after their dormant period.

■ **Comments:** When tops of tubers die down in the fall, store plants indoors in dry vermiculite or sand. Begonias do well in warm houses but are happier with cooler temperatures at night. These plants don't generally appeal to insects, but watch for mealybugs just in case. Multiply rex by stem pieces, although leaf or leaf-section cuttings also will work. Wax stems root easily in about two weeks. Start tubers for summer bloom in February or March. Set them in a shallow container of loose, moist rooting medium with round sides down and pinkish buds exposed. Bottom heat will speed the process. After the tubers have rooted, pot up in pots 5 inches in diameter or larger. Increase water as plants grow. Feed every four weeks.

AZALEA

FIBROUS BEGONIA

FLOWERING PLANTS PORTFOLIO *(continued)*

BROMELIAD—*aechmea fasciata*

CITRUS—orange

CYCLAMEN

BROMELIADS

The bromeliad family, which includes the pineapple, has enjoyed a great surge of popularity. The easy care and almost foolproof growth of these plants fits today's hectic homelife. Their exotic stiff leaves and vase-shaped trunks are sophisticated enough for the most modern apartment, yet adapt to other decors as well. This alone would recommend them. But they also bloom with bright, bold, unusual flowers. If you summer a pineapple outdoors, you may even get a small fruit after a few years.

■ **Light:** Requirements vary. Offer bright, but not full, sun to the easy billbergia, pineapple dyckia, neoregelia, and tillandsia. Place earthstar, guzmania or scarlet star (whose blooms last for months), nidularium, and flaming-sword or vriesea in medium filtered light. The stiffer the leaves, the more light the plants need.

■ **Water:** Keep water in center of cup formed by the leaves at all times, and water lightly around the base once a week. Too much water on the roots will cause rot. Plants like humidity, but don't mist them in bright sunlight.

■ **Comments:** Use osmunda or shredded tree fern, although plants will thrive in a commercial soil mix that is half fir bark, sphagnum moss, or perlite and half sand. The goal is good drainage. Bromeliad roots need little space.

Feed bromeliads little. A bit of fish emulsion in the cup water works best—every six or eight weeks and only in summer.

Bromeliads readily form offsets at the base. You can pot these separately to multiply your stock or leave them to replace the main plant, which dies after flowering.

CITRUS

Fruit is unnecessary to make citrus a fascinating indoor plant. But fruit is quite possible if your conditions are right. Children love to start plants from orange or grapefruit seeds, and the plants' shiny leaves are attractive from the first. In several years, the plants make handsome indoor trees. Ponderosa lemon is a choice indoor plant with huge fruits. Calamondin orange makes a nice diminutive tree with small but edible fruit. Buy a grafted plant to be sure to get deliciously fragrant flowers. The blooms often appear on the plants at the same time as the green and orange fruits.

■ **Light:** Grow in a sunny window in winter, outdoors in summer. Toughen plants by easing them outside. Set plants first where they will get a little east sun a few hours each day for a week. Expose to more sun gradually.

■ **Water:** Soak well, then let dry before soaking again. Fruit tends to drop if plant is over- or underwatered. Citrus prefers humid air; mist foliage daily.

■ **Comments:** Use slightly acid soil with plenty of peat moss. Once a month, apply ½ teaspoon of vinegar mixed in a quart of water. Use a slow-release plant food. Too much warmth without ventilation will cause leaves to drop. Move plants back inside gradually before the furnace goes on in the fall and mist often. Enclose in plastic to increase humidity if necessary.

To ensure pollination indoors, take a child's paintbrush and dab ripe pollen to sticky surface of stigmas in centers of bloom.

CYCLAMEN

Also called poor man's orchid
Cyclamen persicum

Cyclamen is a popular gift plant, especially for Christmas and Valentine's Day. Its round to heart-shaped leaves are mottled and mounded on long, slender stems. It has exquisite blooms with recurved butterfly petals that rise above the foliage in great profusion.

■ **Light:** Give bright light to full sun filtered by curtains. Cyclamen also likes artificial light.

■ **Water:** Water from the bottom and never get the leaves wet. The succulent stems grow from a corm slightly concaved at the top, and if the corm holds water, rot sets in.

■ **Comments:** Start from seeds. Cyclamen takes 18 months to grow to its full beauty, though it is attractive as a foliage plant in the meantime. Coolness is the secret to cyclamen survival. It likes 50-degree temperatures at night and not more than 60 degrees in the daytime. This need for low temperatures is the reason cyclamen usually doesn't survive indoors for long periods. Enjoy the plants while you can, then discard them without guilt when they go.

FUCHSIA

Also called lady's-eardrops
Fuchsia species

Fuchsias grow on shrubs that need cool conditions. Varieties exist with arching upright habit, but most cascade and grace hanging baskets. The long, pendent blooms have recurved petals about halfway down, then a bell skirt bottom that the stamens and pistil extend from.

■ **Light:** Provide bright light, but protect from midday sun. East or west windows are best.
■ **Water:** Keep soil evenly moist but not soggy. Plants have shallow roots.
■ **Comments:** Keep your house cool at night, 50 to 65 degrees. Fuchsias will perish in overheated rooms. Feed them twice a month when flowering. Reduce both water and food between blooming periods. Pinch to keep bushy. Propagate from stem cuttings.

GARDENIA

Also called cape jasmine
Gardenia jasminoides

Gardenias, shiny-leaved plants with delicate, wildly fragrant flowers, often are sold as houseplants. Yet they are very difficult for most people to grow. Do not invest more than you can afford to gamble.
■ **Light:** Place in sun in winter, bright shade in summer.
■ **Water:** Water heavily. Gardenias can sit with water always in the saucer. Mist plants daily.
■ **Comments:** If you buy a plant in bud, remove all but a very few. The buds will fall off anyway as the plant adjusts to your house. Repot every spring in a porous, peat-rich (by half), acid (no lime) soil mix. Feed with vinegar—as with citrus trees (see opposite)—or a special

acid food. Summer plants outdoors with their pots sunk to the rim for constant moisture. Pinch flower buds to encourage winter bloom.

GERANIUM

Pelargonium species

Common garden geraniums from the pelargonium genus are long-time favorites indoors as well as out. Types include dwarfs, Martha Washington, Lady Washington, ivy, and variegated. All have pleasantly scented foliage, but the scented-leaf varieties are so aromatic when brushed or crushed that their blooms are incidental.

Although outdoor plants will overwinter bare-rooted in paper bags on the basement floor, you can enjoy blooms on as many stock plants as you can fit into sunny south windows. Also, you can start from seed new hybrids that have vastly superior vigor and bloom; plant them in December for flowers the next spring and summer.
■ **Light:** Offer as much light as possible.
■ **Water:** Water heavily, though geraniums' thick, succulent stems can withstand some drought. For healthy growth and heaviest bloom, water plants every time the soil surface becomes dry. Check drainage; plants do not like waterlogging.
■ **Comments:** Keep room warm; plants also tolerate dry air. Feed plants only if they have stopped growing or the foliage is pale. Too much food or water, or too little light, will make plants tall and leggy with few flowers. Summer plants outdoors. Geraniums bloom best if slightly pot-bound. Pick dead flower stems. Pinch tall stems after bloom to promote branching and shape young plants as they grow. Stem cuttings root easily from still green, not yet woody, shoots. Let them dry a day or two to form a callus before sticking them in moist rooting medium. Plain water sometimes works but often causes rot. Avoid direct sun on cuttings.

FUCHSIA

IVY GERANIUM

FLOWERING PLANTS PORTFOLIO *(continued)*

GLOXINIA

CHINESE HIBISCUS

HOYA

GLOXINIA

Sinningia species

Gloxinias, with their huge, scallop-edged, velvetlike trumpets, are one of the loveliest flowering plants. They bloom—often white on the outside and edged with brilliant color inside—above a low mound of large leaves.

■ **Light:** Offer bright light but not direct sunlight. Too little light creates leggy stems.

■ **Water:** Keep soil evenly moist, but avoid waterlogging. Keep water off the hairy foliage and the top of the tuber by watering around the edge of the pot or from the bottom.

When the plant stops blooming, withhold water gradually until the foliage dries. Store in the pot on its side in a dark place no cooler than 50 degrees until new growth starts. Then repot or top-dress with vermiculite or peat and perlite. Set the pot in a warm, softly lighted spot; water only enough to keep the perlite moist. Encasing each pot in a plastic bag at first will aid plant growth. Don't overwater. If you do not give this treatment, the plant will drop its leaves on its own, but rot is more likely.

■ **Comments:** Use the same soil mix as for African violets (see page 366). Feed lightly every few weeks beginning as soon as flower buds develop. Gloxinia, a tropical plant, likes plenty of humidity and warmth. Start new plants from seed, or root leaf cuttings at the base, bracing the leaves with sticks above the medium.

HIBISCUS

Hibiscus species

A cousin of the hollyhock, hibiscus has similar but much showier flowers. The blooms come in bright shades of red, pink, purple, orange, yellow, and white, and are 4 to 8 inches across. Each one lasts only a day and stays lovely even without water. Chinese hibiscus is one of the best types.

■ **Light:** Provide full sun for bloom. But even without flowers, hibiscus is an attractive foliage plant.

■ **Water:** Keep soil evenly moist when plant is in flower, on the dry side at other times. Hibiscus likes humidity.

■ **Comments:** Keep plants in a warm spot when growing and blooming, a cool place at other times. In March, before new growth starts, prune plants back by half and repot if necessary. Use a standard potting soil and feed lightly only when in growth or bloom. Pinch tips to keep plants compact and bushy. Root stem cuttings. Summer plants outdoors for maximum bloom in the summer and fall. Move in and out gradually.

HOYA

Also called wax plant
Hoya species

Hoya offers a dozen interesting varieties, all attractive as foliage plants with thick, succulent, waxlike leaves of varied markings. The clusters of star-shaped, fragrant flowers come in creamy velvet with a perfect dark pink star in the center, blue-white with red centers, or yellow-green.

■ **Light:** Give bright light, up to four hours of sun a day if you can. Hoyas will live for years in the shade but never bloom.

■ **Water:** Water generously during bloom. Keep almost dry otherwise.

■ **Comments:** Feed every second month. Use extra-rich soil with sand and leaf mold. Tie plants to supports for best growth. Keep plants pot-bound to yield the most flowers. Never remove a stub where the flowers appear or you will be cutting off your next blooms. Propagate with stem cuttings.

HYDRANGEA

Hydrangea macrophylla

Hydrangea, a small shrub with huge balls of papery blossoms in pink, blue, red, or greenish cream, often is a gift at Easter.

■ **Light:** Provide bright indirect light, cool nights.

■ **Water:** Water heavily. Forget hydrangea and it soon will look quite dead, but it revives when the pot is plunked in a bucket of water. Try to keep soil evenly moist.

■ **Comments:** Don't feed until blossoms fade. Then cut plants back severely, to 1 inch above woody growth. Move plants to the garden until the next buds appear. In the southern half of the United States, hydrangea is hardy outdoors. Grow in rich, porous soil and light shade. Aluminum sulfate added during bloom deepens colors; lack of soil acidity may change colors from blue to pink.

Where winters are cold, bring hydrangea back inside in the fall. Put plants in a cool but frost-free cellar. Keep soil moist. In February, move plants gradually to more warmth and light. Propagate with stem cuttings.

IMPATIENS

Also called patience plant or patient lucy
Impatiens wallerana

With the right conditions, impatiens will bloom almost continuously (it's one of the few plants that will). New hybrids have interesting foliage as well as dainty, five-petaled flowers. Some dwarf varieties will grow in terrariums.

■ **Light:** Place in full sun during the winter, partial sun during the summer.

■ **Water:** Water abundantly. Plant wilts quickly if allowed to dry.

■ **Comments:** Place in cool to moderately warm room. Avoid sharp temperature fluctuations. Use any good, nonacid soil. Feed monthly. Cuttings root easily. Plants need some shaping and can take severe pruning. Watch for aphids, mites, or whiteflies.

ORCHIDS

Although they seem more mysterious and exotic, both in beauty and culture, many orchids are easier to grow than African violets. You don't have to know all the fancy terms to get the flowers. Just bring one home and you'll learn as you go. Moth orchid (phalaenopsis) and lady-slipper (paphiopedilum or cypripedium) do well in most homes. The florist orchid (cattleya) is not difficult; the flowers last for weeks, and the fragrance, which florists must chill away, fills your room. See orchids in bloom before buying if you can. Some flowers are no bigger than a quarter. Try to get some that bloom at different times of the year. If one kind does not work for you, try another. There are 25,000 species and about as many hybrids. An orchid show or grower's greenhouse should give you enough information and inspiration to start.

■ **Light:** Provide cymbidiums with the most light, preferably full sun in a cool house. Give others very bright, indirect light. Cattleya needs light bright enough to keep foliage yellow-green. If the foliage is darker, the light is insufficient and the plant won't flower. Most orchids benefit from a summer outdoors in shade. Move them gradually. Orchids do well in artificial light.

■ **Water:** Keep moist, watering every day or every other day. Do not let water stand in leaf axils of moth orchids or lady-slippers, or they'll rot. Cymbidiums and cattleyas have pseudobulbs, and water runs off them easily. Do not let pots stand in water. Use tepid water, and, to avoid discoloring, never get leaves wet in sunlight. Don't forget to water outdoor orchids in the summer. Mist foliage every morning. Humidity is a must for orchids. Set on trays of wet pebbles.

■ **Comments:** Use osmunda fiber or fir bark; orchids do not grow in soil. A potted plant may not need any more medium for two years, but buy some when you get the plant just in case. Orchids also need special food. Cattleyas need two formulas: one for growing and another, a blossom booster, for flowers. Orchids need ventilation, but resent drafts.

HYDRANGEA

IMPATIENS

MOTH ORCHID

FLOWERING PLANTS PORTFOLIO (continued)

POINSETTIA

SPATHIPHYLLUM

POINSETTIA

Euphorbia pulcherrima

This popular Christmas plant has been bred and improved greatly in the past few decades. It is less fussy but showier, comes in more forms and colors, and is almost sure to stay beautiful right into the spring.

■ **Light:** Provide bright light until plant reaches peak of bloom, when it can survive with less. More important is to avoid drafts, either hot or cold. And most important is to enjoy the plant. Place it accordingly.

■ **Water:** Be sure both the pot and foil paper allow drainage. Water enough to drain through, then check daily and water again when the surface begins to dry.

■ **Comments:** Place plants in a cool room, especially at night. Feed plants within 10 days after purchase. Feed monthly after that. Poinsettias root from stem cuttings and grow easily, but they will not form buds unless they have 12 to 14 hours of complete darkness each day.

If you have no rooms in your house where lights are *never* on, or are unwilling to cover the plants at dusk and uncover them every morning for weeks, don't bother to save them. If you do, cut them back and plant outdoors for the summer. Keep plants pinched and shaped. Bring back in before frost to a bright, cool place that receives no evening light.

SPATHIPHYLLUM

Also called white anthurium, peace lily, or spathe flower

Spathiphyllum species

Spathiphyllum is a less fussy cousin of the anthurium. Its foliage looks much like smaller aspidistra; sword-shaped leaves grow 1½ feet tall on sturdy stems rising from the soil like a milling crowd. Some are variegated and dwarf (see photo, page 346). The pale green sheath turns white as it opens. The true flowers are tiny and surround a slender protruding stalk. New varieties get larger and pleasantly scented flowers. Each bloom lasts for weeks, usually in January and February. 'Mauna Loa' blooms intermittently all year.

■ **Light:** Provide bright light in winter, diffused light in summer. Plants will bloom in shade, but with sparse, undersized flowers.

■ **Water:** Keep soil evenly moist with frequent waterings. Increase humidity.

■ **Comments:** Place in a warm room. Feed every two months from March to September. For pot-bound plants, use a sharp knife to divide the roots after flowering. Pot up in standard potting soil with a handful of sand or perlite added for good drainage. Leaves that turn brown at the edges and then yellow are simply aging; cut them off. When leaf tips yellow, check for too much or not enough water, or insufficient food.

SUCCULENTS—GENERAL

The giant succulent family offers endless diversity, and, fortunately, its members like to live like we do: in low humidity, shirt-sleeve warmth, and bright sunshine much of the time. The unique forms and sculpted shapes result partly from stored water. Some, like burro's-tail, are striking in hanging baskets. You can make a wreath of tiny succulents in a frame of damp sphagnum that will live and grow as it hangs. In an open terrarium with sand and only occasional waterings, succulents re-create the best of desert beauty. If a pot of succulents falls over and spills, these plants are hardy enough that you can sweep them into a corner for a week and then replant.

■ **Light:** Place most succulents in south windows. Some need protection from intense afternoon sun. When you move them outdoors for the summer, ease them into sun or open shade gradually; otherwise, they will cook in their own juices and turn transparent.

■ **Water:** During fall and winter, their natural rest period, water succulents only enough to keep the roots and soil from drying—not enough to encourage new growth. The plants will take considerably more water during their active growing and blooming time, in spring and summer. Be sure their pots provide enough drainage so water almost runs right through; water every other week.

■ **Comments:** To handle prickly cactus, make a band of newspapers and wrap around a plant like a vise. Place succulents such as burro's-tail and jade where people or animals won't brush against them. Leaves fall off at the slightest pressure. Pot with a layer of drainage in the bottom, preferably gravel, broken pottery, or similar jagged-edged material rather than smooth rocks or pebbles.

Buy potting mix for cactus and succulents or make your own of equal parts humus, perlite (not vermiculite; it holds too much water), and washed sand, which you can buy at garden and building supply stores. Leave an inch at the top of the pot. Mulching with limestone chips reflects heat and light and sets off the dramatic aspects of the plants to advantage.

Feed succulents frequently, but lightly. Watch for mealybugs, although they probably will eat a tenderer plant first. Succulents multiply easily from cuttings, seeds, grafts, or offsets. Because the stems store water, make the cuttings with a sharp razor or knife, then let them sit out for a day or more in a nice dry spot. Dip the cuttings in rooting hormone, then stick them just barely into the medium. If a cutting needs support, use small sticks to hold it up and steady it until roots form.

SUCCULENTS—HOLIDAY CACTUS

Holiday cactus is a favorite gift plant because it's easy to grow and lasts for years. There are three close relatives. The Thanksgiving cactus has the most deeply notched edges. The true Christmas cactus has more-rounded teeth, usually two or three on each side. Easter cactus' leaves have almost smooth edges with little bristles, and it may bloom between the leaf segments as well as on the tips. All come in a wide range of colors. The satiny flowers are often bicolored with a combination of white and a pastel.

■ **Light:** Make sure plants don't receive too much light in summer. Some buds may drop as plants adjust to a new place. If the dropping persists, check for too much or too little water, or insufficient light. Plants need long nights to bloom.

■ **Water:** Water evenly throughout the year. Holiday cactus is a native of the rain forest, not the desert.

■ **Comments:** Set in very little soil. Prune in midsummer for more branching and flowers.

SUCCULENTS—KALANCHOE

Also called aurora borealis plant or Christmas kalanchoe
Kalanchoe blossfeldiana

In full sunlight, kalanchoe's leaf edges are reddish, and bright clusters of tiny flowers bloom for long periods. These flowers form only when days are short, so the plant, like the poinsettia, will not bloom if it gets any night light at all.

■ **Light:** Give full sun in spring, fall, and winter, but avoid direct sun during the hottest part of the day in summer.

■ **Water:** Let soil dry between waterings. Water more frequently until the flowers fade, then keep soil on the dry side for a month or two with just enough moisture to keep the leaves from shriveling. If leaves turn yellow, you're overwatering.

■ **Comments:** Place where nights are cool, down to 50 degrees. Prune well back after flowers fade, then put in shade outside. Bring back to sunny window in September. Or take stem or leaf cuttings for new plants.

SUCCULENT—aeonium species

SUCCULENT—*Stapelia gigantea*

FORCING BULBS INSIDE

Tulips and daffodils can bloom on your windowsill even while winter rages outdoors when you use a technique called forcing to create artificial, shorter seasons.

Choose large, firm, unblemished bulbs specially recommended for forcing. Pot them according to the instructions included—precooled bulbs can skip cold storage—or as shown below. Paper-white narcissus and hyacinth also can be set on a tray of wet pebbles. Keep the tray filled with water to the base of the bulbs.

Next subject pots to simulated winter cold and darkness for eight to 15 weeks in a refrigerator, a cool basement or garage, outdoors in a cold frame or under bales of hay, or on the balcony in a picnic cooler. Temperatures should be from 35 to 50 degrees and never below freezing. Keep pots moist.

When stems are 1 or 2 inches high and roots show at the drainage holes, bring in a few pots at a time for a long period of bloom. Move each pot gradually to "spring" light and warmth. Water as needed. You can almost see plants growing, and within a few weeks, you will have flowers and fragrance.

If hyacinths are stubby, surround them with a cylinder of dark paper so the flowers must stretch to the light. Narcissus may need stakes.

POTTING BULBS

1

2

3

4

1 Use a pot twice as tall as your bulbs. Cover the drainage hole with a shard and fill the pot half full of soil.

2 Put in as many bulbs as you can without letting them touch each other or the pot sides. Put flat side of tulips out. Set bulb tips even with pot rim.

3 Cover with additional soil and tamp down gently with your hands.

4 Water thoroughly and label each pot with kind, color, and date. Then move pots to cold storage.

HOUSEPLANT DISEASES AND INSECTS

Disease/Insect	Description and Trouble Signs	Control
Aphids	Also called common plant lice, aphids are about ⅛ inch long and green, red, black, or brown. They are found mostly on new growing tips and the undersides of leaves. By sucking the plant juices, they cause the foliage to curl, yellow, and die. They also secrete a sticky substance called honeydew that attracts ants and fungus.	If infestation isn't serious, wash the aphids away with a strong stream of water or a soapy bath. Or use spray or systemic insecticide according to label instructions. A cotton swab dipped in alcohol will kill individual insects, but also will damage your plant if it touches the stem or leaf. Insect traps work well.
Crown or stem rot	If leaves appear dull and centers turn dark green and then black, check the base of stems, the petiole, rhizome, or tuberous roots for rot. Rot is indicated if parts are slimy and soft or hard and dry. Avocado, African violet, cyclamen, gloxinia, peperomia, and amaryllis are especially susceptible.	Plant disease-free stock at the correct depth in clean, well-drained soil. Avoid wounding, overfertilizing, and overwatering, or letting plant stand too long with water in the saucer. Water less in winter and when bulbs are near dormancy.
Cyclamen mites	Cyclamen mites are sucking insects that can stunt plants, and make leaves curl and buds stay folded. Check cyclamen for deformed leaves or flowers; also check chrysanthemum, fuchsia, and geranium.	Use strong water spray or miticide. Wash hands and tools; sterilize empty pots or soak in a solution of one part chlorine to nine parts water. Destroy badly infested plants.
Mealybugs	Mealybugs are barely big enough to see, with only up to ¼ inch of gray body wrapped in woolly white. They hide in joints and under leaves, suck plant juices, and multiply by 600 eggs at a time. They are the worst enemy of African violet, fuchsia, coleus, and wax vine.	Be on guard at all times. Isolate new plants to check. Keep brush and soapy water handy, and give plants regular cleanings to prevent outbreak. Use alcohol swab only as emergency treatment. Re-treat constantly. Destroy badly infested plants.
Red spider mites	Red spider mites are too small to notice until they've done their damage. If leaves look rusty and the plant droops, run your finger under the leaves and see if it turns red. In advanced stages, tiny webs form around the joints. Watch hydrangea, ivy, and azalea.	Keep plants properly watered and humidity high. Dip in plain or soapy water on a regular basis, or spray large plants. Use a miticide if necessary. Destroy plants that are far-gone before pests spread.
Scales	Scales are oval or round, ⅛-inch-long insects with shell-like coverings. May be white, gray, brown, or black. They deposit a sticky, shiny substance called honeydew on leaves and suck plant juices. Can kill plant. Prime targets are ferns, palms, rubber plant, and citrus.	If just a few, remove with soapsuds. Or use a sponge or old toothbrush dipped in an oil emulsion to dislodge shells. Support the leaf with one hand, scrub with the other. Or use a houseplant insecticide as a spray or dip.
Viruses	Plants look stunted. Foliage is mottled, streaked, or spotted with white or light green. Flowers also may be marked. Ring spot on peperomia is a virus.	Remove and destroy infected plants to prevent spread. Do not take cuttings. No chemical control exists.
Whiteflies	Whiteflies are flying, dandrufflike insects that make a cloud around stirred plants; they hide under leaves in the meantime. They suck plant juices and turn foliage yellow, eventually killing plants left untreated. Worse in some seasons, usually near spring, and like tender new shoots of tomato plant, fuchsia, and geranium.	Several applications of insecticide may be necessary. Use spray or systemic insecticide according to label instructions. Wash hands after handling infested plant to keep from spreading invisible eggs. Buy insect traps.

INDEX

If you would like to
order any additional copies of
our books, call 1-800-678-2803
or check with your local
bookstore.